The Transnational Redress Movement for the Victims
of Japanese Military Sexual Slavery

Genocide and Mass Violence in the Age of Extremes

Edited by Frank Jacob

Volume 2

The Transnational Redress Movement for the Victims of Japanese Military Sexual Slavery

Edited by
Pyong Gap Min, Thomas R. Chung, and Sejung Sage Yim

ISBN: 978-3-11-076374-4
e-ISBN (PDF): 978-3-11-064348-0
e-ISBN (EPUB): 978-3-11-063987-2
ISSN 2626-6490

Library of Congress Control Number: 2019949233

Bibliographic information published by the Deutsche Nationalbibliothek
The Deutsche Nationalbibliothek lists this publication in the Deutsche Nationalbibliografie;detailed bibliographic data are available on the Internet at http://dnb.dnb.de.

© 2021 Walter de Gruyter GmbH, Berlin/Boston
This volume is text- and page-identical with the hardback published in 2020.
Cover Image: © WCCW, Inc. (Washington Coalition for Comfort Women Issues),
photographed by Mr. Doo Chan Hahm
Photograph of demonstration in the U.S. organized by Washington Coalition for Comfort Women Issues, Inc. (WCCW) in 1994
Druck und Bindung: CPI books GmbH, Leck

www.degruyter.com

Acknowledgments

The Research Center for Korean Community (RCKC) held an international conference focusing on "The Redress Movement for the Victims of Japanese Military Sexual Slavery—Looking Back at the 27-Year Movement" at Queens College on 13–14 October 2017. About 20 scholars and key "comfort women" activists from South Korea, Japan, and the United States participated in the conference. This edited book is based on revisions of 13 papers selected from those presented at the conference. First of all, without the authors' participation in the conference and their subsequent revisions of their papers, this book would not have been possible. We would like to express our sincere thanks to the authors of this book for participating in the conference, and also for writing and revising their papers for publication in this book.

Holding the conference and the subsequent editing of the papers were financially supported by the Research Foundation for Korean Community (RFKC), the Academy of Korean Studies, and Queens College. We would like to give special thanks to the first two organizations for making the publication of this book possible. Jea-Seung Ko, the President of RFKC, and its other members have also financially supported many other research activities of our research center, and we are always thankful for their devotion to our activities and mission. In addition, donations by two dozen Korean community leaders supported the 2017 conference and other research activities of our center. We would like to express great thanks especially to Peter Ki Hyo Park, Spencer An, and Sophia Lee.

All chapters of this book are partly based on testimonies given by Korean "comfort women" in the form of documentary films, anthologies of testimonies, press conferences, personal interviews, photo images, or their own paintings. The redress movement for the victims of Japanese military sexual slavery would have been impossible without the courage with which Kim Hak-sun and other "comfort women" survivors emerged to society and actively participated in it. Among the 240 Korean "comfort women" survivors who reported to the government or the Korean Council, only 23 women are currently alive (as of February 2019). We would like to devote this book, the record of the redress movement in which many of them actively participated, to Korean "comfort women" who have passed away and those who are still with us.

The research support by Hyeonji Lee, one of the staff members of our center, has facilitated the completion of this book and Pyong Gap Min's other research projects. She has helped Min with library research, analyses of testimonies given by Korean "comfort women," and online searches of Korean newspaper articles. Young Oak Kim, Min's wife, has also been deeply involved in this and his other book projects to help him with analyses of testimonies, internet searches of redress movement activities, and translation of Korean words into English. Her unselfish daily support for his research activities has been essential to the completion of this book project, as well as to his other academic achievements.

Min wrote Chapter 2 based on his personal interviews with Korean redress activists and participant observations made in Seoul, many monthly collections of data sources and newsletters published by the Korean Council for the Women Drafted for Military Sexual Slavery by Japan and the Korean Research Institute for the Chongshindae, and many newspaper articles. In particular, he owes great thanks to two key redress activists, Mee-hyang Yoon (who wrote a chapter for this volume) and Sun-ju Yeo, for doing interviews with him several times and sending him their newsletters and collections of data sources. Min would also like to express his sincere thanks to Shin-kwon Ahn, the director of the House of Sharing, who did several interviews and shared valuable information and insights, in person and on the phone.

Min also would like to acknowledge that four PSC-CUNY Research Awards (1996, 1999, 2001, and 2007), the 1997 Korea Foundation Research Award, and the 1995 Fellowship by the Asian Research Institute at Kyungnam University enabled him to visit South Korea several times for research on the "comfort women" issue. We also extend special thanks to Frank Jacob, the Series Editor of Genocide and Mass Violence in the Age of Extremes, and Rabea Rittgerodt, Project Editor of De Gruyter, for recognizing the value of this book project and accepting it for publication in the book series. Both waited patiently to get the manuscript ready for publication, and have moved quickly to get the book published. Without a doubt, the editing team of De Gruyter has improved the quality of the book.

Congratulatory Remarks

The Research Center for the Korean Community (RCKC) at Queens College, CUNY is the only one of its kind in the United States. As this year (2019) marks its 10th anniversary, the publication of this book, *Japanese Military Sexual Slavery: The Transnational Redress Movement for the Victims*, is all the more meaningful.

This book came together thanks to the hard work and tireless efforts of its many contributors, as well as Professor Pyong Gap Min, the Research Foundation for Korean Community (RFKC) board of directors, and all those who donated to the RCKC and RFKC. I would like to extend heartfelt thanks for their contributions.

This book is a collection of the research papers presented at the 8th annual RCKC Conference, which focused on "The Redress Movement for Victims of Japanese Military Sexual Slavery: Looking Back at the 27-Year Movement," that took place on 13–14 October 2017. When one first comes across the title of this conference, one might feel struck by its uncomfortable subject matter or feel desensitized by the volume of work already published on this subject. However, the issue of Japanese military sexual slavery is still ongoing. During the Asian and Pacific War, research shows that 50,000 to 200,000 women fell victim to sexual slavery. Their trauma, scars, and fight are still not over. With the Japanese government denying their historic responsibility for the crimes of their predecessors and using this issue for political purposes, "comfort women" survivors are still fighting for reparations and to restore their pride. This book aims to show the truth.

The motivation for this book's publication is not political. Rather, this book is a record of historical facts presented from an objective and academic perspective. Through this book and the topics of the research papers presented within it, Korean, Japanese, American, and Chinese researchers on the subject of "comfort women," and the activists fighting for the "comfort women's" cause are sending a firm message to Japan.

As of February 2019, there are currently 23 "comfort women" survivors who are still alive, the majority of whom are over ninety years old. The thought of losing these women and their stories was a driving force in this book's publication.

I hope that this book will help all those invested in this issue, women's rights researchers, and those in the future who choose to continue this work. In addition, I hope that this book can bring a little solace to the survivors of Japanese military sexual slavery, for whom this book was made.

Jea-Seung Ko
President
The Research Foundation for Korean Community (RFKC)

Table of Contents

Pyong Gap Min, Thomas R. Chung, and Sejung Sage Yim
Introduction —— 1

Part I: The Redress Movement in South Korea and Japan

Mee-hyang Yoon
Unfulfilled Justice: Human Rights Restoration for the Victims of Japanese Military Sexual Slavery —— 21

Puja Kim
The "Comfort Women" Redress Movement in Japan: Reflections on the Past 28 years —— 43

Pyong Gap Min
Japanese Citizens' and Civic Organizations' Strong Support for the Redress Movement —— 71

Mina Watanabe
Initiatives by Citizens of a Perpetrator State: Advocating to UN Human Rights Bodies for the Rights of Survivors —— 95

Part II: The Redress Movement in the United States

Jungsil Lee and Dongwoo Lee Hahm
Tracing 28 Years of the Redress Movement Led by the Washington Coalition for Comfort Women Issues —— 117

Judith Mirkinson
Building the San Francisco Memorial: Why the Issue of the 'Comfort Women' is Still Relevant Today? —— 149

Phyllis Kim
Looking Back at 10 Years of the "Comfort Women" Movement in the U.S. —— 179

Part III: Legacies of "Comfort Women" in Arts

Bonnie B.C. Oh
Legacies of "Comfort Women" —— 203

Margaret D. Stetz
Making Girl Victims Visible: A Survey of Representations That Have Circulated in the West —— 215

Part IV: The Neo-Nationalist Movement in Japan and the United States

Tomomi Yamaguchi
The "History Wars" and the "Comfort Woman" Issue: The Significance of *Nippon Kaigi* in the Revisionist Movement in Contemporary Japan —— 233

Emi Koyama
Japanese Far-Right Activities in the United States and at the United Nations: Conflict and Coordination between Japanese Government and Fringe Groups —— 261

Part V: New Sources and Theories

Peipei Qiu
Documenting War Atrocities Against Women: Newly Discovered Japanese Military Files in Jilin Provincial Archives —— 275

Angella Son
The Japanese Secret: The Shame Behind Japan's Longstanding Denial of Its War Crime against Korean *Comfort Girls-Women* —— 295

Major Publications Included in Book Chapters (Reading List) —— 325

Authors' Bios —— 329

Editors' Bios —— 333

Index —— 335

Pyong Gap Min, Thomas R. Chung, and Sejung Sage Yim
Introduction

The "Comfort Women" Issue and the 28-Year Redress Movement

The most brutal crime committed by the Japanese military during the Asia-Pacific War (1931–1945) was the forced mobilization of a large number of Asian women (50,000–200,000 women) to military brothels to sexually serve Japanese soldiers as "comfort women."[1] Koreans are believed to have been the largest group of "comfort women" victims, because the Japanese military was able to recruit women and girls from its own colonies (the other colony was Taiwan, which had a much smaller population) most effectively.[2] The majority of these women died of physical abuse, malnutrition, illness (including sexually transmitted diseases), bombings, or other tragic circumstances.[3] Many others are presumed to have committed suicide or to have been killed by Japanese soldiers. Most Korean survivors returned home after Japan was defeated in August 1945, while others remained trapped in the countries of their sexual servitude, mostly in China.

Due to patriarchal norms stigmatizing sexual victims, Korean survivors kept silent for almost half a century about their brutal experiences in Japanese military brothels. However, the active women's movement in South Korea, facilitated by the replacement of the military dictatorship with a civilian government, helped to start the redress movement for the victims of Japanese military sexual slav-

---

[1] "Comfort women" is a euphemism for female victims of Japanese military sexual slavery. The term is a translation of the Japanese word, *ianfu* (*wianbu*, in Korean), and during the Asia-Pacific War, the Japanese military used this term to denote that these women provided "comfort" to Japanese soldiers by providing sexual services. We do not condone this term, because it seems designed to minimize or even conceal the brutality and exploitation of the Japanese military sexual slavery system. However, since it has been so widely used in many different settings and contexts for so long, many people are familiar with this euphemism, thus, the term is enclosed in quotation marks throughout this volume. We provide more detailed information about "comfort women" and other terms in a section titled "Clarification of Terms" near the end of this introductory chapter.
[2] Yoshiaki Yoshimi, *Comfort Women: Sexual Slavery in the Japanese Military during World War II*, trans. Suzanne O'Brien (New York: Columbia University Press, 2002), 92–95.
[3] Yuko Hayashi, "Issues Surrounding the Wartime 'Comfort Women,'" *Review of Japanese Culture and Society* 11–12 (1999–2000): 54.

ery in the late 1980s. In 1990, 37 women's organizations in South Korea established the Korean Council for the Women Drafted for Military Sexual Slavery by Japan (hereafter referred to as the Korean Council) for the redress movement. The Korean Council helped Kim Hak-sun, a Korean victim of Japanese military sexual slavery, to come forward in August 1991 and to recount her past experiences at a Japanese military brothel. Her testimony encouraged many other Korean survivors to come forward and to talk about their own brutal experiences in Japanese military brothels. Altogether, 240 Korean victims reported to either the Korean government, or were located in China and other Asian countries, while about 150 Korean victims in North Korea reported. "Comfort women" survivors in Taiwan, China, the Philippines, and other Asian countries also emerged to give testimonies, following the lead of their Korean counterparts.

The emergence of "comfort women" victims in South Korea in 1991 stimulated research on the "comfort women" issue in Japan. In January 1992, Yoshiaki Yoshimi, a Japanese historian, located documents in the Japanese Self-Defense Agency archives that verified the Japanese military government's planning, construction, and operation of "comfort stations." The testimonies by surviving Korean "comfort women" and the discovery of historical documents in Japan accelerated the redress movement for the victims of Japanese military sexual slavery.

The main goal of the movement was to make the Japanese government acknowledge its predecessor's crime and take necessary other measures to bring justice to the victims. The Korean Council made the following six specific demands to the Japanese government in 1990: (1) to acknowledge its predecessor's forced mobilization of Korean women as military "comfort women," (2) to make a formal apology to the victims for the historical event, (3) to reveal all the details about the "comfort women" system, (4) to build a memorial for the victims of the "comfort women" system, (5) to make reparations to the surviving victims and the bereaved families, and (6) to include information about military sexual slavery in Japanese history textbooks.[4] In April 1993, Kōno Yōhei,[5] then-Chief Cabinet Secretary of the Japanese government, announced that a governmental investigation had found the Japanese Imperial Army to have forced "comfort women" to work in Japanese military brothels and to provide sexual services for Japanese soldiers during World War II. In the same year, Japanese scholars and activists established Japan's War Responsibility Center and actively engaged

---

4 Hyun-Sook Lee, *Hanguk Gyohoe Yeoseong Yeonhaphoe 25 Nyonsa* [*A 25 Years' History of Korean Church Women United*] (Seoul: Korean Church Women United, 1992), 314–315.
5 For Japanese names in this text, we use the family/last name followed by given/first name.

in discovering historical documents that demonstrated the Japanese military's responsibility for establishing and operating military brothels.

However, the emergence of historical revisionism[6] and neo-nationalism in the mid-1990s has increasingly rejected progressive scholars' and activists' interpretation of the "comfort women" system as sexual slavery. In 1997, all seven Japanese middle-school history textbooks included information about the "comfort women" issue; however, by 2002, only two of the eight history textbooks did, and in 2006, there were no mentions of "comfort women" whatsoever in any of the textbooks (see the chapter by Puja Kim in this volume). Since Abe Shinzō became the Prime Minister of Japan in 2006, he and most other high-ranking Japanese political leaders have argued that Asian "comfort women" participated in "comfort stations" voluntarily or through human trafficking.

In contrast, the redress movement has received positive responses from the United Nations, the United States, and many other Western countries. The United Nation's human rights bodies and other international human rights organizations have sent over two dozen resolutions to the Japanese government since 1996, urging it to acknowledge the "comfort women" system as sexual slavery and to take responsible measures.[7] Based on an investigation, the U.S. House of Representatives also sent a tough resolution to the Japanese government in July 2007. Following the lead of U.S. Congress, the Canadian, Dutch, and European Union Parliaments adopted and sent similar resolutions to the Japanese government in 2007. Moreover, twelve U.S. state and city governments have also sent similar resolutions to the Japanese government. In addition, fourteen Korean or Asian "comfort women" monuments or "comfort girl" statues have been installed in American neighborhoods.

However, surprisingly, the Japanese government has not accepted any of the above-mentioned six demands. It has tried to resolve the "comfort women" issue twice, but it tried to pay the compensation money indirectly to the victims without acknowledging its predecessor's crimes and making a sincere apology. The Murayama Administration established the Asian Women's Fund (referred to as the AWF), using private donations made by Japanese citizens to pay each

---

6 Nobukatsu Fujioka, *Ojoku no Kingendaishi: Ima Kokufuku no Toki* [Shameful Modern History: Now Is the Time to Overcome] (Tokyo: Tokuma Shoten, 1996).
7 The Korean Council, *Major International Documents on the Japanese Military Sexual Slavery* ('Comfort Women') Issue (Seoul: The Korean Council, 2015).

Asian victim of Japanese military sexual slavery two million yen (about U.S. $20,000) between 1995 and 2007.[8]

The Korean Council and other Asian advocacy organizations strongly rejected the AWF, labeling it "charity money."[9] They demanded direct payment to the victims by the Japanese government, using its own fund, not one consisting of donations from individual citizens. Japanese leaders of the AWF succeeded in persuading 68 Korean "comfort women" (a little more than one-third of all Korean "comfort women" who had publicly reported or testified) to accept the compensation money by contacting them individually without the knowledge of members of the Korean Council.[10] But most Korean surviving "comfort women" and the Korean Council never considered it as a solution to the "comfort women" issue.

Greatly influenced by the U.S. government's effort to establish a strong alliance among the United States, Japan, and South Korea, the Japanese and South Korean government hastily reached a controversial agreement on the "comfort women" issue in December 2015. It included an ambiguous apology for the victims' suffering, without indicating the source of their suffering. It also included a promise from the Japanese government to give one billion yen to the South Korean government to compensate the 56 Korean surviving victims. However, Abe Shinzō should have made a more specific apology and arranged to pay the reparations directly to the victims rather than through the South Korean government. Another controversial aspect of the so-called agreement was that it included a promise from the South Korean government to accept the agreement as final and irreversible.[11] Finally, the South Korean government did not ask the Korean Council or the victims whether the agreement was acceptable or not. Abe did not follow these formal procedures for reparations, mainly because he and his government did not accept the "comfort women" system as sexual slavery.

Korean victims and the Korean Council did not accept the agreement as an adequate solution to the "comfort women" issue for the reasons described

---

[8] Haruki Wada, *Ianfumondai no kaiketsu no tame ni Ajia-jyosei-kikin no keiken kara* [*The Resolution to the Comfort Women Issue: From the Experience of Asian Women's Fund*] (Tokyo: Heibonsha, 2015).
[9] The Korean Council, *Chongshindae Jaryojip III* [*The Korean Council's Data Source III*] (1996).
[10] Ibid., 38.
[11] Chang-rok Kim, Hyun-a Yang, Na-young Lee, and Sihak Cho, "Wianbu Hapeu Idaero-neun Andenda" [We Cannot Accept the 2015 Resolution between Korea and Japan] (Seoul: Gyeonjin Munhwasa), 158; Sang-Hun Choe, "Japan and South Korea Settle Dispute Over Wartime 'Comfort Women,'" *New York Times*, December 28, 2015. Accessed February 14, 2019. https://www.nytimes.com/2015/12/29/world/asia/comfort-women-south-korea-japan.html

above, as well as other reasons, which will be clarified in the document submitted to the United Nations by the Women's Active Museum of War and Peace (WAM), the major Japanese advocacy organization for the victims. To enforce the agreement, with the fund given by the Japanese government, the South Korean government established the *Hwahae Jaedan* (the Reconciliation and Healing Foundation) in July 2016. The Korean Council has rejected compensation money and services from the Reconciliation and Healing Foundation (hereafter referred to as the Foundation). However, the Foundation persuaded—with much difficulty—31 of the 46 surviving Korean victims to accept 120 million Won (about U.S. $100,000) each.[12] It was difficult for the Korean victims not to accept such a significant amount of reparation money because many knew that they would not live much longer. Nevertheless, 15 Korean "comfort women" refused to accept the significant amount of money from the Foundation. Instead, they wanted to receive it directly from the Japanese government in the form of reparation.

The controversy over the 2015 Agreement continued in January 2018, after the change of power from the Park Geun-hye Administration to the Moon Jae-in Administration. The former President, Park Geun-hye, who accepted the 2015 agreement, was involved in the Choi Soon-sil scandal, which came to light in October 2016, and she was impeached and removed from office for bribery and abuse of power in March 2017. President Moon Jae-in, newly elected in May 2017, who had been critical of President Park's acceptance of the controversial 2015 agreement with the Japanese government, ordered an investigation of the process of reaching the agreement through a Special Task Force in the fall of 2017. According to the major findings by the Task Force, the two governments accepted several secret agreements which included the following: (1) the Japanese government prohibits the South Korean government from using the term "sexual slavery" in international settings; (2) it prohibits the South Korean government from supporting "comfort women" memorial projects in foreign countries; and (3) the money the Japanese government paid was not reparation money, but charity money.[13] These secret agreements clearly indicate that the Japanese government's main motivation for passing the agreement was to prevent the South Korean government and advocacy organizations from using the

---

12 The Chosun Ilbo, "Iljeongbu Chaigim Batanaitjiman Haewe Sonyosang Jiwonankiro Bigongae Yaksok" [The Japanese Government's Responsibility Acknowledged, but the Secret Oral Agreement to Give No Support to Get "Comfort Girl" Statues Erected], *The Chosun Ilbo*, December 28, 2016. Accessed February 14, 2019.
13 BBC Korea, "Wianbu TF 'Han Il Hap Ui, Bi Gong Gae Nae Yong Iss Da'... Gung Geum Han 3 Ga Ji" [TF 'comfort women' agreement, unlisted contents'... three questions], December 27, 2017. Accessed February 14, 2019. https://www.bbc.com/korean/amp/news-42490967

term "Japanese military sexual slavery" in international meetings and installing "comfort women" monuments within and outside of South Korea. The Abe administration had been very irritated by these two issues in exercising global leadership in its first three years.

Invigoration of the Redress Movement and the Need for English-Language Books

As noted above, the 2015 Agreement included three secret bargains between the Japanese and South Korean governments. These agreements prevent South Korean advocacy organizations from using the term "Japanese military sexual slavery" in international meetings and getting "comfort women" memorials installed inside and outside of South Korea. In addition, the last secret agreement emphasizes that the compensation money was actually "charity money." These secret agreements clearly indicate the Japanese government's bad intentions to try to resolve the "comfort women" issue solely through financial compensation, without acknowledging its predecessor's crime of sexual slavery and issuing a sincere apology to the victims. Accepting these agreements means nullifying all of the recommendations that UN human and international human rights organizations have given to the Japanese government. The passage of the 2015 Agreement between the Japanese and South Korean governments, as well as President Moon Jae-in's strong support for the Korean Council's position, have invigorated the redress movement in South Korea and elsewhere.

Angered by Japanese politicians' intention to get the Korean "comfort girl" statue in front of the Japanese Embassy in Seoul relocated, a young Korean group installed another Korean "comfort girl" statue in December 2016 in front of the Japanese Consulate General in Busan, the second-largest city in South Korea, to remind Japanese officials of the tragic event that occurred seventy years ago. Moreover, since December 2016, about 80 Korean "comfort girl" statues or "comfort women" monuments have been installed all over South Korea.

In 2016, while working on writing a book manuscript focusing on sexual slavery in Japanese military brothels and the redress movement for the victims, Pyong Gap Min realized that it was a good time to organize an international conference focusing on the redress movement through the Research Center for Korean Community (for which he serves as the director) at Queens College in 2017. He ended up inviting nine "comfort women" scholars and seven top redress movement activists from South Korea, Japan, and the United States for a two-day conference. He set three major goals for the conference: he wanted to (1) publicize the "comfort women" issue and the 27-year-old redress movement, (2) to provide an opportunity for social networking among "comfort women" scholars and activists from a variety of disciplines and different geographical settings, and finally, (3) to publish a comprehensive edited book focusing on the redress movement based on the papers presented at the conference.

We have achieved the first two goals, and we are writing this introduction chapter to achieve the third goal of the conference—producing an informative edited book focusing on the redress movement for the victims of Japanese military sexual slavery. Many Japanese- and Korean-language monographs and edited books focusing on the "comfort women" issue have been published in South Korea and Japan. However, as of 2019, although 28 years have passed since the redress movement started, there are a limited number of English-language materials on this subject. Researchers have published several dozen English-language articles focusing on different aspects of the "comfort women" issue. In addition, about ten English-language edited anthologies of testimonies or autobiographical books have been published.[14] Six English-language monographs and edited books focusing on the "comfort women" issue have also been published.[15] Among them, the English-language translation of Yoshimi's book[16] seems to have gained some popularity among "comfort women" researchers. However, rather than focusing on the redress movement or more recent "comfort women" issues, this book demonstrates how the Japanese Imperial Army planned, established, and managed "comfort stations," and transported "comfort women" from one place to another.

---

14 Sangmi Choi Schellstede, ed. *Comfort Women Speak: Testimony by Sex Slaves of the Japanese Military* (New York and London: Holmes & Meier, 2000); Maria Rosa Henson, *Comfort Women: A Filipina's Story of Prostitution and Slavery under the Japanese Military* (Lanham, MD: Rowman and Littlefield, 1994); Keith Howard, ed. *True Stories of the Korean Comfort Women* (London: Cassell, 1995); Dai Sil Kim-Gibson, ed. *Silence Broken: Korean Comfort Women* (Parkerburg, Iowa: Mid-Prairie Books, 1999); Jan Ruff-O'Herne, *50 Years of Silence* (New York: Editions Tom Thompson, 1994); The Commission on Verification and Support for the Victims of Forced Mobilization Japanese Colonialism in Korea, *Can You Hear Us: The Untold Narratives of Comfort Women* (Seoul: Commission on Verification and Support for the Victims of Forced Mobilization Japanese Colonialism in Korea, 2014).
15 George Hicks, *The Comfort Women: Japan's Brutal Regime of Enforced Prostitution in the Second World War* (New York: W. W. Norton & Company, 1990); Peipei Qui, Su Zhiliang, and Chen Lifei, *Chinese Comfort Women: Testimonies from Imperial Japan's Sex Slaves* (New York: Oxford University Press, 2014); Margaret Stetz and Bonnie B. C. Oh, eds. *Legacies of the Comfort Women of World War II* (London: M. E. Sharpe, 2001); C. Sarah Soh, *The Comfort Women: Sexual Violence and Postcolonial Memory in Korea and Japan* (Chicago: University of Chicago Press, 2008); Yoshimi, *Comfort Women*.
16 Ibid.

In particular, scholars have neglected to conduct research on the redress movement. Only three books focusing on the redress movement have been published in South Korea in the Korean language.[17] The only English-language book focusing on it is C. Sarah Soh's 2008 book, *The Comfort Women: Sexual Violence and Postcolonial Memory in Korea and Japan*. However, this book, written mainly to criticize the Korean Council's redress activities and to reject the orthodox interpretation of the Japanese "comfort women" system as sexual slavery, provides the author's biased views of the redress movement. Moreover, the book has not covered the Japanese politicians' and citizens' recent neo-nationalist movement to deny the Japanese government's responsibility for the "comfort women" issue. Nor has it covered the "history war" going on in the United States between Korean and American redress movement leaders and Japanese neo-nationalist leaders over the installment of "comfort girl" statues and "comfort women" monuments in American neighborhoods. There are a few English-language books that have examined the issues related to war memory in Japan in general.[18] However, there is no book that has examined the responses to the redress movement for the victims of Japanese military sexual slavery systematically.

The Transnational Redress Movement

Korean women's organizations and women's leaders started the redress movement for the victims of Japanese military sexual slavery in South Korea at the end of the 1980s. The redress movement quickly spread to Japan (the perpetrating country), other Asian victim countries, the United Nations, the United States, Canada, Australia, and European countries, including the Netherlands and Germany. The level of the movement's transnational linkages has increased over time for the past thirty years, partly because technological advances have increasingly facilitated transnational activities in all fields. Moreover, the redress

---

17 Chung Chin-song, *Ilbongun Seongnoyeje* [*The Japanese Military Sexual Slavery System*], Second Edition (Seoul: Seoul National University Publishing Company, 2016); The Korean Council, ed. *Ilbongun "Wianbu" Munche-ui Chinsang* [*The Real Picture of the Japanese Military "Comfort Women" Issue*] (Seoul: Ryeaksa Bipyongsa, 1997); The Korean Council, *Hanguk Chongshindae Daecheak Hyeopeuihe 20-Nyonsa* [*A 20-Year History of the Korean Council*] (Seoul: Hanul, 2014).
18 Yoshiko Nozaki, *War Memory, Nationalism and Education in Post-War Japan, 1945–2007* (London/New York: Routledge, 2008); Franziska Seraphim, *War Memory and Social Politics in Japan, 1945–2005* (Cambridge, MA: Harvard University Press, 2006); Kamila Szczepanska, *The Politics of War Memory in Japan: Progressive Civil Society Groups and Contestation of Memory of the Asia-Pacific War* (London/New York: Routledge, 2014).

movement has been increasingly accepted mainly because under the impact of the global feminist movement, people's awareness and consciousness of sexual violence against women as a very important women's human rights issue has continued to increase over time.

From the beginning of the redress movement, the Korean Council has made coalitions with women's groups in Japan and other Asian victim countries through the Asian Solidarity Conference on the Issue of Military Sexual Slavery by Japan (hereafter, the Asian Solidarity Conference). Asian women's advocacy organizations have held fifteen such pan-Asian conferences between 1992 and 2018, at the rate of more than once every two years. As pointed out in Pyong Gap Min's chapter, even though much smaller numbers of women from other Asian victim countries participated in the pan-Asian conferences than Korean women, participants in each Asian Solidarity Conference were able to collectively have a much louder voice to Japan and the rest of the world by virtue of pan-Asian solidarity. Moreover, participation of large numbers of Japanese women and Japanese women's organizations in each pan-Asian conference has legitimated the redress movement mainly as women's and general human rights struggle to stop sexual violence against women during wartime rather than as a Korean ethno-nationalistic movement.

The 1990s was a good time to publicize Japanese military sexual slavery globally partly because two significant world conventions focusing on women's human rights were held, and partly because rape, ethnic cleansing, and other forms of sexual violence against women in Bosnia, Rwanda, and other areas forced UN human rights bodies to take Japanese military sexual slavery—a historical event—very seriously to prevent ongoing sexual violence in those war zones. The Korean Council and other Asian advocacy organizations introduced and publicized Japanese military sexual slavery effectively at the World Convention for Human Rights held in Vienna in 1993.[19] The Fourth World Conference on Women held in Beijing in 1995 provided the Korean Council with an even better opportunity to publicize the "comfort women" issue and the Japanese government's responsibility to women's organizations, feminist scholars, women leaders, and politicians from all over the world.

The Korean Council has actively lobbied UN human rights bodies since 1992. Staff members of the Korean Council have visited the UN in New York City and

---

19 Hei-su Shin, "Ilbongun 'Wianbu'munje Haegyal-eul Wihan Gukjehwalddong-eu Seonggwa-wa Gwaje" [The Achievements and Unresolved Problems of International Activities for the Solution to the 'Comfort Women' Issue], in *Ilbongun 'Wianbu' Munje-eu Jinsang* [*The Real Picture of the Japanese Military Comfort Women Issue*], ed. The Korean Council (Seoul: Yeoksa Bipyongsa, 1997), 282–283.

the UN Human Rights Commission located in Geneva, Switzerland many times over the past 28 years. The Korean Council has also organized several testimonies by Korean "comfort women" at the UN and the UN Human Rights Commission. Many Korean lawyers and even more Japanese lawyers have helped the Korean Council in terms of international law. Many other UN NGOs have supported the redress movement by introducing the "comfort women" issue as an agenda. In particular, two Special Rapporteurs appointed by the UN Human Rights Commission, Radhika Coomaraswamy (a Sri Lankan legal scholar) and Gay J. McDougall (a U.S. legal scholar), submitted reports based on their investigations in 1996 and 1998, respectively.[20] These reports defined the "comfort women" system as "sexual slavery" and "comfort stations" as "rape centers," recommending the Japanese government to take tough legal responsibility.

The Women's International War Crimes Tribunal on Japan's Military Sexual Slavery (hereafter, the Women's Tribunal) held in Tokyo in December 2000 after two and a half years of preparation was a product of intensely coordinated transnational redress activities spanning several different countries.[21] The organization of the Women's Tribunal by many advocacy organizations, which involved Japan and nine other Asian victim countries, the participation of several prosecutors from each Asian victim country, the committee of six judges consisting of internationally renowned legal scholars, the international prosecuting team, the participation of 74 "comfort women" victims from the nine victim countries, as well as the participation of numerous global human rights NGOs, indicates the extreme transnational character of the Women's Tribunal.[22] Several international

---

[20] The Korean Council, *Major International Documents on the Japanese Military Sexual Slavery ("Comfort Women") Issue* (Seoul: The Korean Council, 2015), 5–105; Radhika Coomaraswamy, "Report on the Mission to the Democratic People's Republic of Korea, the Republic of Korea and Japan on the Issue of Military Sexual Slavery in Wartime," E/CN.4/1996/53/Add.1, the Economic and Social Council, the United Nations; Gay J. McDougall, "Contemporary Forms of Slavery: Systematic Rape, Sexual Slavery and Slavery-Like Practices during Armed Conflict," *Final report submitted to United Nations Commission on Human Rights, Sub-Commission on Prevention of Discrimination and Protection of Minorities, 50th Session* (June 22, 1998), UN Doc. E/CN.4/Sub.2/1998/13. Appendix: "An Analysis of the Legal Liability of the Government of Japan for 'Comfort Women Stations' Established during the Second World War," 52, paragraph 55.

[21] Christine Chinkin, "Editorial Comments: Women's International Human Rights Tribunal on Japanese Military Sexual Slavery," *The American Journal of International Law* 95 (2001): 335–341; Rumi Sakamoto, "The Women's International War Crimes Tribunal on Japan's Military Sexual Slavery: A Legal and Feminist Approach to the 'Comfort Women' Issue," *New Zealand Journal of Asian Studies* 3, no. 1 (2000): 49–58.

[22] The Korean Council for the Women Drafted for Military Sexual Slavery by Japan, *Jaryojip 2000: 2000 Nyeon Ilbongun Seongnoye Jeonbeom gukjebeopjeong [Collection of Sources 2000:*

symposiums and meetings were held in Tokyo, Seoul, and Taipei to prepare and to rehearse the Women's Tribunal. The judges found Emperor Hirohito and 39 other Japanese officers guilty of the charges and Japan responsible under international laws applicable at the time of the events for violations of its treaty obligations and principles of customary international law relating to slavery, trafficking, forced labor, and rape, amounting to crimes against humanity. The final judgment reflects the determination and aspiration of global civilians to punish perpetrators of rape and other forms of sexual violence against women during wartime, thereby protecting women's human rights.

The final component of the "comfort women" redress movement's transnational linkages is that overseas Koreans in Japan, the United States, and other Western countries, such as Canada, Australia, and Germany, have engaged in the redress movement. Since the 1960s, large numbers of Koreans have emigrated to the United States and other Western countries. Immediately after Kim Hak-sun *halmeoni*[23] emerged and publicly testified on 14 August 1991, Korean women in Japan established a few advocacy organizations and have actively engaged in the redress movement (see Chapter 2 and 3 of this book). The news that many other Korean women suffered sexual slavery in Japanese military brothels must have been shocking to Korean-Japanese women, especially because most of them were descendants of Koreans forced to move to Japan, the perpetrating country, during the colonization period. For this reason, Korean-Japanese women have been very actively involved in the redress movement, especially in the 1990s.

By the early 1990s, when the redress movement started in South Korea, significant Korean communities had been established in several metropolitan areas in the United States, with much smaller, but still sizeable Korean communities established in Canada, Australia, Germany, and Great Britain. Many Korean immigrant women in these host countries joined the redress movement in the early 1990s. The redress movement led by Korean immigrant women has been most active in the United States, partly because the Korean diasporic community there is much larger (over two million Korean Americans) than that in any other Western country and partly because the U.S. government and citizens can exercise much greater influence on the Japanese government. Korean advo-

---

the Women's International War Crimes Tribunal on Japan's Military Sexual Slavery], (Seoul: The Korean Council, 2000).

23 *Halmeoni* is a Romanization of the Korean word for "grandma" or "grandmother." Korean "comfort women" survivors are often affectionately and respectfully referred to as *"halmeoni"* because of their advanced ages, usually preceded by their family name or even their full name; thus, in this case, Kim Hak-sun is referred to as "Kim *halmeoni.*"

cacy organizations in the United States have invited Korean "comfort women" to give testimonies numerous times. Many major universities and colleges in the United States hosted Korean "comfort women" survivors testifying about their brutal experiences, with many universities having hosted testimonial events twice. Korean advocacy organizations successfully lobbied the U.S. House of Representatives and twelve state assemblies and city councils to pass resolutions to send to the Japanese government. Finally, and perhaps most symbolically, they got thirteen Korean "comfort girl" statues or "comfort women" monuments installed in public places in different U.S. neighborhoods, with two Korean girl statues installed inside buildings of Korean ethnic organizations.

Korean immigrant women settled in other Western countries have engaged in the transnational redress movement by inviting Korean "comfort women" to give testimonies and also by getting Korean "comfort girl" statues or "comfort women" monuments installed in their host countries. We understand that at least one Korean "comfort woman" monument or a "comfort girl" statue has been installed in Canada, Australia, Germany, and France, respectively. In particular, Korean immigrant women's groups in Berlin and other cities in Germany have continued the redress movement since 1991. According to two members of Korean advocacy organizations in Germany,[24] Korean immigrant women advocates for the victims of Japanese sexual slavery there have engaged in a number of important events to publicize the "comfort women" issue to German citizens. These events include testimonies by Korean "comfort women," an international symposium and seminars on human beings' dignity, women's dignity, and war and rape, a campaign against Japan's entry as a UN Security Council member, and translation of Korean "comfort women's" testimonies into German.

Summary of Chapters

This edited book, consisting of 13 substantive chapters, intends to bridge the large gap in research on the redress movement for the victims of Japanese military sexual slavery. As shown in their short author bios, the six scholars who have contributed chapters to this book are eminent specialists and have done much research on the "comfort women" issue and the redress movement. Most of them have also been emotionally involved in the redress movement. The seven redress activists who have written chapters for this book have played

---

24 The Korean Council, *Hanguk chongshindaemunje DaeChaekhyopuihe 20 Nyeonsa* [*The Twenty-Year History of the Korean Council*] (Seoul: Hanul, 2014), 340–387.

central roles in the redress movement in South Korea, Japan, or in the United States. Based on their own personal observations, memories, and records of their advocacy organizations' redress activities, they have written chapters that report many journalistic stories related to "comfort women's" testimonies, Wednesday demonstrations,[25] installation of "comfort girl" statues or "comfort women" monuments, and getting resolutions passed by local governments and even the House of Representatives in the United States. Moreover, their chapters indicate their strong intentions to continue the redress movement to bring justice and dignity to "comfort women" victims. All nine book chapters in Parts I through III focus on the redress movement in South Korea, Japan, and the United States.

Part I includes four chapters that focus on the redress movement for the victims of Japanese military sexual slavery in South Korea or Japan. In the first chapter, Mee-hyang Yoon, who has served as the executive director and a co-representative of the Korean Council for over 25 years, has summarized the activities of the Korean Council in three major sections: (1) its various efforts to help Korean "comfort women" heal their suffering and wounds, (2) its appealing Japanese military sexual slavery to the UN and other human rights organizations and its reception of their strong support, and (3) its international social justice activities to support other victims of wartime sexual violence in other countries. Chapter 2 by Puja Kim examines both the positive and reactionary responses to the redress movement in Japan comprehensively. As an ethnic Korean born and raised in Japan, Kim has been actively engaged in the redress movement in Japan, as a member of a few different advocacy organizations. In addition, she has also conducted active research on the "comfort women" issue, often in collaboration with members of Japan's War Responsibility Data Center. Chapter 3 by Pyong Gap Min focuses on examining various redress activities of many Japanese citizens and organizations to support the redress movement led by two major Korean advocacy organizations. It provides readers with many moving stories which reflect how far Japanese citizens and small groups have gone to support the redress movement. Chapter 4 by Mina Watanabe is a slight revision of the document that the WAM (Women's Active Museum on War and Peace), a historical museum established in Tokyo, submitted to the UN Human Rights Committee, to indicate that the 2015 Agreement between Japan and South Korea was un-

---

25 Beginning on 8 January 1992, every Wednesday at noon, there has been a protest led and organized by the Korean Council held in front of the Japanese Embassy in Seoul, South Korea. Only twice, during the massive earthquakes in Japan, once in Kobe in August 1995 and another time in March 2011, the protest was not held. The Wednesday Demonstration is the longest-running protest about a single theme/issue.

acceptable to resolve the "comfort women" issue. Watanabe serves as the Secretary General of the WAM. The document explains that the "comfort women" issue is not a Japanese-South Korean bilateral diplomatic issue, but an important women's human rights issue, and that therefore the Japanese government has a legal obligation to make fact-finding investigations, an apology, compensation, education, and memory to resolve the "comfort women" issue.

Part II includes three chapters written by three redress activists, focusing on the redress movement in the United States. Chapter 5 by Jungsil Lee and Dongwoo Lee Hahm summarizes the redress activities in which the Washington Coalition for Comfort Women Issues (WCCW) has been engaged in since its establishment in 1992. WCCW is the most active "comfort women" redress organization in the United States, and Jungsil Lee has served as its president for several years. Hahm (the founding president of WCCW) and Lee devote much space to the passage of the House Resolution 121 by the U.S. House of Representatives, in which WCCW played the key role. As a well-known artist and curator, Lee also highlights her organization's educational effort to publicize the "comfort women" issue through arts. Chapter 6 by Judith Mirkinson journalistically covers the process of installing an Asian "comfort women" monument in San Francisco in 2017 with much difficulty. Twelve other "comfort girl" statues or "comfort women" monuments installed in the United States are memorials to Korean "comfort women" installed largely by the efforts of Korean immigrant activists. In contrast, the statue in San Francisco is an Asian "comfort women" monument that commemorates Chinese, Korean, and Filipina "comfort women" and was established by Chinese, Korean, Jewish, and Japanese community coalitions. As a long-term human rights advocate specializing in sexual violence and women's trafficking, Mirkinson served as the President of the Board of the Comfort Women Justice Coalition. Chapter 7 by Phyllis Kim describes the passage of the House Resolution 121 in 2007, the installment of a "comfort girl" statue in Glendale, Los Angeles in 2013, and the installment of a "comfort women" statue in San Francisco in 2017. As a 1.5-generation Korean-American woman, Phyllis Kim was deeply involved in each of these redress projects for "comfort women" victims, and has worked as one of the major "comfort women" activists in the United States over the last several years.

Part III includes two interrelated chapters focusing on legacies of "comfort women" in the arts and humanities. In Chapter 8, Bonnie B. C. Oh examines legacies of "comfort women" that establish educational materials and fields of study in higher educational institutions. She indicates that women's studies, history (including oral history), arts, literature, politics, international relations, and interdisciplinary studies are major fields of study for the "comfort women" issue and the redress movement. In Chapter 9, Margaret Stetz, a prominent feminist scholar in English literature, has taken an overview of the representations of "comfort women"—emphasizing that they were underage female victims of Japanese military sexual slavery—in photographs, commercial films, and novels in the West in the last twenty years. She has made extended comments on two films: *Spirits' Homecoming*, written and directed by Cho Jung-rae in 2016 and *Snowy Road*, written by Yoo Bo-ra and directed by Lee Na-jeong in 2017. In particular, *Spirits' Homecoming* seems to have been used in many college classes in the United States. Reading Stetz's chapter before viewing the movie is likely to help students' understanding of the movie.

Part IV includes two chapters, both of which focus on the Japanese neo-nationalist reactionary movement in Japan and the United States. Tomomi Yamaguchi, the author of Chapter 10, is an anthropologist who has conducted research on the "comfort women" issue. Emi Koyama, the author of Chapter 11, is a Seattle-based social activist who has worked on sexual violence against women. In addition, both authors are Japanese Americans and belong to the Japanese-American redress activist group in the Western United States, which has documented and criticized Japanese neo-nationalists' "history war" activities there. Yamaguchi examines the historical revisionism of Japanese neo-nationalists and their denial of the Japanese military's involvement in sexual slavery. In her view, Japanese neo-nationalists consider the acts of remembering and commemorating "comfort women" survivors' experiences of war-time violence as contentious political issues that mobilize them intensively in Japan and the United States. In Chapter 11, Koyama focuses on attacking Japanese neo-nationalists' and the Japanese government's effort to deny the "comfort women" system as sexual slavery in the United States.

Part V includes two chapters that cover topics not directly related to the redress movement, but to new sources and theoretical approaches related to the history of the Japanese military sexual slavery system and the abuse of Asian women by the Japanese Army. Therefore, they are very important chapters for the understanding of the "comfort women" issue and its legacies. In Chapter 12, Peipei Qiu demonstrates the Japanese military government's establishment of "comfort stations," the ratio of "comfort women" to Japanese soldiers, and the forcible mobilization of Chinese women for sexual servitude in Jilin, China based on Jilin Provincial archives that were discovered and analyzed recently. Japanese scholars have thus far demonstrated the Japanese military government's responsibility for the "comfort women" system largely based on historical archives in the Japanese Self-defense Agency.²⁶ Given this, her chapter based on newly discovered Japanese historical documents in Jilin is likely to attract a great deal of scholarly attention. In Chapter 13, Angella Son argues that the Japanese government has refused to acknowledge the crime of sexual slavery because of its deep sense of shame. She has analyzed Japan's inability to embrace shame, using Heinz Kohut's self-psychology and Gershen Kaufman's discussion on defense against shame.

Clarification of Terms

During the Asian and Pacific War, the Japanese military and Japanese historical documents referred to the victims of military sexual slavery euphemistically as "military comfort women" (*jūgun ianfu* in Japanese) or simply as "comfort women" (*ianfu* in Japanese and the *chongshindae* or *wianbu* in Korean). In addition, Japanese military brothels were referred to as "comfort stations" *(iansho* in Japanese and *wianso* in Korean)*. In post-war Japan, the victims have been continuously referred to as "military comfort women" or "comfort women." Japanese researchers have continuously used the terms "military comfort women," "comfort women," and "comfort stations" in the titles of many books and articles.²⁷

In Korea, the terms "*chongshindae*" (which means "voluntary labor corps," implicitly in service to the nation), "*yeoja* (women) *chongshindae*," "*geunro* (labor) *chongshindae*," or "*yeoja geunro chongshindae*" (women voluntary labor corps) were used interchangeably beginning in 1941 to refer to "women's voluntary labor corps" mobilized for labor service to Japan.²⁸ Despite the term's indication of the voluntary nature of the recruitment of Korean women, the *geunro chongshindae* (Korean women labor corps) were mostly forcibly drafted by the Japanese government. However, the terms "*chongshindae*" or "*cheonyeo gongchul*" ("releasing one's unmarried daughter") were also used more often in

---

26 Hirofumi Hayashi, *Nihongun "Ianfu" Mondai-no Kakushi* [*The Core of the Japanese Military Comfort Women Issue*] (Tokyo: Kadensha, 2015); Yoshimi, *Comfort Women*.

27 Suzuki Yūko, *Chōsenjin jūgun ianfu* [*Korean Military Comfort Women*] (Tokyo: Iwanami Shoten, 1991); Suzuki Yūko, *Sensō sekinin to gendā* [*War Responsibility and Gender*] (Tokyo; Miraisha, 1997); Yoshimi Yoshiaki, *Jareojip: Jonggun Wianbu* [*Source Book: Military "Comfort Women"*], trans. Soon-Oh Kim, (Seoul: Suhmoondang, 1993); Yoshimi, *Comfort Women*.

28 M. K. Kang, "Ilbongun 'wianbu' ui gaenyumgwa hoching munje" [The Issues Related to Concepts and Terms for Japanese Military "Comfort Women"], in *Ilbongun "wianbu" munje ui jinsang* [The Reality of the Japanese Military "Comfort Women" Issue), ed. The Korean Council (Seoul, South Korea: Yuksa Bipyoungsa, 1997), 14–15.

Korea in 1938 and after to refer to what the Japanese military called Korean "comfort women." One of the main reasons Japanese authorities and recruiters used these terms was that they were able to deceive young Korean women into thinking that they were being mobilized or recruited for non-sexual forms of labor, when they were in fact being mobilized to Japanese military brothels. The term "*chongshindae*" continued to be highly associated with Korean "comfort women" victims in the post-war years. For this reason, Korean women's leaders named their organization *Chongshindae Munje Daechaek Hyeopuihe* (the Association for the Resolution to the Chongshindae Issue) when it was established in 1990.

However, the Korean leaders of the redress movement translated the name of the organization into the Korean Council for the Women Drafted for Military Sexual Slavery by Japan; they have continuously used this name at the United Nations and in the English-speaking world in 1992 and after. They seem to have used this name especially to present the Japanese "comfort women" system as sexual slavery. In fact, in validation of Korean movement leaders, two UN Special Rapporteurs on Violence against Women referred to Japanese military "comfort women" as "sexual slaves" and referred to "comfort stations" as "rape centers" in 1996 and 1998.[29] The labeling of "comfort women" as "sexual slaves" and the "comfort women" system as "sexual slavery" by UN Human Rights Rapporteurs[30] has encouraged the members of Korean and other Asian advocacy organizations and scholars to use the terms "sexual slaves" and "sexual slavery" to refer to "comfort women" and the "comfort women" system, respectively. Nevertheless, Japanese scholars and advocacy organizations have continued to use "comfort women," "military comfort women," and "comfort stations" since the beginning of the redress movement in 1990, mainly because Japanese historical data and previous Japanese writers used those terms. Following Japanese scholars, Western media and scholars have continued to use these euphemistic terms.

We are well aware that the terms, "comfort women," "comfort stations," and the "comfort women" system poorly represent the victims' experiences. Not only that, these terms are disrespectful to the women who experienced these ordeals, and it is completely understandable that surviving victims like Lee Yong-su do not like them. However, these terms have been used so much, not only by Japanese movement leaders and scholars, but also by others interested in the "comfort women" issue and the redress movement. Thus, we have also decided to use

---

29 The Korean Council for the Women Drafted for Sexual Slavery by Japan, *Major International Documents on the Japanese Military Sexual Slavery ('Comfort Women') Issue*, 2015, 9, 49–50; Coomaraswamy, "Report;" McDougall, "Contemporary."
30 Coomaraswamy, "Report;" McDougall, "Contemporary."

these terms in this book to communicate with Japanese scholars and others effectively. We use the terms "comfort women" and sexual slaves, "comfort stations" and Japanese military brothels, and the "comfort women system" and sexual slavery interchangeably. Following the Korean Council's decision, we have put the terms "comfort women," the "comfort women" system and "comfort stations" within quotation marks.

In using the names of Korean "comfort women," we have put their family/last names first, as is customary in Korea (as well as in some other Asian countries) because Kim Hak-sun and many other Korean redress movement activists have been referred to that way by international media. In Romanizing Japanese and Chinese books, names, and words into English, we have followed the McCune-Reischauer format. But in Romanizing Korean books, names, and words, we have followed the revised format used by the South Korean government,[31] which is easier for lay readers to read. However, when citing Korean and other Asian names and words that have already used particular spellings in the past, we have continued to use the same spellings without applying any of the current widely used Romanization styles.

Social researchers usually use pseudonyms in order to hide, protect, or maintain the privacy of informants' identities. However, when the Korean Council and the Korean Research Institute edited eight volumes of testimonies, they kept the real names of Korean "comfort women" with their approval. In case the participants in the project did not want to disclose their real names, they used pseudonyms. As we have used testimonies by Korean "comfort women" that have either already been cited by others or from the eight volumes of testimonies, in this book, we have used the same names included in the original citations or directly from the eight volumes, whether real or pseudonyms. Since the vast majority of Korean "comfort women" who participated in the testimony project have passed away, with only 23 of them surviving as of February 2019, keeping their identities confidential is much less important now than it was 28 years ago.

---

[31] "Romanization of Korean," Ministry of Culture, Sports and Tourism. Accessed January 21, 2019. https://www.mcst.go.kr/english/koreaInfo/language/romanization.jsp

Part I: **The Redress Movement in South Korea and Japan**

Mee-hyang Yoon
Unfulfilled Justice: Human Rights Restoration for the Victims of Japanese Military Sexual Slavery[1]

In April 2010, the United Nations Special Rapporteur on Violence Against Women, Rashida Manjoo, submitted a report to the UN, in which she wrote, "[t]he single most organized and well-documented movement for reparations for women is that for the so-called 'comfort women.'" The Special Rapporteur reminded the international body that the victims of the "comfort women" system have long demanded an official apology: "Since the late 1980s, survivors have come forward to bear witness and mobilize international public opinion, asking for an official apology and reparation." She further noted, "As victims of sexual crimes, they do not want to receive financial aid without an official apology and official recognition of State responsibility." Rashida Manjoo made the point clear that there remained an unmet demand for legal justice for the victims of the "comfort women" in her report.[2]

On 6 August 2014, Navi Pillay, then UN High Commissioner for Human Rights, issued a statement, arguing that "[t]his is not an issue relegated to history. It is a current issue, as human rights violations against these women continue to occur as long as their rights to justice and reparation are not realized." The former High Commissioner reaffirmed the victims' rights to legal reparations and demanded the Japanese government stand accountable for the issue.[3]

Notwithstanding that the "comfort women" system was an organized and systematic crime forcefully carried out by the Japanese military, on 28 December 2015, the governments of South Korea and Japan announced that the issue was

---
[1] The Korean Council for the Women Drafted for Military Sexual Slavery by Japan is an independent non-governmental and non-profit organization formed by 37 women's rights activist groups in 1990 to resolve the so-called "comfort women" issue.
[2] Report of the Special Rapporteur on violence against women, its causes and consequences by Rashida Manjoo, Human Rights Council Fourteenth session, Agenda item 3 – Promotion and protection of all human rights, civil, political, economic, social and cultural rights, including the right to development. Accessed February 17, 2019. https://digitallibrary.un.org/record/683885/files/A_HRC_14_22-EN.pdf
[3] Japan's approach to the issue of "comfort women" causing further violations of victims' human rights by Navi Pillay, former UN High Commissioner for Human Rights (2008–2014). Accessed February 17, 2019. http://www.ohchr.org/EN/NewsEvents/Pages/DisplayNews.aspx?NewsID=14920

"finally and irreversibly" resolved through a bilateral agreement between the two governments. The agreement made between the two governments ignored the basic historical facts of the issue and denied Japan's legal responsibilities. At the agreement, 28 years of independent efforts to prove that victims of wartime sexual violence have legal right to reparation were shrugged off, and the "comfort women" victims ended up being treated as people needing economic assistance rather than as the victims of war crimes.

After the agreement between South Korea and Japan was announced on 28 December 2015, Gil Won-ok, who was abducted at age 13 and taken into combat zones where she was raped by soldiers as a "comfort woman" until she was 18 years old, said she felt pained due to the agreement: "What I have demanded from the Japanese government was not money because I was hungry. What I have demanded from the Japanese government was for them to accept the historical truth and make an official apology and for legal reparations. This is the demand for no more wars like this ever again."[4] Kim Bok-dong, one of the victims of Japan's sexual slavery system from the time she was 15 until she was 22, made the following statement when she appeared as a witness at the National Assembly Audit: "We do not fight to receive consolation money. We have fought to regain our honor and dignity. The reason we have been fighting is to obtain an official apology and legal reparations from the Japanese government. How could the Korean government sell our history with money? We will fight until Japan admits its fault and apologizes."[5]

It has been 73 years since the war ended, and 28 years since the victims of the Japanese military "comfort women" system emerged to demand from Japan an admission of its war crimes and taking up subsequent legal responsibilities. Despite resolute protests by and for the victims, the Japanese government has denied its war crimes and disrupted and attacked the victims' efforts to make their case heard around the world to resolve the issue. In order to evade its responsibilities, the Japanese government continues to reply with absurd statements, such as claiming that there is "no evidence of the victims being forcibly taken." Such remarks made by the government of Japan injure the victims over and over again.

Justice for the victims of the Japanese military "comfort women" system has not been fulfilled, and the surviving victims, many of whom are now over 90 years old, have never stopped raising awareness about what has been done to

---

[4] Personal communication with officials from the Ministry of Foreign Affairs of The Republic of Korea, December 2015.

[5] National Assembly Audit of Foreign Affairs and Unification Committee during the 346th Regular Session, Testimony, September 26, 2016.

them. They have been out on the streets in different lands for 28 years, meeting and talking to strangers who may not have yet heard about this issue. When will the victims see their justice fulfilled? How can we open the path that stops sexual violence during wartime, which is occurring even at this moment, from ever reoccurring?

28-Year Effort to Resolve the "Comfort Women" Issue

The Korean Council for the Women Drafted for Military Sexual Slavery by Japan (hereafter "the Korean Council") is an organization that works closely with the "comfort women" victims towards a resolution of the Japanese military "comfort women" issue. 16 November 2018 marked the 28th anniversary of the establishment of the Korean Council. The "comfort women" issue was first brought to public attention in South Korean society in the late 1980s, when pro-democracy movements emerged against the previous military dictatorship and Koreans began to discuss many other important historical and political issues for the first time. In addition, liberal and progressive civil organizations were established and expanded their activities during this time period. Therefore, many issues regarding Korean society at large that had been suppressed in the postwar years began emerging. The "comfort women" issue was one of many that came to light. However, it remained marginal and did not receive much attention until several years after the initial outpouring. It was only when the Korean Council was established that the "comfort women" issue arose for real public discussion in South Korean society. On 16 November 1990, 37 liberal and progressive women's organizations created the Korean Council to resolve the "comfort women" issue, and so was ordained as an important responsibility of the women's rights movement. Women's organizations coming together to form the Korean Council also meant the "comfort women" issue had become a symbolic consolidation of overall women's issues that had been suppressed and coercively silenced in the postwar era in Korea.

Despite the camaraderie in the initial formation of the Korean Council, South Korean society in the early 1990s did not welcome the taking up of the "comfort women" issue. Many people still thought it was a shameful issue due to social stigma associated with victims of sexual abuse or assault, and the social environment made the victims reluctant or unwilling to come forward. On 8 January 1992, the first Wednesday Demonstration took place in front of the Embassy of Japan in Seoul, South Korea. However, South Korean society did not suddenly change its opinion on the issue just because this demonstration happened. At this time, a call center was set up by the Korean Council for the victims to report harm done to them during the war, but old men who lived through the war period called in and said, "The more that the 'comfort women' issue is openly revealed, the greater our people's shame becomes. Stop this reporting movement right now." During the early stages of the Wednesday Demonstrations in front of the Japanese embassy in Seoul, some old men complained, "[w]hat's there to be proud about being 'comfort women?' It is no use making an issue out of it. It is only shame." The Korean Council requested the "comfort women" issue be included in the Independence Hall of Korea's exhibition hall of Japanese colonial-imperial history, but organizations from Korea's independence movement rejected this request, all of which demonstrates how the "comfort women" victims were treated in the post-war Korean society.

The societal pressure felt by "comfort women" victims was finally understood when several brave victims visited the Korean Council office to tell their story. In spring of 1992, Kim Soon-duk, one of the "comfort women" victims, came to our office to report her hardship during the war. She was not able to say that she was a "comfort women" victim during her first visit to our office. It was very difficult for her to tell us about that period in her life. She visited several times and struggled to speak because of shame, and she barely convinced herself to disclose her story. She testified that she was taken away to China and forced to become a sex slave for the Japanese military. Afterwards, she participated in the Wednesday Demonstrations and gave public testimony as protest in Japan later on, but we remember with pain that she was never able to look up into someone's face when she was interviewed by the media.

Lee Yong-su walked in to a newspaper's office in Daegu, South Korea and was guided to call the Korean Council office to report a "comfort women" story. She called us and said in a very soft voice, "[i]t was not me but my friend, she was taken away by the Japanese military and came back... what should she do?" This is hard to imagine because she is now one of the most courageous and noble activists on the issue. Twenty-eight years have passed and the accumulation of these years have come with changes.

Chronology of the Victims' Disclosure

- On 21–23 April 1988, Women's organizations actively took up the "comfort women" issue for the first time at "International Seminar on Women and Tourism Culture," held in Jeju Island, South Korea.

- On 16 November 1990, The Korean Council for the Women Drafted for the Military Sexual Slavery by Japan was organized.
- On 14 August 1991, Kim Hak-sun unveiled she was a victim of the "comfort women" system through an open press conference – on 18 September 1991, the Korean Council call center was established and publicized – Second report of "comfort women" damage, Mun Ok-chu and other victims reported, as of end of June 2017, total 239 victims.
- In January 1992, Sin Do Song reported to a call center 110 established by women's organizations of Japan.
- On 10–11 August 1992, the 1st Asian Solidarity Conference for Resolution of the Japanese Military "Comfort Women" Issue was held in Seoul. Women's rights activists of Asia, including Philippines, Taiwan, Hong Kong, Japan, and so on, participated in the Asia Solidarity Conference held in South Korea. Women who disclosed themselves as victims of the "comfort women" system participated.
- The victims started movements that were 1) searching for other victims across Asia, 2) supporting victims in other Asian countries, 3) filing a lawsuit against the Japanese government, and 4) attending UN events, etc.

As a result of these meetings and the creation of the Korean Council, new movements arose that demanded a resolution of the Japanese military "comfort women" issue, and this began to change Korean society. In particular, the Korean Council's movement started with women's protests, which demanded an end to the culture of sexual violence and the reform of the systemic discrimination against women which had been rampant in Korean society in the 1970s and 1980s. The movement for the resolution of the "comfort women" issue asked fundamental questions of Korean society and the government, which treated women as "national" and "economic" resources. Though time has passed and socio-political situations have changed, sexual violence and the violation of women's rights have only changed their forms but continue in substantially similar ways. The fight on the "comfort women" issue is a protest against the true root of these issues.

The Korean Council did not begin by confronting the "comfort women" issue. In fact, the first issue the organization examined was the experience of women in prostitution and the sex tourism industry. The Korean Council has continuously asked, "Why does this keep happening?" Attempting to answer this question led them to understand that it was necessary to change the patriarchal system which reinforces these conditions. The "comfort women" victims independently and autonomously made efforts that played a major role in the movement for women's emancipation, and their vocal support and solidarity with other victims of sexual violence has become a beacon of empowerment.

Although the issue of women who have survived the Japanese military's sexual slavery system, or the "comfort women" issue, can be understood as a standalone issue for the advocacy of specific surviving victims, it is, in fact, deeply related with other broader issues. The pursuit of a resolution to the "comfort women" issue is a matter of women's rights as well as peace (it is an anti-war and anti-war crime issue as well). Therefore, the attempt to resolve the "comfort women" issue was not only to hold the perpetrator country accountable for their war crimes, but to constructively change Korean society's perceptions about women. In order to change traditional Korean perceptions about women, the Korean Council repeatedly highlighted the problems of the patriarchal system in Korean society so that the general public would become aware and remember the history for the next generations. Solidarity with other organizations in different fields throughout Korean society was necessary to produce these changes.

These movements ultimately led to efforts in Korea and all over the world to prevent the recurrence of sexual violence during wartime. Furthermore, these efforts helped the Korean Council include the issue of the U.S. "camptown prostitution" system, which was the continuation of the "comfort women" system created by the Japanese government during their colonization of Korea as Korea transitioned from a colonized nation to a divided peninsula. These movements also led to the construction of the War and Women's Rights Museum and establishment of the Nabi Fund to support non-Korean victims of sexual violence during wartime, and constructing Peace Monuments as well as memorial stones for the "comfort women" victims. Through these movements that have gone beyond national borders, the Korean Council pushed forward the movement to prevent the recurrence of sexual violence during wartime and to protest against any anti-peace factors that encourage the atmosphere of armed conflict.

Subsequently, South Korean society has changed through an accumulation of these efforts. How people see and what they say about the so-called "comfort women" have transformed a society that used to blame and avoid the victims, calling them shameful and dirty women, putting them under extreme pressure to remain silent. As a result of these efforts, many people in South Korea have become supportive voices, and have said things like, "[t]hank you for surviving the war," "[t]hank you for telling us our history, we cannot forget," and "[w]e will be with you as you have fought so hard despite your age and illness." Since 2000, new organizations that support the "comfort women" victims have grown across the country and have begun to organize to resolve the issue.

Through all the efforts throughout the last 28 years mentioned above, the path to regaining dignity and human rights for the "comfort women" victims has become clear. This path is possible when three conditions are met. The first condition must be met by the perpetrator(s); in other words, the perpetrator(s) must take complete responsibility for their crimes, make an official apology and offer legal reparations, establish an education curriculum that corrects the historical record, and implement public commemoration ceremonies for the victims to prevent recurrence of the same crimes. The second condition is the necessary change in the social perceptions that stigmatize victims and the structures that oppose the victims achieving their justice. The third condition is met when the dignity and human rights of the victims are restored, and this is achieved by the victims' social and political self-actualization. The work towards meeting these conditions have been in progress for the last 28 years.

Support for the Victims of Japanese Military Sexual Slavery

The severe physical and bodily damage inflicted upon the "comfort women" victims during their enslavement in the "comfort stations" remained long after the war. From 1995 to 1999, the Korean Council carried out medical examinations for the victims who reported themselves as victims of the Japanese sexual slavery system to the Korean Council office. According to the results of the exam by Seoul Central Hospital (currently, Asan Hospital), 19 victims among 53 victims (35.9%) who took medical exams tested positive for Treponema pallidum (syphilis). After-effects of the "comfort women's" time in the "comfort stations" have been latent in the victims' body for more than a half a century since the liberation of Korea. Syphilis requires long-term treatment, and even when the syphilis virus goes into remission from treatment, one will still test positive whenever a blood test is done, so the victims were stigmatized as prostitutes or "comfort women" when they returned to the patriarchal post-war Korean society.

In accordance with the medical examination conducted by the Orthopedics Department of Incheon Sarang Hospital in September 2000, seven of 14 victims reported ongoing suffering from physical beatings endured in "comfort stations." Moreover, their injuries were not limited to their bodies but were accompanied by psychological trauma. The results of an inquiry on 192 victims out of those reported by the Korean Council in 2001[6] revealed that most of these "comfort

---

6 Center of War and Women's Human Rights of the Korean Council for the Women Drafted for Military Sexual Slavery by Japan, "Chapter 6–4: Health Condition" in *Sourcebook of Testimony, Statistics on the Japanese Military "Comfort Women" System* (Seoul: Center of War and Women's

women" victims had serious mental disabilities and emotional disorders such as severe anthrophobia (fear of other people), anxiety, resentment, strong feelings of humiliation, guilt, anger, self-loathing, resignation, depression, self-degradation, loneliness, and so on. The Korean Council faced this deteriorated situation of the victims and had to put the matter of victims' welfare first before any other activities.

First of all, the Korean Council began to hold meetings for the "comfort women" victims: from 2–3 May 1992, an event was held for victims to get together who had shared the same pain. Their meeting was a significant start of a healing process as they had an opportunity to share their painful experiences and to feel belonging with each other that they could not do with anyone else, not even with their family. As soon as the survivor victims who attended that event met each other, they started talking about their "comfort women" experiences. The same situation occurred among "comfort women" victims from other countries; when the Korean victims met with Jan Ruff O'Herne, a "comfort woman" victim from Australia, and other victims from Taiwan and the Philippines, they all poured out the difficult suppressed feelings and memories from their common experience. "Although we don't speak the same language, we can feel each other." Events like these, called Human Rights Camps, continued two or three times every year as part of the victims' healing process.[7]

Second, the Korean Council prepared a common residential space for the victims. This subject was brought up as a top priority at the first victims' meeting. At the time, most of the victims lived in very poor conditions, and most did not even have their own private room. The representatives of the Korean Council met to discuss securing long-term shelter for the victims. At the discussion, a representative from the Women's Commission of the Buddhism Human Rights Commission (one of the member organizations of the Korean Council at that time) volunteered to raise funds and build a common apartment building for the victims. Later, this apartment became the House of Sharing in Gwangju, Gyeonggi-do, and it became an independent project separate from the work of the Korean Council. In 2003, the Korean Council opened its own long-term shelter for sexual violence victims located in Seoul named Our Home of Peace, where many events for the healing of the "comfort women" victims have been conducted.

Third, the Korean Council formed civilian support networks as part of a healing process for the victims. Particularly through cooperation with medical insti-

---

Human Rights of the Korean Council for the Women Drafted for Military Sexual Slavery by Japan, 2001), 128–130.
7 Ibid., 128–130.

tutions, the victims were able to get treatment when they were sick or in an emergency situation that usually required high medical costs. Medical institutions who participated in the victims' healing process were Cheonho Oriental Clinic, Haemosu Dental Clinic, and Hyundai Asan Foundation, among others.

Fourth, the Korean Council has ensured that the healing process has continued through seeking continual economic support. At the first Human Rights Camp, the Korean Council verified the victims' vulnerable economic situation and therefore raised funds to support the victims financially. The first fundraising event was in 1992, and all of the victims received 2,500,000 Won (about U.S. $2,182) each. The second fundraising event occurred in 1996, and at that time, the Japanese government commemorated the 50th anniversary of the end of the war and announced that it would establish the Asian Women's Fund (also known as the Asian Peace and Friendship Fund for Women) to pay the "comfort women" victims. However, the Asian Women's Fund did not come from Japan's governmental budget, but was instead collected from voluntary contributions by Japanese citizens. The Japanese government declared it would give this money as a "consolation money" (not a reparation), which was a denial of Japan's legal responsibilities for the "comfort women" issue. The Korean Council continued fundraising for the victims, and it demanded that the Japanese government admit the truth of history, make an official apology to the "comfort women" victims, and offer them reparations as one form of taking legal responsibility for its crime.

Fifth, the Korean Council organized victim support networks at the city and local community level. This was done to support the victims in all areas, particularly those who lived alone without a family or caregiver. The local support networks made it easier for volunteers to coordinate making regular visits to the victims in their community. This local support system is called "Peace Nabi," and it has been established in Suwon, Sungnam, Haenam, Gwangju, and other areas, and Peace Nabi continues to give care and attention to the victims in their communities. A project like this could come into existence because Korean society began to reflect on how it had neglected the victims for such a long time after liberation from Japan. Thereafter, more victim-supporting organizations were established in Daegu, Tongyoung, and Changwon, independent of the Korean Council.

Sixth, since the victims' first meeting event in May 1992, the Korean Council has demanded that the South Korean government establish an institutional system for fact-finding investigations on the issue and advocated for support for the victims at the government level. Accordingly, the South Korean government set up a task force on the "comfort women" issue under the Ministry of Foreign Affairs in 1992, and it received victims' testimonies collected by local governments.

The task force disclosed the results of their first investigation, and in 1993, enacted the "Act on Livelihood and Stability for Sexual Slavery Victims Drafted for the Japanese Imperial Army Under the Japanese Colonial Rule" to carry out victim-supporting programs. These programs included giving the victims priority to move into permanent rental housing, free healthcare and nursing services, and providing monthly living expenses, and so on. In 2004, the act was amended and the title was changed to the "Act on Livelihood, Stability and Commemorative Projects for Sexual Slavery Victims Drafted for the Japanese Imperial Army Under the Japanese Colonial Rule."[8]

Lastly, along with the direct and urgent help described above, the Korean Council has supported the victims towards regaining their dignity and human rights. Although the victims may be able to have a stable daily life economically, psychologically, and culturally, the ultimate healing of the victims is impossible if society's perception of the victims does not change. Therefore, the Korean Council used various ways to provide history education for the general public, organized the Wednesday Demonstrations, and promoted the cause of the "comfort women" through media to correct people's perception of the issue.

Raising the "Comfort Women" Issue in the International Community

On 28 December 2015, the "comfort women" agreement between the Korean and Japanese governments (hereafter, "the 2015 Agreement") declared that both governments had agreed to not to bring up the "comfort women" issue in the international community again. However, this agreement has become meaningless because the "comfort women" issue has since been continuously brought up and questioned throughout the international community. Actually, the 2015 Agreement helped people realize the importance of the "comfort women" issue as a human rights matter because the idea that two governments can "finally and irreversibly" resolve and conclude such a human rights issue, committed by one of these countries upon the other, is itself a mistake.

The first time the "comfort women" issue was brought up in the international community was 25 years ago. In August 1992, the Korean Council and the victims made official accusations of the Japanese government for their crimes in

---

[8] Accessed February 19, 2019. http://www.moleg.go.kr/english/korLawEng;jsessionid=4Qj6ayHzKje2WAdg6VZsndEkfKqaavcbZpGUUew0b4N6vWiLZl084vURN09DNc6c?pstSeq=52824&pageIndex=6

creating the "comfort women" system. The Korean Council held press conferences, briefing sessions with other NGOs, and made remarks at the UN Subcommittee on Human Rights regarding two agendas at that time: (1) modern slavery and (2) reparations for victims of serious human rights violation. As a result of these activities, the "Report on the Issue of the Japanese Military 'Comfort Women' System" was submitted to the UN Human Rights Committee in 1996 by Radhika Coomaraswamy, the UN Special Rapporteur on Violence against Women. The "Special Report on Sexual Slavery during Wartime" was submitted to the UN Human Rights Subcommittee in 1998 by Gay McDougall, UN Special Rapporteur on The Issue of Systematic Rape, Sexual Slavery, and Slavery-like Practices in Armed Conflict. These two reports are considered groundbreaking studies on the "comfort women" issue as these investigations revealed precise details and demonstrated the Japanese government's legal responsibilities for the crimes committed at the national level. In addition, both reports suggested that Japan must make an effort to resolve the so-called "comfort women" issue.

From that point on, the victims reported their situations and the Japanese government's responses to the UN on a regular basis and continued to communicate with the UN. Consequently, recommendation reports on resolution of the Japanese military "comfort women" issue were continuously adopted by UN human rights conventions, including the Convention on the Elimination of all Forms of Discrimination against Women (CEDAW), the Convention Against Torture (CAT), the Convention on Civil and Political Rights (CCPR), the Committee on Economic, Social, and Cultural Rights (CESCR), and so on. In particular, the CAT was concerned that the Japanese government's official denial and concealment of the "comfort women" crimes, non-indictment of the responsible actors, and inaction regarding appropriate measures for the victims' recovery was an ongoing abuse of the survivor victims, as it caused continuous retraumatization. The CAT recommended that the Japanese government seek punishment for the responsible actors without any sort of statute of limitations and that they establish means of recovery for the survivors.

Since 1996, experts from the Committee on the Application of Standards of the International Labour Organization (ILO) pointed out that the "comfort women" issue was a crime of sex slavery and an example of violation of international law, as the Japanese government violated the ILO Convention No. 29, which they also ratified. The ILO experts also demanded the Japanese government implement legal reparations and other measures for the victims. In recent years, recommendations from international organizations have continued. On 25 July 2014, the UN Committee on Civil and Political Rights criticized the attitude of the Japanese government on the "comfort women" issue, and demanded immediate and effective implementation of full reparations for the victims, disclosure of all evidence of the crimes to the utmost, inclusion of descriptions of relevant facts in history textbooks, a public apology and official admission of responsibilities for the crimes, prohibition on insulting the victims and denial of the issue, an independent and fair investigation on human rights violations committed by the Japanese military during the war including the "comfort women" issue, and punishment of the responsible parties.

When the above UN resolution was adopted, about 200 members of right-wing organizations from Japan made a disturbance at the UN conference room, yelling that the UN committee members were leftists. "One is not necessarily obligated to follow the recommendations of the UN," said Prime Minister Abe in officially contradicting the UN judgement when questioned about the UN recommendations during a National Diet session, "[i]t is unfortunate that the UN does not understand the Japanese government's stance."[9]

On 21 August of the same year, the UN Committee on the Elimination of Racial Discrimination (CERD) urged Japan to seek a comprehensive resolution to the "comfort women" issue that includes making an apology and offering reparations to the victims, as Japan avoided resolving the issue despite criticisms by the international community. In addition, CERD emphasized that so-called "hate speech," making volatile remarks or protesting against a specific ethnic group or race, was not freedom of expression, but subject to regulation, and called on an investigation and indictment of individuals or groups involved in anti-Korea protests, if necessary. The CERD also ordered Japan to impose a proper sanction on public figures including civil servants and politicians who instigated any anti-Korea remarks and hate speech against South Korea.

There were statements and recommendations by the UN's human rights organizations condemning the 2015 South Korea-Japan agreement. On 7 March 2016, the CEDAW announced its stance that the 2015 agreement did not sufficiently take a victim-centered approach, and CEDAW called for an official apology and reparations by the Japanese government. The CEDAW also urged the Japanese government to ensure cessation of any statements or actions of Japan's leaders and public officials disparaging Japan's responsibilities for the "comfort women" issue to avoid retraumatizing the "comfort women" victims.

On 10 March 2016, Zeid Ra'ad al Hussein, the UN High Commissioner for Human Rights, also remarked on the 2015 agreement. He claimed that only the survivors had a right to say if true reparations were made to them, and urged both Korean and Japanese governments to make greater efforts to develop

---

9 Article containing Prime Minister Abe's statement in Korean. Accessed February 19, 2019. http://www.yonhapnews.co.kr/politics/2014/01/30/0503000000AKR20140130041700073.HTML

an understanding of the brave and noble survivors, as communication with them is important in the agreement process.

On 11 March 2016, three of the Special Procedures of the UN Human Rights Council (the CEDAW working group, Special Rapporteur on the promotion of truth, justice, reparation and guarantees of non-recurrence, Special Rapporteur on torture and other cruel, inhuman or degrading treatment or punishment) criticized the 2015 agreement because it did not meet the demands of the survivors nor the standards of national responsibilities for serious violation of human rights. Moreover, the agreement was condemned because there was no negotiating process with the victims and their supporting organizations during the agreement process. They emphasized that the victims' rights to truth, justice, and reparation can only be protected when there is a clear official apology and sufficient reparations are offered. They also observed that Peace Monuments are not only for commemorating the past history of "comfort women," but that they are also a symbol of survivors' ongoing pursuit of justice, and thus condemned the demolition of Peace Monuments.

Announcements of the UN's positions on the 2015 agreement has continued in 2017. In May 2017, the CAT pointed out to the Korean government that the 2015 agreement failed to provide the surviving victims with rights that ensure truth and non-recurrence (including compensation, reparations, restoring dignity, and a means of complete rehabilitation) because the 2015 agreement did not sufficiently comply with the scope and contents of General Comment 3 on Implementation of Convention Against Torture article 14. The CAT, therefore, recommended the Korean government revise the 2015 agreement in order to ensure the surviving victims' rights to compensation, regaining their honor and dignity, fact-finding investigation, and other assistance, including reparations and promise of non-recurrence according to Article 14 of Convention Against Torture. In other words, the CAT determined that it was necessary to renegotiate the 2015 agreement.[10]

---

10 Under Article 14, No. 1 of the UN Convention Against Torture, each state party "shall ensure in its legal system that the victim of an act of torture obtains redress and has an enforceable right to fair and adequate compensation, including the means for as full rehabilitation as possible". On 19 November 2012, the CAT repeated, "[a]ll States parties are required to 'ensure in its legal system that the victim of an act of torture obtains redress and has an enforceable right to fair and adequate compensation, including the means for as full rehabilitation as possible.'" through General Comment No. 3 of the Committee against Torture, which was adopted to clearly explain the duties and range of countries that ratified the UN Convention Against Torture under Article 14. This document addresses the importance of victims' participation in the aid process and concludes that the ultimate purpose of aid for the victims is to regain their dignity.

In response to the CAT's comments, the Ministry of Foreign Affairs of South Korea announced, "[t]he Korean government has noted the recommendations by the UNCAT and is in the process of reviewing the details of the suggested recommendations with relevant departments." The response demonstrated that the Korean government would affirmatively review the UN's recommendations made on 16 May regarding the 2015 agreement.

In the second half of 2017, the international community expected continued discussion of this issue. In November 2017, human rights in Korea and Japan were discussed at the Universal Periodic Review (UPR) of the UN Human Rights Council. The UN Human Rights Council re-examines the human rights situation of UN member states and makes recommendations to each member every four and a half years. The second half of 2017 included sessions that reviewed the human rights record of South Korea and Japan.

Victims' Voice Grows in Solidarity: Beyond Gender, Generation, and Borders

On 8 January 1992, the first Wednesday Demonstration took place. The first Wednesday Demonstration coincided with the fact that Japanese Prime Minister Miyazawa was visiting South Korea at that time. The Wednesday Demonstrations have occurred every week since then, more than 1,300 times for over 27 years. The Wednesday Demonstrations are carried out all over the world by diverse civil organizations, students, and normal everyday citizens. Every year on South Korea's National Liberation Day, and on other commemorative days, the Global Solidarity Action for Comfort Women also takes place. A few times a year, the Wednesday Demonstration joins with other groups around the world to protest war. On 14 December 2011, on the day when the 1,000th Wednesday Demonstration was held, the Peace Monument, which contains a message about the "comfort women" victims' long journey towards peace, was placed in front of the Japanese embassy in Seoul. Since then, additional Peace Monuments have been built in 70 areas throughout South Korea and overseas, and now students from 239 high schools are participating in constructing more Peace Monuments. On 5 May 2012, the War and Women's Human Rights Museum was built in Seoul through independent fundraising from the general public. The museum informs people of the "comfort women" issue as an extended issue of war and women's human rights, and directs people in how they can participate to resolve the issue.

As the 1,000th Wednesday Demonstration took place, one could not help but notice how the crowd had changed over time. Young people came out to express their heartfelt support of the survivors; in fact, 80% of the Wednesday Demonstration participants were adolescents, which meant that the history of the "comfort women" issue has successfully been passed on to the next generation. The number of participants has grown every year, particularly from the U.S., other Asian countries, and even in Africa, and many student groups have joined the Wednesday Demonstrations for the purpose of learning history on a regular basis. It is clear that the Wednesday Demonstrations go beyond being a protest that amplifies the voice of individual victims. Rather, the demonstrations are a place of solidarity to achieve the mutually-reinforcing values of peace and human rights.

In addition, there were many other activities for students and everyday citizens, such as visiting places where sexual violence occurred in Korea, including areas where the Japanese system of licensed prostitution were established, places of pain and sorrow during the Korean War, and also places in Vietnam where civilians were massacred during the Vietnam War. More international activities in solidarity with movements towards resolving sexual violence have sprung up. The Korean Council provided monthly seminars on issues of Korean society, starting with Korea's involvement in the Vietnam War and the U.S. military bases in Korea, then expanding to human rights violations against women in armed conflict areas in Thailand, Bosnia, Congo, Uganda, Afghanistan, and Pakistan. This work allowed the Korean Council to work with international women's rights activists and to raise greater awareness about the "comfort women" issue. On International Women's Day, 8 March 2012, these collective actions led to the establishment of the Nabi Fund to support victims of sexual violence during wartime. Nabi Funds have been sent to Congo, Vietnam, Syria, and Palestine for emergency rescue and support since its creation. In the case of Vietnam, in particular, annual "Apology Trips" have been made to support Vietnamese sexual violence victims, and to demand that the Korean government admit the war crimes committed by the Korean military during the Vietnam War, and to demand that the Korean government take legal responsibility and make an official apology.

Solidarity between "comfort women" victims in North and South Korea played a crucial role. On 14 August 1991, Kim Hak-sun, one of the victims of the "comfort women" system, held the first press conference on the "comfort women" issue to testify about her painful experiences during the war. Since her courageous move, other "comfort women" victims in both North and South Korea continued to report their testimonies. This movement led by the victims themselves has led to cross-border solidarity efforts. For humanitarian reasons, despite political tensions and a lack of communication between North and

South Korea since 1992, South Korean organizations have been able to meet with "comfort women" from the North in support and solidarity. Both parties have recognized the "comfort women" issue as an historic humanitarian crisis. The "comfort women" victims in Asia also continued to unify and work together to resolve the "comfort women" issue for the last 26 years. Through this solidarity, the first Asian Solidarity Conference was held in Seoul on 11–12 August 1992, and the victims' voice became even louder in the international community through the continuation of this conference.

The movement to resolve the "comfort women" issue continues to be relevant because there is still sexual violence during wartime—violence created by patriarchal social systems—and the crimes that created the "comfort women" system continue to recur. Ten years ago, Solidarity for Human Rights of Camptown Women (SHRCW) was established by the Korean Council and other women's rights organizations that support women who survived U.S. military camp towns. SHRCW filed a claim for compensation for the victims against the Korean government. There exist social and political structures that encourage imperialist invasion and war (including Japan's colonization of Korea), sexual crimes against women during war, military camptown prostitution (e.g., the U.S. occupation), and domestic gender discrimination. Our solidarity network has expanded because people understand that if the fundamental structures behind these crimes do not change, these crimes will continue to recur.

These activities of the "comfort women" victims and the Korean Council became widely known, and in 2015, Reporters Without Borders selected Kim Bok-dong (one of the "comfort women" victims and a human rights activist who was the founder of Nabi Funds) as one of the "100 Heroes for the Freedom of Press" and wrote about her in their book. As a result of these movements and activities, a substantive victim support system in Korea was realized; victim-supporting laws have been established and social attention has been raised through gradually changing society's ideas and the government's policies. However, the victims' fury and sorrow, which have continued to exist deep in their minds, had not been able to be resolved through these supports. Although a number of victims by their own will determined to regain their self-esteem, dignity, wholeness, and human rights by directly participating in the movements, the major wounds in their minds still exist and cannot heal. These wounds have never left the victims because the perpetrator, the Japanese government, has denied its crimes against the victims. With everything else that has improved, the "comfort women" victims have still not received an apology nor reparations from the perpetrator, and the need to be justly compensated for how they were victimized remains deep in their mind. Japan's denials remain an unjust reality that continue to harm the victims.

Whenever there was any news of political changes in either Korea or Japan, the "comfort women" victims always called their supporting organizations and asked if Japan would make an apology or try to resolve the issue. Victims who were bedridden due to illness, who had forgotten all else because of dementia, still could not forget the Wednesday Demonstrations, saying, "I should go to the Japanese embassy today." An ill victim would remember the abuse she endured and suddenly jolt awake, and in her outrage, would begin unleashing a torrent of scornful words for what she was forced to experience. In the end, the experience and agony of the victims cannot be completely erased but will always follow them. Appropriate measures for victims' recovery need to be done in a sufficient and evident way by the perpetrator country as it is beyond the scope of the victim country's organizations.

The first step of the recovery measures is the victims' most common wish to the Japanese government, which is for it to admit its predecessor's responsibility and culpability, making a sincere apology, and providing reparations. The victims have continued to appeal the importance of telling the truth to the next generation and ensuring non-recurrence of the same crimes.

The Victims' Wishes to the Japanese Government

Son Pan-im: I still feel shivering when I think of what Japan did to us. The Japanese government must correctly investigate the facts on the issue, make reparations for all damages, and punish the responsible. It still makes me sick and furious every time I testify even now.[11]

Yeo Bok-sil: There are many victims whose lives were ruined after being taken into the Japanese military brothel. We need to receive Japan's apology and reparations. Would Japan leave things be for over 50 years if the Korean military took Japanese women and did to them what they did to us?[12]

Choi Jung-rye: I felt mortified and angry because I was deceived about where I was going to at that time, and it destroyed my life like this. That is why I decided to report that I was a "comfort woman" victim. The Japanese government has to stop making excuses, and truly apologize and make reparations.[13]

---

11 The Korean Council for Women Drafted for Military Sexual Slavery by Japan and the Korean Research Institute, *Gangjero Kkullyeogan Joseonin Gunwianbudeul* [The Forcibly Drafted Korean "Comfort Women"], *Testimonies* (Seoul: Hanul, 1997), 82.
12 Ibid., 207.
13 Ibid., 223.

Kim Hwa-ja (alias): When I pray nowadays, I say, "[p]lease help the Japanese people apologize to us anyhow." I pray like this when I pray alone. I say, "[p]lease let us to have world peace" three times and "[p]lease, God, help Koizumi apologize to us, to Korea anyhow, please, God, my father."[14]

Chung Seo-woon: Ah... I really hope that this issue is resolved before I die. Only so I die with my two eyes closed and relaxed. Japan has to apologize and make a reparation no matter how much it is, even a penny is fine, only if they truly apologize before I die. This is the only thing I hope. I will become just a handful of dirt when I die, but I can't die in peace with my eyes closed if they don't apologize.[15]

Noh Chung-ja: It is fair and right to demand compensation. We have suffered enough.[16]

Gil Won-ok: I don't have much time left in life. I only wish to release my deep sorrow. Just one word of apology, that is all I have wanted, only if it is with an honest heart. Ah, so many victims already have gone and only a few are left with me now. They say, "[o]ne word is worth a thousand pieces of gold." An apology would be only a ten-thousandth of what they have done to us, though how glad I would be if they said, "[y]ou indeed became like this because of us, please untangle your mind even a little bit."[17]

Shin Hyun-soon: What I want to say to the Japanese government is... live with honesty. When they first took us into the "comfort stations," they lied to us. Then they did not write this correctly in their children's history textbook. It would be great if they corrected their textbook, apologized to us, and surrendered before the truth. They cheered up their soldiers by using us Korean women, and they won then lost the war. Terrible. Even we who didn't learn much know what shame is. They took Korean people and made Koreans do all kinds of crazy things.[18]

In accordance with the victims' wishes, the Korean Council has made the following demands to the Japanese government in the last 20 years:

---

[14] The Korean Council for Women Drafted for Military Sexual Slavery by Japan, *Yeoksareul Mandeuneun Iyagi* [History Making Stories], *Testimonies*, Vol. 6 (Seoul: Doseo Chulpan, 2004), 76.
[15] Ibid., 98.
[16] Ibid., 233.
[17] Ibid., 342.
[18] The Korean Research Institute and the Korean Council for Women Drafted for Military Sexual Slavery by Japan, *Gangjero Kkullyeogan Joseonin Gunwianbudeul* [Forcibly Drafted Korean "Comfort Women"], *Testimonies* (Seoul: Hanul, 1999), 316.

1. Admission of war crimes committed by Japan
2. Disclosure of all documents relevant to the crimes and a fact-finding investigation
3. Official apology
4. Legal reparations
5. Punishment of the responsible
6. Correcting the record in history textbooks
7. Establishment of commemorative monuments and history museums

These seven demands are only minimum measures to recover the victims' human rights and prevent recurrence. However, the Japanese government has not implemented even one of them. Rather, Prime Minister Abe denied the fact that the victims were taken away by force and stated that calling the victims "sex slaves" was slander against Japan. Moreover, the "comfort women" issue has disappeared from their history textbooks.

The issue of the Japanese military "comfort women" system is an undeniable crime against humanity and it is the most organized and extreme example of violence against women during wartime. In accordance with resolutions of the UN General Assembly and international human rights principles, the Japanese government is obligated to provide prompt and full reparation. The Japanese government is also obligated to resolve the issue in a way that is acceptable to the victims, and the Japanese government must follow through with the recommendations by the UN human rights mechanisms, legal perspectives suggested by the ILO and International Commission of Jurists (ICJ), and recommendations by the U.S. and the European Union.

Efforts to Rebuild Hope

Although the governments of Korea and Japan attempted to block the victims' voices and to end the issue through the 2015 agreement, their intentions backfired, and instead, their agreement made more people aware of how important the issue was and expanded the movement all over the world. People called for the invalidation of the 2015 agreement and for it to be replaced by a righteous resolution so that a positive future for South Korea-Japan relations could be possible. The 2015 agreement was put in place as a roadblock to the "comfort women" but has become their stepping stone towards a resolution.

The biggest change occurred in South Korean civil society. Prior to the 2015 agreement, the "comfort women" issue was not considered a women's issue or an important social issue by the general public. However, since the 2015 agreement, masses of Korean people understood that it was their task to resolve this and began to work together for the "comfort women." Plays, dances, songs, and films about the "comfort women" issue were made by artists for the general public to understand the issue clearly; the issue was on the news day after day; and everyday citizens designed and sold products (such as badges, bracelets, and stationary supplies) that incorporated the "comfort women" and donated the profits to support the "comfort women."

On 9 June 2016, the Foundation of Justice and Remembrance was established by 500 civil organizations and 500 individuals who collected 1 billion Won (about U.S. $875,000) in donations. The foundation started supporting not only victims in Korea, but also other victims in Asia, where there has been no government support or other supporting organization for them. In addition, memorial scholarship funds were made in the victims' names to assist impoverished adolescents. The foundation also runs a Korea-Japan student exchange program for the future generations to remember the victims and history, and eventually, to build a relationship between the two countries with a long-term vision for the future. The Foundation of Justice and Remembrance conducted research and investigation on missing victims taken during the war, and trained educators of women's rights and sent them to schools from 25 November to 10 December 2016 (International Day for the Elimination of Violence against Women 16-day campaign).

On 28 December 2015, the victims who said they were hurt because the 2015 agreement excluded their opinion, began to smile again. They expressed their hopes again and are appealing for peace now.

Toward an End: Peace Together

For the last 28 years, the victims have spoken for women's rights and peace all over the world. Now they are over 90 years old, and only 35 "comfort women" victims of the 239 who reported 28 years ago are still alive. Only about five of the 35 living victims can work as activists now. Other victims in Asia are in the same situation.

On its own, the pain of being a sex slave during a war would be enough to destroy one's life. However, the perpetrator denying the truth of this experience means that they face another abuse on a daily basis because they have to hear these denials, and so they are being abused and destroyed for a second time. This justice has been withheld too long, and now it is at risk of being unfulfilled and totally lost with the death of each victim who could hear an apology. The "comfort women" victims who have gone through unspeakable pain, have spoken out as well as offered support and hope to other victims. Now it is our turn to finish their hope for peace.

For the righteous and just resolution of the Japanese military "comfort women" issue, we must not stop our effort to recover the victims' human rights, to prevent recurrence of sexual violence victims during wartime, and to make the world free of war. Resolution of the "comfort women" issue will be a good example of crimes being punished without time limitation, in this reality where women's bodies are exploited in war. This effort will move forward to finally end violence. The victims sincerely hope that the resolution of war crimes and systematic violence against women no longer remains merely as a discourse, but that it becomes converted into action by the international community to eradicate the problem.

Puja Kim
The "Comfort Women" Redress Movement in Japan:
Reflections on the Past 28 years[1]

Introduction

Korean "comfort women" (*ianfu*), forced to provide sex to Imperial Army troops at military "comfort stations" (*ianjo*) during the Asia-Pacific War (1931–1945), were abandoned after Japan's defeat in August 1945. Those fortunate enough to return home spent more than half a century in poverty, hiding their experiences of systemic sexual abuse from their own communities. In the late 1980s, as South Korea's democratization movement flourished, Korean women's groups drew attention to the plight of these victim-survivors and began a campaign to help them obtain justice and rejoin society. To coordinate and expand that work, in November 1990, these groups formed the Korean Council for the Women Drafted for Military Sexual Slavery by Japan (hereafter, the Korean Council). In December, concerned women in Japan exchanged views with their South Korean counterparts and laid the groundwork for a Japanese redress movement.

Less than a year later, an unexpected development galvanized the new advocacy groups. In August 1991, Kim Hak-sun appeared at a press conference in Seoul and spoke openly about her past as a "comfort woman," becoming the first South Korean to "come out" using her real name. In December 1991, during a visit to Japan, Kim brought suit against the Japanese state for her wartime suffering. Tokyo denied responsibility, but in January 1992, historian Yoshimi Yoshiaki uncovered Imperial Army documents that proved direct military involvement in the "comfort women" system, forcing the government to acknowledge the complicity of the Imperial state and its armed forces.[2]

---

[1] This chapter is a substantially rewritten and updated version of an article that originally appeared in Japanese in the September 2013 issue of *The History Journal*. Puja Kim, "Nihon no shimin shakai to 'ianfu' mondai kaiketsu undō" [Japanese Civil Society and the Struggle to Resolve the Issue of Japan's Military Sexual Slavery], *Rekishi Hyōron* [The History Journal] no. 761 (September 2013): 24–40. I wish to thank Tomomi Emoto for her English translation. I am also grateful to Robert Ricketts for revising and adapting the manuscript.
[2] Yoshiaki Yoshimi, *Comfort Women: Sexual Slavery in the Japanese Military During World War II*, trans. Suzanne O'Brien (New York: Columbia University Press, 2000), 43–75. In the main text

Following Kim Hak-sun's example, survivors in South Korea and other countries also stepped forward and announced themselves. Redress groups quickly formed around these women, many of whom later filed lawsuits in Japanese courts demanding a formal apology from the government, state-mandated compensation, and a full accounting of the truth about military sexual abuse. As the advocacy movement gathered steam and public interest in the "comfort women" issue grew, both in Japan and abroad, the Japanese government conducted two internal surveys of its own.[3] On 4 August 1993, Chief Cabinet Secretary Kōno Yōhei announced the conclusions of these studies in a formal policy pronouncement.

Speaking on behalf of the government, Kōno expressed Japan's "apologies and remorse" for the "comfort women" system and recognized the Imperial military's role in establishing, maintaining, and managing the sex venues.[4] The so-called Kōno Statement was ambiguous about the ultimate responsibility for the "comfort women" system, but it acknowledged the coercive recruitment (*kyōsei renkō*) of women, their transportation to foreign battlefields, and the lives of misery they led at "comfort stations" under "a coercive atmosphere." Kōno also stated Japan's "firm determination never to repeat the same mistake by forever engraving such issues in our memories through the study and teaching of history." This pledge was an official commitment to the international community to remedy this historical injustice and work to prevent recurrences.

In August 1995, Prime Minister Murayama Tomiichi addressed the issue of war responsibility in general, conveying his "deep remorse" and "heartfelt apology" for Japan's pre-1945 "colonial rule and aggression."[5] Responding to the Kōno and Murayama statements, junior high textbook editors began includ-

---

of this essay, Asian names are given in the traditional Asian order: family name first, given name second.

3 Official documents assembled in these surveys were later published in five volumes between 1997 and 1998. They are available online at the website Digital Museum: The Comfort Women Issue and the Asian Women's Fund. *Archives: Historical Documents Regarding the Comfort Women*, 2007. English and Korean versions of key documents are also available at http://www.awf.or.jp/e6/index.html. Accessed February 20, 2019.

4 Kōno Yōhei, "Statement by Chief Cabinet Secretary Yōhei Kōno on the Result of the Study on the Issue of 'Comfort Women'," August 4, 1993. Online website of the Asian Women's Fund. *Digital Museum: The "Comfort Women" System and the Asian Women's Fund*. 2007. Accessed February 20, 2019. http://www.awf.or.jp/e6/statement-03.html.

5 Murayama Tomiichi, "Statement by Prime Minister Tomiichi Murayama on the Occasion of the 50th Anniversary of the End of the War." August 15, 1995. Website of the Asian Women's Fund. *Digital Museum: The "Comfort Women" System and the Asian Women's Fund*. 2007. Accessed February 20, 2019. http://www.awf.or.jp/e6/statement-03.html.

ing brief accounts of the "comfort women" in school history books. This change seemed to presage a turning point in post-war education: the "comfort women" issue would now become part of the nation's historical memory.

The Japanese government's efforts to deal with this issue through the quasi-private Asian Women's Fund (1995–2007) faltered and ended in confusion, however. In the late 1990s, there was a strong reaction from historical revisionists, who disputed the facts of military sexual servitude. Far-right politicians, academics, social commentators, and business leaders challenged the Kōno and Murayama pronouncements and called for the elimination of textbook references to "comfort women," the Nanjing Massacre, and other unresolved war issues. Abe Shinzō, Japan's current prime minister, and other influential young lawmakers of the day, participated actively in this movement. Abe channeled this "revisionist turn" and ascended rapidly inside the ruling Liberal Democratic Party,[6] serving as a magnet for ultranationalists of various persuasions. These forces quickly aligned with his revisionist agenda, insisting that public education and the media reflect their right-wing views of history.

When Abe became prime minister in 2006 and formed his first government (2006–2007), his position on the "comfort women" was soon formalized as government policy. On 5 March 2007, Abe told the National Diet that "testimony to the effect that there had been a hunt for 'comfort women' is a complete fabrication."[7] This assertion was ratified as a Cabinet decision on 16 March 2007, nullifying one of Kōno's fundamental admissions: that "comfort women" had been "recruited against their own will, through coaxing, coercion, etc., and that, at times, administrative/military personnel directly took part in the recruitment."

In June of that year, a group of 60 prominent revisionists close to Abe placed a full-page advertisement in *The Washington Post*, making the following additional claim to a world audience: "The *ianfu* [comfort women] were not, as is commonly reported, 'sex slaves.' They were working under a system of licensed prostitution that was commonplace around the world at the time."[8] When Abe

---

6 The Liberal Democratic Party is a conservative party that has ruled almost continuously since its founding in 1955. The LDP's post-war hold on power has been broken momentarily only twice: by a coalition government from 1993 to 1994 under Prime Minister Murayama Tomiichi and by the centrist Democratic Party of Japan from 2009 to 2012.
7 Martin Fackler, "No Apology for Sex Slavery, Japan's Prime Minister Says," *The New York Times*, March 6, 2007, A10.
8 This view has been thoroughly debunked by Japanese historians. See Footnote 16 below and Yoshiaki Yoshimi, "The Kōno Statement: Its Historical Significance and Limitations" in *Denying the Comfort Women*, eds. Rumiko Nishino, Puja Kim, and Akane Onozawa, trans. Robert Ricketts (New York and London: Routledge, 2018), 23–28, and Akane Onozawa, "The Comfort Women and State Prostitution" in ibid., 70–86.

became Prime Minister again in December 2012, an explicit priority was to revise the Kōno Statement. By then, the official denial and disparagement of "comfort women" had metastasized into a full-blown hate movement.

With that background in mind, this chapter discusses Japan's redress movement, focusing on three themes. The first is the cooperative ties forged in the early 1990s between former "comfort women," and an extensive network of researchers, legal specialists, educators, women's groups, human rights activists, and local residents in Japan. The period from the early 1990s through the end of Abe's first term begins with the personal revelations of former "comfort women" in 1991 and ends with the failure of the Asian Women's Fund in 2007.

The high point of this early period was the Women's International War Crimes Tribunal on Military Sexual Slavery by Japan, held in Tokyo in 2000. The Tribunal was a pivotal event that pursued the criminal responsibility of those who created and ran the "comfort women" system, opening a new front in the redress campaign.

A second theme is the revisionist rejection of the historical realities of the "comfort women" saga and the attempts of the redress movement to counter this reaction by strengthening the appeal of a fact-based discourse. "Comfort women" revisionism became a highly politicized feature of the first Abe government. I analyze changing public perceptions of the sexual slavery issue in the early 2000s, as both the government and some segments of society engaged in what became known as "comfort women bashing." Since Abe's second term as prime minister (late 2012-present), this current has broadened into a hate-speech movement that now attracts younger Japanese, including women.

The final theme is the search for an enduring settlement of the controversy. It includes the continuing response of the redress movement to the state's assault on historical truth, the problems facing survivors and support groups, and the deceptive Japan-South Korea Agreement of December 2015, which professes to have settled the issue definitively.

On a personal note, I write from my perspective as an ethnic Korean born and raised in Japan who has been deeply involved in efforts to find a solution to the "comfort women" dilemma consonant with the needs and wishes of living victims. This essay is also informed by my personal experiences as an organizer of the 2000 Women's International Tribunal.

The Redress Movement

The Early Years

The existence of "comfort women" was known in Japan long before the 1990s. Senda Kakō's 1973 reportage, *The Military "Comfort Women,"* sold 700,000 copies, becoming a long-running best-seller.[9] His book remained the representative work on the "military "comfort women"—a term he popularized—until the 1990s. The issue, however, did not arouse widespread public interest. Nor did it stimulate historical research on the subject or inspire a broad-based advocacy movement committed to finding a solution.

Two factors in the early 1990s led to a progressive shift in popular perceptions of the "comfort women" in both Japan and South Korea. The first was the emergence in 1990 of a unified Korean women's movement inspired in part by the pioneering "comfort women" research of Yun Chong-ok, a professor at Ewha Woman's University in Seoul. In June 1990, when asked in the Japanese National Diet if his ministry planned to investigate that question, a Labor Ministry bureaucrat replied that there were no records because private brokers, not the military, had mobilized the women. In October, a coalition of South Korean women's groups issued an open letter to the Diet protesting that statement and drawing renewed attention to the problem. Yun Chong-ok visited Japan and delivered a series of lectures that December based on her extensive studies. Invigorated by Yun's talks, women's groups in Japan launched their own campaign to advocate for the rights of victim-survivors.[10]

A second factor impelling the redress movement was Kim Hak-sun's dramatic public testimony in 1991. Her surprise revelations in August and subsequent lawsuit against the Japanese government spurred Japanese and ethnic Koreans in Japan to act on her demands for official restitution. Large numbers of women gathered to hear Kim talk in Tokyo and Osaka during her December visit, and many lent her their support.

Deeply moved by Kim's earlier televised interviews in Seoul, Yoshimi Yoshiaki scoured Japan's Self-Defense Agency archives for information on military "comfort stations." In January 1992, he publicized military documents proving

---

9 Interview with Senda Kakō conducted by the author in 2000. See Senda Kakō, *Jūgun ianfu* [*The Military "Comfort Women"*] (Tokyo: Futabasha, 1973).
10 The *Hankyoreh* newspaper (Seoul) serialized Yun Chong-ok's Japan lectures, which ethnic Koreans in Japan had translated into Korean. The talks were also published later in Japanese.

beyond a doubt that Imperial Armed Forces had been intimately involved in planning, establishing, and operating those venues in China as early as 1932.[11]

In South Korea, China, the Philippines, Taiwan, and the Netherlands, victimized women came forward, spoke publicly, and in some cases, took the Japanese government to court. In each country, support groups coalesced around the survivors, and as lawsuits multiplied, researchers and legal experts in Japan offered their assistance. Following the example of South Korean and Japanese women's organizations, advocacy networks sprung up and were soon cooperating across borders. The result was the emergence of a transnational movement that won the backing of the United Nations and other world human rights bodies.

In August 1992, one year after Kim Hak-sun's press conference, the first Asian Solidarity Conference for the Issue of Military Sexual Slavery by Japan convened in Seoul. Support groups from South Korea, Taiwan, the Philippines, Hong Kong, and Japan participated. In 2014, the Conference drafted a proposal for a solution that survivors could accept, providing the outlines of a viable settlement. By 2016, the coalition had met fourteen times in South Korea, Japan, the Philippines, Taiwan, and other countries.

From "Comfort Women" to Sex Slaves

Scholars in Japan engaged in intensive and sustained fact-finding to uncover the realities behind the "comfort women" system. Yoshimi Yoshiaki worked closely with Hayashi Hirofumi and other pioneering researchers, including feminist historians and writers such as Suzuki Yūko, Nishino Rumiko, and Kawata Fumiko. Together they produced a substantial body of new information on the background and inner workings of this system.[12] In 1993, historian Arai Shin'ichi joined Yoshimi, Hayashi, Nishino, and Kawata to inaugurate the Center for Research and Documentation on Japan's War Responsibility (abbreviated as

---

[11] Yoshimi Yoshiaki, *Jūgun "ianfu" shiryōshū* [*Historical Documents on the Military "Comfort Women"*] (Tokyo: Ōtsuki Shoten, 1992).

[12] See Yoshimi Yoshiaki and Hayashi Hirofumi, eds. *Kyōdō kenkyū: Nihongun ianfu* [*Joint Research: "Comfort Women" of the Japanese Army*] (Tokyo: Ōstuki Shoten, 1995); Suzuki Yūko, *"Jūgun ianfu" mondai to seibōryoku* [*The Military "Comfort Women" Issue and Sexual Violence*] (Tōkyō: Miraisha, 1993); Nishino Rumiko, *Jūgun ianfu: Moto heishitachi no shōgen* [*Military "Comfort Women": Testimonies by Former Soldiers*] (Tokyo: Akashi Shoten, 1992); and Kawata Fumiko, *Kōgun ianjo no onnatachi* [*Women of the Imperial Army's Comfort Stations*] (Tokyo: Chikuma Shobō, 1993).

Japan War Responsibility Center, or JWRC).[13] The JWRC journal, *Report on Japan's War Responsibility* (1993–2018), published numerous seminal studies. The JWRC also copied and analyzed the war diaries and memoirs of Imperial soldiers in the National Diet Library, clarifying the nature of military sexual violence.

Japanese civic groups and supporters also played a crucial part in fact-finding and discovery. In January 1992, for example, several local organizations established a hotline, "Dial Emergency for 'Comfort Women,'" which collected the personal war memories of 235 Imperial veterans and former military nurses across Japan.[14] Support groups in Saitama, Kyoto, and Kumamoto also conducted telephone surveys, publishing their findings in self-funded books and pamphlets. Korean women living in Japan helped bridge the Japanese and South Korean movements by organizing public conferences (*shōgen shūkai*) for Kim Hak-sun during her Japan tour. They interpreted, translated Kim's talks into Japanese, and helped publish the proceedings.

Groundbreaking research and citizen data-gathering raised public awareness of the problem, but the single most important factor was extraordinary progress in recording and publishing the oral histories of survivors. The tight cooperation that developed between Korean, Chinese, Taiwanese, Filipino, and Dutch survivors, on the one hand, and a wide variety of redress groups in Japan, on the other, gave the Japanese advocacy movement a distinctive dynamism. This collaboration was particularly evident in the civil law cases that survivors brought against the Japanese government.

In the decade between 1991 and 2001, survivors began ten civil actions against the state. Kim Hak-sun and two others filed the first suit in December 1991. They were followed in short order by plaintiffs from South Korea (1991 and 1992), the Philippines, and a Zainichi Korean in Japan (1993), a Dutch survivor (1994), Taiwanese victims (1999), and four groups of Chinese women from Shanxi Province and Hainan Island (1995–2001). In March 2010, the Supreme Court dismissed a final appeal by the Hainan group, ending litigation.

The plaintiffs lost all of their cases but one, that of the Yamaguchi District Court's Shimonoseki Branch, where they won a partial victory and limited damages—only to have the decision overturned later by a higher court. But Japanese judges unanimously recognized as fact that "comfort stations" had been established and managed by the military. Many judgments also cited or quoted direct-

---

13 The JWRC's official English website is http://www.japanwarresp.g1.xrea.com. Accessed January 20, 2019.
14 Jūgun ianfu 110 ban henshū iinkai, ed. *Jūgun Ianfu 110 ban* [*Dial 110 for Military "Comfort Women"*] (Tokyo: Akashi Shoten, 1992).

ly from plaintiff depositions, attesting to their veracity. During adjudication, lawyers, researchers, and women's groups in Japan examined and compiled the plaintiffs' oral statements, many of which were later published by support groups. The evidentiary trial record became an indispensable part of the struggle to uncover historical truth, and for that reason, courtroom testimonies remain a rich oral archive of historical importance.[15]

It is clear from this voluminous written and oral documentation that the "comfort women" system was not a case of wartime prostitution. It was a regime of systematic rape instituted as state policy by Japanese military and civil authorities between 1932 and 1945. The world human rights community concurred. After careful examination, UN human rights mechanisms concluded in 1992 that the "comfort women" system was a system of "sexual slavery." That determination quickly gained traction in Japan and Asia. Redress advocates began employing the terms "Japanese military comfort women" and "Japanese military sexual slaves" interchangeably, a shift in emphasis that brought this terminology closer to the lived experiences of victims.

The key issue is not forcible recruitment, per se, but the fact that many tens of thousands of girls and women across Asia and the Pacific were subjected to an elaborately organized regime of military control, confined in "comfort stations," and obliged to perform sex acts on demand. Deprived of freedom of movement, captive women lived under threat of extreme sanction and could neither refuse work nor walk away.[16]

The Failure of the Asian Women's Fund (1995–2007)

Survivors and redress groups demanded redress for all victims regardless of ethnicity, nationality, or place of residence, and Kōno incorporated that phrase into his final report. Faced with a transnational advocacy movement, escalating law-

---

15 Tsubokawa Hiroko and Ōmori Noriko, *Shihō ga nintei shita Nihongun "ianfu": Higai/kagai jijitsu wa kesenai* [*Japan's Legal System Recognizes the Military "Comfort Women": The Facts Concerning Victim and Aggressor Cannot be Erased*] (Tokyo: Kamogawa Shuppan, 2011).
16 The great majority of "comfort" girls and women were Asians and Pacific Islanders, but the Japanese military also recruited considerable numbers of ethnic Japanese. Most were licensed prostitutes, indentured to their owners, often under slave-like conditions. Although the military enticed many to sign contracts, once they reached the "comfort stations," the women were subject to the same harsh military regulations and violence as non-Japanese inmates, until their contracts expired. See VAWW RAC, *Nihonjin "ianfu": Aikokusin to jinshin baibai to* [*Japanese "Comfort Women": Patriotism and Human Trafficking*], eds. Nishino Rumiko and Onozawa Akane] (Tokyo: Gendai Shokan, 2015).

suits, and growing domestic and world concern, the government attempted to find a solution. On 19 July 1995 the National Asian Peace Fund for Women (commonly referred to as the Asian Women's Fund) was inaugurated under Foreign Ministry auspices as a semi-public, semi-private foundation. This policy initiative ultimately betrayed the hopes of survivors and advocacy groups alike.

The Asian Women's Fund (AWF) purported to settle the Japanese state's moral, but not legal, responsibility for the "comfort women" system by financing individual "atonement" payments, not with national funds, but with privately raised money, thus avoiding any suggestion of state compensation.[17] The semi-private Fund operated from 1995 to 2007. Although "comfort women" came from a dozen countries and territories in Asia and the Pacific, only victims from South Korea, Taiwan, and the Philippines were eligible for "sympathy" money and a written apology from the prime minister. The many victims who refused to accept the AWF solatia, or who were considered ineligible, never received an apology. Moreover, the fund did nothing to correct the impression that the "comfort women" system was a form of prostitution tolerated and often encouraged by modern warring armies. Thus, survivors continued to be evoked in the public eye not as victims of sexual violence but as "paid professionals" or camp followers—who were now asking for a handout.

New Directions: Prosecuting the Guilty

From the late 1990s, two obstacles stood in the path of the redress movement. One was a demand by South Korean groups that civil and military officials responsible for the "comfort women" system be prosecuted and punished. The second was an ultra-nationalist backlash in Japan that rejected the very notion of redress, a topic that is addressed below.

Punitive action against the wartime architects of the "comfort women" system proved controversial in Japan. Women's groups and world human rights bodies, on the other hand, viewed such action as essential in the worldwide struggle against male impunity. Eliminating violence against women by pursuing the worst offenders had the broad support of the global women's movement. A crucial advance in this area was the UN General Assembly's adoption in 1993 of the Convention on the Elimination of All Forms of Discrimination against Women.

---

[17] See Puja Kim, "The Failure of the Asian Women's Fund: Legal Accountability and the Colonial Legacy," in *Denying the Comfort Women*, eds. Rumiko Nishino, Puja Kim, and Akane Onozawa, trans. Robert Ricketts (New York and London: Routledge, 2018), 98–101.

Based on the Convention, crimes such as mass rape and impregnation used as weapons of ethnic cleansing in the former Yugoslavia and gang rapes and forced marriages in Rwanda were tried by the UN criminal tribunals for Yugoslavia and Rwanda as crimes against humanity in 1993 and 1994, respectively. The need for punitive measures was also written into the Beijing Platform for Action adopted at the World Conference on Women in 1995. A 1996 report[18] on the Japanese military "comfort women" by Radhika Coomaraswamy, UN Special Rapporteur on Violence against Women, also endorsed that conclusion.

In the fall of 1997, leaders of the women's movement in Japan invited 40 redress activists from 20 countries to an international conference in Tokyo on violence against women in wartime, leading to the establishment of VAWW-NET Japan (Violence against Women in War Network-Japan). In 1998, the new organization's chair, well-known feminist and journalist Matsui Yayori, conferred with Yun Chong-ok of the Korean Council and Indai Sajov, leader of a major Filipina women's coalition. They agreed to create a women's international war crimes trial. Staffed by internationally known jurists, this court would hear testimonies from victim-survivors and prosecute Japanese military and civil leaders responsible for the "comfort women" system. The idea of a people's tribunal enlarged the scope of advocacy. In addition to demanding legal relief for victims, the movement would indict and try *in absentia* those who had engineered the system for crimes against humanity in accordance with international humanitarian law.

The International Women's Tribunal (2000)

In late 2000, as Japan prepared to enter the 21st Century, the Women's International War Crimes Tribunal on Sexual Slavery by Japan (hereafter, the Women's Tribunal or the Tribunal) convened in Tokyo's Kudan Kaikan Hall, with 64 survivors from eight countries in attendance. Held from 8–12 December 2000, the trial included a common indictment by the chief prosecutor, survivor testimonies given in person or via video, extensive evidence displays, cross-examination by judges, and a verdict. The Women's Tribunal also took testimony from expert witnesses—many of them Japanese historians and legal scholars—and former Imperial soldiers. The Japanese government declined to send representatives or ob-

---

[18] Radhika Coomaraswamy, "Report on the Mission to the Democratic People's Republic of Korea, the Republic of Korea and Japan on the Issue of Military Sexual Slavery in Wartime," E/CN.4/1996/53/Add.1, the Economic and Social Council, the United Nations.

servers despite a formal invitation from the court. Its viewpoint was represented by a friend of the court brief (*amicus curiae*).

On 12 December 2000, the judges—leading authorities in international law—summarized their conclusions. The Women's Tribunal ruled that international laws in effect at the time the "comfort women" system was established required the present government of Japan to accept "state responsibility" for wartime sexual enslavement and its unresolved problems. One year later, on 4 December 2001, the complete 200-page-long judgment was released publicly in the International Court of Justice at The Hague, Netherlands. The decision did not find all of the accused guilty but convicted Emperor Shōwa[19] and nine high-ranking civil and military officials guilty of either condoning or executing a policy of "rape and sexual slavery," adjudged a crime against humanity.

Fig. 1: Survivors celebrate after hearing the Emperor's guilty verdict delivered by the Women's International War Crimes Tribunal. December 12, 2000. Courtesy of VAWW RAC.

The Women's International Tribunal was significant for many reasons.[20] First, it was a people's initiative held in Tokyo, the capital of the aggressor nation, to pass judgment on war crimes committed by the Imperial state and its armed forces. The Tribunal was modeled on the 1967 Russell Tribunal in Stockholm, which scrutinized American atrocities in the early years of the Vietnam War (1964–1975). A key difference was the Russell Tribunal's lack of a gender perspective: it did not try crimes of violence against women. VAWW-NET Japan

---

[19] Emperor Shōwa's name was Hirohito, and until his death in 1989, he was known as Emperor Hirohito. His name was changed posthumously to Shōwa, the historical era defined by his 63-year reign (1926–1989).
[20] Michiko Nakahara, "Japanese Military Sexual Slavery on Trial: Women's International War Crimes Tribunal in Tokyo in 2000," in *Sexuality, Oppression and Human Rights*, eds. Júlia Tomás and Nicol Epple (Oxford: Inter-Disciplinary Press, 2015), 163–172.

reached out to the survivors of military sexual violence in Asia to help them prosecute some of the former high authorities responsible for that system in Japanese courts.

The Tribunal brought together Japanese women and Asian victims. However, it also attracted jurists, historians, women's rights specialists, citizens' groups, and a host of NGOs/NPOs from around the world. Global civil society assembled in Tokyo to pass judgment on Japan's wartime system of sexual enslavement, which the government of the host country refused to address. Although its verdict was unenforceable, the civil proceeding had great symbolic value, granting international legitimacy to surviving victims and affording many a degree of personal closure. It also refocused the world's attention on their ten-year struggle for justice.

The Tribunal was important for a second reason: the collaboration between survivors and supporters in Japan who drew up individual bills of indictment for the victims in each country. The indictments documented specific acts of violence against the plaintiffs by those responsible based on survivor testimonies and historical records. Indictment teams, organized for each country, worked with victims and their supporters in the months leading up to the Tribunal, with some visiting former Asian battlegrounds to interview survivors. Through this process, it was discovered that an iconic photograph of a pregnant "comfort woman" taken by U.S. soldiers in China in 1944 was Pak Yong-sim, a North Korean survivor. Pak was invited to Tokyo to testify at the Tribunal.[21] Researchers learned in this way that the "comfort women" system had also been implemented in Portuguese Timor (East Timor) and many parts of the Dutch East Indies (Indonesia).

The Tribunal was unusual in a third sense: it relied on the copious empirical research that Japanese scholars and researchers had produced in the 1990s. Their findings adduced evidence of the Emperor's war responsibility, the deep involvement of the military, the Emperor's awareness of sexual slavery, and his criminal negligence in condoning it.

The Women's International Tribunal was neither a public hearing nor a mock trial. It was an innovative people's action grounded in international law that held up for world scrutiny three important questions that the Allied Powers had ignored in the early post-war Tokyo War Crimes Trials (1946–1948): the exemption of the Emperor from war responsibility, Western and Japanese colonial

---

[21] Nishino Rumiko, *Senjō no "ianfu": Ramō zenmetsusen o ikinobita Pak Yong-sim no kiseki* [*"Comfort woman" on the Frontline: the Journey of Pak Yong-sim, a Survivor of the Annihilation of Ramo*] (Tokyo: Akashi Shoten, 2003).

rule, and organized sexual violence against women.²² Jurists, researchers, and women's groups representing many ethnicities and nationalities carefully summarized an enormous quantity of oral and written evidence to help the judges produce a final judgment on these issues as they related to wartime sexual violence. The proceedings were published in six volumes by VAWW-NET Japan in 2002.²³ The Tribunal represents the high-water mark of the 1990s redress movement. Its achievements, however, would soon come under attack as the far-right mobilized to discredit them.

The Revisionist Turn

"Comfort Women" Revisionism and Textbooks (1997 – 2007)

Meanwhile, after the late 1990s, a reaction against the advocacy movement set in as ultra-rightist politicians and educators pushed back against public calls for reparations and textbook revision. In January 1997, revisionist educators established the Japanese Society for History Textbook Reform (*Tsukurukai*), and began agitating for the removal of "comfort women" and other "masochistic" themes from the nation's schoolbooks. In February, ultra-rightists in the ruling Liberal Democratic Party (LDP) established the Young Diet Members' Group for Considering Japan's Future and History Textbooks. Led by Abe Shinzō, the group's secretary-general and a rising star in the LDP, this conclave characterized "comfort women" as prostitutes and demanded that such references be banned from public school texts. Finally, in May, far-right businessmen, academics, writers, cultural figures, and religious leaders inaugurated the Japan Conference (*Nippon Kaigi*), bringing powerful private-sector interests into the revisionist fold.

In their 1997 editions, all seven publishers of junior high school history and civics books had included some mention of the "comfort women." Alarmed at this development, in the early 2000s, LDP leaders, the Young Diet Members'

---

22 Utsumi Aiko, "Senji Seibōryoku to Tōkyō Saiban" [Wartime Sexual Violence and the Tokyo War Crimes Trials], in *Nihongun seidoreisei o sabaku: 2000 nen josei kokusai senpanhotei no zenkiroku* [*Judging the Japanese Military System of Sexual Slavery: The Complete Proceedings of the 2000 Women's International War Crimes Tribunal on Japan's Military Sexual Slavery*], ed. VAWW-NET Japan, vol. 1, (Tōkyū: Ryokufū Shuppan, 2000), 58 – 102.
23 In English, see *Judgment. Parts I-VIII*, ed. Women's International War Crimes Tribunal, December 4, 2001, pdf at the Violence against Women in War Research Action Center (VAWW RAC) website. Accessed October 30, 2018. http://vawwrac.org/war_crimes_tribunal.

Group, the Ministry of Education, and the *Tsukurukai* prevailed on textbook publishers to remove the offending passages.[24] As a result, such citations gradually disappeared, and by 2006, only two out of eight history books used the term in their main text. By 2012, the last references had been effaced. Since the mid-2000s, Japan's history of military sexual abuse has faded from public memory.

The Politics of Denial (2007)

As the 21st century dawned, an incident occurred heralding the advent of "comfort women" bashing. In January 2001, a Japan Broadcasting Corporation (NHK) television production for its educational channel, "Wartime Sexual Violence in Question," featured the Women's International Tribunal, but at the last minute revised the content. The publicly-financed NHK is Japan's national broadcast network, and its charter obliges it to maintain strict political neutrality in news coverage and programming.

When the segment aired on 30 January 2001, it was apparent that NHK had altered the original version by deleting the testimonies of key witnesses, including two former Imperial soldiers. Furthermore, the network censored the remarks of commentator Lisa Yoneyama, portraying the U.S.-based scholar as being critical of the Tribunal when in fact her evaluation had been positive. The Tribunal's guilty verdict against the Emperor was also cut. Suspicions of outside political interference deepened when the program took the unusual step of inserting an interview with historian Hata Ikuhiko, a hostile critic of the "comfort women" problem. Just before the segment was televised, Sakagami Kaori, one of the directors of the original version, warned that something was amiss.

In July of that year, Tribunal organizer VAWW-NET Japan and Matsui Yayori lodged a civil complaint against NHK, fearing that "[i]f we remain silent now, we will be guilty of self-censorship later, in effect having condoned [this abuse of] state power." In March 2004, the Tokyo District Court handed the plaintiffs a partial victory. In 2005, as the lawsuit proceeded on appeal to the Tokyo High Court, a program director, Nagai Satoru, blew the whistle, revealing that a high-ranking NHK executive had been persuaded to modify the script after pressure from senior government officials. According to Nagai, the officials had "intimated that changes would be advisable" (*ito no sontaku*), a phrase that the court cited in

---

[24] Yoshifumi Tawara, "Comfort Women, Textbooks, and the Rise of the 'New Right' Revisionism," in *Denying the Comfort Women: The Japanese State's Assault on Historical Truth*, eds. Rumiko Nishino, Puja Kim, and Akane Onozawa (London: Routledge, 2018), 151–165.

its final judgment. Fearful that the government would cut its budget, the broadcaster had complied. As many surmised, political intervention had indeed caused NHK to violate its charter and realign with the revisionist agenda. In 2007, the High Court sided with the plaintiffs, criticizing NHK for political bias, and assigned damages. NHK appealed, however, and in 2008, the Supreme Court nullified the High Court decision.

The senior government figures involved were said to include Abe Shinzō, a Cabinet member, and other officials in his sway. Efforts to prove their involvement were inconclusive, however, and media sources and many researchers took this as a signal to steer wide of the "comfort women" problem, which politically had become too hot to handle. The NHK incident was a turning point in the public perception of the issue, a change that paved the way for an official policy of "comfort women" denial.[25]

As we saw earlier, Abe announced this policy in March 2007, when he told the Diet there was no evidence that "comfort women" had been forcibly recruited and then had that statement adopted as a Cabinet decision. A full-page public comment that leading revisionists placed in *The Washington Post* in June completed the narrative by adding that "comfort women" were not "sexual slaves" at all but licensed prostitutes. Abe's attempt to undermine the 1993 Kōno Statement was condemned by governments in North America, Europe, and Asia. The U.S. House of Representatives, for example, responded to these provocations in July by adopting House Resolution 121, which admonished the Japanese government to acknowledge, apologize for, and accept its historical responsibility for the "comfort women" system.

Preserving Historical Memory: The Women's Active Museum (2005)

In the first decade of the 2000s, as the NHK incident unfolded, the advocacy movement intensified its public education campaign while searching for a viable solution acceptable to the victim-survivors of sexual slavery. Women's groups and other civic organizations set up mobile exhibitions across Japan, where experts explained the issues using teaching materials based on current research.

---

[25] VAWW-NET Japan, *Sabakareta shinjitsu: NHK bangumi kaizan jiken* [*The Truth Revealed: The NHK Program-tampering case*], eds. Rumiko Nishino and Rutsuko Shōji (Tokyo: Gendai Shokan, 2010).

This movement was one of the precursors to the Women's Active Museum on War and Peace (WAM), which was established in Tokyo in August 2005.

WAM, Japan's only "comfort women" museum, regularly holds symposia, lectures, and seminars on military sexual slavery, organizes both permanent and temporary exhibits open to the public, maintains an extensive working archive, and produces a steady stream of educational materials, reports, and other publications. Established by colleagues of Matsui Yayori (1934–2002), WAM's multifaceted research and outreach activities provide a strong counter-narrative that is anchored in historical fact to the revisionist distortions. The Museum has also sponsored initiatives by younger Japanese. An early undertaking was the "Indelible Memory" National Rallies, a series of public talks by former "comfort women" held simultaneously in several large cities across Japan. WAM continues to work closely with a loose coalition of women's and human rights groups in Japan and abroad.

The "Comfort Women" Become a Diplomatic Issue (2009–2011)

Pressed by civil society groups, between 2000 and 2006, lawmakers of three opposition parties, the Social Democrats, the Communists, and the Democratic Party, sponsored eight "wartime sexual coercion" bills. LDP Diet members blocked all but one of these from reaching the legislative docket. As public dissatisfaction with the LDP mounted on a host of issues, in 2009, the centrist Democratic Party of Japan (DPJ) ousted the LDP in a general election. It was the first transfer of political power to a single opposition party since 1955.

Encouraged by this development, in February 2010, redress groups in Japan joined forces to form the 2010 Japan National Action to Resolve the Japanese Military "Comfort Women" Issue and pressure the DPJ to legislate a solution. In November, together with the Korean Council, National Action handed the new government some 610,000 signatures from around the world demanding action on the issue. Despite its liberal credentials, the DPJ failed to respond, leaving the questions in limbo.

On 30 August 2011, the Constitutional Court of Korea ruled that the South Korean government's failure to solve the problem of individual war claims against Japan violated the constitutional rights of living war victims. At a Japan-South Korea summit that December, President Lee Myung-bak pressed Japanese Prime Minister Noda Yoshihiko to take immediate action to settle the "comfort women" dispute, but Noda demurred. A year later, in December 2012, the DPJ was roundly defeated in a general election, returning the Liberal Democratic Party to power and Abe Shinzō to the premiership.

The Hate Movement (2007–2018)

Beginnings

Following the NHK incident, public support for war reparations to the victims of military sexual slavery began to waver. In the mid-to-late 2000s, escalating revisionist counterclaims attempted to delegitimize redress demands by denigrating victim-survivors. The cascade of pejorative comments by ultra-nationalist political and public figures became known as "comfort women bashing." At a popular level, Internet-savvy ultra-rightists—the so-called right-wing netizens (*netto uyo*)—picked up this rhetoric, turning social media into a vehicle for attacking not only the "comfort women," but Koreans and Chinese, in general. The upsurge of historical revisionism spawned an incipient hate-speech movement "from below" that took its cue from the policies and public remarks of central authorities.

In January 2007, young ultra-rightists at the grassroots level created the Association of Citizens against the Special Privileges of Zainichi Koreans (*Zainichi Tokken o yurusanai Shimin no Kai*, hereafter *Zaitokukai*). It comes as no surprise that the rise of xenophobia began with Abe Shinzō's first administration (2006–2007). Utilizing social media, the *Zaitokukai* organized a hate campaign targeting ethnic Korean residents in Japan (*Zainichi Chōsenjin*) and other minorities, among them, former "comfort women."

Ironically, an influx of South Korean popular culture swept Japan at about the same time, somewhat dampening the chorus of ethnic vilification. Known in Korean as *hallyu* (Japanese, *kanryū*), the "Korean Wave" produced a boom in imported South Korean TV dramas, which were largely consumed at first by older Japanese women. *Hallyu* began to trend in 2004, and by 2010, had reached younger generations through the musical artistry of K-pop. With the flare-up of a territorial dispute over Takeshima (Dokdo) Island in August 2012 and a new Abe Cabinet in December, enthusiasm for Korean pop culture waned.

In 2013, driven in part by the Japan-South Korea "comfort women" dispute, hate speech became a national buzzword. In this paper, I limit my discussion of this phenomenon to what I call "comfort women" hate speech. Although the targets have expanded beyond the victims of military sexual violence, "comfort women" bashing was an important early influence on this movement, which continues to rage against survivors. This variant of hate speech is characterized by 1) the fomenting of racial animosity toward South Korea, China, and Koreans living in Japan, 2) the narrowing of the term "comfort women" to include only Koreans, and 3) the defamation of survivors.

The Normalization of Hate Speech (2013-present)

From 2013 to 2014, the primary objectives of the hate campaign dovetailed with the Abe government's policy of disavowing the 1993 Kōno Statement. Four political and social developments explain the proliferation of verbal intimidation directed at minority groups during Abe's second administration.[26]

First, in September 2012, two months before his elevation to Prime Minister, Abe repeated that, "[w]e must affirm the fact that the Cabinet decision [of 16 March 2007] has revised the Kōno Statement."[27] On 7 February 2013, following his resumption of power, Abe again told the Diet that the government had no evidence of women being forcibly carried off by the military. Leaders of the revisionist camp applauded these pronouncements and kept the pot boiling with a steady barrage of derogatory comments about victim-survivors. Right-wing netizens amplified the Abe government's contentions, asserting that because "comfort women" were prostitutes, no coercion was involved, and thus neither the Japanese state nor the Imperial military could be held responsible for that system.

Secondly, social media activists were not the only source of "comfort women" disparagement to impact mass culture. Many conservative weeklies, books, TV talk and variety shows, and even comic books (*manga*) now echoed anti-Korean sentiment. As advertising revenues, book sales, and audience ratings soared, hate speech became a thriving cottage industry. Even mainstream media sources revised their position on this issue. In January 2014, Momii Katsuto, the new NHK director-general, affirmed that "['comfort women'] existed in the war zones of every country." This exculpatory comment was not innocent. Momii was an Abe protégé appointed to bring Japan's state broadcasting corporation into sync with the government's political views. Some private broadcasters also began to suggest that coercion was not a factor in "comfort women" mobilization.

---

26 Booja [Puja] Kim and Sachiyo Tsukamoto, "Sexual Slavery Versus Necessary Evil: 'Comfort Women'—Hate Speech under the Abe Administration" in *Sexuality, Oppression and Human Rights*, eds. Júlia Tomás and Nicol Epple (Oxford: Inter-Disciplinary Press. 2015), 173–182.
27 Yoshimi, "The Kōno Statement," 17.

In August 2014, the *Asahi Shimbun*, Japan's leading liberal daily newspaper, published a self-critical review of its past coverage of the "comfort women" and retracted some of its earlier reporting. A feeding-frenzy ensued as far-right politicians, social commentators, and conservative newspapers denounced the *Asahi* for selling the country out and siding with Japan's enemies. Prime Minister Abe joined the fray, lamenting to a Diet committee in October that, "The unfounded slander that Japan as a whole 'enslaved women' is being spread throughout the world." Revisionists and far-right social media took up that mantra, alleging that false allegations of "sexual slavery" were tarring all Japanese.

A third development was psychological, verbal, and physical harassment by xenophobic groups. Today, the *Zaitokukai*, for instance, continues to organize hate demonstrations in the Korea Towns of Tokyo, Kawasaki, Kyoto, Osaka, and other large cities. The *Zaitokukai* employs a combination of racist invective, intimidation, and occasional violence and has advocated the expulsion and even massacre of Japan's Korean minority. "Comfort women" advocacy itself has been targeted, with *Zaitokukai* bullies disrupting exhibitions, rallies, and other redress activities.[28]

The inroads made by hate speech among the general public is especially worrisome. Since 2007, this trend has led many people to see no harm in publicly maligning North and South Korea, China, Japan's ethnic minorities, atomic bomb victims, and survivors of wartime sexual abuse. To be sure, *Zaitokukai* activists are a small minority, and powerful civil society movements have formed to confront and deter them. Nevertheless, vilification campaigns have stirred up dormant feelings of historical and racial resentment that society and the education system have failed to address properly. Thus, hate rallies are sometimes convened spontaneously without *Zaitokukai* support. Social media platforms are now potent tools for inducing "ordinary" Japanese to engage in hate messaging and other xenophobic behavior.

A fourth vector is the spread of "comfort women" revisionism to women, and even to Japanese living abroad, particularly in the United States. In 2011, the former *Zaitokukai* vice-president established Nadeshiko Action (Japanese Women for Justice and Peace). This all-women group has actively boosted Abe's ideas, not only in Japan, but also overseas, to wit its briefs to the UN Human Rights Council depicting sexual slaves as camp followers. In the United States, a small group of expatriate Japanese, the Global Alliance for Historical Truth

---

28 Yasuda Kōichi, *Netto to aikoku: Zaitokukai no "yami" o oikakete* [*The Internet and Patriotism: Exploring the Dark Side of the Zaitokukai*] (Tokyo: Kōdansha. 2012); Naoto Higuchi, *Japan's Ultra-Right*, trans. Teresa Castelvetere (Melbourne: Trans Pacific Press, 2016).

(GAHT), has attempted to transplant the "history wars" being waged in Japan. It brought suit against the city government of Glendale, California to halt construction of a "comfort women" memorial (see below). The U.S. Supreme Court dismissed the lawsuit in March 2017.[29]

The acrimony unleashed against scholars, researchers, and journalists who have exposed the unsavory facts of the "comfort women" system is particularly alarming.[30] On 5 May 2015, 187 historians and Japan specialists working in the United States issued an "Open Letter in Support of Historians in Japan." Researchers from European and other countries also added their names, focusing world attention on the suppression of historical truth in Japan.[31] On 25 May, 464 Japanese historians and educators representing 16 professional associations followed up with their own statement *criticizing the disinformation campaign waged by the Abe regime and "comfort women" detractors.*

A Solution the Victims Can Accept

The Asian Solidarity Conference (2014)

With the start of the second Abe government in 2012, redress groups reassessed their struggle and sought to reunify the movement around the basic demands for justice articulated by survivors. In August 2013, a new organization, Fight for Justice, created a website to provide the public with accurate and up-to-date information on the "comfort women" system and the progress of the advocacy movement.[32]

One of the signal achievements of this period was the proposal to the Japanese government of a settlement based on the needs and wishes of former "comfort women." Entitled "Recommendations to the Government of Japan for Reso-

---

29 See Yamaguchi Tomomi, Nogawa Motokazu, and Koyama Emi, eds. *Umi o wataru "ianfu" mondai—Uha no "rekishisen o tou* [*The "Comfort Women" Problem Crosses the Pacific: Examining the Right's "History Wars"*] (Tokyo: Iwanami Shoten, 2016).
30 See Tomomi Yamaguchi, "Press Freedom Under Fire: 'Comfort women', the Asahi Affair and Uemura Takashi," in *Press Freedom in Contemporary Japan*, ed. Jeff Kingston (London/New York: Routledge, 2017), 135–151.
31 "Open Letter in Support of Historians in Japan Updated," *The Asia-Pacific Journal*, May 11, 2015. Accessed October 30, 2018. http://apjjf.org/-Asia-Pacific-Journal-Feature/4828/article.html.
32 *Fight for Justice Website*, http://fightforjustice.info/?page_id=2477. Accessed 30 October 2018. An English version is available at http://fightforjustice.info/?lang=en. Accessed October 30, 2018. In addition to Japanese and English, the site also includes information in Korean and Chinese.

lution of the Japanese Military 'Comfort Women' Issue," the plan was drafted by the 12th Asian Solidarity Conference on the Issue of Military Sexual Slavery by Japan. Meeting in Tokyo from 31 May to 3 June 2014, the Conference was attended by representatives from eight countries. Its operating concept was "[a] Realistic Settlement is One that Victimized Women Can Accept." The proposal was submitted to Prime Minister Abe on 2 June 2014, together with 529 official records and 53 supplementary documents pertaining to the "comfort women" acquired since the Kōno Statement. Below is a resume of the main recommendations.[33]

To resolve the Japanese military "comfort women" issue, the Japanese government must recognize 1) that during the war, the Japanese government and military planned, established, managed, and controlled "comfort stations;" 2) that women were forced against their will to provide sex to military personnel in those facilities and kept there by coercive methods; 3) that different forms of victimization existed depending on whether the women were from colonies, occupied areas, or Japan proper, that the scale of victimization was extensive, and that the suffering continues today; and 4) that this system was a serious violation of human rights that contravened domestic and international laws in effect at the time.

In order to provide surviving victims with just reparations, the Japanese government must 1) apologize to individual victims in a way that is unambiguous, official, and cannot be overturned afterwards; 2) provide compensation to victims as proof of the legitimacy of the apology; 3) give a complete accounting of the truth (full disclosure of all official documents and further truth-finding, including hearings with survivors and others with firsthand and expert knowledge; and 4) take measures to prevent the recurrence of organized wartime violence against women by revising school curricula and textbooks, prohibit statements by public figures that deny or cast doubt on the points listed above, and officially rebut such statements.

The Japanese advocacy movement played a key role in drafting the recommendations, which were revised, refined, and finalized in close consultation with representatives from the countries Japan had victimized during the war. The end document clarified the objectives of the international redress campaign and helped forge a new sense of purpose and direction. The term "legal responsibility" is conspicuous here by its absence, but "compensation" in Point 2 of the reparation demands covers the state's legal liability toward victim-survivors. The

---

[33] "Recommendations to the Government of Japan for Resolution of the 'Comfort Women' Issue" (12th Asian solidarity Conference on the Issue of Military Sexual Slavery by Japan), June 2, 2014, website of the Women's Active Museum on War and Peace (WAM). Accessed October 30, 2018. https://wam-peace.org/main/wp-content/uploads/2014/07/20140602_ EN. pdf.

release of additional official materials, obtained through the persistent efforts of many researchers, introduced important new information, enhancing our understanding of the "comfort women" system.[34]

The Japan-South Korea Agreement (2015)

The so-called Abe Statement of 14 August 2015, which marked the 70th anniversary of Japan's defeat in the Asia-Pacific War, included such key words as "colonial rule," "aggression," "reflection," and "apology," but it gave no indication of the historical referents.[35] Abe's address was a clear retreat from the 1995 Murayama Statement, which expressed Japan's "deep remorse and heartfelt apology" for its "colonial rule and aggression" in Asia. In Abe's speech, the relation between subject (aggressor) and object (victims) is blurred, producing semantic confusion.

The Prime Minister writes, for example, that "there were women behind the battlefields whose honor and dignity were severely injured," but that sentence is a general remark devoid of specific context. There is no explanation of how the women ended up "behind the battlefields," how their dignity was injured, or what agent was responsible. Nowhere in this rambling statement does the term "comfort women" even appear. The Abe Statement appears designed to paper over the structural underpinnings of Japanese colonial rule, the Asia-Pacific War, and the "comfort women" system.[36]

The Japan-South Korea Agreement of December 2015 followed the broad contours of Abe's August discourse, subtly reflecting his historical worldview. On 28 December the foreign ministers of Japan and South Korea, acting on behalf of Prime Minister Abe Shinzō and President Park Geun-hye, met in Seoul to unveil an unsigned bilateral memorandum on the "comfort women" question.

---

34 Recent research has raised the number of military and other official documents found since 1993 to more than 1,000. Although many are from Ministry of Defense archives, the government refuses to recognize them. See Hayashi Hirofumi, *Nihongun "Ianfu" Mondai no Kakushin* [*The Essence of the Japanese Military "Comfort Women" Issue*] (Tokyo: Kadensha, 2015), 83–85. Some of these materials are available on the *Fight for Justice Webite* (see Footnote 32).
35 Abe Shinzō, "Statement by Prime Minister Abe Shinzō," in *Speeches and Statements by the Prime Minister*, August 14, 2015. Accessed February 26, 2019. http://japan.kantei.go.jp/ 97_abe/ statement/201508/0814statement.html.
36 Itagaki Ryūta, "Abe Danwa no nani ga Mondai?" [What's Wrong with the Abe Statement?], in *Q&A: Chōsenjin "Ianfu" to Shokuminchi Shihai Sekinin* [*Korean "Comfort Women" and Responsibility for Colonial Cule*], eds. Kim Puja and Itagaki Ryūta (Tokyo: Ochanomizu Shobō, 2015).

By mutual consent: 1) The Japanese government recognized its "responsibilities" for "an involvement of the Japanese military authorities" in the "comfort women" issue and reaffirmed Prime Minister Abe's "most sincere apologies and remorse to all the women who underwent immeasurable and painful experiences and suffered incurable physical and psychological wounds as 'comfort women.'" 2) The Japanese government agreed to "a one-time contribution of ¥1 billion through its budget" to a foundation to be established by the South Korean government for "recovering the honor and dignity and healing the psychological wounds of all former 'comfort women.'" 3) In return, the South Korean government agreed to acknowledge "the fact that the Government of Japan is concerned about the statue built in front of the Embassy of Japan in Seoul from the viewpoint of preventing any disturbance of the peace of the mission or impairment of its dignity" and promised to "strive to solve this issue in an appropriate manner."[37] 4) Both governments confirmed that "this issue is resolved finally and irreversibly" and that each would refrain from "accusing or criticizing [the] other regarding this issue in the international community, including at the United Nations."[38]

After the agreement, however, Abe, his foreign minister, and some LDP lawmakers began backtracking. At the press conference in Seoul announcing the agreement, Japanese Foreign Minister Kishida Fumio praised the accord for enhancing security arrangements between Japan, South Korea, and the United States; insisted that Japan's ¥1 billion grant was not state compensation but a humanitarian contribution; and reiterated that the "comfort women" problem had been resolved once and for all. The bilateral agreement had little to do with "apologies and remorse," but rather, it was a political deal that paved the way for closer trilateral economic and defense cooperation, under the watchful eye of Washington.

One month later, in January 2016, Abe was asked in the Diet if he would make a personal apology to former "comfort women." The Prime Minister refused, insisting that "sexual slavery and [the story of] 200,000 victims are not facts." Abe also reminded the Diet that his Cabinet decision of 16 March 2007 had officially rejected charges of coercion. He repeated his expectation that the statue in front of the Japanese Embassy would be removed. Foreign Minister

---

37 The statue of a "comfort girl," widely known as the Peace Memorial or Peace Statue of a Girl, was erected in front of the Japanese Embassy by South Korean civic organizations in December 2011 to protest the Noda government's failure to resolve the "comfort women" problem.
38 "Japan-ROK Foreign Ministers' Meeting: The Japan-ROK Agreement," in *Japan-Republic of Korea Relations*, Ministry of Foreign Affairs of Japan, December 28, 2015. Accessed February 21, 2019. http://www.mofa.go.jp/a_o/na/kr/ page4e_00036.html

Kishida publicly agreed. At the same time, a prominent LDP politician told party members at LDP headquarters that "comfort women" were "prostitutes by trade."

How did the international community and human rights organizations view the 2015 agreement? In March 2016, the UN Committee on the Elimination of Discrimination against Women in its concluding observations on Japan's "military sexual slavery" criticized the accord for failing to adopt a victim-centered approach, and urged Japan to take "due account of the views of victims/survivors and ensure their rights to truth, justice, and reparations."

In October 2016, as controversy continued over the "comfort girl" statue in Seoul and a second memorial later set up next to the Japanese Consulate in Busan, South Korea, the unexpected occurred. President Park was implicated in a major corruption scandal involving a close friend, sparking massive demonstrations across South Korea. Protesters took to the streets to accuse the South Korean president of malfeasance and demand her resignation. After four months of public agitation and political turmoil, Park was impeached for abuse of power, later arrested, and finally removed from office in March 2017. On 9 May 2017, Moon Jae-in, a well-known lawyer and human rights advocate, was elected president of South Korea in a special election.

President Moon did not reject the bilateral accord out of hand, but conducted a thorough review of the diplomatic process that had produced it. By then, Seoul had already established the Foundation for Reconciliation and Healing (28 July 2016) to administer the ¥1 billion grant from Tokyo. In November 2018, South Korean officials notified Japan that the Foundation would be dismantled and that the decision was based partly on feedback from survivors. There has been talk in government circles of returning the money to Japan.[39] Meanwhile, the two "comfort girl" memorials remain in place.

Despite the wide perception gap that separates Japanese and South Koreans, both countries must work together to support UN recommendations calling for a victim-based solution, complete with a consultative mechanism for victims and their families. Neither side conferred with survivors about the 2015 agreement, and Abe has refused to apologize personally. But only an approach that accommodates the victims' needs and wishes is likely to produce a lasting settlement. Moreover, this problem cannot be reduced to a bilateral dispute between Japan and South Korea. Wartime military sexual violence remains a diplomatic issue

---

[39] Hyunmin Michael Kang, "South Korea Decides to Dismantle 'Comfort Women' Reconciliation and Healing Foundation," *The Diplomat*, November 27, 2018. Accessed December 15, 2018. https://thediplomat.com/2018/11/south-korea-decides-to-dismantle-comfort-women-reconciliation-and-healing-foundation/.

that negatively impacts Japan's reputation in Asia and the Pacific. It is in the interest of all concerned parties to resolve it meaningfully.

Conclusion

Japan's redress movement has been propelled by two forces: victim-survivors from Asia and the Pacific who stepped forward to expose the realities of the military "comfort women" system, and the historians, researchers, women's organizations, and civil society groups who responded to their cry for justice. This partnership has had wider ramifications. It encouraged victims of organized sexual violence in other armed conflicts to follow suit and publicize the wartime abuses they, too, had suffered. Examples include the aging survivors of Nazi-era forced prostitution in German camp brothels and the genocidal rapes that accompanied ethnic cleansing campaigns in the former Yugoslavia and Rwanda in the early 1990s.

The achievements of the Japanese movement also influenced the establishment of the South African Truth and Reconciliation Commission of the mid-1990s and the creation in 2002 of the International Criminal Court in The Hague. To the international community, whether or not the "comfort women" were "prostitutes" is a moot point. The general consensus among world human rights experts is that such women were sex slaves, and that the "comfort women" system was an institutionalized regime of military sexual servitude.

Yet successive redress campaigns have failed to alter public perceptions of the "comfort women." For the past 20 years, no other issue involving Japan's historical consciousness of colonization and war has elicited the same emotional responses from both the central authorities and the public as the "comfort women" question. Historical revisionists have attempted to deny Japan's war responsibility and suppress public discussion of a wide range of war-related disputes, but the question of military sexual slavery seems to arouse the fiercest resistance. Defying world opinion, "comfort women" revisionism in Japan remains rampant.

Why do revisionists attack this issue with such rancor? Kobayashi Yoshinori, a cartoonist and founding member of the Tsukurukai (Japanese Society for History Textbook Reform), depicted the "comfort women" as prostitutes in his 1997 political manga, *Shin Gōmanizumu Sengen* (The New Arrogance Manifesto). Kobayashi told readers to "overlook the sexual desire of men who fought for their homeland and future generations," and asked the rhetorical question, "[t]hose people who call our grandfathers rapists for visiting comfort stations before dying in battle are some kind of lowlifes, aren't they?"[40] Like Kobayashi, "comfort women" revisionists—most of them male—seem to share a common mindset: they regard the problem not only as demeaning to Japan, and thus a question of national pride, but also as a gender issue that consciously or unconsciously seeks to shame Japanese men, in general.

Two kinds of self-justification are at work here. First, revisionists portray Japanese aggression in the Asia-Pacific War as a fight for "the homeland and future generations." Secondly, they justify the "comfort women" system as allowing men to indulge their sexual appetites while asking us to overlook this fact and not label them rapists. Kobayashi's cartoons lack self-reflection on Japan's peculiar brand of nationalism with its built-in colonialist ideology— throwbacks to the country's history of colonial conquest and wars of aggression. Nor does it occur to the manga artist that the "comfort women" issue is fundamentally a question of women's human rights. But Kobayashi is hardly alone in holding such views. To see this, I take a closer look below at both propositions.

First, I will examine the question of national pride and nationalism. Japan's post-war education system did not foster a robust awareness of the nation's history of colonial oppression and military aggrandizement. Unlike students in post-war Germany, Japanese students generally have not been encouraged to cultivate a sense of personal or national responsibility for confronting and rectifying that past. Japanese schoolbooks focus on the terrible destruction and trauma caused by the U.S. atomic bombings of Hiroshima and Nagasaki, but teach little about the horrific acts their own country committed against other Asian peoples. The media, too, tend to emphasize the nation's wartime suffering, but downplay the mayhem its armies wreaked abroad.

In the early 1990s, as the "comfort women" became an international issue, the Japanese government did attempt to act responsibly, as shown by the Kōno and Murayama statements of 1993 and 1995 and the 12-year tenure of the Asian Women's Fund (1995–2007). Although ineffectual, these responses envisaged limited restitution, official expressions of remorse, and promises to educate the public and future generations about the "comfort women" system.

Since the mid-2000s, however, LDP-led governments—notably the two Abe administrations—have attempted to undermine the Kōno and Murayama legacies and whitewash Japan's pre-1945 colonial policies and war depredations. The growing popular appeal since 2007 of extremist groups such as the *Zaitokukai* and the rise of unabashed hate speech after 2013 cannot be understood apart

---

40 Kobayashi Yoshinori, *Shin Gōmanizum Sengen*, vol. 3 [*The New Arrogance Manifesto*, vol. 3] (Tokyo: Shōgakkan, 1997).

from the promotion of far-right values and policies by the Abe regime. Against this backdrop, an internationally discredited neocolonialist nationalism continues to thrive just below the surface of social and political life.

Secondly, I would like to take a close look at the question of gender. Japan is a preeminently male-dominant society. In 2016, for instance, the UN Global Gender Gap Index ranked Japan 111th out of 144 countries. At the start of his second term in late 2012, Prime Minister Abe pledged to help promote women to leadership positions in politics and the workplace, creating "a society where all women can shine." Despite such campaign slogans, in politics, business, academia, law, medicine, the media, and other fields, men still dominate, and gender inequalities abound.

In patriarchal Japan, women are expected to refrain from reporting sexual assaults: rape victims should hide their shame, not broadcast it. When caught, rape suspects routinely insist that the victim agreed to sex. The argument that "comfort women" were not sex slaves but paid professionals is a variant of the "she agreed" defense. This hides inconvenient historical truths: wartime military sexual enslavement, the use of coercive measures to secure compliance, and the intentional recruitment of underage "comfort girls," who were sexually inexperienced and thus free of venereal disease.[41] Common to such arguments is the desire to escape accountability by blaming the victim.

Japan is a society that resists and suppresses public accusations of sexual violence. Historical revisionists have found fertile ground here for a narcissistic nationalism infused with unexamined colonialist assumptions. The gender identity of many Japanese men has roots in the same soil. This prompts some to displace their fear of a spoiled masculinity by verbally abusing the victims of military sexual servitude—a kind of "second rape" and source of post-traumatic stress for many victims.

The Japanese redress movement will continue to confront Japan's revisionist forces over the "comfort women" issue until a lasting solution that victim-survivors can embrace wholeheartedly is reached. The struggle to achieve gender equality and overcome a pervasive and sometimes toxic neocolonialist nationalism will prove decisive in the ongoing quest for justice.

---

[41] Puja Kim, "The Mobilization of Korean Adolescents as Comfort Women—Colonialism and the Victimization of Teenage Girls," in *Denying the Comfort Women: The Japanese State's Assault on Historical Truth*, eds. Rumiko Nishino, Puja Kim, and Akane Onozawa (London: Routledge, 2018), 136–147.

Pyong Gap Min
Japanese Citizens' and Civic Organizations' Strong Support for the Redress Movement

As of 2019, it has been 28 years since the redress movement for the victims of Japanese military sexual slavery formally started in South Korea. The redress movement has received global support, not only from Asian victim countries, but also from the United States and Western countries. Most importantly, it has received strong support from UN human rights bodies and many other international human rights organizations. The public testimonies of many "comfort women" survivors in Korea and other Asian countries since August 1991 and the discovery of key Japanese historical documents in January 1992 also forced the Japanese government to announce the so-called Kōno Statement in July 1993. In his statement, Kōno Yōhei, the Chief Cabinet Secretary of the Japanese government, acknowledged the Japanese military government's responsibility for the forced mobilization of Asian "comfort women" and made a sincere apology. The Kōno Statement led members of the Korean Council for the Women Drafted for Military Sexual Slavery by Japan (hereafter referred to as the Korean Council) and other Asian redress activists to believe that the "comfort women" issue would be resolved successfully within a few years.

However, the surprising reactionary turn of the Japanese government and neo-nationalist citizens with the emergence of historical revisionism since the middle of the 1990s has led them to increasingly reject the "comfort women" system as sexual slavery. The Japanese government has tried to resolve the "comfort women" issue twice, only by paying compensation to the victims of Japanese military sexual slavery. Despite all the documentary and testimonial evidence for military sexual slavery, the Japanese government has intentionally rejected the interpretation of "comfort women" as sexual slaves. A dozen UN human rights bodies and international human rights organizations, the United States, and several other countries have sent the Japanese government tough resolutions, telling it to take responsible actions as soon as possible. Nevertheless, the Japanese government has thus far not taken any significant measures to accommodate their recommendations. Given its near-religious nationalist ego, strongly supported by neo-nationalist organizations, the Japanese government is unlikely to acknowledge its predecessor's crime of sexual slavery and make a sincere apology and compensation to the victims of Japanese military sexual slavery, the minimum requirements for resolving the "comfort women" issue.

https://doi.org/10.1515/9783110643480-006

I have realized that, because of the Japanese government's refusal to acknowledge the "comfort women" system as sexual slavery and to take responsible measures, few people outside of Japan seem to know that more citizens and organizations in Japan have supported the redress movement for the victims of Japanese military sexual slavery than those in any other country, with the exception of South Korea. In the previous chapter, Puja Kim gave an excellent overview of the activities of major redress organizations in Japan. This chapter pays special attention to the positive responses of Japanese individuals and small groups/organizations to the redress movement led by two major Korean redress organizations. In addition, this chapter intends to introduce many individual citizens' and small groups' supporting activities in the perpetrating country to recognize their good will and unbending conscience. Since it focuses on Japanese civilians' and organizations' efforts to help Korean advocacy organizations' redress activities, it will provide enough information about the redress activities of two Korean advocacy organizations (the Korean Council and the House of Sharing), as well as the redress activities in Japan.

The "comfort women" issue is not a Korean-Japanese bilateral historical or diplomatic issue, but a globally important women's human rights issue. That is why many people, especially women, in the United States and other Western countries have supported the redress movement. However, it is also true that the "comfort women" issue has been the major hurdle to forging a friendly relationship between South Korea and Japan for three decades. Finding many Japanese individuals' and groups' support of Korean redress organizations to make the Japanese government take responsible actions, I have realized that there is much hope to improve the relationship between the two nations in the future. Thus, I have decided to focus on this topic to share many moving stories with the readers. While Puja Kim examined redress activities in Japan based on her participant observations and Japanese media materials in Chapter 2, this chapter focuses on Japanese citizens' and organizations' support of the redress activities of the Korean Council and the House of Sharing mainly based on data available in Korea.

This chapter is based on different data sources that I have collected for over twenty years since 1995 to complete a major book project. In particular, I have used the following three data sources for this chapter: (1) my personal interviews with about 30 redress movement leaders in South Korea and Japan, (2) various newsletters and source reports compiled by the Korean Council and the Korean Research Institute, and (3) several edited books and monographs made by the Korean Council and the Korean Research Institute. This chapter consists of the following four sections. The first section summarizes Japanese individual citizens' and small groups' support of Korean advocacy organizations' redress activities in South Korea, Japan, and the United Nations. The second section looks at Japanese women leaders' and women's organizations' support of the redress movement through their participation in the Asian Solidarity conferences. The third section focuses on major Japanese organizations' activities to support the Korean Council in connection with international redress activities. I have not covered the redress activities of Korean-Japanese women's advocacy organizations here partly because they are covered by Puja Kim in the previous chapter and partly because I intend to highlight Japanese citizens' and Japanese organizations' redress activities in this chapter.

Japanese Individual Citizens' and Small Groups' Participation in Redress Activities

First of all, I want to bring the readers' attention to the fact that a small group of Japanese citizens consisting of a few or several people, mostly women, has often participated in the weekly Wednesday Demonstrations[1] held in front of the Japanese Embassy in Seoul. Japanese participants are usually women redress activists, teachers, and college students, many of whom are Christians. A few Japanese groups are reported to have participated in the Wednesday Demonstrations regularly. The presider of the demonstration has usually introduced Japanese participants to other participants; sometimes, arrangements are made for the leader of the Japanese group to speak at the podium to the other protest participants. I witnessed Japanese citizens' groups a few times when I attended the demonstration in the late 1990s. For example, when I attended it on 26 July 1995, I found members of the Korean Catholic Justice and Peace Association participating with its Japanese counterpart. After the demonstration, they usually ate lunch together at a restaurant. I had a chance to talk with a Japanese Catholic participant while eating lunch. According to him, since the school education on East Asian history in Japan is so distorted, Japanese students do not know many things that Korean students know. He indicated that, while talking with the Korean Catholic group visiting Japan, he realized that his historical knowl-

---

[1] Beginning on 8 January 1992, every Wednesday, there has been a protest led and organized by the Korean Council for the Women Drafted for Military Sexual Slavery by Japan held in front of the Japanese Embassy in Seoul, South Korea. The only time the protest was not held since 1992 was during the massive earthquake in Kobe, Japan in 1995. The Wednesday Demonstration is the longest-running protest about a single theme/issue.

edge had a serious problem. That's why his group was visiting South Korea and learning Korean history by visiting Korean historical sites.

When I attended the Wednesday Demonstration in Seoul in August 2018, a coalition of progressive college students was hosting the demonstration. They emphasized not forgetting the "comfort women" issue and taking actions. I witnessed eleven Japanese Christian college students from Hokkaido, Japan participating in the demonstration. The leader came to the podium to introduce his group and said that they went to the House of Sharing to see Korean "comfort women" residents first, but that none of them were healthy enough to see them. He regretted that his group had not visited the House of Sharing earlier to meet Korean "comfort women." He said that he learned in Korea that making an apology one time is never enough, and that Japanese citizens should continue to feel guilty about the suffering of many Korean women.

It requires much courage and a strong sense of social justice for any Japanese citizen to join the Wednesday Demonstration held in front of the most important Japanese Consulate building in Korea. Japanese participants have to endure Korean participants' chanting against the Japanese military government's crime of sexual slavery and the contemporary Japanese government's refusal to take responsible actions for the span of an hour or so. In addition, some of the staff members of the Japanese Embassy in Seoul could easily take incriminating photos of Japanese participants in the Wednesday Demonstration and send them to the Japanese government. However, the Japanese participants did not seem to worry about any negative effects of their participation in the movement in South Korea.

A large number of Japanese citizens have also visited the House of Sharing, where several Korean "comfort women" live and a historical "comfort women" museum has been established. It is not easy for foreigners to visit the organization because it is located in a fairly remote area about a one-and-a-half-hour drive from Seoul. Ahn Shin-kwon, director of the House of Sharing, told me in October 2016 that approximately 10,000 people visited his organization in the previous year. He said that about two-thirds of foreign visitors (3,000) were Japanese citizens. The visitors wanted to talk with the surviving victims after looking at the museum exhibition. Ahn said that when there was one or more visiting groups at the House of Sharing, he usually arranged for one of the "comfort woman" residents to give a short testimony to the visitors. While I was staying at the House of Sharing for one week during the summer of 2001, I met with many Japanese visitors there. They seem to have had special feelings when meeting and talking with Korean "comfort women" because as citizens of the perpetrating country, they felt guilty. Some Japanese visitors, usually women, to the

House of Sharing stay there for one week or longer for volunteer activities, including cooking for and serving food to "comfort women" residents there.

Both the House of Sharing and the Korean Council have established a historical museum dedicated to "comfort women." The House of Sharing established the Historical Museum of Japanese Military "Comfort Women" in 1998 and expanded it during the subsequent few years. The Korean Council started building the War and Women's Human Rights Museum in 2005 and completed it in 2012. Both organizations may not have completed the respective museum projects without financial support by Japanese citizens and organizations. In particular, the House of Sharing's Historical Museum would have been impossible without the financial and technical support by Japanese citizens. Ahn Shin-kwon, the director of the House of Sharing, reported that he established the Supporting Group for Construction of Historical Museum of Japanese Military "Comfort Women." The group was composed of 500 people, mostly of Japanese citizens, who collected six million yen. The House of Sharing also depended mainly upon Japanese scholars and writers specializing in issues related to "comfort women," such as Hayashi Hirofumi, Nishino Rumiko, and Ito Takahashi, for "comfort women's" relics and historical information about the "comfort women" system.[2]

Many Japanese elderly women and Japanese women's organizations also significantly contributed to the fund-raising for constructing the Korean Council's historical museum. They included a Japanese elderly woman, who donated half of her estate inherited from her parents and entered a nursing home, and a retiring Japanese school teacher who donated half of her pension money.[3] Their support for the establishment of the museum in South Korea with such generous donations reflects their strong intention to eliminate brutal sexual violence against women in the form of sexual slavery. In addition, many Japanese citizens donated money for the maintenance and continued operation of the two major Korean advocacy organizations. Especially in the early 1990s, when there was lukewarm support for the redress movement in South Korea, Japanese citizens' financial support was essential to their maintenance.

While major women's organizations in South Korea are highly concentrated in Seoul, women's organizations in Japan are dispersed throughout several major

---

2 Shin-kwon Ahn, "The Establishment of the Museum of Japanese Sexual Slavery and the House of Sharing," Paper Presented at the Conference on "The Redress Movement for the Victims of Japanese Military Sexual Slavery: Looking Back at the 27-Year Movement" held at Queens College in October 2017.
3 The Korean Council, *Hangukchungshindaemunje Daecheak Hyeopeuihe 20-Nyonsa* [*A 20-Year History of the Korean Council*] (Seoul: Hanul, 2014), 256.

cities because of the stronger autonomy of local prefectures and cities. Thus, small and medium-sized advocacy organizations (most of which lack physical offices or headquarters) for the victims of Japanese military sexual slavery are scattered in different cities in Japan. They usually engaged in the redress movement in Japan using two strategies. One was to organize testimonial events, mostly by inviting Korean former "comfort women." The other was to help and support Korean and other Asian victims' lawsuits in Japanese courts against the Japanese government.

The Korean Council used testimonies by Korean "comfort women" as the most effective method of the redress movement. The redress movement has received global support mainly because a large number of "comfort women" courageously emerged as sexual victims and accused Japanese soldiers of inflicting hyper-sexual exploitation and brutal physical violence; this was significant because there was (and still is) social stigma around victims of sexual violence, and furthermore, this was the first time that survivors of the "comfort women" system had come forward publicly to talk about their experiences. About 50 Korean "comfort women" were actively engaged in giving testimonies in South Korea, Japan, and the United States in the 1990s and 2000s. Their testimonies were more wholeheartedly received in Japan and the U.S. than they were in Korea. Part of the reason they were received more enthusiastically and sympathetically in Japan than in Korea was that in almost all cases, Japanese redress activists (most of whom were women) organized these testimony events and specifically invited Korean "comfort women" survivors. Far more Korean "comfort women" gave testimonies in Japan than in the U.S., mostly because of the shorter and more convenient travel time and more manageable travel expenses.

Kim Hak-sun is known globally as the first Korean "comfort woman" who came forward to give a testimony in August 1991. According to my interview with her conducted in 1995, NHK World, a major public broadcasting company in Japan, visited her apartment for an interview immediately after her first testimony and invited her to Japan for further testimony. Along with two other Korean "comfort women," she filed a lawsuit to a district court in Tokyo for compensation on 5 December 1991, and gave five testimonies in five different cities in Japan for one week, each testimony hosted by a local redress organization. Kim Hyewon, an executive director of the Korean Council who took her to Japan for these testimonies, reported:

The Japanese media, non-profit organizations, and Korean-Japanese residents in Tokyo, Osaka, Kobe, Nara, and Sakai accepted Kim halmeoni's[4] testimonies with so much interest and enthusiasm that I was too optimistic about the possibility of resolving the "comfort women" issue soon. A Korean-Japanese resident in Nara asked me about the prospectus for resolving the issue. I said: "Thanks to your great interest and fever, I have the hope that the issue is likely to be resolved sooner or later." It was my careless answer.... Whenever each testimony ended, many participants came forward to halmeoni, gave gifts and made a sincere apology.[5]

In her book, Kim Hye-won introduced a moving event she experienced just before Kim Hak-sun gave a testimony at the YMCA in Kobe, Japan in December 1991. Read the following narrative:

A Japanese woman in her early 40s wearing a sweater quietly came into the room to see Kim halmeoni. She apologized to Kim halmeoni, shedding tears. She then began to talk about her father. She said that she lived only with her widowed father who had served as a Japanese navy officer during the Asian-Pacific War. She confessed that, whenever her father was drunk, he treated her as a woman. She said that she planned to enter a monastery for nuns. She put a white envelope on a desk before she left the room, and asked me to use the money in legally fighting in the court for Kim halmeoni. There was 500,000 yen [$5,000] inside the envelope. It was a big amount of money at that time. However, I saw a bigger gift than the money inside the envelope. It was her aspiration for a peaceful world with no war and no sexual violence against women.[6]

Even before the *chongshindae* movement developed in South Korea in the 1990s, there were progressive forces in Japan that were concerned with Japan's post-war responsibility to Asian countries.[7] For example, Takagi Ken'ichi, Onuma Yasaki, and other conscientious Japanese citizens established the Association Clarifying Japan's Post-war Responsibility to Asian Countries. The association emphasized the Japanese government's moral obligations to take measures to compensate the Asian-Pacific War victims for their suffering inflicted by Japan's colonization and invasion of Asian countries. Several Japanese lawyers concerned with civil

---

4 Halmeoni is a Romanization of the Korean word for "grandma" or "grandmother." Korean "comfort women" survivors are often affectionately referred to as "halmeoni," usually preceded by their family name; thus, in this case, Kim Hak-sun is referred to as "Kim halmeoni."
5 Kim Hye-won, "Ggotjung-eu Ggot Mugunghwaggot-euro Mugunghi Pisoseo" [May You Blossom Eternally as Mugunghwa, the Best among All Flowers], The Korean Council, Newsletter 18 (1999): 17.
6 Kim Hye-won, Ddaldeul-ui Arirang: Iyagiro Sseun 'Wianbu' Undongsa [Daughters' Arirang: The "Comfort Women" History Written with Stories] (Seoul: Heowon Media, 2007), 205.
7 Takagi Ken'ichi, Jeonhu Bosang-ui Noni [The Logic of Post-war Compensations], translated into Korean by Choi Young-gi (Seoul: Hanul, 1992).

rights issues, including Takagi Ken'ichi, helped Asian victim groups file lawsuits against the Japanese government for compensation. In 1989, the Roh Tae-woo (the President of South Korea at the time) Administration gave him an award for his legal counsel to Korean Pacific War victims. Several other lawyers have helped other Asian "comfort women" groups (Filipino, Taiwanese, and Chinese) file lawsuits in Japanese courts. One major redress activity of the Women's Active Museum on War and Peace, one of the major advocacy organizations in Japan, has been to help Asian "comfort women" groups file lawsuits in Japanese courts against the Japanese government (see the chapter by Watanabe in this book).

Korean and other Asian "comfort women" groups made ten civilian lawsuits for compensation at Japanese courts against the Japanese government.[8] But only one lawsuit filed by three Korean "comfort women" at the district court in the Shimonoseki Branch of the Yamaguchi Prefecture received a partial winning verdict.[9] All the remaining lawsuits received the verdict that supported the Japanese government's rejection of the "comfort women" system as sexual slavery. Despite consecutive failures, the efforts of Asian "comfort women" and their advocacy organizations to bring justice through Japanese courts have helped to publicize the "comfort women" issue to the public and to gain more supporters for the redress movement in Japan.

Asian "comfort women's" lawsuits in Japan have helped to publicize the forced mobilization of many Asian women to Japanese military brothels and their brutal experiences there mainly because many Japanese individual citizens and small groups supported their lawsuits by collecting donations and participating in the trials. For example, in the Gwanbu Trial (known as "Gwanbu Jaepan" in Korean) in the High Court in Hiroshima, Japanese citizens in the Fukuyama area established the Fukuyama-based Association to Support the Gwanbu Trial on Post-War Responsibility (hereafter referred to as the Fukuyama Association).[10] Members of the Fukuyama Association not only gave moral support by attending the trial, but also invited members of the advocacy organization in Daegu, South Korea, offering them food and accommodations for six days during their stay in Hiroshima.[11]

---

[8] The Korean Council, *Unfulfilled Justice* (2013), 4–5.
[9] Kim, Chang-rok, "Baro Ilgeun Shimonoseki Pangyeol" [The Shimonoseki Judgment's Correct Understanding of the Issue], The Korean Council, *Newsletter* 13 (1998): 9–11.
[10] Chun-sun Lee, "Appeal Trial in Hiroshima," The Korean Council, *National Activities against Military Sexual Slavery by Japan* (1998), 13.
[11] Because of their experience of the atomic bomb attack in August 6, 1945, many Japanese citizens in the Hiroshima area, including Fukuyama, are engaged in anti-war and peace activism.

Song Shin-do, a Korean "comfort woman" survivor who had lived in Tokyo since the end of the Asian-Pacific War, filed a civilian lawsuit to the Tokyo District Court on 5 April 1993. From the beginning of her trial, Korean-Japanese women established a supporting group for her lawsuit (the Song Shin-do Lawsuit Supporting Association). Many other Japanese citizens joined the supporting group. For all 20 court proceedings, the courtrooms were full of people who came to witness the trials, attracting approximately 10,000 audience members over the course of six years.[12] Many Japanese citizens who lived in neighboring prefectures are reported to have travelled to Tokyo to attend her court trials. By virtue of the exposure of her face and name to the Japanese public and media, she has become well-known in Japan. Many other lawsuits filed by "comfort women" in Japan have also gained a supporting group consisting of Japanese citizens, and their trials attracted a great deal of attention by Japanese citizens.

Mun Ok-chu was one of several Korean "comfort women" who could not get back the money she deposited in the Shimonoseki post office during her sexual servitude. During her testimony tour to Shimonoseki, Japan in 1993, a Japanese supporting group tried to assist her in getting her deposit money back from the post office.[13] However, the Shimonoseki post office refused to give the money back to her on the grounds that she was no longer a Japanese citizen after the 1952 San Francisco Peace Treaty. Although she did not get the money back from the post office, she had many Japanese supporters in Shimonoseki. She was so popular in Japan that Morikawa Machiko, a Japanese writer, published her biography in Japanese, *Mun Oku-chu: Biruma Sensen Tateshiden no "Ianfu" Data Watashi* [*Mun Ok-chu, I Was a Comfort Woman of the Shield Division on the Burmese Front*].[14]

The Korean Council has used the weekly Wednesday Demonstration in front of the Japanese Embassy in Seoul as another major technique of the redress movement in Korea. Japanese citizens and advocacy organizations have organized demonstrations for the redress movement in Japan on special occasions. For example, 61 Japanese civic organizations held a big rally in Tokyo and Osaka, under the name of Japan-Korean Civil Solidarity Committee, when newly elected Korean President Kim Dae-jung was visiting Japan in October 1998 to attempt to make the Japanese government address its reparations to for-

---

12 Jing-ja Yang, "Gongjeonghan Jaepan-eul Narisio" [Please Render a Fair Judgment], Korean Research Institute, *Newsletter* 6 (1999): 4.; Chung-sun Lee, "Appeal Trial in Hiroshima," The Korean Council, *International Actions* 6, no. 2 (1999): 13.
13 Yang, "*Gongjeonghan Jaepan-eul Narisio*," 138.
14 C. Sarah Soh, *The Comfort Women: Sexual Violence and Postcolonial Memory in Korea and Japan* (Chicago: University of Chicago Press, 2008), 183.

cibly mobilized Korean soldiers and "comfort women."[15] On the occasion of the 100th Wednesday demonstration, about 1,000 people demonstrated in Tokyo and 300–400 people demonstrated in Osaka on 18 March 1999.[16]

For the 1,000[th] anniversary of the Wednesday demonstration, similar types of demonstrations were held on 14 December 2011 in 30 other areas in nine provinces and special cities in South Korea at the same time on the same Wednesday. Internationally, demonstrations were held in 42 cities in eight countries on the same day.[17] At noon, a Japanese advocacy organization, Ilbongunwianbu Munjehaegyul Jeongukhaengdong 2010 (The National Action Committee for the Solution to the Comfort Women Issue 2010), organized a demonstration at the Kasumigaseki area, Tokyo. Approximately 1,300 Japanese citizens surrounded the building of the Japanese Foreign Ministry, holding hands.[18] They asked the Japanese government to recognize its legal responsibility, to make an apology to the victims, and to coordinate with the South Korean government to resolve the "comfort women" issue quickly.

One Japanese advocacy organization held a Wednesday demonstration in Tokyo. Dorajihe (Bell Flower Association), a "comfort women" advocacy organization, started the weekly Wednesday demonstration at the East Gate of the Tokyo Ikebukuro station.[19] In her report included in a Newsletter of Korean Research Institute, Oogami Iko, the leader of the organization, indicated how her group started the Wednesday demonstration in Tokyo:

> Our members sold bell flower buttons[20] to Japanese citizens to make them support the redress movement. In April 1994, we visited South Korea to treat Korean "comfort women" with a meal with the money from the sale of the bell flower buttons and also participated in the Wednesday Demonstration for the first time. At that time, Kim Hak-sun, Mun Ok-chu, and Kang Deok-gyeong halmeonis were still alive. We could not forget the scene of several sick old Korean "comfort women" protesting loudly in such a cold, windy weather in the demonstration. In that year, the Murayama administration was actively working on the Asian Women's Fund. Japanese redress activists, who never considered the Asian Women's

---

15 The Korean Council, "Yes Let Our Cries Bring the Justice," *International Activities* 6, no.1 (1999): 1–2.
16 Ibid.
17 "Wianbu Sonyo Hyongsangwha 'Pyonghwabi' Geonlip" [Installment of "Comfort Girl" Peace Statue], *Seoul Shinmun*, December 15, 2011.
18 "Wianbu Halmeoni Cheonbeonjjai 'Nunmul-ui Wechim'" [The "Comfort Women's" 1,000[th] Screaming out of Their Tears], *KBS News*, December 14, 2011.
19 Oogami Iko, "Iboneseodo Jeongi Siwi-reul" [Regular Wednesday Demonstrations even in Japan].Korean Research Institute, *Newsletter* 4, no.14 (1999), 2.
20 The Korean Council has made bellflower buttons and sold them to encourage people to wear them as a sign of supporting the redress movement for the victims of Japanese military slavery.

Fund as an acceptable measure to solve the "comfort women" issue, were very much disappointed.[21] It was around January 1995 that our Bell Flower Association, which had started as a local movie-watching group [movies about "comfort women"], dared to make a coalition with the Korean Council by holding the weekly Wednesday Demonstration in Tokyo. Until May last year (1998), seven or eight of our members had staged a demonstration in the East Gate of the Ikebukuro subway station between six and seven in the evening. We distributed fliers including "Stop the Asian Women's Fund" and "Accept Coomaraswamy's Recommendations."[22]

Radhika Coomaraswamy was appointed as a UN Special Rapporteur on Violence against Women in 1994 by the UN Commission on Human Rights to investigate the causes and consequences of sexual violence against women and to find its solution. Based on her interviews with Korean "comfort women," she completed her report in which she recommended the six measures the Japanese government to take, including the following: "Identify and punish, as far as possible, perpetrators involved in the recruitment and institutionalization of 'comfort stations' during the Second World War."[23] Since Coomaraswamy's recommendations to the Japanese government have been widely known to redress activists, the members of the Japanese advocacy organization seem to have included her recommendations in the banner. However, most Japanese citizens who passed the subway station may not have understood what the flier meant.

Oogami further reported that she found most passersby to have had little information about the "comfort women" issue, which was indicated by such questions as "It is not over yet?," "How long do we have to apologize?," and "Why do we have to stop donating to the Asian Women's Fund?" She said that in 1997, they had big arguments with two former Japanese soldiers who tried to prevent their picketing activities in a police station. She indicated that members of her group had difficulty telling people that they were Japanese citizens when they were asked what nationality they were and what they were doing.[24] People's responses to their Wednesday Demonstration are not surprising at all. However, their courage to hold the Wednesday Demonstration in the Tokyo area is surprising. It is much more difficult and risky for such a small redress organization to organize the Wednesday Demonstration in Tokyo than for the Korean Council to organize it in Seoul.

---

21 Oogami, "Ilboneseodo Jeongi Siwi-reul."
22 See Radhika Coomaraswamy, "Report on the Mission to the Democratic People's Republic of Korea, the Republic of Korea and Japan on the Issue of Military Sexual Slavery in Wartime." E/CN.4/1996/53/Add.1, the Economic and Social Council, the United Nations.
23 Oogami, "Ilboneseodo Jeongi Siwi-reul."
24 Ibid.

Japanese Women's Contribution to Asian Solidarity

One main reason the Korean Council's redress movement has gained global support is its effective pan-Asian coalition from the beginning of the movement. The women's leaders and women's organizations not only in South Korea, but also in other Asian victim countries have participated in the annual or biannual Asian Solidarity conferences. Other Asian victim counties include the Philippines, Taiwan, China, Indonesia, Malaysia, Thailand, North Korea, and even the Netherlands.[25] The pan-Asian coalition has strengthened the redress movement, both symbolically and practically. It has strengthened the redress movement symbolically because several Asian countries can collectively make their demands to the Japanese government effectively and legitimately than individual nations. Pan-Asian solidarity can facilitate redress activities practically because the Korean Council can share information, resources, and womanpower with advocacy organizations and women's leaders in other Asian countries.

Women leaders and women's organizations in Asian victim countries as well as in Japan have actively participated in the Asian Solidarity conferences and coordinated with other advocacy organizations for the common goals of making the Japanese government accept their predecessor's crime of military sexual slavery and also to take responsible measures to try to resolve the issue. First, the active involvement of Japanese women's leaders and organizations have served to strengthen the overall redress movement because it has shifted the overall issue to being a struggle for women's human rights and social justice rather than as anti-Japanese nationalistic struggles. At the end of each Asian Solidarity conference, the participants pass a major resolution or set of recommendations to be sent to the Japanese government and/or international human rights organizations. Because of the participation of many women leaders and women's organizations from Japan in the conference, their resolution or recommendations can carry greater weight.

Second, the participation of many Japanese women leaders and women's organizations has made an immense contribution to pan-Asian solidarity activities in terms of well-educated staff members and financial resources. In the early

---

[25] After Japan occupied Indonesia, the Japanese military took about 40,000 Dutch people in Indonesia as prisoners of war and forcefully took approximately 400 Dutch women as sexual slaves. Because of this historical background, they established the Foundation of Japanese Honorary Debts in the Netherlands in 1990 to deal with the compensation issue. The foundation has participated in the Asian Solidarity Conference since the 11th conference held in Taipei in 2012.

1990s, there were more highly-educated feminist activists and women's organizations in Japan comparable to South Korea. Moreover, Japanese women's organizations had enough financial resources to host the Asian Solidarity conference as well as many other pan-Asian and international symposia and meetings related to the "comfort women" issue. Thus, they have hosted five of the sixteen Asian Solidarity conferences, along with one conference report meeting, while the Korean Council have hosted nine of them.[26]

Large numbers of Korean and Japanese women leaders and women's organizations have participated in each Asian Solidarity conference. In contrast, advocacy organizations from the other Asian victim countries have not attended the conference regularly. On the occasions when these other Asian countries have participated in the conference, they have usually sent only a few participants. Thus, Korean and Japanese women redress activists have comprised the vast majority of participants in each pan-Asian conference. For example, according to the list of participants in the 3rd Asian Solidarity conference held in Seoul in February 1995, 44 Japanese women representing 21 organizations participated, compared to only four Taiwanese women and only two Filipina women.[27] Not surprisingly, a much larger number, 135 Koreans representing about 20 organizations, participated in the conference. These statistics suggests that, without participation of many Japanese women and women's organizations, the Asian Solidarity conference would have lost much of its pan-Asian characteristics.

Japanese Prime Minister Tomiichi Murayama tried to resolve the "comfort women" issue with the Asian Women's Fund (referred to as AWF) collected mainly by Japanese citizen's donations in 1995.[28] The Japanese government would compensate the "comfort women" victims in South Korea, Taiwan, and the Philippines with two million yen (about $18,000) to each victim using AWF, while it would provide an additional fund for their medical care. It planned to cover medical costs for "comfort women" in Indonesia and the Netherlands. The Korean Council and other Asian advocacy organizations adamantly rejected AWF, labeling it "charity money." They demanded the Japanese government's direct compensation to the victims with a sincere apology. The major issue in the 1995 and 1997 Asian Solidarity conferences was criticizing AWF and the Japanese government. The Korean Council and a Taiwanese advocacy organization suc-

---

[26] The Korean Council, *Hangukchungshindaemunje Daechaek Hyeopuihe 20-Nyeonsa* [*20-Year History of the Korean Council*], 395–426.
[27] The Korean Council, *Sourcebook 5: Report on the Third Asian Solidarity Conference on the Comfort Women Issue* (1995), 97–99.
[28] Asian Women's Fund, *Jugun Ianfu ni Sareta Gatanata Tsugunai no Tameni* [*Compensation for Military Comfort Women*] (Tokyo: Asian Women's Fund, 1996).

cessfully persuaded their respective governments to pay compensation comparable to two million yen to each victim so that their "comfort women" did not have to receive the "charity money" from the Japanese government. Since the Filipino government did not have enough financial resources, almost all Filipina "comfort women" survivors received the fund by the end of 1996.[29] This situation weakened Asian Solidarity to some extent.

More detrimental to Asian Solidarity, the Japanese government's creation of AWF as a solution to the "comfort women" issue divided advocacy organizations in Japan. Many Japanese advocacy organizations, which had focused on monetary compensation to the victims due to humanitarian concerns, supported the AWF as a solution. By supporting it, they could no longer work with the Korean Council and other Asian advocacy organizations which flatly rejected it. Thus, they gradually disappeared as advocacy organizations in Japan. Surprisingly, even all members of the Japanese Socialist Party, with the exception of Motooka Shoji, who had strongly supported the Korean Council from the beginning of the redress movement, endorsed the AWF. They may have done so partly because their party head, Prime Minister Murayama, started the AWF. Even Murayama had himself emphasized the Japanese government's direct compensation to the victims before he became Prime Minister.[30] Thus, he seems to have pragmatically compromised his position by accepting the idea of giving compensation to elderly "comfort women" survivors with Japanese citizens' donations to make it helpful to them as soon as possible before they passed away.

VAWW-Net Japan and the Women's International War Crimes Tribunal on Japanese Military Sexual Slavery

The most important contribution of Japanese women leaders and Asian Solidarity to the redress movement is the planning and successful completion of the Women's International War Crimes Tribunal on Japan's Military Sexual Slavery (hereafter, the Women's Tribunal). Matsui Yayori and other Japanese feminist leaders established Violence against Women in War Network-Japan (hereafter,

---

29 Haruki Wada, *Ianfumondai no kaiketsu no tame ni Ajia-josei-kikin no keiken kara* [*The Resolution to the Comfort Women Issue: From the Experience of Asian Women's Fund*] (Tokyo: Heibonsha, 2015), 38.

30 Chin-song Chung, *Inbongun Sungnoyeje* [*The Japanese Military Sexual Slavery System*], Second Edition (Seoul: Seoul National University Publishing Company, 2016), 203.

VAWW-NET Japan), a very radical women's advocacy organization for the victims of Japanese sexual slavery in January 1998. Matsui, representing VAWW-NET Japan, formally proposed to organize the Women's Tribunal in the 5th Asian Solidarity conference held in Seoul in April 1998. Given that VAWW-NET Japan was established only in early 1998, we can presume that organizing the Women's Tribunal may have been the major motivation to establish the advocacy organization. The Women's Tribunal was held in Tokyo for five days between 8–12 December 2000, which means that Asian advocacy organizations worked on preparing the Women's Tribunal for two and a half years.

There are two major factors that led VAWW-NET Japan and other Asian advocacy organizations to decide to organize the Women's Tribunal. First, despite the Kōno Statement's acknowledgment of the forced mobilization of Asian women to Japanese military brothels, both the Japanese government and Japanese neo-nationalists denied the Japanese government's legal responsibility for Japanese military sexual slavery. The Murayama government's effort to resolve the "comfort women" issue through the Asian Women's Fund and many Japanese advocacy organizations' and activists' support of the AWF seem to have led Asian women activists to realize the need for the judgment of the "comfort women" system as sexual slavery by internationally renowned legal specialists. Since the 1946 Tokyo War Crimes Trial did not prosecute the "comfort women" system as a war crime despite sufficient evidence, the Japanese government denied its predecessor's legal responsibility for military sexual slavery despite additional pieces of evidence accumulated by historians.[31] In order to make the Japanese government accept its legal responsibility, they realized the need for something like the Women's Tribunal to render the judgment that the "comfort women" system involved crimes violating several international laws.[32]

Second, Asian women's advocacy organizations, especially members of the Korean Council, seem to have been encouraged to organize an international tribunal by UN organizations' emphasis on prosecuting the offenders responsible for the establishment and management of Japanese military brothels. In order to force the Japanese government to accept the legal responsibility for Japanese military sexual slavery, they need to locate the perpetrators of the "comfort women" system and make a criminal suit against them. Two reports by Special Rapporteurs of the UN Human Rights Commission, one submitted by Radhika

---

31 Nicola Henry, "Memory of an Injustice: The 'Comfort Women' and the Legacy of the Tokyo Trial," *Asian Studies Review* 37 (2013): 362–380.
32 Yayori Matsui, "On the Constitution and the Procedure of the Women's International War Crimes Tribunal on Japan's Military Sexual Slavery in 2000," The Korean Council, *Symposium* held in Seoul on June 4, 1999, 107–115.

Coomaraswamy in 1996 and the other submitted by Gay J. McDougall in 1998, emphasized prosecuting those responsible for atrocities related to the "comfort women" issue. McDougall was especially adamant about this in the following paragraph:

> Japan is clearly the most appropriate location to conduct criminal prosecutions of those for responsible for implementing the system .... The Japanese Government should act as a matter of urgency on this complaint and should seek to bring charges against any surviving individuals who operated or frequented the military's rape centers.[33]

Moreover, two United Nations' International War Crimes Tribunals for the former Yugoslavia and Rwanda, which were prosecuting offenders of sexual violence in the late 1990s, must have encouraged Matsui and other Asian women's leaders to organize the Tribunal in 2000.

The following summary of the organizations of the Tribunal is based on the sourcebook on the Tribunal by the Korean Council.[34] The Tribunal was represented by Matsui Yayori, Yun Chong-ok, and Indai Sajor, the three representatives of women's advocacy organizations in Japan, South Korea, and the Philippines, respectively. VAWW-NET Japan assumed half of the U.S. $400,000 budget, while the Korean Council and VAWW-NET International Networks (a Filipino advocacy organization) respectively assumed U.S. $100,000 each. The International Organizing Committee, consisting of eleven members representing South Korea, Japan, the Philippines, Taiwan, and China, was established in February 1999. It selected six judges, including Gabriel Kirk McDonald, an international legal expert (USA) who served as the President of the International War Crimes Tribunal for Former Yugoslavia, as the chief judge. Three of them were internationally known female judges. Two women legal experts, Patricia Viseur-Sellers and Ustinia Dolgopol, were also selected as the lead prosecutors. In deciding on who would be judges and prosecutors involved in the Women's Tribunal, the organizers took into consideration the fact that the Tokyo War Crimes Trial (which consisted of all male judges and prosecutors) did not prosecute Japanese criminals responsible for the "comfort women" system despite more than enough evidence. Thus, the Interna-

---

[33] Gay J. McDougall, "Contemporary Forms of Slavery: Systematic Rape, Sexual Slavery and Slave Like Practices during Armed Conflict," *Economic and Social Council, United Nations*, included in *Major International Documents on the Japanese Military Sexual Slavery*, ed. The Korean Council (2015), 104.

[34] The Korean Council for the Women Drafted for Military Sexual Slavery by Japan, *Jaryojip 2000: 2000 Nyeon Inbolgun Seonnoye Jeonbeom gukjebeopjeong [Collection of Sources 2000: The Women's International War Crimes Tribunal on Japan's Military Sexual Slavery]*, (Seoul: The Korean Council, 2000).

tional Organizing Committee deliberately selected a significant number of women judges and prosecutors.

The opening ceremony of the Tribunal started on the evening of 7 December 2000 dramatically with a projection of a famous painting titled "Punish the Responsible," made by Kang Duk-kyung, a Korean "comfort woman" survivor. Kang *halmeoni* also asked Yoon Mee-hyang, Representative of the Korean Council, to "get the Japanese military punished" while she (Kang) was dying of pneumonia in 1997. For the next three days (8–10 December), the Tribunal heard prosecuting statements with oral and documentary evidence given by prosecutors from each of the nine victim countries. Many "comfort women" victims gave testimonies as evidence. Two former Japanese soldiers who participated in military brothels also gave testimonies as witnesses. Synthesizing all victim countries' indictments, Ustinia Dolgopol, one of the International Prosecutors, presented the final indictments.

On the fourth day (11 December), the judges deliberated and prepared a preliminary judgment, assisted by legal advisors. On the fifth and final day (12 December), they presented the preliminary judgment and comments in a hall packed with more than 1,000 people. The preliminary judgment indicated that the judges had found Emperor Hirohito and 40 other Japanese officers guilty of the charges, and that they had also determined Japan to be responsible under international laws applicable at the time of the events for violations of its treaty obligations and principles of customary international law relating to slavery, trafficking, forced labor, and rape, amounting to crimes against humanity.[35]

The judges presented the preliminary judgment on the final day of the 2000 Tribunal partly because they needed more time to polish the judgment statement and partly because they wanted to proclaim it in The Hague, Netherlands, where the International Criminal Tribunal for the former Yugoslavia was held, to make it more meaningful. As planned, the final judgment was presented at a meeting held in the Lucent Danstheater in The Hague one year later, on 3 and 6 December 2001, with almost all of the original participants congregating together.[36] The final judgment issued in The Hague was 265 pages long, in English.[37]

---

[35] Christine M. Chinkin, "Editorial Comments: Women's International Tribunal on Japanese Military Sexual Slavery," *The American Journal of International Law* 95 (2002): 335–341.
[36] Young-hee Sim, "Hague, Netherland of Women's International War Crime Tribual on Japan's Military Sexual Slavery in 2000," The Korean Council, *Newsletter* 12 (2002): 8.
[37] Rumiko Nishino, "Women and Active Museum on War and Peace: Creating a Space for Hub of Activism for Peace and Gender Justice," *Women's Asia* 21 (2006): 36.

When the leaders of Asian advocacy organizations originally planned to organize the Women's Tribunal, they worried about many things: whether they could bring enough internationally eminent legal scholars to serve as judges and prosecutors for the civilian court; whether they could get verdicts from the civilian court that would hold Emperor Hirohito, many Japanese officers, and the Japanese government legally responsible for military sexual slavery; and whether they could overcome possible Japanese neo-nationalists' obstructions to prevent the court proceedings. However, they overcame all difficulties, and the civilian court trials went smoothly and achieved the original goals. The Japanese government was notified of the Tribunal and was invited to participate. Since it did not respond to the invitation, they invited a Japanese law firm to send a team to defend the Japanese position as an *amicus curiae* (independent advisor). Thus, the Japanese government and neo-nationalist politicians could not do anything to stop the establishment of a global civilian court in the heart of Tokyo and its judgments of former Emperor Hirohito, many officers, and the state's accountability for the crime of sexual slavery.

The only thing Japanese neo-nationalists could do was to make NHK (Nippon Hōsō Kyōkai, a.k.a., Japan Broadcasting Corporation), Japan's national public broadcasting television channel, distort and alter the content of the broadcasting of the Tribunal.[38] In broadcasting the Tribunal, NHK shortened a 44-minute program to a 40-minute program by cutting a crucial segment of the verdict that found the Emperor guilty and strategically deleting interview footage, including two Japanese soldiers and two "comfort women" victims. It also altered the commentary of Lisa Yoneyama, a discussant who spoke highly of the Tribunal. Suspecting that the members of the LDP and historical revisionists had intervened in the distorted program, Matsui Yayori, representing VAWW-NET Japan, filed a lawsuit against the NHK and its two production companies in July 2001, demanding compensation of 20 million yen for altering the content of the documentary.[39] The Lower Court sided with the plaintiffs by proving that Abe and Nakagawa had put pressure on NHK before it aired the TV program. However, in June 2008, the Higher Court reversed the ruling by the Lower Court on the grounds that "broadcasters have the right to edit their productions freely...."[40] Members of VAWW-NET Japan believed that the lawsuit was still wor-

---

[38] See Puja Kim's chapter in this book.
[39] Akemi Nakamura, "NHK Censorship Ruling Reversed: No Right for Sex Slave Trial to Survive Cutting, Top Court," *Japan Times* online, June 13, 2006. Accessed February 21, 2019. www.japantimes.co.jp/news/2008/06/13/national/nhk-censorship-ruling-reversed/#.U1VYihBLT1U.
[40] Nakamura, "NHK Censorship."

thy because it proved the intervention of high-ranking Japanese politicians in the alteration of the documentary.

Matsui Yayori, the key figure of VAWW-Net Japan, worked so hard in preparing the Women's Tribunal for two and a half years and seeing it through to its successful completion in December 2000 that she may not have found the time to check her health condition. In 2002, she was diagnosed with end-stage liver cancer. Before she passed away in 2002, she organized a major meeting in which about 500 women's movement leaders from all over Japan participated.[41] In the meeting, she announced that she had incurable liver cancer and asked the attendees to continue her incomplete campaign for women's human rights.[42] She also announced her will and dream to donate all her property and assets to help fund the installation of a museum for women's war and peace installed in Tokyo. Sadly enough, on 27 December 2002, shortly after she had detected the liver cancer, she passed away.

Following Matsui's will and with the assets that she had left behind, members of VAWW-NET Japan established the Women's Active Museum on War and Peace (WAM) in Tokyo in August 2005. Its website (http://www.wam-peace.org/eng/) indicates that they established the museum to "preserve the history and memory of the wartime violence committed by the Japanese military against women." It gave three reasons why they opened WAM. One main reason was to preserve records accumulated for the Women's International War Crimes Tribunal on Japan's Military Sexual Slavery of 2000. The second main reason was to honor the "comfort women" in Korea and other Asian countries who had dealt with trauma, psychological suffering, and physical torment... as a result of their maltreatment." The third was to "establish a base for peace and human rights activism in order to wipe out wartime violence against women and to promote a more trusting relationship between Japan and its neighbors in Asia." It has held exhibitions on "comfort women," lectures, and public forums to educate the general public. My interview with Mina Watanabe, its executive director in 2017, reveals that WAM has also helped many Asian advocacy organizations (Filipino, Chinese, Taiwanese, and Malaysian) and "comfort women" victims file lawsuits in Japan.

---

41 Kim Yun-ok, "Jeonguigam-e Neomchineun Matsui Yayori-reul Chumohameyeo" [In Memory of Matsui Yayori Who Had a Great Sense of Social Justice], *Chongshindae Jaryojip* 27 (2003), ed. The Korean Council: 4–5.
42 Kim Yun-ok, "Jeongeugam-e," 4.

Japanese Citizens' and Organizations' Efforts to Help the Korean Council with International Redress Activities

This final section of my chapter examines the efforts of Japanese citizens and organizations to help the Korean Council's redress activities gain support from UN human rights bodies and other international human rights organizations. The Korean Council's redress movement for the victims of Japanese military sexual slavery has gained global support partly because, from the very beginning, it appealed the "comfort women" issue to UN human rights bodies and international human rights organizations. To introduce the "comfort women" issue or any other human rights issue as an agenda to the UN Commission on Human Rights (hereafter referred to as UNCHR), an organization or an individual needs to find a UN NGO to argue on behalf of the organization or an individual. In addition to many Korean lawyers, even more Japanese lawyers have helped the Korean Council in international law.

In particular, I would like to highlight the role of Totsuka Etsuro in this chapter. As an expert on international law, he devoted approximately ten years to explaining the "comfort women" system's violations of many UN laws and international treaties at the UN Commission on Human Rights in the 1990s.[43] In fact, he used the term "sexual slavery" for the first time to refer to the "comfort women" system in 1992 at the United Nations.[44] Korean Women's Associations United selected Totsuka Etsuro as the winner of the annual women's award in 1994 for his devotion to publicizing the "comfort women" system's violations of several international laws.

The Japan Federation of Bar Associations (hereafter referred to as JFBA) adopted the "Declaration calling for the remedy to the Human Rights Violations during the war," including the "comfort women" issue at the 36th World Convention on the Protection of Human Rights held in October 1993.[45] However, the Japanese government had not taken any legal responsibility. Instead, in July 1995, the Murayama administration announced its plan to compensate each "comfort woman" victim through the Asian Women's Fund based on Japanese citizens'

---

[43] Totsuka Etsuro, *"Wianbu"-ga Anira "Seongnoyeda* [*Not "Comfort Women," but "Sexual Slaves"*], transl. into Korean by Park Heung-Gyu (Seoul: Sonamu, 2001).
[44] Ibid. 23.
[45] Japan Federation of Bar Associations, "Recommendation on the Issue of 'Comfort Women,'" *Supplemental Explanation of the Recommendation on the Issue of "Comfort Women,"* (1995), 1.

donations. In response, JFBA submitted "Recommendation on the Issue of 'Comfort Women'" to the Japanese government, asking it to "take immediate legislative measures to make reparations to individual victim...."[46] Of course, it gave the recommendation, after explaining that the Japanese government has legal responsibilities based on results of a few international symposia and research on the "comfort women" issue.

The International Commission of Jurists (ICJ) is an international standing group of 60 eminent jurists dedicated to ensuring respect for international human rights. The Korean Council also asked ICJ to send resolutions and recommendations to the Japanese government in support of the redress movement in 1993. Responding to the Korean Council's request, ICJ sent two lawyers to South Korea, North Korea, the Philippines, and Japan in 1993 to investigate the "comfort women" issue. Based on interviews with 40 "comfort women" victims and other relevant people, ICJ released its report, entitled "Comfort Women: Report of a Mission" in 1994.[47] The 205-page report ended with tough recommendations similar to those made by the report by Radhika Coomaraswamy in 1996. Encouraged by ICJ's emphasis on the Japanese government's legal responsibility and direct reparation to each victim, the Korean Council decided to take the "comfort women" issue to the Permanent Court of Arbitration (PCA) in September 1994. Following the Korean Council's decision, Japanese advocacy organizations established a communication network to support and prepare PCA's judgment on the "comfort women" issue. The Japanese Communication Networks involved 47 advocacy organizations and about 200 members, including the Japanese legal counsel of 70 lawyers.[48]

JFBA recommended that the Japanese government accept the intervention of the PCA to resolve the "comfort women" issue and also lobbied Japanese Diet members to accept it. JFBA and Korean Federation of Lawyers (KFL) established the final legal counsel consisting of 68 Japanese lawyers and 37 Korean lawyers.[49] In order to prepare for the PCA's arbitration, JFBA and KFL had a preparation meeting together in Seoul in November 1995. In the preparation meeting, Ishikawa Itsuko reported that the dismissal of the Korean "comfort women's" criminal lawsuit filed in Febru-

---

46 Japan Federation of Bar Association, "Recommendation," 30.
47 Ustinia Dolgopol and Snehal Paranjape, *Comfort Women: An Unfinished Ordeal* (Jury, Switzerland: International Commission of Jurists, 1994).
48 Chuburaya Gyoko, "Ilbongun 'wianbu' Munje-ui Haegyeol-eul Wihaeseo" [For the Solution to the Japanese Military 'Comfort Women' Issue," the Korean Council, *Sourcebook*, vol. 5 (1995): 64.
49 The Korean Council, "For the Solution to the "Comfort Women" Issue through International Laws: Report on Korean-Japanese Defense Team's Discussions to Send the Comfort Women Case to PCA," January 1995.

ary 1994 by the Tokyo District Court also led Japanese activists and lawyers to seriously consider sending the "comfort women" case to the PCA.⁵⁰ At the end of her article, Ishikawa introduced her poem about a Korean "comfort woman" who was killed with her neck cut off by a Japanese soldier's sword at a Japanese military brothel for speaking Korean. I have below translated the first verse of her poem from a Korean translation of the Japanese original:

> Your cut-off neck is blown over sky. A girl randomly called "Tokiko."
>
> A girl detained in a Japanese military brothel near Tumen River.
>
> A girl who got her neck cut off by a Japanese sword by way of example for punishment for speaking Korean.⁵¹

However, the Japanese government rejected the intervention of the PCA in making a judgment in January 1995,⁵² apparently because it knew that the PCA would render a judgment that would make the Japanese military government accountable for the crime of sexual slavery. The main reason I have introduced the efforts of JFBA to send the "comfort women" case to the PCA is to show that many Japanese lawyers took the initiative in getting a judgment about the "comfort women" system as sexual slavery by a powerful international human rights organization that can make the Japanese government legally responsible for the crime. In addition to being a poet, Ishikawa may have also been a lawyer, which was why she participated in the preparation meeting organized by JFBA. It is surprising to find that a Japanese professional was so emotionally engaged in the "comfort women" issue as a social justice issue that she published a collection of poems focusing on the theme of Korean "comfort women."

Summary and Conclusion

To summarize my analyses of Japanese citizens' and organizations' various activities taken to support the Korean redress movement, first of all, many Japanese citizens as individuals or members of small groups donated money or participated in the weekly Wednesday Demonstrations held in South Korea or Japan. Many Japanese citizens also visited the House of Sharing to meet Korean "comfort

---

50 Itzko Ishikawa, "Ilboneseo-eu Jiwonhwaldong-e Gwanhaeseo" [Regarding Supporting Activities in Japan]; The Korean Council, "For the Solution," 13.
51 Ibid., 15.
52 Chuburaya Gyoko, "Ilbongun 'Wianbu' munje-ui Haegyol-eul Wihaeseoh" [For the Solution to the Japanese Military Comfort Women Issue], The Korean Council, *Sourcebook*, vol. 5, 64.

women" living there and to learn about the history of the "comfort women" system. Also, many Japanese individuals and small groups invited Korean "comfort women" survivors to give testimonies in Japan and/or attended the testimony events. Their support of the redress movement led by Korean advocacy organizations also took the form of supporting Korean "comfort women's" lawsuits filed in Japanese courts against the Japanese government.

Some Japanese citizens, overwhelmingly women, have played the role of redress activists by joining one or more redress organizations in Japan. They usually participated in the Asian Solidarity Conferences, which were held annually, bi-annually, or tri-annually. Some of them supported the Asian Women's Fund as a solution to the "comfort women" issue, which other Asian advocacy organizations adamantly rejected. As a result, they could no longer support the redress movement. Many of the other Japanese redress activists who followed other Asian redress activists in rejecting the Asian Women's Fund as the solution to the "comfort women" issue played an important role in preparing and hosting the Women's International War Crimes Tribunal on Japan's Military Sexual Slavery in 2000. Matsui Yayori played the central role in the redress movement in Japan, in general, and holding the Women's International War Crimes Tribunal, in particular. Her sudden passing in 2002 as a result of liver cancer was a major loss of a towering Asian women's human rights activist.

I have also provided information about both the individual and collective efforts of many Japanese lawyers and other professional women activists to support the Korean Council's international activities to bring justice and honor to "comfort women" victims. It is surprising to find that as many as 47 redress organizations in Japan rejected the Asian Women's Fund and actively engaged in supporting the Korean Council's effort to take the "comfort women" case to the Permanent Court of Arbitration to get a judgment that would hold the Japanese government responsible for its predecessor's crime of sexual slavery.

Given the Japanese government's and neo-nationalist citizens' denial of the Japanese military government's crime of military sexual slavery for such a long period of time, many readers of this chapter may be surprised to find that such a large number of Japanese citizens supported the redress movement, and that so many Japanese advocacy organizations actively engaged in the redress movement. These findings clearly indicate that the "comfort women" issue is one of the most important women's human rights issues, rather than an unresolved historical or political issue between Japan and other Asian countries. Many people all over the world have supported the redress movement for the victims of Japanese military sexual slavery mainly because the brutalities behind "comfort women's" stories have deeply touched their hearts. These stories seem to have not only touched more Japanese citizens' hearts, but also made a deeper impression, partly because they were citizens of the perpetrating country and partly because the victims were citizens of their neighboring countries. No doubt, the vast majority of Japanese participants in the redress movement in the 1990s and early 2000s were middle-aged and elderly women, mainly because as women, they felt far more sympathetic than men to the sufferings of fellow Asian "comfort women" victims.

Mina Watanabe
Initiatives by Citizens of a Perpetrator State: Advocating to UN Human Rights Bodies for the Rights of Survivors

Preface

Concerned citizens in Japan have taken various actions in order to hold the government of Japan accountable for crimes and human rights violations committed during WWII under Japan's military sexual slavery system, euphemistically called the "comfort women" system. In the early 1990s, citizens of Japan joined the redress movement initiated by the victims/survivors of the "comfort women" system and their supporters in victimized countries. Citizens and scholars began undertaking fact-finding research, while lawyers supported victims filing lawsuits against the Japanese government. With respect to international human rights bodies, in an attempt to make the government of Japan accountable under international human rights law, as early as 1992, attorney at-law, Mr Totsuka Etsuro, began providing information to the then-UN Commission on Human Rights and the then-Sub-Commission on Prevention of Discrimination and Protection of Minorities.

Violence against women, especially rape and sexual violence during war and armed conflict, was one of the biggest concerns of global women's movements in the 1990s. The victims/survivors of Japan's military sexual slavery system who testified in international fora gave important impetus not only to women's rights activists but also to those who specialized in human rights law. Since then, a number of recommendations on this matter have been issued by UN special rapporteurs, UN human rights treaty bodies and international human rights NGOs.

The Violence Against Women in War Network Japan (VAWW-NET Japan)[1] began submitting reports and lobbying UN Human Rights institutions in August 2002 following the December 2001 final judgement of the Women's International War Crimes Tribunal for Japan's Military Sexual Slavery delivered in The Hague, the Netherlands. The purpose of the first submission was to inform UN Human

---
[1] Renamed "Violence Against Women in War Research Action Center" in September 2011.

Rights institutions regarding the contents of the Tribunal judgment, one of the most comprehensive documents encompassing legal analysis on the system of Japan's military sexual slavery. With its founding in 2005, the Women's Active Museum on War and Peace (WAM) took over this role as a women's NGO in Japan of submitting alternative reports and lobbying UN human rights bodies. WAM has so far submitted alternative information to the Human Rights Committee (CCPR), the Committee on Economic, Social and Cultural Rights (CESCR), the Committee on the Elimination of All Forms of Discrimination against Women (CEDAW), the Committee Against Torture (CAT), the Committee on the Elimination of Racial Discrimination (CERD), the Committee on Enforced Disappearances (CED), the Committee on the Rights of the Child (CRC), and to the Universal Periodic Review (UPR) conducted under the auspices of the Human Rights Council. To date, many of these UN human rights bodies have made recommendations to Japan on the "comfort women" issue.

The report below is an alternative report for the process of the Replies to Lists of Issues Prior to Reporting (LOIPR)[2] for the 7th Periodic Report of Japan to be conducted in the near future by the Human Rights Committee (CCPR). Particular focus is given to the Korea-Japan diplomatic announcement regarding "comfort women" issued on 28 December 2015. Although this bilateral "announcement" has been criticized by many UN human rights institutions, the government of Japan continues to claim that this "announcement" provides a "final and irreversible solution" to the issue of "comfort women." Accordingly, the report below provides updated information on the statements and actions/inactions made by the Japanese government in terms of an apology, compensation, fact-finding, prosecution of the perpetrators, education and memory in order to clarify ways in which the government of Japan has failed to fulfill its obligation as a State party to the International Covenant on Civil and Political Rights (ICCPR) with regard to providing reparations to the victims.

The report below is not modified to academic style. Rather, it retains the format submitted by us as a civil society organization to the UN Human Rights body in order to provide a concrete example of the reporting efforts of citizens in Japan. Some errors have been corrected and long appendices omitted.

---

[2] It is a simplified procedure adopted by the Human Rights Committee. For further information, see: http://www.ohchr.org/EN/HRBodies/CCPR/Pages/SimplifiedReportingProcedure.aspx. Accessed February 23, 2019.

HUMAN RIGHTS COMMITTEE
NGO Alternative Report for LOIPR on the 7th Periodic Report of Japan
On Japan's Military Sexual Slavery Issue
Submitted on 24 July 2017

Submitted by:
Women's Active Museum on War and Peace (WAM)
avaco bldg. 2F, 2–3–18, Nishi-Waseda, Shinjuku, Tokyo 169–0051 Japan
Tel +81-(0)3–3202–4633 Fax +81-(0)3–3202–4634 email:wam@wam-peace.org

The Events after the Last Review in 2014

1. After the review by the CCPR in July 2014, one of the major events held by the State party was a 28 December 2015 press conference at which the Foreign Ministers of Japan and the Republic of Korea jointly announced a bilateral agreement between the two countries to solve the issue of "comfort women."
2. Since the CCPR stipulated that matters regarding sexual slavery practices against "comfort women" be followed up within a year[3], the State party reported on 17 March 2016 about the above-mentioned announcement.[4]
3. In response to the information provided by the State party, the CCPR special rapporteur sent a letter on 17 April 2016 (KF/fup-116)[5] requesting information on paragraph 14 as follows:

> Paragraph 14:[B2]: The Committee notes the information provided by the State party, but requests further information on measures taken after the adoption of the concluding observations on Japan, on 23 July 2014 (CCPR/C/JPN6), including on the agreement made in December 2015 between the State party and the government of the Republic of Korea, in which the Prime Minister of Japan reportedly made an apology and the State party promised an 1 billion yen payment that would provide support for former comfort women. The committee also requires information on measures taken to (a) investigate all cases and prosecute and punish perpetrators; (b) provide full reparation to victims and their families; (c) disclose all available evidence; (d) condemn attempts to defame victims or to deny the events; and (e)

---

[3] The follow-up procedure is adopted by CCPR in order to monitor more closely the implementation of recommendations that they consider urgent, priority or protective, and therefore to be implemented within one or two years. Please see: http://www.ohchr.org/EN/HRBodies/Pages/FollowUpProcedure.aspx. Accessed February 22, 2019.
[4] http://tbinternet.ohchr.org/Treaties/CCPR/Shared%20Documents/JPN/INT_CCPR_FCO_JPN_23340_E.pdf. Accessed February 22, 2019.
[5] http://tbinternet.ohchr.org/Treaties/CCPR/Shared%20Documents/JPN/INT_CCPR_FUL_JPN_23627_E.pdf. Accessed February 22, 2019.

educate students through references in textbooks. The Committee reiterates its recommendation.

4. On 27 December 2016, the State party replied to the questions of the special rapporteur (MT/UN 598).[6]
5. This report will therefore: (a) provide additional information on the bilateral announcement of 28 December 2015; (b) provide information about the questions raised by the special rapporteur on 17 April 2016 and respond to the State party's reply of 27 December 2016; and (c) propose relevant questions to be considered[7].

1. Korea-Japan Bilateral "Announcement" on Japan's Military Sexual Slavery Issue

The Character of the "Announcement"

6. On 28 December 2015, the Foreign Ministers of the Republic of Korea (ROK) and Japan held a televised press conference to announce that the "comfort women issue is resolved finally and irreversibly" with this announcement. The content of the announcement (hereafter the "announcement") between the governments of the ROK and Japan was concluded with no consultation with the victims/survivors. Moreover, no written document has been made public by either government, leaving nothing for the survivors to read, consider or sign. The wordings of the "announcement," translated into English and disclosed by each government, differ significantly according to each government's position.
7. Japan's military sexual slavery is not a bilateral issue between the ROK and Japan. Japan practiced military sexual slavery throughout the Asia-Pacific region until its defeat in 1945. Survivors who have testified come from many different countries and regions, including the Republic of Korea (ROK), the Democratic People's Republic of Korea (DPRK), China, Taiwan, the Philippines, Malaysia, Indonesia, the Netherlands, East Timor, Papua New Guinea and Japan. The locations of "comfort stations" identified from documents or witnesses include Myanmar, Thailand, Vietnam, Cambodia, Singapore, India, Guam, Palau and other Southern Islands. Under international law, the State party remains responsible for remedy for all victims/survivors,

---

[6] http://tbinternet.ohchr.org/Treaties/CCPR/Shared%20Documents/JPN/INT_CCPR_ASP_JPN_26211_E.pdf. Accessed February 22, 2019.
[7] Please see the recommendation made in the 2014 review at the end of the chapter.

whose rights to receive reparation remain violated. Therefore, the ROK-Japan bilateral "announcement" neither discharges the Japanese government's responsibility, nor resolves the "comfort women" issue.

Nature of the Payment

8. Foreign Minister Kishida made it clear at the press conference that the 1 billion yen payment ($9.8 million) is not compensation based on legal responsibility for the harm done to survivors.[8]

Apology

9. No apology was given directly to victim/survivors. Although Prime Minister Abe was repeatedly asked to apologize publicly to survivors during January 2016 sessions of the Japanese Diet, he refused. When the foundation established by the Korean government as a result of the "announcement" requested that Abe apologise for the sake of the survivors, he replied "I have no intention whatsoever" of making such a statement.[9]

Reactions from UN Human Rights Bodies and Victims/Survivors

10. The State party claims that the "announcement" was "welcomed by the international community" and "positively received by many former comfort women in the ROK."[10] However, this assessment contradicts the statements or reactions of the UN Human Rights institutions and those of the survivors of Japan's military sexual slavery system.
11. According to the Korean Council for the Women Drafted for Military Sexual Slavery by Japan, survivors have rejected the notion that this "announcement" represents the "final and irreversible solution of the comfort women" issue.[11]
12. The Japanese government reply to the follow-up, on the other hand, argues that about two thirds of the survivors have received money transferred from the Japanese government to the foundation set up by the Korean Government. However, according to a report by Korean NGOs, victims/survivors only accepted this money because they were falsely informed that the "Jap-

---

[8] At the press conference with Japanese reporters pursuant to the "announcement," December 28, 2015.
[9] At House of Representatives Budget Committee, October 3, 2016
[10] The reply from the Government of Japan dated December 27, 2016 (MT/UN 598)
[11] The report to the 63rd Session of CEDAW in 2016 (INT_CEDAW_NGO_JPN_22816_E (3)).

anese government has officially apologized and the payment is compensational."[12] The Korean Council for the Women Drafted for Military Slavery by Japan also reported that although one victim/survivor refused to receive money, "the staff of the foundation kept coming back to her urging to receive money, which we consider that as human rights violation."[13]

13. The CEDAW reviewed Japan in February 2016 and discussed the bilateral "announcement." The concluding observations expressed concern that the "announcement" did not fully adopt a victim-centered approach and recommended that the State party take "due account of the views of the victims/survivors and ensures their rights to truth, justice and reparations."[14]

14. On 10 March 2016, during the 31st session of Human Rights Council, Mr. Zaid Ra'ad Al Hussein, the High Commissioner for Human Rights, commented that [the "announcement's"] "terms have been questioned by various UN human rights mechanisms, and most importantly by the survivors themselves. It is fundamentally important that the relevant authorities reach out to these courageous and dignified women."[15]

15. Three UN special rapporteurs, namely, Ms. Eleonora Zielinska, Chair-Rapporteur of the Working Group on the issue of discrimination against women in law and in practice; Mr. Pablo de Greiff, Special Rapporteur on the promotion of truth, justice, reparation and guarantees of non-recurrence; and Mr. Juan E. Méndez, Special Rapporteur on torture and other cruel, inhuman or degrading treatment or punishment, have also expressed their concerns on the "announcement." These rapporteurs urged the government of Japan to implement CEDAW's new recommendations, take a victim-centered approach and follow international human rights standards.[16]

---

12 From paragraph 300 of the report submitted by 64 Korean NGOs to the 60th session of the Committee Against Torture, March 20, 2017. Accessed February 22, 2019. http://tbinternet.ohchr.org/_layouts/treatybodyexternal/Download.aspx?symbolno=INT%2fCAT%2fCSS%2fKOR%2f26966&Lang=en.

13 Follow-up information submitted by the Korean Council for the Women Drafted for Military Slavery by Japan to the CCPR, May 12, 2017. Accessed February 22, 2019. http://tbinternet.ohchr.org/_layouts/treatybodyexternal/Download.aspx?symbolno=INT%2fCCPR%2fFIS%2fJPN%2f27485&Lang=en.

14 CEDAW/C/JPN/CO/7–8. Accessed February 22, 2019. http://tbinternet.ohchr.org/_layouts/treatybodyexternal/Download.aspx?symbolno=CEDAW%2fC%2fJPN%2fCO%2f7–8&Lang=en.

15 http://www.ohchr.org/en/NewsEvents/Pages/DisplayNews.aspx?NewsID=17200&LangID=E. Accessed February 22, 2019.

16 http://www.ohchr.org/EN/NewsEvents/Pages/DisplayNews.aspx?NewsID=17209&LangID=E. Accessed February 22, 2019.

16. Immediately after its release on 28 December 2015, Ban Ki-moon, then Secretary-General of the United Nations, welcomed the "announcement" and expressed the hope that "the agreement will contribute to improving the bilateral relationship between the two countries."[17] However, after meeting survivor Ms. Gil Won-ok, on 11 March, 2016, Ban pointed out that "the agreement between Japan and the Republic of Korea on 28 December 2015" needed to be "faithfully implemented under the guidance of human rights principles." He further called on "all concerned parties to continue the dialogue towards a comprehensive resolution of this issue in line with human rights principles, with the victims at the centre."[18] Comparing these responses, it is clear that two months after December 2015, the UN Secretary-General was not simply "welcoming" the "announcement," but stressing the need for its implementation according to human rights principles.

17. On 27 May 2017, Prime Minister Shinzō Abe and Mr. António Guterres, UN Secretary-General, had a short meeting in Italy. It was reported that UN Secretary-General Guterres expressed "his support for the agreement and welcomed it."[19] However, the following day on 28 May a spokesperson for the UN Secretary General issued a note to correspondents saying that "the Secretary-General agreed that this is a matter to be solved by an agreement between Japan and the Republic of Korea. The Secretary-General did not pronounce himself on the content of a specific agreement but on the principle that it is up to the two countries to define the nature and the content of the solution for this issue."[20] In spite of this notice, the State party has failed to update its website, and continues to insist on the Ministry of Foreign Affairs website that UN Secretary-General Guterres expressed "his support for the agreement and welcomed it."[21]

18. In May 2017, the Committee against Torture reviewed the report submitted by the Republic of Korea, making recommendations that the State party (ROK) "revise the agreement of 28 December 2015 between Japan and the Republic of Korea in order to ensure that the surviving victims of sexual slavery during the Second World War are provided with redress, including the right to com-

---

17 http://www.un.org/apps/news/printnewsAr.asp?nid=52910. Accessed February 22, 2019.
18 http://www.un.org/apps/news/printnewsAr.asp?nid=53428. Accessed February 22, 2019.
19 http://www.japantimes.co.jp/news/2017/05/28/national/politics-diplomacy/u-n-chief-supports-japan-south-korea-comfort-women-agreement/#WWtPIITyhaQ. Accessed February 22, 2019.
20 https://www.un.org/sg/en/content/sg/note-correspondents/2017-05-28/note-correspondents-response-questions-meeting-between. Accessed February 22, 2019.
21 http://www.mofa.go.jp/fp/ipc/page3e_000683.html. Accessed February 22, 2019.

pensation and rehabilitation, and that they are guaranteed the right to truth, reparation and assurances of non-repetition."[22]

Questions:
✓ What is the legal status of the 2015 bilateral "announcement" between Japan and the Republic of Korea?
✓ Does the State party intend to revise the content of the "announcement" in order to fully comply with the covenant and start negotiations that adopt a victim-centred approach?

2. Investigation and Prosecution of the Perpetrators

19. The State party replied on investigation and prosecution of the perpetrators as follows (underlined emphasis added by the author):

> With regards to the war crimes committed by Japanese citizens during the Second World War, we are aware that there have been (1) the International Military Tribunal for the Far East, held in Tokyo, (2) GHQ military tribunals in Tokyo, and (3) tribunals held by the Allied countries. For example, in the Dutch East Indies, some former military officials coerced foreign women into prostitution, <u>against their superior's orders and in violation of military rules that require the woman's consent</u>. In this case, after the military found out about the situation, <u>the military shut down the comfort station</u>, and the officials involved in the case were tried in a BC-level court martial after the war. One was sentenced to death, and 8 were sentenced to imprisonment. <u>That said, it is extremely difficult to investigate the facts of individual cases retrospectively</u>, and therefore, the Government of Japan does not consider prosecuting and punishing perpetrators.[23]

No Prosecution by the State Party in the Post-War Period

20. Unlike post-war Germany and other European governments that prosecuted those individuals who committed crimes against humanity during WWII, the State party to date has never itself attempted to bring to justice anyone who committed atrocities in its war of aggression. The State party has never tried any individual for any war crimes, and Japan's military sexual slavery is no exception. This is in spite of the State party's repeated pledges to contribute to the international community's efforts to end the cycle of impunity for violence against women.

---

[22] CAT/C/KOR/CO/3–5. Accessed February 22, 2019. http://tbinternet.ohchr.org/_layouts/treatybodyexternal/Download.aspx?symbolno=CAT%2fC%2fKOR%2fCO%2f3–5&Lang=en.
[23] Reply from the Government of Japan, December 27, 2016 (MT/UN 598).

21. The post-war trials, including the International Military Tribunal for the Far East (IMTFE) held in Tokyo, did not adequately prosecute sexual crimes by the Japanese Imperial Army, possibly due to a lack of gender sensitivity among legal professionals at the time. No superior commander was tried for planning or setting up Japan's military sexual slavery system.
22. The case in the Dutch East Indies to which the State party refers is known as the "Semarang case" and was prosecuted by the Batavia Temporary Court Martial. The case concerns young Dutch women in civilian detention centres who were forced into sexual slavery for Japanese troops. Certain Japanese military officials stationed locally, including a Major-General, planned comfort stations and eventually took young women detainees from the detention centres and into the facilities. While it is true that the "comfort stations" in Semarang were shut down after two months, none of the military officials was disciplined by the State party prior to Japan's defeat. Instead, the Major-General was promoted to Lieutenant-General in March 1945.[24]
23. Throughout the Dutch East Indies, none of the "comfort stations" where local Indonesian women were confined were shut down. The closure of facilities in the Semarang case is a rare exception and may well be due to the fact that the victims were of European origin in civilian detention centres; as such the case provides no support for the State party's contention that it was acting lawfully at the time. Further, while the State party underlines that those officials were acting "against their superior's orders" and "in violation of military rules" as if to say other "comfort stations" were operated lawfully, such allegations cannot stand in light of the testimony of the many women survivors who courageously came forward across Asia in the 1990s to testify about their ordeals.

Possibility of Investigation and Prosecution
24. It is still possible to investigate and prosecute perpetrators and the State party cannot argue it is difficult to do so. It would have had much more time had it started investigations in 1994 when a group of Korean survivors and their supporters tried to file an official complaint with the Tokyo Public Prosecutor's Office. The State party's unwillingness to prosecute is evident even when the identity and whereabouts of surviving responsible former officers is well known to the government.

---

24 Toyama Misao, ed. *Riku-kaigun shōkan jinji sōran (rikugun-hen)* [*Comprehensive List of Personnel Matter concerning Officers of the Army and Navy (Army Volume)*], Fuyō Shobō Shuppan, 1981, p.36.

25. A typical case is that of former Prime Minister Nakasone Yasuhiro. In his 1978 memoir, Nakasone wrote about his days as a Navy officer in present-day Indonesia: "It was a big troop with about three thousand men or more. After a while some of them started to assault native women or give themselves over to gambling. I took great effort to set up comfort stations."[25] When questioned at a 23 March 2007 press conference, Nakasone replied that the "comfort station" was not a brothel, but a place to play games like Japanese checkers and for other recreational activities.[26] However, in October 2011, a civil society group found official documents in the Library of the Ministry of Defence, stating that, *"with the paymaster's arrangements, women natives were collected and comfort stations was opened"* on 11 March 1942. The name of the paymaster was Nakasone Yasuhiro, and the documents included a map that showed the location of the comfort station in Balikpapan, Borneo Island.[27] The "comfort station" set up by Nakasone was in fact a brothel for soldiers. Despite the discovery of such evidence, the State party has done nothing to hold the former prime minister accountable either in the form of judicial proceedings or through a parliamentary process. Ms. Suharti, an Indonesian survivor of Japan's military sexual slavery who was confined in the "comfort station" in Balikpapan, visited Japan in 2009 and tried to meet Nakasone, but such a meeting was refused. Nakasone Yasuhiro is still alive.

26. Another example of the State party's failure to investigate and prosecute perpetrators is found in an official document located by scholars in 2014.[28] This document is a report of an interview of a former Naval Chief Petty Officer stationed in Bali, conducted by Ministry of Justice personnel in 1962. In the interview this ex-officer testified that he had about 200 local women sent to the island of Bali as "comfort women." He also noted that he was not prosecuted for crimes regarding those women, possibly because he ran local schemes to conceal this fact using the 700,000 yen that he received

---

25 Nakasone Yasuhiro, *"Nijūsan sai de sanzennin no sōshikikan* [The Supreme Commander of Three Thousand at the Age of Twenty-Three]." In *"Owarinaki kaigun"* [Endless Navy], Edited by Matsuura Takanori, Bunkahōsō Kaihatsu Sentā Shuppanbu,, 1978, p. 98.
26 *Mainichi Shimbun*, March 23, 2007.
27 *Kaigun koku-kichi dai-ni setsuei shiryō* [Naval air base second construction party materials] copied in April 1962 by Miyaji Yonezo, former chief engineer of the naval air base second construction party.
28 Found by Prof. Hayashi Hirofumi from the National Archives of Japan. The document is now available at http://wam-peace.org/ianfu-koubunsho/pdf/M-PDF/J_J_012.pdf. Accessed February 23, 2019.

from the military budget in 1945. The State party should have understood as early as the time of this interview in 1962 that there must have been many other similar cases of victimizing women and commenced investigation immediately. The many memoirs published from 1960s and onwards that refer to the soldiers' own encounters with "comfort women" also highlight the State party's negligence concerning investigation.

"Women's International War Crimes Tribunal" Held in Tokyo in 2000

27. The "Women's International War Crimes Tribunal on Japan's Military Sexual Slavery" was held in Tokyo in 2000 by international civil society organizations. The Tribunal identified the responsible military units for certain sites from the testimony of survivors and witnesses, collected evidence accordingly and indicted the individual military officers in charge of those units. Due to limited time and resources, the Women's Tribunal was able to proceed with only the ten highest ranking officials among those accused. The bench, consisting of law experts from Europe, North and South America and Africa, and led by Judge Gabrielle Kirk McDonald, former President of the International Criminal Tribunal for the former Yugoslavia, considered that the evidence submitted was sufficient to declare each of those ten individuals, including Emperor Hirohito, guilty of crimes against humanity for setting up Japan's military sexual slavery system. An official invitation was sent to the State party, which also received a copy of the Tribunal's Judgment. Not only did the State party completely ignore these overtures, the ruling bloc also put pressure on the media to curtail coverage of the event.

Questions
✓ How will the State party comply with the covenant and implement the recommendations of the number of concluding observations by the UN entities regarding prosecuting the perpetrators?

3. Disclosure of Evidence

28. The State party replied on disclosure of evidence as follows (underlined emphasis added by the author):

> [the] Government of Japan has <u>conducted a full-scale fact-finding study</u> on the comfort women issue since the early 1990s when the issue started to be taken up as a political issue between Japan and the ROK. The fact-finding study included research and investigation on related documents owned by <u>relevant ministries and agencies of the Government of</u>

Japan, document searches at the U.S. National Archives and Records Administration, as well as hearings of relevant individuals including former military parties and managers of comfort stations and analysis of testimonies collected by the Korean Council. The result of this study, as well as the documents found in the process, have been made public.[29]

29. The State party has never conducted "a full-scale fact-finding study on the comfort women issue." Many of the military documents acknowledged as "comfort women" related at the time of Kōno Statement of 4 August 1993 had already been located by the efforts of independent scholars. In June 2014, 21 years after the Kōno Statement, a citizen's group submitted over 500 documents discovered by independent scholars and citizens that had not been discovered during official research by the State party. However, the State party refused to accept those documents, and claimed that the newly discovered documents had to be reported officially by the ministries themselves, not by private citizens.[30] The State party returned all the submitted documents to the citizen's group on 31 March 2016.

30. Regarding archival research abroad, the State party has conducted only very limited research at the National Archives and Records Administration in the United States (NARA). The State party has never conducted research at the national archives of the Netherlands, UK, China, ROK, Taiwan, or Australia, where scholars and journalists have already found much relevant evidence. The State party has not acknowledged these documents in foreign archives as "comfort women"-related with the exception of a few Japanese military documents in the National Archives of the UK that were confiscated by the Allied Forces at the end of World War II. Furthermore, many other relevant documents have been discovered at NARA by independent scholars since 1993.

31. The State party has not fully disclosed evidence related to post-WWII war crimes tribunals or provided public access to them. For instance, the documents of the "Semarang case" (please refer to §22) is clear evidence that Japanese soldiers forcefully took women from detention centers to "comfort stations" in Semarang. This directly contradicts the State party's repeated assertion that there are no official documents confirming "forceful taking-away" by military and government authorities. Furthermore, the Ministries of Foreign Affairs (MOFA) and of Justice, as well as the Cabinet Office, all claim that they cannot locate the materials related to the "Semarang case" despite the fact that there is a record of the MOFA obtaining a copy

---

29 Reply from the Government of Japan, December 27, 2016 (MT/UN 598).
30 Stated by Tanaka Naoko, staff to the Assistant Chief Cabinet Secretary, March 31, 2016.

of the court martial documents from the National Archives of the Netherlands.[31] To date, the State party has not provided public access to the "Semarang case" documents.

32. In terms of collecting testimonies as evidence, the State party only says that it analyzed "testimonies collected by the Korean Council." Although the State party in fact conducted interviews with 16 victims/survivors living in the ROK in 1993, the results of these interviews have never been disclosed, even anonymously, and the State party never cites these testimonies as evidence. Although civil society groups have repeatedly requested public hearings or interviews of other victims/survivors from the Republic of Korea (ROK), the Democratic People's Republic of Korea (DPRK), China, Taiwan, the Philippines, Malaysia, Indonesia, the Netherlands and East Timor, the State party has never conducted such hearings or interviews. Many victims/survivors have thus passed away without recognition as victims from the State party.

33. The State party is presumed to hold voluminous amounts of contemporaneous records. Independent scholars have pointed out these to include: police records; colonial records of the Department of Overseas Affairs and the Home Ministry; a huge collection held by the Defence Ministry of diaries of officials and personnel accompanying the military; materials held by the Justice Ministry relating to the war crimes trials; and Welfare Ministry documents relating to repatriation and war victims' relief. Even though Japanese government and military officials were ordered to destroy all incriminating official documents at the end of World War II, scholars assume that the State party still holds many documents in the archives of the above-mentioned ministries.

Questions
✓ Does the State party consider the victims/survivors testimonies as evidence?
✓ What are the concrete reasons for the State party for conducting interviews only in the ROK but not in the other countries where victims have already come forward?
✓ Does the State party intend to seek cooperation from foreign governments for thorough fact-finding about Japan's military sexual slavery system, including research in the foreign archives and interviewing victims/survivors as well as witnesses?

---

31 *Shugiin Naikaku-iinkai Kaigiroku*, [Minutes of the Cabinet Committee, House of Representatives], April 23, 2014.

4. Providing Full Reparation to Victims

34. There is no new initiative by the State party since the last review in 2014.

Questions
- ✓ How will the State party implement the recommendations of the number of concluding observations by UN entities, and fulfil its obligations under international human rights law concerning victims of all countries where the victims/survivors are still alive and claiming their rights for reparation?
- ✓ The practice of Japan's military sexual slavery was widespread and involved women in many countries and regions. Does the State party intend to seek expertise and assistance from UN human rights institutions to ensure the victims' rights for remedy and reparation, as suggested by UN human rights experts?

5. Public Apology / Official Recognition of Responsibility / Refuting Denials

35. In January 2016, right after the bilateral "announcement," the Prime Minister of Japan stated as follows (underlined emphasis added by the author).

> Prime Minister Abe: "This agreement does not mean that [we/GOJ] have admitted to, for instance, things that constitute war crimes. There is no such fact as sex slaves or 200,000 [victims]; it is a fact that [the Western media/the world] has been showering [us/Japan] with this criticism. Against it [i.e. this criticism] the government would like to firmly demonstrate that it is not fact. In 2007 at the time of the first Abe Cabinet, the government ratified, as the official cabinet reply to a parliamentary enquiry submitted in writing by MP Tsujimoto Kiyomi, the Cabinet Decision that no reference had been found until that time among materials discovered by the government that directly suggested the so-called forcible taking away [of women] by military or government personnel. I would like to state anew that there has been no change whatsoever to this position [on the part of the GOJ]".[32]

36. Recalling the 26 years of struggle for justice for victims/survivors of Japan's military sexual slavery, any words of apology that do not fully acknowledging the crimes committed against the women are meaningless. The GOJ's website says that the Japanese government is "painfully aware of its responsibility."[33] However, as long as denials of the historical facts continue, no one can be certain of the acts for which the State party is "painfully

---

[32] *Sangiin Yosan-iinkai Kaigiroku*, [Minutes of the Budget Committee, the House of Councilors], January 18, 2016.
[33] Accessed February 23, 2019. http://www.mofa.go.jp/a_o/na/kr/page4e_000364.html.

aware of its responsibility," or of the acts for which the government apologized.

Questions
- What is the legal argument of the State party in insisting that the women in "comfort stations" were not sexual slaves?
- Does the State party recognize that unambiguous acknowledgement of the facts is fundamentally important for remedy and full reparation?

6. Memory and Education

37. The State party has made no effort to pass on the history of Japan's military sexual slavery to the next generation. Instead, there are many attempts to whitewash history and to disrupt initiatives for remembrance made by civil society organizations not only in the ROK and Japan, but also in other countries.
38. On 19 July 2017, the new Moon Jae-in administration issued a five-year policy plan including designating a "comfort women" memorial day in 2018, setting up a research institute in 2019 and setting up a history museum on the "comfort women" issue in 2020. On the same day, the State party immediately protested to the ROK government on the grounds that the plan is "against the purpose of the 2015 agreement," and urged the ROK to faithfully implement the bilateral deal.[34]

Textbooks
39. Most victims hope that history will be told accurately to succeeding generations to ensure that the same mistakes are not repeated. However, even though from 1997 through to 2001 all history textbooks used in compulsory education in Japan included some reference to the "comfort women" issue, the number of such textbooks decreased in 2002 and again in 2006. In 2012, the term "comfort women" was erased from all compulsory education textbooks. In 2016, a reference to "comfort women" appeared in only one of all the history textbooks issued by eight publishers, although the content

---

34 "ROK to Designate "Comfort Women" Memorial Day: National Plan with History Museum in 2020" (J), *Mainichi Shimbun*, July 21, 2017. Accessed February 23, 2019. https://mainichi.jp/ch150910073i/%E9%9F%93%E5%9B%BD.

was largely modified under the scrutiny of a textbook vetting committee set up by the government.

Memorials

40. The Japanese Government demands the removal of the "Girl Statue for Peace" that stands in front of the Embassy of Japan in Seoul. This statue was put in place on 14 December 2011 by citizens including "comfort women" survivors themselves. This was the very day of the 1000th demonstration of protest held outside the embassy by survivors every Wednesday since 1992.[35] In response to the installation of this statue, the Japanese government made official requests to the ROK for its removal, claiming that the monument negatively affects the "dignity of diplomatic establishments abroad" and that it is in violation of the Vienna Treaties concerning consolatory relations. Implying that this was one of the matters agreed upon, the government of Japan has continued to demand the removal of the statue even after the "announcement."

41. When another girl statue was installed on 30 December 2016 by citizens in the city of Busan, ROK, the Japanese Government demanded its removal and, in protest, summoned back Japan's ambassador to the ROK. On 17 February 2017, Foreign Minister Kishida repeated the request "in a strong manner" to the Foreign Minister of the ROK.[36] Japan's ambassador returned to the ROK in April and on 2 May requested the "faithful implementation of the 2015 agreement" and the removal of the Busan statue.[37] On 9 May

---

[35] The "Wednesday Demonstration" began on 8 January 1992 in front of the Japanese Embassy in Seoul. Korean survivors of Japan's military sexual slavery and their supporters have continued to stand in front of the Embassy each Wednesday at noon calling for the restoration of their honor and dignity. The Wednesday Demonstrations have been carried out no matter the weather with two exceptions on Wednesdays just after the 1995 Great Hanshin Earthquake and the 2011 Great East Japan Earthquake and Tsunami. On 14 December 2011, at the 1000th demonstration, the "girl statue for peace" was erected.

[36] Press conference held by Foreign Minister Kishida, February 17, 2017, reported on the website of Ministry of Foreign Affairs. Accessed February 23, 2019. http://www.mofa.go.jp/mofaj/press/kaiken/kaiken4_000458.html#topic1

[37] "Ambassador to ROK asks ROK Foreign Minister for Removal of Girl Statue, First meeting with Minister after Return to ROK" (J), *The Asahi Shimbun*, May 2, 2017. Accessed February 24, 2019. http://www.asahi.com/articles/ASK526JHTK52UHBI038.html?iref=pc_rellink

Chief Cabinet Secretary Suga stated that "the government's policy continues to demand that the ROK steadily implement the 2015 agreement."[38]

42. The Japanese Government has repeatedly stated that the "comfort women" statues erected overseas are "against" Japan's "position." On 22 February 2017, the Japanese Government filed an *amicus curiae* brief to the U.S. Supreme Court (in *Gingery et al. v. City of Glendale*) in support of the plaintiffs who sued the city of Glendale for the removal of the "comfort women" memorial that the city erected in July 2013. In its documentation the Japanese Government argued that the girl statue "presents a significant impediment to Japan's diplomatic efforts" as it is "not in line" with the "spirit" of the bilateral agreement of 2015. The Japanese Government also "strongly disagrees that the inscription on the Glendale monument accurately describes the historical record, which Japan has studied at length."[39] When the U.S. Supreme Court dismissed the case on 27 March 2017, Chief Cabinet Secretary Suga again stated that setting up comfort women statues is "irreconcilable" with Japan's stance and "extremely regrettable," and that the Japanese Government will continue to promote an "accurate understanding" of its basic stance and projects with regard to this issue.[40]

43. On 8 March 2017, a "girl statue" was erected by a private entity on private premises in Wiesent, Germany. The Japanese Government again showed resentment and demanded its removal. At a press conference on 10 March 2017, Foreign Minister Kishida noted that "recent developments centering around comfort women statues are extremely regrettable. We will continue to make every effort to explain the position of our country."[41] Following persistent meddling by the Japanese government, in April of the same year the owner removed the plaque at the statue base that had provided a historical explanation of the "comfort women" issue.

---

[38] "Hope New ROK Administration Will Steadily Implement 2015 Agreement: CCS Suga" (J), *The Asahi Shimbun*, May 9, 2017. Accessed February 24, 2019. http://www.asahi.com/articles/ASK593G98K59UTFK003.html

[39] Ministry of Foreign Affairs. Accessed February 24, 2019. http://www.mofa.go.jp/mofaj/files/000231732.pdf

[40] "US Comfort Woman Statue: CCS Calls for Understanding of Japanese Government's Position", *NHK*, March 28, 2017. Accessed February 24, 2019. http://www3.nhk.or.jp/news/html/20170328/k10010927181000.html

[41] Ministry of Foreign Affairs. Accessed February 24, 2019. http://www.mofa.go.jp/mofaj/press/kaiken/kaiken4_000467.html#topic2

44. On 30 June 2017, a girl statue was erected in a Brookhaven park in Atlanta, Georgia, U.S.A. In order to block this installation, Shinozuka Takashi, the consul general of Japan in Atlanta, stated the following on June 16, 2017:

> No evidence has been found about that. So first of all, this is [a] fact of history. Not 200,000, not sex slaves and not taken by force. Maybe you know that in Asian culture, in some countries, we have girls who decide to go to take this job to help their family.[42]
>
> [....]
>
> The memorial which the city of Brookhaven would like to have is not a simple art object but a political tool which has many controversial implications. As you can see, this has been [a] symbol of hatred and resentment against Japanese.[43]

This remark has not been condemned, refuted or taken back by the State party.

UNESCO Memory of the World

45. The government of Japan is openly resisting an initiative to register documents related to Japan's military sexual slavery in the UNESCO Memory of the World Register. For example, on 15 May 2015, Prime Minister Abe noted "with emphasis" to members of his Liberal Democratic Party including the head of the party's Foreign Affairs Division: "It is important to start making all-out efforts now so as not to have [the materials concerning 'comfort women'] registered [in MOW]."[44] The government of Japan is suspending its fiscal contribution of U.S. $34 million to UNESCO in order to pressure the organization not to register "comfort women" documents with the Memory of the World.[45] They also suspended fiscal contributions when documents related to the 1937 Nanjing Massacre were registered in 2015.

---

[42] Website of Reporter Newspapers, June 20, 2017. Accessed February 24, 2019. http://www.reporternewspapers.net/2017/06/27/japan-consul-generals-comfort-women-comments-trigger-international-criticism/

[43] Ibid.

[44] "PM Abe: Memory of the World 'Requires Close Examination,' Efforts for 'Comfort Women' Non-Registration," Jiji Wire Service, May 15, 2015. Accessed February 24, 2019. http://archive.fo/nArGp.

[45] *Sankei Newspaper*, May 7, 2017.

Museums

46. As the "comfort women" issue did not appear in textbooks used in compulsory education until 1997, most adults have not had a chance to learn about this issue. Thus, it is important to provide other means of educating people about "comfort women." However, neither the National Museum of Japanese History nor any other national museums related to the history of WWII make any reference to the fact of Japan's military sexual slavery.

47. Furthermore, the Japanese Government objected to, and harshly criticized, the establishment of museums focusing on the "comfort women" issue in Shanghai and Taiwan. When then-President Ma Ying-jeou of Taiwan expressed interest in setting up a memorial museum on "comfort women," Chief Cabinet Secretary Suga said: "This is of course in conflict with Japan's position." He continued: "If such efforts seem likely to be formalized, then we intend to explain our position [to the government of Taiwan] through a variety of channels, and thrash it out [with them] so that the plan is cancelled."[46]

Questions

✓ How will the State party implement measures to pass the memory and history of Japan's military sexual slavery on to the next generation in order to assure non-recurrence of such crimes?

✓ What aspects of "comfort women" statues and museums are "in conflict" with the State party's position?

---

[46] Cabinet Secretary's Press Conference, June 5, 2015.

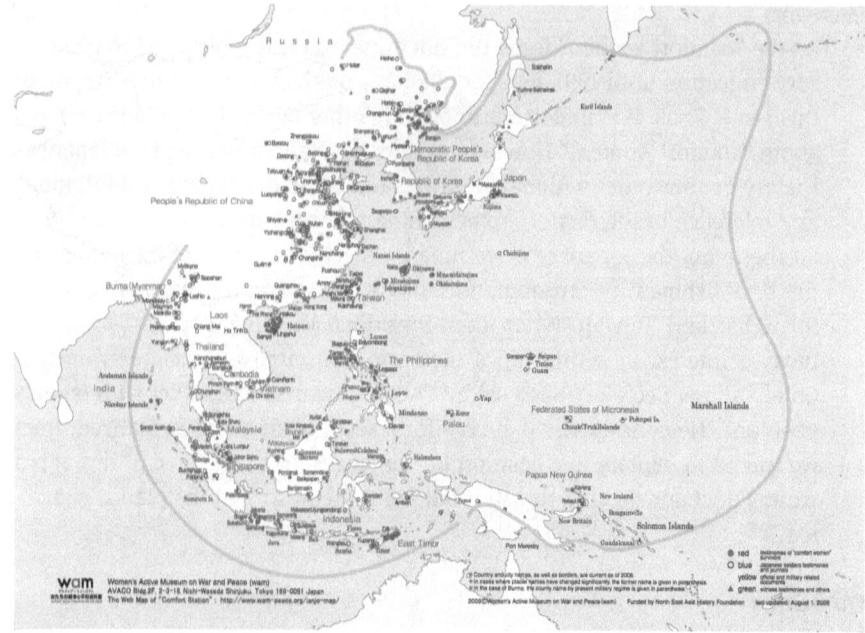

Fig. 1: This map shows the locations of different "comfort stations" in the Asia and Pacific Island region established by the Japanese military. Courtesy of Women's Active Museum on War and Peace (wam).

Part II: **The Redress Movement
in the United States**

Jungsil Lee and Dongwoo Lee Hahm
Tracing 28 Years of the Redress Movement Led by the Washington Coalition for Comfort Women Issues

This study examines the activities and significance of the Washington Coalition for Comfort Women Issues, Inc. (hereafter referred to as WCCW), a non-profit organization based in the Washington D.C. metropolitan area. It will mainly focus on people closely related to the organization who have been a voice for victims of Japanese military sexual slavery from its inception in 1992 and up to the present. WCCW was founded as the first organization of its kind in the U.S. in a collaborative effort with Korean American groups in New York and Toronto, Canada.[1] They have fought for the justice and dignity of the wartime victims euphemistically called "comfort women," and provided support for those unable to defend their legal rights and human dignity. In 1992, the groundbreaking testimony by Hwang Keum-ju at the Korean Methodist Church of Greater Washington in Virginia sparked the beginning of WCCW's activities. WCCW has worked with other organizations, elected officers, scholars, artists, and more throughout the years. We mention those names in this chapter and highlight their achievements.

WCCW has endeavored to raise awareness of this issue from within the D.C. area in concert with the U.S. House of Representatives. Members of the U.S. House of Representatives who have helped with WCCW's goals and activities include former and current Congressmen and Congresswomen, such as Mike Honda, the late Lane Evans, William Lipinski, Nancy Pelosi, former Speaker of the House Newt Gingrich, and the 167 House representatives who co-sponsored to pass House Resolution 121.[2] Other people who have helped raise awareness of this issue include Eli Rosenbaum, director of the U.S. Department of Justice; Susan Lee, Maryland State Senator; Mark Keam, Virginia House of Delegates; Retired Bishop Young J. Cho of the United Methodist Church; Emeritus Professor Bonnie Oh of Georgetown University; Margaret Stetz at the University of Delaware; Mindy Kotler, director of Asia Policy Point; Dennis Halpin, congressional

---

[1] Interview with Pastor Youngho Kim, January 9, 2019; He described the first demonstration in UN of 1991 with "comfort women" survivor, Hwang Keum-ju and participating Korean groups and individuals. They started to rally in the small square of the Church for UN, in front of the UN and expanded to a larger plaza.
[2] See names of co-sponsors at https://www.congress.gov/bill/110th-congress/house-resolution/121/cosponsors. Accessed February 24, 2019.

staff and visiting scholar of School of Advanced International Studies (SAIS), Johns Hopkins University,[3] and all former presidents, chairs, board members, officers, and supporters of WCCW.

WCCW's Redress Activities

It was two days before Thanksgiving in 1992 when a former "comfort woman," Hwang Keum-ju, was invited to the U.S. to give a testimony at the UN Commission on Human Rights.[4] The women leaders of Korean United Methodist Church of Greater Washington, The Association of Women's Mission, invited her for convening and prayer.[5] Hwang exposed her experiences as a 17-year-old sex slave and detailed her life in the "comfort station." She "was raped by several tens of Japanese soldiers a day and Japanese government now calls [her] a liar!"[6] All attendees were shocked by the harrowing accounts, and three days later, her story was aired on Fox News Channel 5 in the Greater Washington, D.C. area and the public was outraged. The WCCW was established two weeks later on 12 December 1992.

Korean community leaders, church leaders, and journalists attended the first meeting at the Korean United Methodist Church of Greater Washington. The consensus was that the individual leading WCCW should be a woman who was fluent in Korean, English, and Japanese; Dongwoo Lee Hahm was unanimously elected as the first president of WCCW. In 1992, very few people had even heard about the issue until Hwang Keum-ju's testimony shattered the silence. WCCW was immediately inundated with inquiries from near and far. Dongwoo Lee Hahm indicated that the initial mission of WCCW was to influence the

---

[3] Halpin was part of the professional staff for Foreign Affairs Committee Chairman Henry Hyde in 2006 and prepared materials for consideration of H. Res. 759 that were used as background for H. Resolution 121.

[4] Per Youngho Kim's memory, in 1992, he and 24 Korean-American organizations formed a coalition called East Coast Korean American Council to support and collaborate with the Korean Council in Korea with ardent devotion with Dae Si-dong, New York, and Min Hye-gi from Association of Women's Mission, Toronto, Canada.

[5] One of them, Kang Soon Im, initiated the gathering and started to print a bound volume that consists of testimonies and historical resources of former "comfort women" in her garage. In addition, Dongwoo Lee Hahm—one of the authors of this chapter and also the founding president of WCCW—was a member of The Association of Women's Mission in the same church.

[6] For the whole content of Hwang's testimony, see Dai Sil Kim-Gibson, *Silence Broken: Korean Comfort Women* (Iowa: Mid-Prairie Books Parkersburg, 1999), 12–31. Kim Gibson, as a translator, recorded the whole testimony.

U.S. government to demand that Japan resolve this issue. This initial mission was inspired by Ms. Doi Takako, the keynote speaker at the *Japanese International Symposium* in April 1993.[7]

Demonstrations, Petitions, and Media

The first effort of WCCW to fulfill its mission[8] was to appeal to the U.S. federal government through the U.S. House of Representatives to give an ultimatum to the Japanese government. For ten years, President Hahm had intensely advocated for the "comfort women" issue through demonstrations, petitions to community leaders and political leaders in the UN, publications, films, forums, conferences, media exposure, and exhibitions. WCCW's successive presidents followed this plan and raced to evangelize the American public.

On 1 March 1993, the first WCCW demonstration was organized. In memory of the Korean March 1st Independence Movement Day, leaders of WCCW[9] protested in front of the Embassy of Japan in Washington, D.C., blaming the Japanese government's rejection of responsibility for crimes against humanity. In addition, the protest intended to spread awareness of the "comfort women" issue and WCCW's mission. Approximately 150 activists led by Korean women dressed in white, traditional Korean attire (*hanbok*), along with Chinese activists, conducted

---

[7] As a motivation of her dedication for the issue, founding president Hahm remembers the symposium "Asian Women for Peace" in April 1993 organized in Japan. The keynote speaker was Doi Takako, the Chair Woman of the Social Democratic Party of Japan, and after her speech, Ms. Takako asked her to urge U.S. Congress members to put political pressure on the Japanese government with a belief that "only American Government pressure works for the Japanese government."

[8] WCCW's original mission statement in 1992: "WCCW believes that the Japanese government must clearly acknowledge its responsibility for crimes committed against 'Comfort Women.' The Japanese government should officially apologize to these victims: provide redress from government resources; correct false statements concerning the issue that have appeared in government-issued textbooks; and open all government records regarding its involvement in these heinous crimes. Until these steps are taken, WCCW believes that Japan should be denied a permanent seat on the United Nations Security Council." This statement was revised twice, in 2013 and 2016.

[9] First officers of WCCW are as such: president-Dongwoo Lee Hahm, Senior Committee (later called vice president)- Kang Soon Im and Rhee Moon hyung, Legal advisor-Lee Jonyeon, Auditor-Yang Seung-gil.

a peaceful rally demanding an official apology and legal reparations from the Japanese government. The emphatic rally lasted for two hours.¹⁰

Fig 1: WCCW organized the First Demonstration "Asian and American United to Redress Japanese War Crimes" in front of the White House wearing Korean traditional dress, June 1994. Washington Coalition for Comfort Women Issues Visual Archives (WCCWVA), photo by Doochan Halm.

It was a formidable task to carefully phrase and deliver WCCW's stance for a large audience. WCCW had a vision of collecting petitions with the goal of 10,000 signatures to submit to the UN on 11 December 1992, even before the organization was formally established. In the next year, September 1993, WCCW delivered the official letter with the victims' demands to the Embassy of Japan in the U.S., along with the signatures of 8,000 others.¹¹ The Japanese Prime Minis-

---

10 The rally was peaceful, but some of the banners featured very bold messages such as "How many Korean women did you kill after sex?"
11 Rhee Moon Hyung (former co-chair of WCCW), "Lecture on archival material of WCCW," Forum of WCCW, KUSCO, Virginia, February 21, 2015.

ter Hosokawa Morihiro[12] visited the United States to speak at the UN in New York in the autumn of that year. Thus, WCCW wrote an open letter addressed to Hosokawa, requesting an official apology and legal reparation to the sex slaves of the Japanese Military during World War II. The letter was published in *The Washington Post* on the same day as Hosokawa's speech at the UN General Conference. The letter brought about further action, as 17 members of the U.S. Congress sent their own letters to Hosokawa, requesting the Japanese government to investigate the sexual slavery of "comfort women" during the Asian-Pacific War. This was the first major Congressional support of WCCW's redress movement.

In June 1994, when the Japanese Emperor visited Washington, D.C. to meet with President Bill Clinton, WCCW organized another demonstration demanding full redress for Japan's war crimes. WCCW invited Hwang Keum-ju and Prof. Lee Hyo-jae, a former representative and one of the founders of the Korean Council, to participate in the rally. Two sessions were held in front of the White House: "Asians and Americans United to Redress Japanese War Crimes," and "United against Japan for Justice and True History." WCCW delivered a letter addressed to President Clinton and Emperor Hirohito along with petitions containing 8,000 signatures, demanding an official apology and legal reparation from the Japanese government.

On 27 April 2015, WCCW published a statement titled "Open Letters of Peoples of United States and Japan," which took up an entire page in *The Washington Post*; the publication of this statement coincided with Japanese Prime Minister Abe Shinzō's visit to the U.S. to deliver a speech to the joint session of Congress. WCCW also organized a rally consisting of 700 people on 27 and 28 April 2015, in front of the Capitol building, while Abe was speaking at the Congress on April 28. WCCW collaborated with more than 30 organizations throughout the nation, and special guests who spoke at the event included Lee Yong-soo (a survivor of Japanese military sexual slavery) and Congressman Mike Honda, as well as other political leaders who supported the issue. Abe's visit prompted many journalists to report on the issue, including delegations from *The Washington Post*, *Washington Times*, *CCTV*, and *Al Jazeera*.[13]

Disappointed by the Korean-Japan Bilateral Agreement on 28 December 2015, WCCW made an official statement and presented it in the UN press conference with the Coalition of Trafficking Against Women, KACE, and KAFC in support of the statement of The Convention on the Elimination of all Forms of Discrimination against Women (CEDAW). WCCW's statement is as follows:

---

12 Hosokawa Morihiro was Prime Minister of Japan from August 1993 to April 1994.
13 Jungsil Lee, "The Future of Comfort Women," *The Washington Times*, October 14, 2015.

Fig. 2: WCCW organized a rally to demand an official apology from the Japanese Government when Prime Minister Abe Shinzō visited U.S. Congress to give a speech at the joint session, April 2015. Washington Coalition for Comfort Women Issues Visual Archives (WCCWVA), photo by Jaeheup Kim.

> After last year's joint agreement issued by the Republic of Korea and Japan on the issues of the "comfort women," WCCW members have been appalled by the Japanese government's continued denial and whitewashing of the historical facts that had already been acknowledged by their previous officials. Their recent statement proves that the agreement was not sincere and genuine. True reconciliation would not be possible without real and perpetual efforts in a clear and unequivocal manner. WCCW, an organization whose mission is to advocate for the rights of wartime victims—military sex slaves—and their lawful reparation, expected and hoped for progress in terms of the lawful reparation and official treatment followed by the agreement of two countries, but the recent activities of the Japanese government failed to reveal this hope is headed for the right direction. We support the recent recommendation by CEDAW (Committee on the Elimination of Discrimination against Women) …. [14]

WCCW regard the bilateral agreement as piecemeal bureaucracy with many flaws that was posited without the consultation of the victims and the NGOs who worked on their behalf.

---

[14] Introduction of statement at the UN press conference Headquarters, March 8, 2016.

Production of a Documentary Film and Holding Conferences

In September 1994, President Hahm went to South Korea with Doochan Hahm, retired editor from *The Korea Times*, to interview victims and to record testimonies from fifteen surviving victims. The interviews focused on their suffering in captivity and the belated campaign for justice. The documentary, titled *Comfort Women*, was screened in the following locations along with the exhibition: George Washington University, Wesley Seminary, Washington D.C.; Falls Church, Virginia; the Fourth UN World Conference on Women, Beijing, China; Old Dominion University, Virginia; Chinese Community Center, Virginia Beach; Atlantic Exhibition "The Forgotten Holocaust," Atlanta, Georgia; "The Asian Holocaust," St. Paul, Minnesota; the UN, New York; Free Library, Philadelphia; the Church of Christ, Charlotte, North Carolina; University of Michigan, Ann Arbor, Michigan; and Cornell University, Ithaca, New York.[15]

Since the first forum on "comfort women," which was co-sponsored by the Georgetown University Law Center Student Association (1994), many forums, lectures, victims' testimonies, and archival exhibitions have been carried out at places like Cornell University, University of Michigan, Northwestern University, University of Wisconsin, Ohio State University, Boston University, MIT, and Tufts University.

WCCW organized an international conference on "comfort women" titled "The Comfort Women of World War II: Legacy and Lessons," from 30 September to 2 October 1996, co-sponsored by Georgetown University and the Korea Society in Washington, D.C. It was the first academic event of its kind, and it included a keynote address by Miki Mutsuko, the widow of late Japanese Prime Minister Miki Takeo, who championed the "comfort women" issue during his administration. The conference also featured a testimony by Kim Yoon-Shim, a former "comfort woman" taken at the age of 13, which brought the audience to tears. Two months later, on 4 December 1996, the U.S. Department of Justice made an announcement of "War Crimes List Bars 16 Japanese From U.S." which made the front page of *The Washington Post*. *The Washington Post* editorial on 6 December 1996 stated, "The Department of Justice's decision to bar 16 alleged Japanese war criminals from the United States—and to announce that decision

---

15 Through the travelling exhibition, the issues of "comfort women" were covered by many reporters and WCCW could provide the historical photos to *Time* magazine and *U.S. News & World Report*. The "comfort women" issue was featured in *Time Magazine*, June 17, 1996 and *U.S. News & World Report*, December 16, 1996.

with considerable fanfare—has angered many Japanese but the United States has a right to say the war criminals are not wanted here."[16]

In May 1997, WCCW organized the first press conference at the U.S. Capitol in collaboration with Chinese and Filipino communities, which led House Representative William O. Lipinski (D-IL, 1983–2005) to submit a resolution (House Concurrent Resolution 126) urging the Japanese government to make an official apology and pay legal reparations to reconcile with the "comfort women." It paved the way for further resolutions on the "comfort women" issue, including H.Res 121, which finally passed in 2007.

WCCW organized a congressional exhibition titled "Comfort Women of World War II: An Indisputable Tragedy" at the Cannon House Office Building Rotunda, Capitol Hill, from 1 to 12 June 1998. The exhibition was co-sponsored by 30 community organizations, including the Congressional Human Rights Caucus, the Congressional Caucus on Women's Issues, the Congressional Asian Pacific American Caucus, the Korea Society, and many individuals. For the opening ceremony, WCCW held a press conference with two "comfort women" survivors, Kim Bok-Dong (from Korea) and Losita Nacino (from the Philippines), and Representatives Lane Evans and Robert A. Underwood. The Capitol Hill garden was packed with congressional staff, students on field trips, tourists from around the world, and American, Korean, and Japanese journalists. The exhibition continued through from 9 March through 3 May 1999, and later, the exhibition "Comfort Women of World War II" was held at the Free Library of Philadelphia.[17]

On 25–28 March 1999, WCCW presented the screening of a documentary film titled *"Comfort Women"* at KASCON XIII (Korean American Students Conference) at Stanford University. The theme of the Conference was "Empowering the Han" and the conference was co-hosted by Stanford University and the University of California, Berkeley. The keynote speaker was a "comfort woman" survivor. President Bill Clinton delivered an encouraging message about the importance of pursuing the history of immigrants and making it a shared lesson.[18]

---

[16] Pierre Thomas, "War Crimes List Bars 16 Japanese from U.S.," *The Washington Post*, December 4, 1996. Accessed February 25, 2019. https://www.washingtonpost.com/archive/politics/1996/12/04/war-crimes-list-bars-16-japanese-from-us/2dc9a6a0-a607-42b8-8f44-83d9c31a65cb/?utm_term=.6cc4e6ff16d0

[17] The exhibition showcased archival photography of "comfort women" collected and duplicated from the National Archives II in Maryland; photos included black-and-white photography of "comfort women" when they were young at "comfort stations" in different locations.

[18] President Bill Clinton: "The life of our nation has been continually renewed and enriched by the generations of people who have chosen to come here and become our fellow citizens. Each has brought a part of his or her own heritage, which over time becomes part of our common heritage.—-You can be proud of your roots and of the outstanding contributions [that] the Korean

At the Rayburn House Office Building, Capitol Hill, a solemn commemoration was held on 20 September, 2000 to honor all girls and women who died in Japanese rape camps and in sexual slavery. Nine surviving "comfort women" from across Asia[19] were invited to attend the ceremony and to give testimonies to American audiences. It was a fitting venue for Asian victims of war crimes to say "Never again." The next day, WCCW organized a testimony event at the U.S. Holocaust Museum, Washington, D.C. In memory of those lost lives without names, WCCW placed a large empty white chair with a bouquet of yellow roses on it and wished honor and peace on their behalf. In conjunction with the Remembrance, WCCW published a book, *Comfort Women Speak: Testimony by Sex Slaves of the Japanese Military* simultaneously with the *Year 2000 Remembrance* project. The book includes testimonies of nineteen "comfort women" survivors, their photography, and excerpts of important documents of the UN and International Commission of Jurists (ICJ).[20]

WCCW has been aware of the power of the arts to represent "comfort women" history and it has organized exhibitions, featuring primary sources and artistic reinterpretations. The artistic response to the theme of "comfort women" started to emerge in the arts world in various genres, including literature, film, visual art, and theater. The play *Comfort Women* (1999, 2004)[21] by Chungmi Kim was first put on in Little Tokyo in Los Angeles (1999), then off-Broadway in New York (2004), and then it became popular in South Korea. The following year, Dai Sil Kim-Gibson made a film called *Silence Broken* (2000), based on her book of the same title.[22] WCCW screened the film *Silence Broken* at George Washington University in 2002 and then at Georgetown University in 2004, along with the exhibition of the art installation *Line of Violence* by Andrew Ward. The most recent screening of *Silence Broken* was in 2014 at George Mason University in commemoration of the 20th anniversary of WCCW.

American people have made to our national life. You can be proud as well of your efforts to encourage the full participation of Korean Americans in the political, social, and economic life of our nation. As you gather at KASCON XIII to reflect on *your shared history and to prepare for the challenges of the future*, you have my best wishes for a productive and enjoyable conference," February 24, 1999.
19 WCCW invited 10 former "comfort women," but only nine could come; Kim Sang-hi, Kim Soon-duk, Kim Eun-ry, Lee Yong-soo, Moon Pil-gi, Hwang Keum-ju, Lola Ammonita, Lola Prescila, Liu Huangar-tau.
20 Sangmie Choi Schellstede, ed. *Comfort Women Speak: Testimony by Sex Slaves of the Japanese Military* (New York/London: Holmes & Meier, 2001).
21 Chungmi Kim, *Comfort Women* [formerly called *Hanako*] (1999, 2004).
22 Dai Sil Kim-Gibson, *Silence Broken: Korean Comfort Women* (Parkersburg, IA: Mid-Prairie Books, 1999).

Fig. 3: WCCW organized Human Rights Awareness "Year 2000 Remembrance: Women of Dignity and Honor," at the Rayburn House Office Building of the Capitol, and presented awards to nine surviving former "comfort women," September 2000. Washington Coalition for Comfort Women Issues Visual Archives, photo by Doochan Halm.

Christine Choi was elected as the president of WCCW for the period of 2009– 2014. Like the previous presidents, she sent out letters to leaders, including then-U.S. President Barack Obama and the Emperor and Empress of Japan, and also held a demonstration on "Global Solidarity Action Day" in commemoration of the 1,000th Wednesday Demonstration in front of the Japanese Embassy in Seoul. When WCCW reached its 20th anniversary, WCCW turned to more subtle but more accessible and powerful ways of educating the public, through art exhibitions.

The 2012 exhibition was the first art exhibition organized by WCCW beyond the showcase of archival materials. Jungsil Lee, WCCW vice president at the time (and one of the authors of this chapter), curated the exhibition and invited distinguished Korean, Japanese, and American artists who have expressed their concerns with the issue through their works, including Yong Soon Min, Yoshiko Shimada, Sasha Yungju Lee, Arin Yoon, Dai Sil Kim-Gibson, Steve Cavallo, In-Soon Shin, Youngmi Song Organ, and Chang-Jin Lee.[23] Dai Sil Kim-Gibson's *Si-*

---

23 *Unveiling the Truth: The Sorrow and Hope of "Comfort Women,"* 26 November – 14 December *lence Broken* (1999) was screened again in 2012. Renowned Japanese artist Yoshiko Shimada and Korean American artist Yong Soon Min were studied as significant feminist artists in the art history literature.[24]

WCCW's Official Statement and College Tours

In June 2002, Dongwoo Lee Hahm resigned from her role as president after her tenth year. Ok Cha Soh, who was the executive secretary at the time, was elected as the next president of WCCW. Once she became the leader of WCCW, she received a letter from the Embassy of Japan, stating that there was no need for an apology and compensation since they had already been carried out in the past.[25] Yet, WCCW regards this apology as an unofficial statement that does not hold authority on a national level passed by the Japanese Diet, and that the money from The Asian Women's Fund was not a legal reparation. WCCW continued to argue that the apology and the compensation were not made, and demanded official statements from the Japanese government.[26]

During the inauguration press conference, President Soh highlighted the mission of WCCW as one focused on educating the next generation in order to prevent future horrors that stem from the lack of education and censorship of history. She proclaimed that WCCW would devote resources to organizing seminars, forums, and exhibitions in U.S. major college campuses. Since the first forum on "comfort women" co-sponsored by the Georgetown University Law Center Student Association (1994), WCCW has been involved in a tremendous

---

2012, Mason Hall Atrium Gallery, George Mason University, sponsored by Korean Studies Center of GMU and the Academy of Korean Studies. To commemorate the 20th anniversary of WCCW, the conference and film screening were held with the art exhibition in the same building for two days, 26–27 November 2012.

24 Elaine H. Kim, Margo Machida, and Sharon Mizota, *Fresh Talk/ Daring Gazes: Conversations on Asian American Art* (Berkeley: University of California Press, 2003); "Min positions her body as landscape or homeland, labeling her chest 'Heartland' and her arms as 'Occupied Territory,'" 125.

25 See the report of the Korean Council regarding their and the victims' resolution not to accept the South Korea-Japan agreement of 1965 on "comfort women" issues that were even emerged to the surface. The author also includes the report on 1992 from Japanese government and South and North Korean government on "comfort women" issues. George Hicks, *The Comfort Women: Japan's Brutal Regime of Enforced Prostitution in the Second World War* (New York, London: W.W. Norton & Company), 220–236.

26 Most WCCW statements throughout years include these two demands: "official apology" and "legal reparation."

amount of college lecture tours with the victims, along with archival exhibits. This goal was amplified by the resolution by the Korean Student Associations at several universities that decided to promote "comfort women" issues as well. The project set off from Harvard and travelled to Yale, Cornell, New York University, Princeton, and Georgetown. The touring seminar and testimony, *Lessons of Courage; Restoring Honor*, accompanied by survivor Hwang Keum-ju, left an indelible mark on the minds of these young people and garnered support from participating students who later became ardent advocates of the cause.

Many other activities, such as symposiums, forums, and talks, were co-sponsored with other institutions such as University of Maryland in October 2002 and Brown University in November 2002. In the same year, the Midwest college tour continued to University of Wisconsin, Northwestern University, Ohio State University, and the University of Michigan. A former "comfort woman," Choi Kap-sun, accompanied the tour for testimonies. In 2013, WCCW continued to visit institutions in Boston: Boston College, Northeastern University, MIT, Wellesley College, and Tufts University. Kim Hwa Sun, a former "comfort woman," joined the tour. In 2003, WCCW participated in a panel at the KASCON at Cornell University.

The Passage of House Resolution 121

The passing of House Resolution 121 in 2007 by Congress was the culmination of WCCW's 15 years of grassroots "comfort women" movement efforts in the United States. Advocates, legislators, and victims deliberated for a long time before coming up with this resolution. Among them, WCCW and its two presidents, Dongwoo Lee Hahm and Ok Cha Soh, played a pioneering role for the passage of the resolution by dedicating their time and passion for organizing demonstrations, lecture tours, press conferences, hearings, campaigns, archival exhibitions, conferences, and inviting former "comfort women" to the Hill. The significant first step for the recognition of the issue at the Hill was achieved by Rep. Lane Evans (D-IL, 1983–2007), who was a close friend of Ok Cha Soh.

The late Rep. Lane Evans, working with WCCW, looked deeply into this issue and saw it as a crime against humanity. He brought up "comfort women" history in the Congressional Record in 1999 and continued to put forth several resolutions regarding the issue.[27]

---

[27] Far before the first submission of the "comfort women" resolution in 2000, Congressman William O. Lipinski introduced House Concurrent Resolution (H. Con. Res) 126 in 1997, which ex-

We (as members of Congress), have a duty to help those who need our help. We have a duty to stand up for those who cannot stand up on their own. We have a duty to speak up for those who have no voice and to do what is just and what is right... Let us lend them our strength. We must act and we must speak out, because in the end, people will remember not the words of enemies, but the silence of their friends. We must not remain silent.[28]

Prior to the final passage of the resolution, Evans submitted House Resolution 357 in 2000, H.Res. 195 in 2001, H.Res. 226 in 2003, H.Res. 68 in 2005, and H.Res. 759 in 2006. The last resolution was passed unanimously by the House International Relations Committee, but not brought to the House floor. Ok Cha Soh said that a stumbling block of the resolution passing was due to powerful lobbying. The Japanese government hired lobbyist Bob Michel from Hogan Lovells, a lobbying company. He had worked as a senior member of staff of the Republican Party for more than twenty years. Michel gave pressure to Henry Hyde, the Chair of the Committee on House International Relations, asserting that it would deteriorate relations between Japan and the United States. Nevertheless, Lane Evans was able to persuade him to be sympathetic to "comfort women" atrocities.[29] Due to Rep. Lane Evans' illness, Rep. Mike Honda (D-CA, 2001–2017), a third-generation Japanese-American, submitted H. Res. 121 on 31 January 2007 after he took the torch from his friend Evans in December 2006. His presence and speech carried symbolic importance as he clarified that the nature of the resolution would not harm the relations between Japan and the U.S. and did not attack the Japanese government, but reconciled and strengthened relations among countries. Because he also experienced the Japanese internment camps when he was a child, he had a taste of what it meant to have one's human rights stripped away and a pretty good idea of what an "official apology" should be. Honda explained the difference between the American apology to Japanese who suffered in internment camps and the Japanese apology to "comfort women" in Asian countries:

---

pressed that the Japanese government should formally apologize for the war crimes committed by the Japanese military in World War II and pay reparations to the victims. By the end of 1998, in the 105th Congress, nearly 80 additional Members of Congress put their support behind the resolution by formally co-sponsoring it; Jason Tai, *Let us Never Forget*, WCCW Newsletter 5 (2002), 1–2.

28 Ok Cha Soh and Lane Evans, "Legislation on 'Comfort Women' in the US Congress," *Forced Prostitution in Times of War and Peace: Sexual Violence against Women and Girls*, eds. Barbara Drinck and Chung-noh Gross (Bielefeld: Kleine Verlag, 2007), 288.

29 Ok Cha Soh, *Becoming Your Voice: Ok Cha Soh, Lane Evans, and "Japanese Comfort Women"* (Seoul: Sechang Media, 2015), 119–120.

1980, after the Congress had passed H.R. 442 and President Reagan signed it into law, did we feel that there was an unambiguous apology and setting the record straight. Japan has not done that officially. And they continue to double talk and white-wash the history of their activities and constantly attempt to change their history books in the junior high school and high school level. That in itself indicates that there is no sincere and historical responsibility being taken by the government of Japan. This is what we're seeking.[30]

Unfortunately, the Japanese government did not think that way and denounced the resolution's passage.[31] When U.S. House Representatives unanimously passed the resolution on July 2007 under chairman Tom Lantos, there was a deep consensus of ethical responsibility for justice and human rights among House representatives.

> H.Res.121 – A resolution expressing the sense of the House of Representatives that the Government of Japan should formally acknowledge, *apologize*, and accept historical *responsibility* in a clear and unequivocal manner for its Imperial Armed Forces' coercion of young women into *sexual slavery*, known to the world as "comfort women," during its colonial and wartime occupation of Asia and the Pacific Islands from the 1930s through the duration of World War II. (Summary of H. Res. 121, 110th Congress (2007–2008)).

As found in the full text of H.Res. 226, Rep. Lane Evans wrote about the enormity of the issue in graphic historical detail with statements from international authorities, such as the International Commission of Jurists (ICJ) and the United Nations Special Rapporteur on Violence against Women. Each version differs slightly from each other, but a few keywords remained in each version and were finally brought together in the final resolution. Among the keywords were *apology, responsibility, sexual slavery, and education;* words that highlight the stance and spirit of H. Res. 121.

This issue was brought up after a shift in the American political timbre in the 20th century towards issues regarding slavery, forced labor, systematic rape, and crimes against humanity. In terms of slavery, the charters of international military tribunals provide a list of crimes against humanity. According to Article 6(c) of the Nuremberg Charter, "enslavement, deportation, and other inhumane acts committed against any civilian population [are to be known] as crimes

---

[30] Mike Honda, "US Demands Apology for 'Comfort Women,'" Interview with NPR, July 31, 2007.

[31] In June 2007, the US ambassador to Washington, Ryozo Kato, warned that passage of the resolution would "almost certainly have lasting and harmful effects on the deep friendship, close trust and wide-ranging cooperation our two nations now enjoy." Justin McCurry, "Japan Rejects US Calls for Apology Over 'Comfort Women'" *The Guardian*, July 31, 2007.

against humanity."³² The United States played a crucial role in the development and support of the ideas and practices of human rights. The U.S. State Department periodically reports on human rights worldwide. Beyond investigating and maintaining extensive records³³ on slavery in the U.S., Congress was also ready to hear the voices of victims of foreign countries. Kinue Tokudome summarized in her article how the "comfort women" issues were revisited and interpreted as "human rights and current issues of humanity."³⁴

Right before H.Res 121 was passed, there was a House hearing on "comfort women" issues on 15 February 2007 in the House Foreign Affairs Subcommittee on Asia and the Pacific chaired by Eni Faleomavaega. WCCW invited three former "comfort women," Lee Yong Soo, Kim Kun-ja, and Jan Ruff O'Herne, who testified along with a speech by Ok Cha Soh, the president of WCCW, and Mindy Kotler, director of Asia Policy Point. During the hearing, Ok Cha Soh confirmed the stance of WCCW in terms of the apology and legal reparation from the Japanese government:

> The statement challenged the issues of the Asian Women's Fund, which was privately funded, therefore, arguing that it cannot be regarded as an official reparation for "comfort women." It addresses the apology issues, which should have been endorsed by the Japanese Diet, thus far only a few Japanese government officials have made near-apology statements on "comfort women" issues. Her (Soh) statements further explored the logical context of the legal issues which had been filed lawsuits on "comfort women" at DC Circuit Court in previous years.³⁵

Mindy Kotler identified "Japan's wartime military rape camps as the precedent of the modern issues of sexual slavery, sexual violence in war, and human trafficking that dominate today's discussion of war and civil conflict—Bosnia, Rwanda, Nicaragua, Sierra Leone, Darfur, Burma."³⁶ With the stories of "comfort women," Kotler engaged in creating an expanded discourse of human trafficking that continues to be relevant to our current issues.

---

32 McDougall Report I, supra note 87, Karen Parker and Jennifer F. Chew, "Compensation for Japan's World War II War-Rape Victims," 17; Hastings Int'l & Comp. L. Rev. 497, 516 (1994), in *Comfort Women: Human Rights of Women from Then to Present*, Jinyang Koh, University of Georgia School of Law, LLM Theses and Essays, 79.
33 *Confronting Historical Injustice: Comparative Perspectives*, Slavery and Justice Report of the Brown University, Steering Committee on Slavery and Justice, 2003.
34 Kinue Tokudome, "Passage of H.Res. 121 on 'Comfort Women,' the US Congress and Historical Memory in Japan," *The Asia-Pacific Journal*, Japan Focus 5, no. 8 (2007): 8.
35 Ok Cha Soh, from the note of summary of *U.S. House Hearing*, February 25, 2007. Subcommittee on Asia, the Pacific, and the Global Environment Committee on Foreign Affairs.
36 Kinue Tokudome, "Passage of H.Res. 121 on 'Comfort Women,'" 4.

Fig. 4: WCCW president Ok Cha Soh helped and organized the Congressional Hearing in preparation of the Passage of House Resolution 121. After Rep. Mike Honda's speech, three former "comfort women," Lee Yong Soo, Kim Kun-ja, and Jan Ruff-O'Herne gave testimonies. Ok Cha Soh and Mindy Kotler supported the demands of the victims, February 2007. Washington Coalition for Comfort Women Issues Visual Archives (WCCWVA), photo by Christine Choi.

The efforts of Lane Evans, Mike Honda, and Ok Cha Soh played pivotal roles in contributing to passage of the 2007 resolution, along with the help of multiple activist organizations and other people for a year leading up to the resolution. It surely can be viewed as the first successful instance of Korean American grassroots movements reaching the federal level. Washington Coalition for Comfort Women Issues (WCCW), Coalition 121, National Korean American Associations, Korean American Civic Empowerment (KACE, formerly KAVC, which is short for Korean American Voters' Council), Korean American Forum of California (KAFC-founded in the year 2007), Global Alliance for Preserving the Truth of WWII, Asia Pacific WWII Atrocities Memorial Inc., and Ms. Annabel Park launched a nationwide campaign to petition the passage of the resolution among many others.

Jungsil Lee was elected WCCW president in 2015 and followed the steps of former presidents: grassroots movements, seminars, exhibitions, media exposure, traveling lectures, and film screenings. Eight years after H. Res. 121, in March 2015, Maryland senator Susan Lee introduced the Resolution of Comfort Women, Maryland Senate Joint Resolution 3, which stated:

> WHEREAS, The people of Maryland honor the surviving victims who are now at the end of their lives, but were victimized at the beginning of their lives when they were too young to consent to prostitution and were ostracized even though they were clearly victims;
>
> WHEREAS, The Maryland General Assembly is determined to combat human trafficking in modern times through all appropriate legislative action, education initiatives, and commemorations to the victims of this horrible injustice and crime that has been perpetrated against so many people throughout history; now, therefore, be it
>
> RESOLVED BY THE GENERAL ASSEMBLY OF MARYLAND, That the General Assembly of Maryland hereby extends its profound hope that the historical record of the crimes against the "ianfu" or "comfort women" of World War II will serve as a lasting reminder to the world that crimes against humanity will not be condoned or tolerated; and be it further.[37]

Susan Lee stated: "The war crime . . . happened in the past and we don't want it to happen anymore and certainly will fight against any modern-day human slavery and human trafficking." Stan Tsai, chairman of the Chinese Culture and Community Service Center and other human rights representatives, along with Jungsil Lee, testified on the "comfort women" history at the Hearing on the Comfort Women Resolution on 6 March 2015. The Maryland Senate sensed that human trafficking was also an issue relevant to the legacy of "comfort women," and they added that to the issues of education, apology, responsibility, and sexual slavery in H.Res. 121.

Building "Comfort Women" Monuments

The first "comfort women" memorials in the U.S. were established three years after the passage of H. Res. 121, first in New Jersey and then in California. The very first U.S. "comfort women" monument was built in October 2010 in Palisades Park, New Jersey, by Korean American Civic Empowerment (KACE) to foster empathy toward "comfort women," and more importantly, to educate younger

---

37 Maryland Senate Joint Resolution 3, Senators Lee, Bates, Montgomery, Nathan–Pulliam, Ready, Conway, Pinsky, Kagan, Rosapepe, Salling, Simonaire, Waugh, and Young, Introduced and read for the first time: February 6, 2015, Assigned to: Education, Health, and Environmental Affairs. Read second time March 13, 2015; they proposed to "Honoring the Surviving Human Trafficking Victims of Asia and the Pacific 3 Islands During World War II."

generations about the atrocious crimes against humanity.³⁸ The monument sparked an uproar from several members of the Japanese Diet who had visited the city and requested that the plaque be removed.³⁹ The Palisades Park monument paved the way for many more similar memorials in the U.S. and other countries, promoting peace building.⁴⁰

During the December 2012 WCCW annual meeting, the WCCW board unanimously passed the proposal of creating a "comfort women" memorial. In May 2014, WCCW unveiled the "Comfort Women Memorial Peace Garden" at the Fairfax County Government Center, Virginia. The initial proposal was to erect the statue on a high pedestal in a Fairfax county park. After the WCCW's presentation for support by Sami Lauri, vice president of WCCW, Sharon Bulova (the Chairman of Fairfax County Board of Supervisors) and her staff were so touched by the survivors' stories that she suggested that WCCW consider placing the memorial on the county government grounds. Chairman Bulova saw that the horror of modern-day human trafficking overlapped with "comfort women" history, and believed that the memorial must be a reminder of the suffering of all women who were denied their human rights since time immemorial. WCCW was grateful for her support and the unequivocal consent of the County Supervisors to this project. In addition, the Fairfax County Board of Supervisors safeguarded the security of the memorial (as we are familiar with the vandalism and controversy associated with the Glendale memorial in California).⁴¹

---

38 John Mitchell, "The Comfort Women and Me," in *Come From the Shadows: Art and Writings Commemorating the First U.S. Memorial for "Comfort Women."* Palisades Park Public Library, the anniversary ceremony catalog, October 2014 edition, 29; "As a student of history, I of course heard about the Comfort Women but as a somewhat vague footnote to WWII. It was not until I became a Bergen County Freeholder in January, 2011 that my real education started ... more and more I was hearing about the 'comfort women' so I decided to study the issue in more detail and hear from many of my Korean American friends."
39 Kirk Semple, "In New Jersey, Memorial for 'Comfort Women' Deepens Old Animosity," *The New York Times*, May 18, 2012. Accessed February 25, 2019. https://www.nytimes.com/2012/05/19/nyregion/monument-in-palisades-park-nj-irritates-japanese-officials.html.
40 Lisa Schirch, *Ritual and Symbol in Peacebuilding* (Bloomfield, CT: Kumarian Press, 2005), 16–17. She defines ritual as a symbolic and physical act that communicates through symbols, myths, and metaphors, allowing for multiple interpretations; ritual aims to form or transform people's worldviews, identities, and relationships.
41 Yoshiko Matsura, a city assemblywoman from the Suginami Ward in Tokyo, said that the delegation is concerned about the statue's effect on Japan's reputation. Two Japanese people, Michiko Gingery, a Glendale resident, and Koichi Mera, a Los Angeles resident, and an organization called Global Alliance for Historical Truth (GAHT-US Corp) filed a lawsuit against the city of Glendale to demand the removal of the "comfort woman" statue. The suit suggests that Japanese-Americans will suffer "irreparable injury from feelings of exclusion, discomfort, and

The initial design of the memorial by the sculptor recommended by the memorial committee[42] was rejected by the County staff because it was considered too overbearing in terms of size and too intricate to be implemented effectively. They recommended something similar to the 9/11 monument with a low tombstone-like slab, situated next to the memorial site. WCCW decreased the size, changed the design, and installed the current granite boulder flanked by two turquoise butterfly benches. The boulder has a plaque on the memorial that reads:

> IN HONOR OF THE WOMEN AND GIRLS WHOSE BASIC RIGHTS AND DIGNITIES WERE TAKEN FROM THEM AS VICTIMS OF HUMAN TRAFFICKING DURING WORLD WAR II.
>
> OVER 200,000 WOMEN AND GIRLS FROM KOREA, CHINA, TAIWAN, THE PHILIPPINES, INDONESIA, MALAYSIA, VIETNAM, THE NETHERLANDS AND EAST TIMOR WERE ENFORCED INTO SEXUAL SLAVERY AND EUPHEMISTICALLY CALLED "COMFORT WOMEN" BY IMPERIAL JAPANESE FORCES DURING WORLD WAR II. WE HONOR THEIR PAIN AND SUFFERING AND MOURN THE LOSS OF THEIR FUNDAMENTAL HUMAN RIGHTS.
>
> MAY THESE "COMFORT WOMEN" FIND ETERNAL PEACE AND JUSTICE FOR THE CRIMES COMMITTED AGAINST THEM. MAY THE MEMORIES OF THESE WOMEN AND GIRLS SERVE AS A REMINDER OF THE IMPORTANCE OF PROTECTING THE RIGHTS OF WOMEN AND AN AFFIRMATION OF BASIC HUMAN RIGHTS.
>
> (30 May 2014, Washington Coalition for Comfort Women Issues, Inc.)

On one side of the plaque is the summary of H. Res. 121, and on the other, a commemoration written by WCCW emphasizing global women's rights. The butterfly-shaped metal benches surround the stone memorial, symbolizing the metamorphosis of those grandmothers[43] from sex slaves to leading activists for women's rights; in addition, the butterflies symbolize rebirth for those who died as a result of the brutal "comfort women" system. It also represents victims who took pride

---

anger if the memorial is not removed;" Brittany Levine, "Third Japanese Delegation Bashes Comfort Women Statue," *Los Angeles Times*, January 16, 2014; she mentioned also Setsuko Sakuraba, a city assemblywoman from Jetsu city was angry because the statue is not supporting world peace; Eamonn Fingleton, "Disgusting! Cry Legal Experts: Is This the Lowest a Top U.S. Law Firm has Ever Stooped?" *Forbes*, April 13, 2014; Brittany Levine, "Lawsuit Seeks Removal of Glendale's 'Comfort Women' Statue," *Los Angeles Times*, February 22, 2014.

42 The Memorial committee initially consisted of WCCW staff only, then later, WCCW invited two co-chairs, Grace H. Wolf (Herndon Town Council) and William Hwang (Korean Community leader) to draw more public awareness; The Committee consisted of Christine Choi, Jungsil Lee, Sami Lauri, and Helen Won.

43 "Comfort women" survivors are often affectionately and respectfully referred to as "grandmother," "*halmeoni*," "*lola*," or other words that mean "grandmother." This refers to the advanced age of "comfort women" survivors who are still alive.

Fig. 5: WCCW campaigned and erected the Comfort Women Memorial Peace Garden at Fairfax Government site, Virginia, in partnership with the Fairfax County Government, tape cutting ceremony on 30 May 2014. Washington Coalition for Comfort Women Issues Visual Archives (WCCWVA), photo by Jaeheup Kim.

in their own beauty, flying away from a painful past. The peaceful site was intended to be a pilgrimage site, a place to remember human bondage at large rather than a politically charged and contentious agora. That is one of the reasons that the committee eventually chose the generic stone slab instead of the famous Girl Statue, which may misrepresent the issues as only those of relations between South Korea and the aggressor.

Creating Further Educational Materials

In 2014, WCCW organized another exhibition and seminar at Catholic University, D.C. and the exhibit featured a wide variety of materials, including artwork created by former "comfort women" at the art therapy sessions at the House of Sharing in South Korea, archival materials, and fine creative works by renowned artists. Kim Soon-duck and Kang Duck-kyung, former "comfort women," re-created a scene from a "comfort station," and artists responded in their own way to their pain. For the exhibition *The Sorrow and Hope of "Comfort Women,"* WCCW invited Korean, Japanese, and American artists, including Steve Cavallo, Chang-Jin Lee, Sunsook Shin, Yoosooja Han, Junghwa Paik, and Eileen Halpin, whose works represented a diverse range of genres and mediums, such as painting, photography, prints, metal work, and sculpture.[44] This exhibition featured the photography of Park Young-sim, a "comfort woman" survivor in North Korea reported by a YTN reporter. Along with the touching paintings done by the survivors, the exhibition not only educated the public, but also raised awareness of the historical issue.

The urgency of education about the "comfort women" issue has led WCCW activists to create new educational materials and protocols. The target audiences include members of Congress (as well as other elected officers and lawmakers), college and high school students, Asian communities, and the younger generation, including non-Korean and pan-Asian communities. The focus on the diverse ways of education were major activities during the presidency of Jungsil Lee (the primary author of this chapter), who is an art historian, curator, filmmaker, and educator. For the 2015 conference, WCCW hosted a panel at the annual Kowinner World Convention, "Wartime Atrocity against Women: Comfort Women Case." In April 2016, WCCW was asked whether we could invite former "comfort women" from the department of Human Rights at the Southern Methodist University in Dallas, Texas and WCCW co-organized the testimony in Dallas.[45] In May, WCCW co-hosted "History Writing: for Justice and Reconciliation of Comfort Women" at the Sigur Center for Asian Studies with the History Department of George Washington University, which was a capstone conference of the webinar project where students and WCCW interns meet and learn from activists and professors who are experts on the issue.[46]

---

44 "The Sorrow and Hope of Comfort Women: Seminar and Exhibition," November 25, 2014 to January 12, 2015. The May Gallery of Mullen Library, Catholic University of Virginia, curator Jungsil Lee, sponsored by Center for International Social Development (CISD) and Korean Women's International Network, DC chapter (KOWIN).
45 Due to more than 20 years of grassroots activities, many people search for resources and ask WCCW to share what we advocate; we are inundated with countless requests for lectures, talks, and materials.
46 "In order to make its historical truth apparent and visible and to ascertain diverse historical evidence, WCCW believes a web-based seminar (webinar) format that encompasses global participants is an appropriate and effective tool to collect the untapped and undiscovered sources and documents scattered all over the world. In addition, this project will bring tremendous value to our plan for creating a repository for documents and artifacts related to the history and current issues of "comfort women." From this, many types of soft-powered material or contents will be created, such as books, papers, theses, articles, film, art, educational material, journal, and other media. The CW Webinar Project will consist of a combination of lectures, presentations,

WCCW launched the "WCCW Webinar Project" to collect, archive, compile, and study primary and secondary sources regarding "comfort women" in order to bring to light the historical evidence in an organized way. WCCW believes that a repository of documents and artifacts related to "comfort women" for posterity will bring many outcomes. Furthermore, this repository will be one of many sources that future historians who wish to document this painful era will be able to refer to. The mission of WCCW is to inform future generations of the women's movements and to rectify recorded history. To this end, it has been an immensely useful and ongoing project.

Each seminar and conference was geared towards the institution's mission, with close attention given to the needs of our collaborators. For example, when WCCW organized a seminar and exhibition *The Sorrow and Hope of Comfort Women* (2014) at Catholic University with the Center for International Social Development (CISD), its main goal was to promote international humanity in the interests of peace and justice. Reconciliation and healing were the key concepts of the seminar and exhibition, whereas the conference at George Washington University focused on accurate history writing.

Many symposia came along with exhibitions featuring WCCW's documentation of this era of women's exploitation. For the first 20 years, most of these exhibitions relied on archival materials, such as photos, letters, statements, primary sources, and artifacts. Beginning in 2012, for the 20th anniversary, WCCW first introduced a fine art exhibit, *Unveiling the Truth: The Sorrow and Hope of "Comfort Women."* The 2016 exhibition, *Collateral Damage: Wartime Atrocity and Trauma*, at John Jay College of Criminal Justice, City University of New York, emphasized the universality of the spirit of the "comfort women" issue. When the "comfort women" exhibit proposal was initially submitted, it was rejected due to strong political controversy and incisive targeting. As the venue was fitting for the issue, the curator Jungsil Lee generalized the title and the theme to broader subjects such as atrocity and vulnerability. From the catalog the first paragraph says;

> This exhibition examines issues of rampant violence during WWII, the Vietnam War, the rise of the Khmer Rouge, and other conflicts where innocent non-combatants were affected. While these conflicts impacted everyone, the women, children, elderly, and infirm suffered

---

workshops, and discussion that is broadcast over the web using specific video conferencing software. A key feature of a webinar is its interactive elements and collaborative nature—the ability to give, receive, discuss, and archive information." From "Objectives of the Project," part of the Syllabus of Webinar pilot program session, November 1, 2015.

to a greater extent due to their vulnerability. In particular, women have been the victims of sexual assault and exploitation, their bodies violated as a war tactic.[47]

This exhibition drew huge attention from diverse audiences and students who studied and wrote a reflection of the show and were urged to attend the opening ceremony by their professors. John Jay College was the home for the Human Rights Center and WCCW invited the director of the Human Rights Center to participate in a symposium on *Collateral Damage: Wartime Atrocity and Trauma* during the exhibition.

In 2017, the president of WCCW was invited to be a chief curator to organize the first Korean government-led travelling exhibition, *Truth: Promise for Future*, where Jungsil Lee incorporated archival historical documents and art works along with interactive installation artworks. As Christian Boltanski declares, "art making is not [just] telling the truth but making the truth felt." WCCW believes that art can be not just an effective tool to educate and raise public awareness, but also to build a strong emotional bond with the victims.

In addition, WCCW was (and remains) dedicated to promoting the victims' stories through films. WCCW did ongoing film screenings throughout the years from *Silence Broken*, the documentary *Comfort Women* (continuously since 2002), *Spirit's Homecoming* (January 2016), *The Apology* (October 2017),[48] *Spirit's Homecoming II* (December 2017), then to sum up, organized *International Film Festival* (November 9 – 11, 2018) at American University, where Christopher Simpson, WCCW's senior vice president, teaches as a professor in the School of Communication. The festival showcased nine "comfort women" films from five different countries.[49] Held on the university campus with huge participation of WCCW interns, the festival drew a large audience, including many members of the younger generation, as well as many non-Asian people.

WCCW has taken a leading role in teaching others and working toward a just and equitable final requiem for the survivors. At the same time, WCCW strives to

---

47 Jungsil Lee, *Collateral Damage*, The Anya and Andrew Shiva Gallery, John Jay College of Criminal Justice, City University of New York, September 8 – October 21, 2016, 3.
48 Anita Lee (producer), *The Apology*. Documentary film. Directed by Tiffany Hsiung. (Montreal, Quebec and New York, New York: National Film Board of Canada, 2016).
49 The film festival committee was Jungsil Lee, Myungho (Lucy) Nam, Christopher Simpson, Jongsuk Thomas Nam, Edward Jang, Jackie Kim, Aileen Chung, Helen Won, JeeEun Chung. WCCW featured dramatic narrative films, such as *I Can Speak* (South Korea) and *Spirits' Homecoming* (South Korea); Documentaries that were screened included *The Apology* (Canada), *50 Years of Silence* (Australia), *Daily Bread* (Australia), *Because We Are Beautiful* (Netherlands), *Twenty Two* (China), and *A Long Way Around* (South Korea). An animated documentary titled *For Her* (South Korea) was also featured.

view this holistically rather than as a single-issue coalition.[50] Our urgent mission is to archive the 26 years (at the time of this writing) of WCCW activities and the "comfort women" movement at large through its primary and secondary sources and make it available to the next generation in order for them to remember the past and to understand that our issues transcend time and place. The vision of WCCW is to reach out to a larger audience through media and to keep this particular issue of "comfort women" alive long after its last victim has passed on. Our ultimate goal is to shine a light on the past, present, and future.

---

50 Jungsil Lee, "The Future of the 'Comfort Women' Movement in Korea," *Washington Times*, October 14, 2015, C20. Accessed February 25, 2019. https://www.washingtontimes.com/news/2015/oct/14/jungsil-lee-the-future-of-the-comfort-women-moveme/

APPENDIX

Special Report

1. Foreign Minister Kishida

The Government of Japan and the Government of the Republic of Korea (ROK) have intensively discussed the issue of comfort women between Japan and the ROK at bilateral meetings including the Director-General consultations. Based on the result of such discussions, I, on behalf of the Government of Japan, state the following:

(1) The issue of comfort women, with an involvement of the Japanese military authorities at that time, was a grave affront to the honor and dignity of large numbers of women, and the Government of Japan is painfully aware of responsibilities from this perspective. As Prime Minister of Japan, Prime Minister Abe expresses anew his most sincere apologies and remorse to all the women who underwent immeasurable and painful experiences and suffered incurable physical and psychological wounds as comfort women.

(2) The Government of Japan has been sincerely dealing with this issue. Building on such experience, the Government of Japan will now take measures to heal psychological wounds of all former comfort women through its budget. To be more specific, it has been decided that the Government of the ROK establish a foundation for the purpose of providing support for the former comfort women, that its funds be contributed by the Government of Japan as a one-time contribution through its budget, and that projects for recovering the honor and dignity and healing the psychological wounds of all former comfort women be carried out under the cooperation between the Government of Japan and the Government of the ROK.

(3) While stating the above, the Government of Japan confirms that this issue is resolved finally and irreversibly with this announcement, on the premise that the Government will steadily implement the measures specified in (2) above. In addition, together with the Government of the ROK, the Government of Japan will refrain from accusing or criticizing each other regarding this issue in the international community, including at the United Nations.

2. Foreign Minister Yun

The Government of the Republic of Korea (ROK) and the Government of Japan have intensively discussed the issue of comfort women between the ROK and Japan at bilateral meetings including the Director-General consultations. Based on the result of such discussions, I, on behalf of the Government of the ROK, state the following:

(1) The Government of the ROK values the GOJ's announcement and efforts made by the Government of Japan in the lead-up to the issuance of the announcement and confirms, together with the GOJ, that the issue is resolved finally and irreversibly with this announcement, on the premise that the Government of Japan will steadily implement the measures specified in 1. (2)

above. The Government of the ROK will cooperate in the implementation of the Government of Japan's measures.

(2) The Government of the ROK acknowledges the fact that the Government of Japan is concerned about the statue built in front of the Embassy of Japan in Seoul from the viewpoint of preventing any disturbance of the peace of the mission or impairment of its dignity, and will strive to solve this issue in an appropriate manner through taking measures such as consulting with related organizations about possible ways of addressing this issue.

(3) The Government of the ROK, together with the Government of Japan, will refrain from accusing or criticizing each other regarding this issue in the international community, including at the United Nations, on the premise that the Government of Japan will steadily implement the measures it announced.

WCCW Statement

Official Statement of WCCW, Inc. (Washington Coalition for Comfort Women Issues) on 2015 Korea-Japan Bilateral Agreement on Comfort Women

March 8th of 2016, Press Conference at UN Headquarters, New York (written by Jungsil Lee, President of WCCW)

After last year's joint agreement issued by the Republic of Korea and Japan on the issues of the "comfort women," WCCW members have been appalled by the Japanese government's continued denial and whitewashing of the historical facts that had already been acknowledged by their previous officials. Their recent statement proves that the agreement was not sincere and genuine. True reconciliation would not be possible without real and perpetual efforts in a clear and unequivocal manner.

WCCW, an organization whose mission is to advocate for the rights of wartime victims- military sex slaves- and their lawful reparation, expected and hoped for progress in terms of the lawful reparation and official treatment followed by the agreement of two countries, but the recent activities of the Japanese government failed to reveal this hope is headed for the right direction. We support the recent recommendation by CEDAW (Committee on the Elimination of Discrimination against Women).

1. WCCW envisions 'comfort women' issues as a global human rights issue and women's rights movement that stretch over 11 nations who had experienced similar atrocities as well as today's violations of women's rights around the globe. Therefore, we do not narrow down the issue to solely a Korean-Japanese political agenda. Rather, we will continue to advocate, research, and educate the importance of human rights through this history.

2. The agreement made no provisions whatsoever for comfort women survivors from North Korea, China, Taiwan, Philippines, Indonesia, Dutch-Indi, Malaysia, Thailand, Burma, East

Timor, Guam, India, and Vietnam. The agreement must include restitution and sincere apology from the Japanese government for all comfort women of all nationalities.

3. WCCW will make sure that these women occupy a prominent place in the annals of history and are provided with legal reparations not only to honor their bravery and endurance but also to commemorate the importance of human dignity. If the agreement is sincere and unequivocal, the world will see that the Japanese government will open their archival records concerning wartime and postwar treatment, create policies to reconcile with the comfort women, and cease to rewrite the past history; the Japanese government will contribute to writing of accurate accounts of the history and will promote educating its own people and the future generation about the war crimes against humanity.

4. WCCW hopes to watch the issue be resolved by a series of gradual, ongoing, and sincere accomplishments toward all victimized nations, not through a single political deal with the expression "finally and irreversibly." Although WCCW promotes a peaceful reconciliation and is eager to see the final and completed resolution, we do not believe that one bilateral agreement cannot and must not cease or delete the whole history of the war or stop activities by human rights advocates and NGO's.

5. WCCW expresses deep regrets to see that the agreement includes the possible removal or relocation of the Girl statue in front of the Embassy of Japan in Seoul that has a huge symbolic value for Koreans, the victims, and importance of civil rights.

6. WCCW would like to see the end of the Japanese government's diplomatic and publicity efforts to humiliate comfort women survivors and to revise the past, or to interfere with people's right to study, research, and speak out about their experiences and opinions. That is precisely the reason that WCCW launched the "Webinar Project" through which we research, archive, and publish the unarguable historical material about comfort women.

WCCW has been so honored to fight for and be the voice for these voiceless women for the last 23 years since 1992. We cannot possibly imagine their sufferings, but we have learned from and been inspired by the survivors. We sincerely hope that these women will finally find what they have been seeking: peace and dignity.

WCCW Members and WCCW Board of Directors
wccwcontact@gmail.com
www.comfort-women.org

H. Res. 121

In the House of Representatives, U. S.,
July 30, 2007.

Whereas the Government of Japan, during its colonial and wartime occupation of Asia and the Pacific Islands from the 1930s through the duration of World War II, officially commissioned the acquisition of young women for the sole purpose of sexual servitude to its Imperial Armed Forces, who became known to the world as *ianfu* or "comfort women";

Whereas the "comfort women" system of forced military prostitution by the Government of Japan, considered unprecedented in its cruelty and magnitude, included gang rape, forced abortions, humiliation, and sexual violence resulting in mutilation, death, or eventual suicide in one of the largest cases of human trafficking in the 20th century;

Whereas some new textbooks used in Japanese schools seek to downplay the "comfort women" tragedy and other Japanese war crimes during World War II;

Whereas Japanese public and private officials have recently expressed a desire to dilute or rescind the 1993 statement by Chief Cabinet Secretary Yohei Kono on the "comfort women", which expressed the Government's sincere apologies and remorse for their ordeal;

2

Whereas the Government of Japan did sign the 1921 International Convention for the Suppression of the Traffic in Women and Children and supported the 2000 United Nations Security Council Resolution 1325 on Women, Peace, and Security which recognized the unique impact on women of armed conflict;

Whereas the House of Representatives commends Japan's efforts to promote human security, human rights, democratic values, and rule of law, as well as for being a supporter of Security Council Resolution 1325;

Whereas the United States-Japan alliance is the cornerstone of United States security interests in Asia and the Pacific and is fundamental to regional stability and prosperity;

Whereas, despite the changes in the post-cold war strategic landscape, the United States-Japan alliance continues to be based on shared vital interests and values in the Asia-Pacific region, including the preservation and promotion of political and economic freedoms, support for human rights and democratic institutions, and the securing of prosperity for the people of both countries and the international community;

Whereas the House of Representatives commends those Japanese officials and private citizens whose hard work and compassion resulted in the establishment in 1995 of Japan's private Asian Women's Fund;

Whereas the Asian Women's Fund has raised $5,700,000 to extend "atonement" from the Japanese people to the comfort women; and

Whereas the mandate of the Asian Women's Fund, a government-initiated and largely government-funded private foundation whose purpose was the carrying out of programs and projects with the aim of atonement for the maltreatment and suffering of the "comfort women", came to an end on March 31, 2007, and the Fund has been disbanded as of that date: Now, therefore, be it

Resolved, That it is the sense of the House of Representatives that the Government of Japan—

(1) should formally acknowledge, apologize, and accept historical responsibility in a clear and unequivocal manner for its Imperial Armed Forces' coercion of young women into sexual slavery, known to the world as "comfort women", during its colonial and wartime occupation of Asia and the Pacific Islands from the 1930s through the duration of World War II;

(2) would help to resolve recurring questions about the sincerity and status of prior statements if the Prime Minister of Japan were to make such an apology as a public statement in his official capacity;

(3) should clearly and publicly refute any claims that the sexual enslavement and trafficking of the "comfort women" for the Japanese Imperial Armed Forces never occurred; and

(4) should educate current and future generations about this horrible crime while following the rec-

4

ommendations of the international community with respect to the "comfort women".

Attest:

Clerk.

Judith Mirkinson
Building the San Francisco Memorial: Why the Issue of the 'Comfort Women' is Still Relevant Today?

Introduction

On 22 September 2017, a new statue in memorial to the hundreds of thousands of "comfort women" of World War II was unveiled in San Francisco. The statue, "Comfort Women": Column of Strength, stands in St. Mary's Square, a public park. This is the story of the building of that statue. It is an account based on my personal experience as a member of the "Comfort Women" Justice Coalition along with many personal interviews with the "movers and shakers." It reflects both recent scholarship and decades of work by the many participants who helped build the statue. As such, this is both a research paper, a current events report, and an oral history. It is a narrative of one struggle for justice for the "comfort women" and for women's human rights, one pitted against historical, specifically Japanese denialism. Finally, it is a success story, for despite all the obstacles put in the way, the statue is built and there for all to see.

ONE, TWO, THREE! And the ribbons were pulled and the drapes came off and the first original memorial statue to the "Comfort Women"[1] in a major U.S. city, San Francisco, was there for all to see. In the statue, three young women—Chinese, Filipina, and Korean—face outward. They stand united, their hands clutching each other, sad but strong, looking at the world. They represent both those who didn't survive and those who lived to tell the truth. Below them, a life-size replica of Kim Hak-sun, the first Korean woman to break the silence about what happened to hundreds of thousands of women and girls in World War II, looks up at them. She sees her past, her present, and her future.

These women represent one memory of the world. A memory which only in recent decades has surfaced out of a silence held for more than fifty years. A memory of the sexual enslavement enacted by the Japanese Imperial Army from 1931–1945. A memory which helped, and which is still helping, change

---
[1] I use quotation marks around the term "comfort women" because it is, while used all the time, a euphemism for those hundreds of thousands of women who had been captured and used as sex slaves.

what has long been considered normal behavior for men during war.² They remind and entreat us to make the world a safer place for women and girls. And their presence demands justice—specifically, an official and legal apology from the Japanese government and reparations for the "comfort women" who are still alive today.

Why do statues engender such passionate feelings? It is because they represent the values of society and the accepted versions of history. And when those versions are no longer deemed to be true, they often come down. So down came the statues of Hitler and the Nazis, as did the statues of Stalin and Franco and Pinochet. Now, finally, we are seeing the demolition of statues of Jefferson Davis and the generals of the Confederacy in the United States. There's even talk of tearing down statues of Christopher Columbus.

Memorials serve a significant purpose. They say that those represented were important and that what happened to them matters. Often, they serve as a reminder, a warning that what occurred should not be forgotten and should not be repeated. There are many statues to white men in San Francisco, but very few to women. A recent article in the *San Francisco Chronicle* highlighted the situation. "Incredibly, of the 87 public statues that dot San Francisco, just two represent real women." Both of these women are white, which is par for the course.³

Beginnings

People keep asking: How did you do it?

It took the building of a women-led, multinational, multi-ethnic, multi-generational organization, led by two Chinese American retired judges and anchored by a committed and driven coalition. This rare combination proved to be unbeatable as it wound its way through countless public commissions and hearings, maneuvered through myriad regulations and overcame numerous artistic obstacles. The new memorial to the "comfort women" and against sex trafficking was built and installed within just two years—much more quickly than anyone had anticipated. In the process, the members of the coalition grew and devel-

---

2 For a further take on memory and the "comfort women" see: Carol Gluck,"Operations of Memory: Comfort Women," in *Ruptured Histories: War Memory and the Post-Cold War in Asia*, eds. Sheila Miyoshi Jager and Rana Mitter (Cambridge, MA: Harvard University Press, 2007), 47–77.
3 Heather Knight, "S.F.'s Monuments to Male Supremacy: The City's Public Art," *San Francisco Chronicle*, June 13, 2017. Accessed February 26, 2019. http://www.sfchronicle.com/news/article/S-F-s-monuments-to-male-supremacy-the-11214724.php.

Fig. 1: "'Comfort Women': Column of Strength" with tribute flowers, St. Mary's Square, San Francisco, CA. Photo by Judith Mirkinson (CWJC).

oped both politically and ideologically, and produced a statue that could influence opinion worldwide.

When the idea came up for a memorial to the "comfort women," it was supposed to be easy. Who could be against a statue in memorial to hundreds of thousands of women who had been sexually enslaved in World War II? This was San Francisco, after all—the first U.S. city to adopt the CEDAW (the Convention for the Elimination of All Forms of Discrimination Against Women), a city with a well-functioning Commission on the Status of Women, and home to many NGOs and nonprofits focusing on women's human rights. Sadly, this wasn't to be the case, and denialists would fight the "comfort women" memorial every step of the way.

The germ of the idea of building a memorial happened many years ago in an organization called Rape in Nanjing Redress Coalition (RNRC), a pan-Asian group formed in the late 1990s to educate and demand justice for the infamous six-week massacre of 300,000 Chinese citizens by the Japanese Imperial Army in 1937. Led by Judges Lillian Sing and Julie Tang, RNRC was inspired both by their own families' experiences and by the work of Iris Chang, whose seminal book, *The Rape of Nanking*, helped the world outside of Asia learn its true history.

"I always knew what had happened," Lillian Sing told me. "It's very personal for me. I come from Shanghai, where the first comfort stations were built in 1932, where one of the fiercest battles took place." She continued, her voice beginning to break up: "My mother told me, 'We had to bow down to them—they completely humiliated us.' But Iris Chang's book really coalesced my thinking and made me want to do even more."

Julie Tang explained: "My family came from a small village which was invaded and occupied by the Japanese. My mother had two daughters long before I was born but they died during the war because of the impact of the gas from centers for biological warfare known as Unit 731. My grandmother could never talk about that time without crying. That's why I knew I had to do something. When we learned about the plight of the 'comfort women,' it broke our hearts. We're women. This was an issue close to us, close to our sisters, our grandmothers, our daughters and our friends."

RNRC was made up of Japanese, Korean and Chinese Americans, African Americans, and white allies. Fred Korematsu, the great Japanese American civil rights leader who mounted a legal challenge to the system of internment in World War II, was among its many Japanese American members. Many members of RNRC were from families that had long memories of the role of Japan in Asia. Their countries had either been colonized, as in the case of Korea, or invaded and occupied. They wanted people in San Francisco (a city which is one-third Asian, the majority being from China) to remember the Asian experience of World War II. In addition, Judge Tang had founded the first domestic violence court in San Francisco. She knew intimately the impact of sexual violence on all members of the community and the plight of the "comfort women" was something she wanted to act on. Judge Sing, the first Asian American woman judge in Northern California (and the second in the state) was moved as well. San Francisco had become a center for sex trafficking and a movement was developing to confront it. The "comfort women" system had also relied on sex trafficking, as many women, especially from Korea and China, were trafficked to other parts of Asia. Tying the two issues together was a way of linking the past to the present and the future.

Various complications and bureaucracies prevented a memorial for years, but the continuing need to address the issue of the "comfort women" was brought home in May of 2013, when Hashimoto Tōru, then mayor of Osaka, Japan, made the following statements, as reported in the *New York Times:*

> Mr. Hashimoto told reporters in Osaka on Monday that they ["comfort women"] had served a useful purpose. "When soldiers are risking their lives by running through storms of bullets, and you want to give these emotionally charged soldiers a rest somewhere, it's clear that you need a 'comfort women' system," he said. When pressed later, he insisted that brothels "were necessary at the time to maintain discipline in the army." Other countries' militaries used prostitutes, too, he said, and added that in any case there was no proof that the Japanese authorities had forced women into servitude.[4]

This did not go over well in San Francisco, a "sister city" of Osaka. Jane Kim, a Korean American member of the San Francisco Board of Supervisors, introduced a non-binding resolution condemning the remarks.[5] The resolution passed but revealed passionate disagreements that would be echoed again two years later when the issue of a memorial was introduced.

Eric Mar, a long-time Chinese American activist and a member of RNRC, had been elected to the San Francisco Board of Supervisors in 2008. Along with other RNRC members, he had been exploring the idea of building the memorial for some time. In July 2015, Mar decided to introduce Resolution 150–764, officially calling for a memorial to be built. The resolution specifically cited the responsibility of the Japanese Imperial Army for the "comfort women" system and demanded that the Japanese government both issue an official apology and give compensation, since neither had happened.

The Resolution reads:

> WHEREAS, According to most international historians, the term "comfort women" euphemistically refers to an estimated 200,000 women and young girls who were kidnapped and forced into sexual slavery by the Imperial Japanese Army during its colonial and war-

---

[4] Hiroko Tabuchi, "Women Forced Into WWII Brothels Served Necessary Role, Osaka Mayor Says," *New York Times*, May 13, 2013. Accessed February 26, 2019. http://www.nytimes.com/2013/05/14/world/asia/mayor-in-japan-says-comfort-women-played-a-necessary-role.html?mcubz=1.

[5] San Francisco Board of Supervisors, "Condemnation of the System of Sexual Enslavement During World War II, File No. 130632, Amended in Board Resolution No. 218–13," (June 18, 2013). Accessed February 26, 2019. http://sfbos.org/ftp/uploadedfiles/bdsupvrs/resolutions13/r0218–13.pdf

time occupation of Asia and the Pacific Islands from the 1930s through the duration of World War II; and

WHEREAS, During the 15 years of invasion and occupation of Asian countries, unspeakable and well-documented war-crimes, including mass rape, wholesale massacres, heinous torture, and other atrocities, were committed by the Japanese Imperial Army throughout the occupied countries and colonies; and

WHEREAS, Of the few top Japanese military leaders who were investigated and convicted as war criminals in the postwar War Crime Tribunals in Tokyo, Nanjing, Manila, Yokohama, and Khabarovsk, many escaped prosecution; and ends:

BE IT FURTHER RESOLVED: That the Board of Supervisors of the City and County of San Francisco during the 70th anniversary of the end of World War II expresses its strong support of creating a public memorial in memory of those girls and women who suffered immeasurable pain and humiliation as sex slaves and as a sacred place for remembrance, reflection, remorsefulness, and atonement for generations to come.[6]

One issue that was immediately raised was that the memorial would fuel anti-Japanese racism. Japanese immigrants and Japanese Americans have a long history in San Francisco starting in the late 19th century. Prior to the enactment of Executive Order 9066, which established the Japanese internment camps, San Francisco had the largest and oldest Japanese community outside of Japan. All that changed after the order, when the city was literally stripped of all its Japanese citizens. After the war, many of the internees who returned to San Francisco played key roles in the redress movement which led to the successful passage of the Civil Liberties Act of 1988. The Act offered a formal apology to those who had been interned and gave $20,000 to each surviving victim as reparations. Members of RNRC and progressives throughout San Francisco were a part of that fight.

But by 2015, right-wing nationalist parties and movements were having a resurgence in Japan and in many other places in the world. A denial of history—the rewriting of the crimes of empire and the systematic attempt to disappear those who suffered the most from those crimes—was fundamental to this rise. For instance, textbooks in Japan have deleted all references to the massacre in Nanjing and to the "comfort women." And intrinsic to this Japanese nationalism was a

---

[6] "Resolution 150764: Resolution urging the City and County of San Francisco to establish a memorial for 'Comfort Women' and to educate the community about stopping global human trafficking of women and girls," Introduced July 14, 2015 and Enacted October 2, 2015. Accessed February 26, 2019. https://sfgov.legistar.com/LegislationDetail.aspx?ID=2375415&GUID=80D4 A290 – 02D8 – 4AC5-BD58-BD2B753C2D33; A video can be found at: http://sanfrancisco.granicus.com/MediaPlayer.php?view_id=10&clip_id=23372&meta_id=450036. (3:27).

retrenchment of racist and colonialist ideology that has never really been overturned.

Japan watchers had already alerted their colleagues in San Francisco that there would be significant opposition to the resolution. They proved to be correct. The Japanese government immediately went to work both privately and publicly. It had already put extensive pressure on the small city of Glendale, California, which had erected a "comfort women" memorial in 2013, and some of the same tactics would be applied to San Francisco. Each of the supervisors received letters and phone calls urging them not to pass the resolution. The Japanese consulate maintained that the "comfort women" issue was not appropriate for mere cities to discuss. The real opening salvo came on 27 July 2015, when the first public comment was allowed on the resolution. Right-wing Japanese speakers claimed that all the women had been privately recruited and were "just prostitutes."[7] Why, they asked, were people singling out Japan, when there had been sexual violence in all wars? Prominent members of the Japanese-American community in San Francisco claimed that the process would sow dissent between various Asian communities.

Supporters argued that just because people are discriminated against in one instance doesn't mean that people or governments can't be held accountable for other human rights violations. For example, the fact that Germany committed genocide in no way lessens or abrogates the U.S. government's responsibility in the internment of the Japanese in World War II. So too, the fact that the U.S. committed these acts in no way lessens the responsibility of the Japanese Imperial Army's culpability in the institutionalization of the "comfort women" system.

We pointed out that the "comfort women" system was unique in that it was the first and largest form of institutionalized sexual slavery in the 20th century. We also argued that real reconciliation and cooperation comes when there is an acknowledgement of the truth, not when there is avoidance and denial. The more the Japanese refused to acknowledge their responsibility to the women, the less the chance of forgiveness and harmony (a word that kept coming into play). It became obvious that fighting for justice for the "comfort women" was not going to be comfortable. If the resolution was going to pass, it would need much larger and much broader support from the greater San Francisco community. RNRC and its contacts would not be enough.

---

7 On the issue of "prostitutes": No woman should ever be raped, be it one time, or in this case, multiple times.

On 15 September 2015, Eric Mar was scheduled to give a Certificate of Honor to Yong Soo Lee, an 87-year-old Korean survivor of the "comfort women" system who had been kidnapped at age 15. This seemed like a perfect occasion to bring out masses of supporters. Several key people went to work, including Miho Kim. A Zainichi Korean[8] and a fierce anti-racist and anti-colonialist, Miho had been organizing for justice for the "comfort women" for years. She had connections in both the U.S. and Japan, and she had ties to the women's and peace communities. It was Miho who formally called the first meeting of the "Comfort Women" Justice Coalition together.

It makes sense that this type of support could be built in the Bay Area. There is a long history here of progressive work and of collaboration between different ethnicities and different sectors. San Francisco has been the center of anti-war and peace activity for generations. Its labor movement goes way back to before the famous general strike of 1934.[9] It has a vibrant women's movement that encompasses women from all nationalities and walks of life. Its LGBTQI movement is legendary. There are myriad Chinese, Korean, Japanese, Vietnamese, Filipino, and Pacific Islander organizations within the city and its surrounding areas. Julie Tang and Lillian Sing were part of this history. They were so well-connected that people would joke, "they know everybody." And the rest of what was to be the coalition knew just about everyone else.

Following the example of Judge Tang, Lillian Sing officially retired from the bench so she could participate publicly in the campaign (judges in California must maintain neutrality on current events to preserve impartiality in court). The judges then reached out to religious, civic, Chinese, and other Asian organizations, as well as to colleagues. RNRC pulled out all the stops. Key activists with long histories of working for peace, especially those with connections to Asia, were invited to join. It was a transnational effort: Japanese peace activists themselves called on their friends in the U.S. to support the resolution. Labor organizers and anti-war activists, like those in Veterans for Peace and Women for Genuine Security (which had a focus of linking the impact of militarism on women), got involved. Critically, Japanese and Japanese Americans who felt it es-

---

8 Zainichi Koreans are those whose families were forced to come to Japan during the period of Japanese colonization of Korea. Generations later, they have continued to experience racism and discrimination to this day, even being denied Japanese citizenship.
9 Jeremy Brecher, *Strike!* (Oakland, CA: PM Press, 2014 [1972]), "The dock workers strike and San Francisco general strike, 1934 – Jeremy Brecher," Excerpts and summary from *Strike* by Jeremy Brecher. Accessed February 26, 2019. https://libcom.org/history/dock-workers-strike-san-francisco-general-strike-1934-jeremy-brecher.

sential for the Japanese government to come to terms with its past became important members of the coalition.

As a white anti-imperialist and anti-racist feminist, I had worked with Miho and others for years. I had been introduced to the issue of the "comfort women" in 1993 by GABRIELA Philippines[10] when they began to uncover the histories of Filipina "comfort women" and formed the organization Lila Filipina with the surviving "lolas."[11] GABRIELA was very familiar with the issue of sexual violence and militarism given the vast presence of the U.S. military in the Philippines. There had always been rumors and family whispers about the issue of rape during the brutal Japanese occupation of the Philippines, so when Korean women began to speak out, Filipina women began to come forward as well. I was a member of GABRIELA Network in the U.S. when we brought one of these women, Lola Amonita, on a nationwide tour.

15 September 2015 arrived, and the room was packed. Hundreds of people showed up for public comment, the vast majority of whom were supporters. Everyone was very excited as Eric Mar presented his certificate to Halmeoni ("Grandma" in Korean) Lee.[12] He said:

> I want to welcome Yong Soo Lee, affectionately known as Grandma Lee, for her courage and a story of breaking silence over generations. She's an example of justice and empathy for the hundreds of thousands of girls who were kidnapped and coerced into sexual slavery by the Japanese Imperial Army from 1932 to 1945. This is historic because she is courageously showing persistence and she represents all those who survived the "comfort women" system. She represents the fighting spirit of the women's movement in Asia and here. She's been leading this fight for over twenty years.
>
> Halmeoni Lee was born in Daegu in 1928. She was 15 years old when she was lured out of her home and taken to a Kamikaze Unit in Taiwan, China [then under Japanese occupation] where she remained until the end of the war. She lived in silence for over 40 years when in 1992, she registered as a former Comfort Woman with the South Korean government. She initially thought what happened to her was an isolated incident, but soon realized so many other women were subject to the same horrors. Some say it was 10–20 rapes a day, that's 50–100 a week. Think about it!

---

10 GABRIELA Philippines is a nationwide alliance of more than 200 women's organizations that cut across sectors and regions, plus chapters and support groups of Pinays and non-Pinays in various continents of the world, http://www.gabrielaph.com/. Accessed February 26, 2019.
11 Tagalog word for "grandmother." Surviving "comfort women" of other nationalities are also sometimes referred to as "grandmothers" in their respective languages. For example, surviving Korean "comfort women" are referred to as "halmeonis," the Korean word for "grandmother."
12 "Video of San Francisco Board of Supervisors Regular Meeting." Accessed February 26, 2019. http://sanfrancisco.granicus.com/MediaPlayer.php?view_id=&clip_id=23651&caption_id=51432796.

Since then, she's been an activist in the movement for justice and to demand an official apology and reparations from the government of Japan. She was one of three former "comfort women" who testified before Congress in 2007.

I want to welcome her.

Fig. 2: Former "comfort woman" Lee Yong Soo and Supervisor Eric Mar speak at a press conference on 15 September 2015 to promote the "comfort women" memorial in San Francisco. Photo by Steve Zeltzer, Labor Video Project.

Grandma Lee replied:

> Thank you. I came here as a living evidence of history and I want to tell this beautiful city of San Francisco to please please lift my sadness and erect a memorial. I came here as a witness to history, but now I am more than that. I came here as an activist who is trying to resolve the history for the sake of all women's rights in the world. And for the sake of these women I am determined to solve this problem. Thank you.

Supervisor Jane Kim added:

> My parents emigrated to the U.S. in the [19]70s. I grew up in my childhood hearing stories about the young women and girls who were taken from their homes to serve as sex slaves for the Japanese military. I grew up hearing from so many women in my family who were fearful that they could have been one of those victims as well. The greatest revolutionary

gift you can give is not just to survive but to survive and tell your story and the stories and experiences are humiliating and challenging to hear and I know even more so to tell. I want to thank you again for your leadership and courage.

What followed was rather incredible. Speaker after speaker talked about why they supported the memorial, ranging from Japanese Americans to Koreans to Filipinas to academics and religious leaders. Despite the fact that there were charges of Japan-bashing, Kathy Masaoka, a leader of Nikkei for Civil Rights and Justice, spoke in favor of the memorial:

> We view this as an issue of human and women's rights and do not see it as one between China or Korea and Japan but one between the Japanese government and the "comfort women." We support them and call for an apology and reparations just as we did the U.S. government on the subject of Japanese internment in this country. I also wanted to dispel any notions that there has been any bullying or harassment of Japanese in Glendale as a result of the "comfort women" statue there. We've had no reports and neither has the Japanese Americans Citizens League (JACL). Instead it has allowed us to share our histories and work together with other communities.[13]

Amos Brown, the president of the local NAACP and the pastor of the Third Baptist Church, also spoke in favor of the memorial:

> For us, color comes in all colors. I stand here as a free thinker. You know, the state of Texas wants to redact history. They want to suggest the idea that slavery did not exist, that it was a merely an economic arrangement. Now I think some redacting is going on here. To suggest to these women that what happened to them is not real is like telling a woman who was raped that it didn't happen. This is no blanket indictment of Japan. It's just permitting people to say "We deserve to be considered and to remember the pain that we felt." I am standing in support of the statue.

The file for the resolution at the Board of Supervisors is 465 pages long, with copies of letters, petitions, and articles. More than 25 organizations from Osaka alone wrote in support. Nationwide Chinese American groups ranging from civic groups to the Chinese Chamber of Commerce all signed a group letter. Korean Americans organized en masse.[14] This connection to both domestic and international activists was one of CWJC's greatest strengths.

On 17 September 2015, the Board of Supervisors' Public Safety and Neighborhood Services Committee heard arguments about the resolution. It was going to

---

13 "Video of San Francisco Board of Supervisors Regular Meeting." Accessed February 26, 2019. http://sanfrancisco.granicus.com/MediaPlayer.php?view_id=&clip_id=23651&caption_id=51432796.
14 "Resolution 150764."

be up to the committee to decide whether to advance the resolution to the full board for a vote. Mera Koichi, a noted Japanese denier, led the opposition. "What the previous speaker [Halmeoni Lee] said is not true," he said. "'Comfort women': totally false. 200,000? Not true. Sex slaves? Not true."[15]

Supervisor Eric Mar then interrupted him and said, "Excuse me, are you calling Grandma Lee a liar? Are you?" Mera went on: "These women were just sold by their families. They were just prostitutes!" Unfortunately, these sentiments were echoed by other speakers and many letters to the supervisors. Halmeoni Lee got up and screamed at him: *"You're the liar!"* Later, Supervisor David Campos made a special comment: "To the gentleman who called Halmeoni a liar, I have one thing to say: Shame! Shame on you. And I hope that this isn't backed by a government hoping to have their way."[16]

The display by these deniers was expected. But the very next day, we experienced one of our biggest disappointments when we, along with Grandma Lee, went to the city's Commission on the Status of Women to seek its endorsement of the statue. As mentioned, San Francisco has a rich history supporting women's rights, so supporting the statue seemed like a natural fit. Emily Murase, the commission's Executive Director, is a firm advocate for women and trafficking victims, but she also has close ties to Japan. She insisted that the "comfort women" issue, though tragic, was old news, and that Japan had apologized many times. She also pitted the issue of trafficking against doing something about the "comfort women," asking why we should single them out when we were not honoring other women. Despite much testimony in favor of the resolution, the Commission refused to endorse it. Murase continues to oppose the statue to this day.

---

[15] Mera Koichi is a noted denier. A former professor at USC, he is one of the lead plaintiffs in the lawsuit against the Glendale Memorial. Not taking no for an answer when it was dismissed by a lower court, Mera brought the suit up to the Supreme Court which refused to hear the case. The Japanese government submitted an Amicus brief. Mr. Mera denies that there were "comfort women" and also denies the Nanjing massacre.

[16] "SHAME ON YOU! By San Francisco Supervisor David Campos-09/17/15," YouTube video, 11:44, posted by SfandBayAreaTruthSeeker, September 24, 2015. Accessed February 26, 2019. https://www.youtube.com/watch?v=dqFFvyq0vaI "'Backlash' Japan Abe's Denialist Supporters Attack Ex-Comfort Woman Grandma Yongsoo Lee," YouTube video, 45:53, posted by laborvideo, September 28, 2015. Accessed February 26, 2019. https://www.youtube.com/watch?v=kIIfZCedXcA

Things had barely calmed down by the next Board meeting on 22 September 2015. But an amendment acknowledging the history of the Japanese internment camps was added and Resolution No. 342–15, "Urging the Establishment of a Memorial to the 'Comfort Women,'" passed unanimously.

We were off and running.

Next Steps: Comfort Women Justice Coalition (CWJC)

The Comfort Women Justice Coalition (CWJC) came together around a few basic principles and goals: (1) Build a memorial to the "comfort women" and against trafficking; (2) Demand that the Japanese government issue an official apology to the survivors and their families and pay reparations; (3) Call on the Japanese government to investigate the crimes and acknowledge the full extent of what occurred; (4) Stress that we were targeting the Japanese government and not the people of Japan; (5) Develop educational materials to ensure that students would learn the true history of the "comfort women" and the issue of sexual violence during wartime.

We wanted to go beyond the horror of what happened to the women and explore the institutionalization of the system that enslaved them. Why didn't Japan just admit the truth? To do so would require not only an examination of the treatment of women, but the relationship of this form of patriarchy to the colonialism and racism that were endemic to Japanese empire and ideology. The utter contempt for women from Korea, China, the Philippines and elsewhere also allowed the Japanese army to enslave them. The use of the term "latrines" in describing them encompasses a profound racism as well as misogyny.

This investigation of the "comfort women" can be combined with an examination of the use of mass rape in the history of colonization and enslavement. For those studying and trying to understand U.S. history, this means a thorough analysis of the rape of Indigenous and Black women. It also requires us to see how history has impacted the treatment of women of color today. This historic intersecting and intertwining of institutionalized misogyny and white supremacy can be observed in all aspects of our society. It is for these reasons that the memorial in San Francisco does not speak of the "comfort women" alone. It also makes the connection between sexual enslavement then and the issue of sex trafficking now. Our members included many scholars and human rights activists who were interested in examining this relationship: what was the trajectory?

We know that, although the American military didn't "officially" use "comfort stations" in the same institutionalized way as the Japanese Army, "comfort stations" in Japan were turned over to American soldiers during the post-war occupation of Japan. There are still U.S. bases in Japan and Okinawa, just as there are huge military bases in South Korea and the Philippines, and there are massive numbers of brothels and prostituted women in all these areas. Rape is omnipresent and the treatment of women is one factor in the demands of "U.S. OUT!"

The "success" of the "comfort women" system as part of what came to be called "R & R" or "rest and recreation" in Vietnam and the Philippines had a direct impact on the IMF/World Bank's plan for development in South East Asia. It was known that tourism would be a big draw, and implicitly that would include sex tourism, which in turn, led to a huge increase in sex trafficking itself.

Breaking Silence

We also learned and understood the power of memory and its role in discovering and telling the truth. From the very beginning, we talked about the impact that the "breaking of silence" by the "comfort women" had on women's human rights. Although it is not often acknowledged, when the "comfort women" spoke out in 1991, they helped lead a movement to change centuries of what had been considered normal behavior for men during wartime, namely the need for sex and systematic rape. As Gay McDougall, the special rapporteur of United Nations High Commissioner for Refugees (UNCHR), put it: "In fact, as I note in my report, the issue of the former 'comfort women' was a major impetus for the United Nations deciding to commission the study of systematic rape and sexual slavery during armed conflict."[17]

In 1991, there was a vibrant women's movement in Asia. Women were examining gender relationships and sexual exploitation within their own societies and in relationship to militarization; this was especially true in places with a large American military presence, like Okinawa, South Korea, and the Philippines. Women were beginning to speak about rape, and the testimony of Kim Hak-sun helped spur others to speak up. Women in all of these countries began to see the relationship between militarization and sex trafficking and

---

[17] Gay McDougall, "Keynote speech at the Seoul International Symposium, leading up to the 'Women's International War Crimes Tribunal on Japan's Military Sexual Slavery in 2000 and the Issue of Japanese Military Sexual Slavery,'" June 1999, 9–10.

made connections between policies of the World Bank and the export of women. By 1993, there was knowledge of large rape camps and the systematic use of rape in the war in Yugoslavia. All these factors led to the declaration in the International Human Rights Tribunal in Vienna in 1993 that sexual violence during war was a crime against humanity. This finally became international doctrine in 2008, when the U.N. Security Council adopted resolution 1820, which noted that "rape and other forms of sexual violence can constitute war crimes, crimes against humanity or a constitutive act with respect to genocide."[18] Women can now speak about what was regarded as unspeakable. The willingness to address openly the issue of systematic rape owes a great deal to the courage of former "comfort women" and those from Bosnia, Rwanda, and Congo.

CWJC was also able to take advantage of the work of Chinese scholars Peipei Qiu and Su Zhiliang. Using careful analysis and with access to the latest revelations in newly released Chinese archives, they had determined that over 200,000 Chinese women had been pressed into sexual service during World War II. This upended the accepted figure of 200,000 total, with the majority, 180,000, coming from Korea. These numbers would become important when we began to discuss the language of the plaque that would accompany the statue. The two also extrapolated from carefully kept records by the Japanese military and determined how long women would typically survive, given how many men they would be raped by in a day. Their research also added to our understanding of the horrors of the system of sexual servitude and femicide.[19]

The issue of rape and shame is one to dissect. Rape has always been anathema in societies. It was outlawed in the Bible and rape as a war crime was discussed in early documents in British law. Yet it was also considered not only necessary but normal. So what to do? On the one hand, most men knew it was wrong. On the other hand? They wanted it—"they just couldn't help themselves." So who to blame? The women. It's one of the cornerstones of patriarchy and its ideology of misogyny. It's been said that one of the reasons that rape is used as part of conquest as part of occupation is to shame the conquered men to prove that they couldn't take care of "their women." Once again, the issue is turned upside down, and the pain and suffering of the women becomes primarily that of the men.

---

18 Judith Mirkinson, "Red Light, Green Light, The Global Trafficking of Women," *Breakthrough, San Francisco*, (1994): 11–15. Accessed November 14, 2018. http://www.armory.com/~leavitt/women.html; Wikipedia contributors, "Wartime sexual violence," Wikipedia, The Free Encyclopedia, https://en.wikipedia.org/w/index.php?title=Wartime_sexual_violence&oldid=868565476.
19 Peipei Qiu, with Su Zhiliang and Chen Lifei, *Chinese "Comfort Women": Testimonies From Imperial Japan's Sex Slaves* (New York: Oxford University Press, 2013), 21–80.

The Coalition and Education

One of the goals of CWJC was to make sure that the history of the "comfort women" and the issue of sexual violence during war was included in both the local San Francisco and the California State K-12 curriculum. In October 2015, flush from our victory at the Board of Supervisors, we went to our local school board at San Francisco Unified School District (SFUSD). In January 2015, Japanese officials had gone to U.S. textbook writers and asked them to delete any references to the "comfort women." We wanted the opposite. We wanted the Board to mandate the teaching of the "comfort women" in our schools, especially in the tenth grade, where our students study Modern World (once known as world history).

The U.S. is notoriously Eurocentric in its depiction and education about World War II, and for many people, the war in Asia and the Pacific region is extremely vague. They've heard about the atrocities committed by the Nazis, but far less about what the Japanese did in Asia. Combine this with the historic racism toward Asian people, and you have a very uneducated public. The textbooks reflect this myopia. In the textbook, *Modern World History*, (with pictures of Gandhi and Aung San Suu Kyi on the cover) the Pacific War rates three pages (as opposed to three chapters for Europe). When speaking about the war, one paragraph says:

> Although the "Japanese had tried to win the support of Asians with the anti colonialist idea of 'East Asia for the Asiatics,'"...they quickly "made it clear they had come as conquerors. They often treated the people of their new colonies with extreme cruelty." ... However, the Japanese reserved the most brutal treatment for Allied Prisoners of War.[20]

We felt that the teaching of the War in the Pacific needed to be greatly expanded and we urged the inclusion of both the "comfort women" and the massacre at Nanjing in the new curriculum. Resolution No. 158–25 A was passed, with the following paragraph added to a resolution on sex trafficking on 13 October 2015.

> **FURTHER BE IT RESOLVED:** That the Superintendent and district staff create a task force with community experts to work in consultation to incorporate an educational component of the history of "Comfort Women" of WWII under the Japanese military in its curriculum to educate the community about the harmful effects of sex trafficking in its historical and

---

[20] McDougal Littell, *Modern World History: Patterns of Interaction*, California Teachers Edition (Boston, MA: McDougal Littell, 2006), 498.

modern day context for the purpose of preventing and protecting the youth community from sexual exploitation and trafficking.[21]

It seemed like we could get on with the business of building the statue when a sudden roadblock appeared. On 28 December 2015, the Japanese Foreign Minister Kishida Fumio and Korean Foreign Minister Yun Byong-sei released parallel statements in a press release claiming that they had resolved the issue of the "comfort women" "finally and *irreversibly*." Kishida offered an apology from Prime Minister Abe to the survivors and Japan agreed to set up a fund of $8.3 million for survivors. The Japanese further demanded that the statue to the "comfort women" in Seoul would be removed.

This is not the place to have a full discussion of the 2015 "Agreement." Suffice it to say that although the media and both U.S. and Japanese officials lauded this development, the survivors and their supporters were outraged. None of the survivors had been consulted in South Korea. Furthermore, the so-called agreement was only between South Korea and Japan. The women and governments of all of the other affected countries were also ignored. CWJC joined with the worldwide movement to denounce the agreement. [22]

We went back to the San Francisco Unified School District on the issue of "comfort women" in the spring and lobbied for a resolution urging the California State Board of Education to also adopt a "comfort women" curriculum. The resolution passed. But there was trouble to come. In the summer of 2016, the State Board of Education was holding its final hearings in Sacramento on its framework for social studies. We went to lobby for the inclusion of the "comfort women." We were told that the State board had adopted our suggestions, but one month later, we heard disturbing news. After the public hearing, the board, which had been lobbied by both the South Korean and Japanese consulates, had inserted a "link" to the electronic version of the phony 2015 Japanese-Korean Agreement into the framework.

---

21 "CW Denial at San Francisco Unified School District Board Meeting, 04/12/2016," YouTube video, 25:59, posted by Japan-U.S. Feminist Network for Decolonization, April 14, 2016. Accessed February 26, 2019. https://www.youtube.com/watch?v=M37TF2vhgbc; Emi Koyama, "Responses to 'Comfort Women' Denier Arguments at the SFUSD Board Meeting on April 12th, 2016," (Report published by Japan-U.S. Feminist Network for Decolonization [FeND], based on the SFUSD Board Meeting, April 12, 2016). Accessed February 26, 2019. https://files.acrobat.com/a/preview/45f7b8a9–8c70–4475–972e-c7165432a683.
22 Ministry of Foreign Affairs of Japan, "Announcement by Foreign Ministers of Japan and the Republic of Korea at the Joint Press Occasion," December 28, 2015. Accessed February 26, 2019. http://www.mofa.go.jp/a_o/na/kr/page4e_000364.html.

CWJC went back to Sacramento. For months, we had meetings and phone calls arguing that the link should be removed. We organized a letter signed by international scholars decrying the addition of the link.[23] The school board representatives kept maintaining that they couldn't remove the link even though they recognized that it might not be accurate or even currently in use. State Deputy Superintendent of Public Instruction Tom Adams kept insisting, "We are not the arbiter of historical debate . . . we will turn it over to students to make their own judgment." The discussions went nowhere, and the link remains. Luckily, the local school boards have the ability not to use this advice. That means that we will have to figure out how to educate textbook writers and local school boards ourselves. However, the curriculum about the "comfort women" will be taught in the spring of 2018 in San Francisco public schools. We are also working on getting this curriculum into classes around the state, particularly in Southern California, and planning conferences in local colleges and universities.

Building the Statue: Art for the People

Once we had a mandate to build a statue, we had to find a venue. Friends suggested a little gem of a park on the border of Chinatown and the financial district called St. Mary's Square. Right next to it, a new building was being built with a huge terrace adjacent to the park. San Francisco requires that all new commercial buildings of a certain size have to have public art, which has to be approved by the San Francisco Arts Commission, and this site seemed perfect. The site had an advantage in that it was still on private property, thus, helping us avoid even more regulations, but it would become public property once the building was operational. We were adamant that the statue be on public and not private land.

Now we had to have a design. Part of the mandate for public art in San Francisco is that it must be original. We held an international competition and received more than 30 submissions. In the end, we went with a very realistic design by local designer Steven Whyte. Steven proposed a statue of three girls facing outward, hands linked, standing on a long column. The young women would represent the countries that were affected most by the Japanese "comfort women" system. In addition, we would have a statue of Kim Hak-sun looking up at her past and remembering those who had passed before her. We wanted

---

[23] The link used to be accessible by clicking Chapter 15 at http://www.cde.ca.gov/ci/hs/cf/sbedrafthssfw.asp, but it has since been removed.

the statue to be a memorial to what had specifically happened to the women in Asia. We wanted to have a memory for those who had perished, but also for those living today, especially future generations. We also knew that many families in the Bay Area had connections to what had happened in Asia during World War II and we wanted to reflect that experience and that history.

Again, we had a fight on our hands. Steven Whyte received over 1,200 letters calling on him to refuse the commission and calling CWJC and the "comfort women" liars and worse. Steven was not moved. He believed in the mission. Along with the statue, which is named "Comfort Women" Column of Strength, would be a plaque explaining the reason for the memorial. CWJC submitted language for our preferred version. We specifically wanted to hold the Japanese government accountable and continue to demand that they give an official apology. We also wanted to say that 400,000 women had been enslaved and that the majority of them had died as a result of their captivity. These points proved to be contentious and, once again, deniers objected. It was only 20,000 women, they said, as if even this number was acceptable. The history wasn't hidden, they claimed. Why should the Japanese government be held accountable? And did the vast majority really die? (Actually, the death rate for "comfort women" was 87%. This is in comparison to the 27% of frontline Japanese soldiers who died). We got letters suggesting that we were only doing the bidding of China and South Korea, and that this was just a nationalist issue.

The Arts Commission itself received hundreds of emails and visits from the Japanese consulate telling them not to approve either the statue or the plaque. There were more public hearings and more negotiations. Finally, we came to an agreement on both, and the Arts Commission accepted the design and the plaque. It reads:

> "Our worst fear is that our painful history during World War II will be forgotten."
>
> —former "Comfort Woman"
>
> This monument bears witness to the suffering of hundreds of thousands of women and girls, euphemistically called "Comfort Women," who were sexually enslaved by the Japanese Imperial Armed Forces in thirteen Asia-Pacific countries from 1931 to 1945. Most of these women died during their wartime captivity. This dark history was hidden for decades until the 1990s when the survivors courageously broke their silence. They helped move the world to declare that sexual violence as a strategy of war is a crime against humanity for which governments must be held accountable.
>
> This memorial is dedicated to the memory of these women, and to eradicating sexual violence and sex trafficking throughout the world.

Gift of the "Comfort Women" Justice Coalition
Korean American, Chinese American, Filipino American and other victim communities
Collection of the City and County of San Francisco

The plaque itself will be translated into English, Korean, Pilipino, Chinese, and Japanese.

Fig. 3: Banner used at the Unveiling Ceremony on 22 September 2017 for the San Francisco "Comfort Women" memorial statue. Banner designed by Kevin Liu. Photo by Frank Jang.

Endings and New Beginnings.

How did we do it? Like all coalitions, we had to work through problems of process and decision-making. We weren't always successful, and there were issues of democracy and transparency. Now that the statue has been built and installed, the sense of urgency is not going to be the same, and there undoubtedly will be have to be some reshuffling. Some people will leave to form their own groups, especially in terms of education. We will have to figure out how to go on from here. In the meantime, we're making plans for tours and events and conferences. We plan to hold anniversary celebrations every year and get delegations here from countries around the world. Those of us in grassroots organizations will have more space to involve our constituencies in all of the issues that we have been raising. The opportunities are almost endless. It will be interesting to see what happens. And throughout it all, we will keep insisting on holding the Japanese government accountable.

One thing we do know now more than ever is that the power of speaking out can never be underestimated. When the "comfort women" spoke out, they helped start a revolution. They weren't the first, but their voices about wartime rape and sexual violence are helping to make what was long acceptable never acceptable. And that voice is getting louder and covering bigger ground all the time. After women in Hollywood came forward in October 2017 with allegations that prominent film producer Harvey Weinstein had sexually abused them, we started to see a global trend of people coming forward to speak out against powerful men who had engaged in sexual abuse and other misconduct, resulting in the #MeToo movement and other social movements that resist the patriarchy. The "Weinstein effect" has been powerful. This is the "comfort women" effect. Kim Hak-sun would have been amazed.

The Statue is There!

> We pledge to continue our struggle against all forms of sexual violence, and for an end to the sexism, racism, colonialism, and war that fuel it. Standing here united in front of the memorial, we envision a world free from fear of sexual violence where all women and girls can live a life with respect and dignity.[24]
> —Statement commemorating the unveiling on 22 September 2017

The statue stands, a living history. Its very existence is both a reminder and a challenge. The Japanese government has not given up. The Mayor of Osaka has written yet another letter threatening to revoke the San Francisco-Osaka Sister City Agreement if the city accepts the gift of the statue. So the fight continues. We will not be deterred. We will continue to press for redress and we will continue to fight.

The day of the unveiling of the statue dawned bright and sunny—a perfect San Francisco day. More than 500 people filed into the plaza. Korean drummers danced and drummed down the aisle. We read the names of all those "comfort women" who had passed in the last year—more than 20. How many more names will we read before there is justice?

When asked about the necessity of an acknowledgement and apology by the Japanese government for their war crimes, one of the Korean "comfort women,"

---

[24] "Statement written by 'Comfort Women' Justice Coalition for unveiling of 'Comfort Women' Column of Strength," September 22, 2017. Accessed February 26, 2019. www.remembercomfortwomen.org.

Kim Bok Dong, who was enslaved for seven years from the age of 14, said, "To be able to receive an apology will allow us to close our eyes."

But WE must do the opposite. We can do that. We can look in the eyes of the young women in the Column of Strength and see both their pain and their determination not to be forgotten.

Fig. 4: Lee Yong Soo greets the statue of her longtime friend, Kim Hak-sun, the first person to speak out about her experiences as a "comfort woman." Photo by Steve Zeltzer, Labor Video Project.

Epilogue

Several months later:

Unfortunately the story doesn't end here. Once the statue was installed, the Japanese government continued to pressure the city of San Francisco. The Board had to accept the statue as an official gift, which it did. Once that was done, Mayor Ed Lee had to sign the acceptance. In November 2017, Osaka Mayor Yoshimura wrote to Mayor Lee urging him not to accept the statue. Doing so, he insisted, would do irreparable harm to the 60-year-old sister city relationship between Osaka and San Francisco. In fact, Mayor Yoshimura continued, if the statue became official public property then he would be forced to totally end that relationship. Mayor Lee passed away unexpectedly in December 2017, and although the actual severance of the relationship is on hold, Osaka has already terminated certain cultural and educational exchanges. Even Prime Minister Abe weighed in and said it was "deeply regrettable that [the San Francisco city assembly's vote to accept the statue] is at odds with our country's position."[25] Mayor Lee didn't bow to the threats, and on 22 November 2017, he signed the resolution accepting the statue, thus making it official San Francisco property.

It's still not over. In February 2018, the newly appointed Japanese Ambassador, Sugiyama Shinsuke, stated that one of his top priorities would be the removal of "comfort women" statues in the United States. On 28 April 2018, the Japanese government successfully pressured the Philippine government to take down their newly erected "comfort women" memorial in Manila.[26] Osaka Mayor Yoshimura then tweeted: "The Comfort Women Memorial Statue which was set up in Manila last year was removed with the backhoe. I want the Comfort Women Memorial Statue in San Francisco to be removed with a backhoe, too."[27]

So the fight continues. But one thing is absolutely clear: The "Comfort Women" Column of Strength will remain in San Francisco, on public land, for all to see for decades to come.[28]

---

25 "PM Abe Says San Fran Acceptance of 'Comfort Women' Statue 'Deeply Regrettable.'" *The Mainichi*, November 22, 2017. Accessed February 26, 2019. https://mainichi.jp/english/articles/20171122/p2a/00 m/0na/003000c.
26 "New 'Comfort Women' Memorial Removed from Thoroughfare in Manila Under Pressure from Japanese Embassy." *The Japan Times*, April 28, 2018. Accessed February 26, 2019. https://www.japantimes.co.jp/news/2018/04/28/national/politics-diplomacy/new-comfort-women-memorial-removed-thoroughfare-manila-pressure-japanese-embassy/#.WvjvdNMvxmM
27 https://headlines.yahoo.co.jp/hl?a=20180428 – 00000527-san-asia ... @YahooNewsTopics. Accessed February 26, 2019.
28 "Japan's New US Envoy Eyes Removal of 'Comfort Women' Statues," *Nikkei Asian Review*, February 16, 2018. Accessed February 26, 2019. https://asia.nikkei.com/Japan-Update/Japan-s-new-US-envoy-eyes-removal-of-comfort-women-statues.

Appendix One

RESOLUTION NO. 342-15
Urging the Establishment of a Memorial for "Comfort Women": Resolution urging the City and County of San Francisco to establish a memorial for "Comfort Women" and to educate the community about stopping global human trafficking of women and girls.

AMENDED AT BOARD 9/22/15
BOARD OF SUPERVISORS
Supervisors: Mar; Kim, Cohen, Christensen, Yee, Farrell, Campos, Aval

FILE NO. 150764

WHEREAS, According to most international historians, the term "comfort women" euphemistically refers to an estimated 200,000 women and young girls who were kidnapped and forced into sexual slavery by the Imperial Japanese Army during its colonial and wartime occupation of Asia and the Pacific Islands from the 1930s through the duration of World War II; and

WHEREAS, During the 15 years of invasion and occupation of Asian countries, unspeakable and well-documented war-crimes, including mass rape, wholesale massacres, heinous torture, and other atrocities, were committed by the Japanese Imperial Army throughout the occupied countries and colonies; and

WHEREAS, Of the few top Japanese military leaders who were investigated and convicted as war criminals in the postwar War Crime Tribunals in Tokyo, Nanjing, Manila, Yokohama, and Khabarovsk, many escaped prosecution; and

WHEREAS, In 2001 the San Francisco Board of Supervisors passed Resolution

No. 842-01, urging the government of Japan, on the 50th anniversary of the US-Japan Peace Treaty, to fully acknowledge and apologize for Japan's wartime atrocities and provide just compensation for the surviving victims of its aggression; and

WHEREAS, In 2007 the U.S. House of Representatives passed Rep. Mike Honda's bipartisan House Resolution 121, which also called on the Government of Japan to formally acknowledge, apologize, and accept historical responsibility for its Imperial Armed Forces' coercion of young women into sexual slavery; and

WHEREAS, In 2013, the San Francisco Board passed Resolution No. 218–13 condemning Japan's denial of its system of sexual enslavement during World War II and calling for justice for "comfort women;" and

WHEREAS, The year 2015 marks the 70th anniversary of the end of World War II

(1941–1945) and the Pacific War (1931–1945) and the defeat of Japanese imperialism and militarism by the Allies; and

WHEREAS, Several cities in the U.S., including, Glendale and Rohnert Park, CA; Long Island, NY; Palisades Park and Union City, NJ; Fairfax, VA; and Michigan City, MI have already erected memorials to help remember the "comfort women" during Japanese occupation in the Pacific War; and

WHEREAS, Victimization of women has occurred in other countries, however, it does not in any way excuse the actions of the Japanese Imperial Army; and

WHEREAS, Today there are an estimated 20.9 million victims of human trafficking globally, of which 55% are women and girls; forced labor and human trafficking worldwide is a $150 billion criminal industry; and

WHEREAS, San Francisco is not immune to the problem, and has been considered a destination for human trafficking due to its ports, airports, industry, and rising immigrant populations; and

WHEREAS, Learning about this victimization and teaching about it will help stop the modern epidemic of human trafficking, which occurs in San Francisco and many other countries around the world; and

WHEREAS, Leaders of the Japanese American community, which faced mass incarceration of 120,000 in US "concentration camps" in WWII and share a history of discrimination with other communities, have worked closely with the broader Asian Pacific Islander community in the past decades to strengthen relationships and build trust, understanding, and community for civil rights and social justice; and

WHEREAS, San Francisco is a city of immigrants and their descendants, many of whom have ancestral ties to Asian and Pacific Islander nations and have direct or indirect experience with Japan's past system of sexual enslavement; and

WHEREAS, City departments and the San Francisco Unified School District are exploring other opportunities to educate the community about "comfort women," current day human trafficking, and efforts to end violence and abuse of women and girls; and

WHEREAS, A growing coalition of immigrant communities, women's organizations, and human rights groups have organized to establish a memorial for "comfort women" and the millions of victims of the Japanese military in San Francisco to ensure that the plight and suffering of these girls and women will never be forgotten or erased from history; now, therefore, be it

RESOLVED, That appropriate City and County agencies will work with the community organizations to design and establish the memorial; and, be it

FURTHER RESOLVED, That the Board of Supervisors of the City and County of San Francisco during the 70th anniversary of the end of World War II expresses its strong support of creating a public memorial in memory of those girls and women who suffered immeasurable pain and humiliation as sex slaves and as a sacred place for remembrance, reflection, remorsefulness, and atonement for generations to come.

City and County of San Francisco
Tails
Resolution

City Hall
1 Dr. Carlton B. Goodlett Place
San Francisco, CA 94102-4689

File Number: 150764   Date Passed: September 22, 2015

Resolution urging the City and County of San Francisco to establish a memorial for "Comfort Women" and to educate the community about stopping global human trafficking of women and girls.

July 21, 2015 Board of Supervisors - REFERRED

September 17, 2015 Public Safety and Neighborhood Services Committee - RECOMMENDED AS COMMITTEE REPORT

September 22, 2015 Board of Supervisors - AMENDED
  Ayes: 11 - Avalos, Breed, Campos, Christensen, Cohen, Farrell, Kim, Mar, Tang, Wiener and Yee

September 22, 2015 Board of Supervisors - AMENDED
  Ayes: 11 - Avalos, Breed, Campos, Christensen, Cohen, Farrell, Kim, Mar, Tang, Wiener and Yee

September 22, 2015 Board of Supervisors - ADOPTED AS AMENDED
  Ayes: 11 - Avalos, Breed, Campos, Christensen, Cohen, Farrell, Kim, Mar, Tang, Wiener and Yee

File No. 150764

I hereby certify that the foregoing Resolution was ADOPTED AS AMENDED on 9/22/2015 by the Board of Supervisors of the City and County of San Francisco.

_____
Angela Calvillo
Clerk of the Board

Unsigned
Mayor

10/2/15
Date Approved

I hereby certify that the foregoing resolution, not being signed by the Mayor within the time limit as set forth in Section 3.103 of the Charter, or time waived pursuant to Board Rule 2.14.2, became effective without his approval in accordance with the provision of said Section 3.103 of the Charter or Board Rule 2.14.2.

_____
Angela Calvillo
Clerk of the Board

10/2/15
Date

File No.
150764

Appendix Two

CWJC Statement at Unveiling of the Memorial for "Comfort Women"

22 September 2017

We stand here today, united, as we bear witness to the suffering of hundreds of thousands of women and girls, euphemistically called "Comfort Women," who were sexually enslaved by the Japanese Imperial Armed Forces in 13 Asia-Pacific countries from the early 1930's to 1945. We stand here determined to win justice for all the victims of the Japanese military sexual slavery system, the majority of whom did not even live to see freedom. Through our memorial, we remember all our grandmothers who are alive, and all those who have passed on but are still with us in both spirit and memory. Through our transnational, multiethnic solidarity, we are also resolved to restore justice to those whose lives and suffering have been erased by nationalist politics or expediency.

This memorial is the product of unity among countless dedicated volunteers, activists, scholars and teachers, students, youth, parents and grandparents, professionals and retirees and others, who have joined under the united banner of the "Comfort Women" Justice Coalition to make this memorial a reality today. Much of the work was done away from the spotlight.

We stand here, guided by the powerful leadership of the surviving grandmothers themselves, who have led the global movement during the past decades. Their voices helped launch a global cry for accountability and justice. When Grandmother Kim Hak-sun courageously broke her silence, she helped pave the way for the international community to recognize sexual violence during war as a crime against humanity.

Echoing the grandmothers' calls, we demand that the Japanese Government take full, official responsibility for the institution of sexual slavery by the Japanese Imperial Army, an act that constitutes a war crime as well as a crime against humanity. The Government of Japan must implement the following actions:
1. Make a sincere, official, and legally binding apology;
2. Pay full reparations to the victims and their families;
3. Conduct a thorough investigation of the crime and punish those found guilty in a court of law;

4. Memorialize the victims and continue to teach its citizens an accurate and truthful history of Japan during its era of imperial expansion and World War II.

CWJC furthermore demands that Japan's apology and redress reflect the findings of the most up-to-date rigorous international scholarship. Recently, scholars have uncovered the fact that even more girls and women than previously known were enslaved, violated, and murdered in makeshift facilities in multiple war fronts across China, the Pacific, and Southeast Asia. These victims have left even fewer traces in official archives than those victims who were confined in the comfort stations set up in larger cities.

We want to go on record:

We condemn the Japanese Government's refusal to issue an official apology, and we denounce its diplomatic attempts to avoid taking full responsibility. These attempts include the 2015 so-called "agreement" between the governments of South Korea and Japan.

We have stood and will stand firm against all of the Government's obstruction and denialism, including its blocking of people's attempts to build memorials all over the world.

Let us remember that through their activism the grandmothers have stood with victims of state-instituted sexual violence all over the world.

Following their footsteps, we stand in solidarity with all those who have suffered from sexual violence. We are thinking of those in our communities who have been forced into sex trafficking, of the Yazidi women, the women in Syria, in Congo, and in Juarez, Mexico, and all those living near military bases. We are also thinking of those who suffered from sexual violence in the past, during the trans-Atlantic slave trade and the genocide of indigenous people.

We dedicate our memorial to all the grandmothers and their unwavering resolve for justice. We pledge to continue our struggle against all forms of sexual violence, and for an end to the sexism, racism, colonialism, militarization, and war that fuel it. Standing here united in front of the memorial, we envision a world free from fear of sexual violence, where all women and girls can live a life with respect and dignity.

Phyllis Kim
Looking Back at 10 Years of the "Comfort Women" Movement in the U.S.

Introduction

When Kim Hak-sun, a survivor of the Japanese military sexual slavery system, broke her silence in 1991 and spoke to the media about the terrible experiences she and other women went through under the Japanese military during World War II, it encouraged many other women to break their own silence and start a movement to recover their honor and dignity, and moved the world to recognize that "Rape during war is a crime against humanity."

Soon after Kim's press conference, support groups and advocacy organizations in other Asian countries where women had been victimized by the Japanese military during the Asian-Pacific War and World War II formed an international solidarity network, led by the Korean Grandmas (Korean survivors of Japanese military sexual slavery are commonly referred to as "comfort women victim grandmothers" in South Korea, but I will use the term "Korean Grandmas" in this chapter) and The Korean Council for the Women Drafted for the Military Sexual Slavery by Japan (hereafter, The Korean Council). The Korean Grandmas, who bravely came out and registered with the South Korean government as victims of the "comfort women" system, began a weekly demonstration every Wednesday, which is still ongoing—the world's longest running demonstration in the Guinness Book of World Records—in front of the Japanese Embassy in Seoul since early 1992. Soon after the groundbreaking testimony by Kim, the Japanese government conducted an investigation and issued the Kōno Statement, a landmark apology announced by then-Chief Cabinet Secretary Kōno Yōhei in 1993. Although Mr. Kōno acknowledged the Japanese military's involvement in the "comfort women" atrocity and expressed apology for it, the statement stopped short of acknowledging the Japanese government's responsibility for creating and operating the system of military sexual slavery, and the apology was neither ratified by the Japanese Diet nor was it an official Cabinet decision. Following the Kōno Statement, the Japanese government set up a charity foundation called the Asian Women's Fund in 1995, which collected donations from private Japanese citizens and corporations and dubbed it "atonement money." The Japanese government made sure this money was not a legal compensation, which would signify the government's acceptance of legal responsibility for this war crime. Many victims rejected the money, saying that this hush money was only an insult. In 2000, prominent jurists for international war crimes, advocacy organizations, and over seventy-five survivors from around the globe came together in Tokyo to hold the historic Women's International War Crimes Tribunal for the Trial of Japan's Military Sexual Slavery, from which a guilty verdict against the defendant Emperor Hirohito and the Japanese government was rendered. The tireless efforts to bring honor and dignity back to the Grandmas in the 1990s and early 2000s manifested in several forms, including direct protests against the Japanese government, building solidarity among the victim countries (including Japan, as there were also many Japanese women who were victimized), pleading to international human rights organizations such as the United Nations and Amnesty International, and raising lawsuits against the Japanese government and corporations involved in this war crime. However, by the early 2000s, all measures seemed to have been exhausted when all of the lawsuits failed, including the one raised in the United States, and Japan was simply turning a deaf ear to the cry of the victims.

Since Abe Shinzō, the grandson of accused Class-A war criminal Kishi Nobusuke, became the Prime Minister of Japan in 2006, Japan started taking a conspicuous turn towards nationalistic conservatism that manifested a tendency of glorifying its past aggression, historical revisionism, and undermining past apologies like the Kōno Statement. However, Japan's deliberate silence and negligence towards the victims' demands went largely unnoticed by the international community and media until Japan's strongest ally, the United States, passed a Congressional resolution that urged Japan to accept its grave historical responsibility in an unequivocal manner.

This chapter examines the major players as well as the strategies and lessons learned from ten years of the grassroots "comfort women" movement (2007–2017) led by the Korean American community to bring justice to the victims of the Japanese military sexual slavery system from the point of view of an activist who was and continues to be a part of the movement. The events described in this paper represent only the major developments during the ten-year period, but there were other efforts and activities to bring justice to the "comfort women" survivors during the same period in the United States.

The main body of this paper will discuss five major events: (1) The campaign to pass House Resolution 121 in the U.S. House of Representatives, (2) subsequent campaigns, including memorial building, (3) the lawsuit filed against the City of Glendale by the Japanese government, (4) the Japanese government's denial campaign, and (5) the 2015 Japan-South Korea Agreement. In conclusion, I will discuss the lessons we have learned from the ten years of activism, and tasks we have left to resolve the "comfort women" issue in a proper manner that is acceptable to the victims and complies with international standards. Although I have been and still am an integral part of the leadership in the Comfort Women Justice Coalition (hereinafter, CWJC) that built the "comfort women" monument in San Francisco in 2017, I won't go into too much detail here because Judith Mirkinson discusses that topic in another chapter.

This chapter has been influenced by books including Yoshimi Yoshiaki's *Comfort Women: Sexual Slavery in the Japanese Military during World War II* (2000); in particular, I read the English-language translation of Yoshimi's 1995 Japanese-language book by Suzanne O'Brien. I was also influenced by *Legacies of the Comfort Women of World War II*, edited by Margaret Stetz and Bonnie B. C. Oh (2001), and *Chinese Comfort Women: Testimonies from Imperial Japan's Sexual Slaves* (2014) by Peipei Qiu, Su Zhiliang and Chen Lifei. However, most of the events described in this paper are based on my own experiences as one of the organizers of the 121 Coalition and the Korean American Forum of California.

Never doubt that a small group of thoughtful, committed citizens can change the world; indeed, it's the only thing that ever was. – Margaret Mead

Campaign to Pass H.Res. 121 in 2007

One phone call in March 2007 changed the landscape of the "comfort women" struggle, the impact of which reached all corners of the U.S. and beyond during the ten years that followed. The caller was Dongsuk Kim from the New York-based Korean American Voters Council (hereinafter, KAVC; KAVC changed its name to Korean American Civic Empowerment, KACE, in 2012). Mr. Kim had started working closely with Congressman Mike Honda and a group of researchers to introduce and pass House Resolution 121, a.k.a., the "Comfort Women" Resolution, in the House of Representatives.[1] He had just successfully organized a congressional hearing in February 2007 in the U.S. Congress Committee on Foreign Affairs, Subcommittee on Asia, The Pacific, and the Global Environment, which was convened and officiated by the late Chairman of the Subcommittee, Eni Faleomavaega, and Congressman Mike Honda.[2] Kim and KAVC raised funds and made arrangements to bring "comfort women" survivors such as

---

[1] Text of the H.Res. 121 can be found as an appendix at the end of Chapter 5 in this volume by Jungsil Lee and Dongwoo Lee Hahm and also at https://www.congress.gov/bill/110th-congress/house-resolution/121. Accessed February 27, 2019.

[2] The 2007 Hearing transcript can be found at http://archives-republicans-foreignaffairs.house.gov/110/33317.pdf. Accessed February 27, 2019.

Jan Ruff O'Herne from Australia and Lee Yong-soo and Kim Koon-ja from South Korea to testify at the hearing.

On the other end of the phone call was Roy (Soon-hyung) Hong, a long-time community activist in the West Coast, whom Dongsuk Kim had asked to organize a grassroots campaign to garner co-sponsorships from Congresspersons across California for the 121 Resolution. One message on which the success of the campaign depended on, emphasized Kim, was that the Korean community understood that the issue we were pushing for in U.S. Congress was not Japan-bashing based on a Korean nationalistic agenda, but a universal human rights issue of a gendered war crime and a crime against humanity, which had largely been buried during the past 60 years. "We are doing this for the Grandmas who don't have voices, not to bash Japan. Japan is an ally for the U.S., as well as South Korea. We are American citizens and we want American government to work with Japan to resolve this issue," said Kim. This became the main mantra of the campaign to pass H.Res. 121 and the subsequent movement to raise awareness about the "comfort women" issue in the United States.

Prior to H.Res. 121 of 2007, similar resolutions had been introduced but remained obscure and had garnered limited support. Starting in 2001, the late Congressman Lane Evans, Democrat of Illinois, introduced resolutions asking the Japanese government to acknowledge and apologize for their crimes against "comfort women;" he did this every year until he retired in 2006, and was prodded by local activists belonging to the Washington Coalition for Comfort Women Issues, Inc. (hereinafter, WCCW) based in Virginia, and supported by a small but dedicated network of activists in the Korean American community and in academia.

For H.Res. 121, Roy Hong quickly organized an ad-hoc committee of activists in Los Angeles to start a campaign that later spread throughout the United States with a kind of fervor that had never been seen before in the Korean American community. The ad-hoc committee included Daniel Lee (an attorney), Phyllis Kim (an interpreter), Paul Yun (a college professor), Sean Kim (a seminary student), Jong-hwa Lee (a college professor), Ji-Hyun Oh (a graphic artist), and Jean Chung (an activist). In conjunction with KAVC in New York, the LA Working Group, namely the 121 Coalition in California, spearheaded the effort to garner endorsements from members of the House of Representatives in California by organizing visits to their district offices with petitions signed by residents from their respective districts. Aggressive but effective grassroots lobbying, fundraising and petition drives were led by Korean American community-based organizations and religious institutions throughout the United States. Catholic churches in the greater Los Angeles area were among the most notable supporters of these efforts; they helped raise funds through second collection at all of the thirteen churches. Eventually, support came from throughout the United States.

At the national level, in the halls of Congress, local efforts were followed up by grassroots activist Annabel Park and others based in Washington, D.C. with help from members of WCCW. Grandma Lee Yong-soo (as mentioned earlier, the victims are affectionately referred to as "Grandmas"), a survivor-turned-activist, made a couple of visits to the United States during this period to work closely with the LA Working Group to generate awareness and support for the movement. Three other individuals, Jihee and Peter Huh and Joachim Sukwon Yoon, were also very actively involved in the grassroots efforts to garner endorsements and raise funds to support the overall lobbying effort. ALPHA – LA (Alliance to Preserve the History of WWII in Asia – Los Angeles) and GA (Global Alliance for Preserving the History of WWII in Asia) in the Bay Area and Los Angeles Chapters also participated in collecting petitions and lobbying key political leaders such as Nancy Pelosi and the late Tom Lantos.

However, on the other side, the Japanese opposition lobby was strong. The Japanese government hired consulting firms in Washington, DC, and lobbyists visited the offices of Congress members to dissuade them from co-sponsoring the bill. Historical revisionists in Japan and the U.S. ran a full page advertisement titled "Facts" in *The Washington Post* (14 June 2007), but they were actually filled with denial talking points, endorsed by dozens of Japanese politicians, including Inada Tomomi of the ruling Liberal Democratic Party. Dongsuk Kim of KAVC provided key strategy and coordination on the national level. The successful effort resulted in securing 167 endorsements in less than five months from throughout the United States and the resolution passed unanimously in the United States House of Representatives on 30 July 2007. Grandma Lee Yong-soo was present at the Congress to witness the historic passage of the resolution.

Motivated by the passage of H.Res. 121 in the United States, many other countries passed their own versions of the resolution, calling for the Government of Japan to address the issue properly.[3] A three-day-long World Conference on Japanese Military Sexual Slavery was held at UCLA from 4 – 6 October 2007, hosted by the 121 Coalition of California; key organizers included Jong-hwa Lee, Paul Hoffman (a human rights attorney), Jihee Huh, Phyllis Kim, and Sean Kim.

---

3 The Netherlands passed a similar resolution in August 2007, The Philippines in August 2007, Canada in November 2007 and the European Union in December 2007.

Fig. 1: Survivor Lee Yong-soo demanding an official apology from the Japanese government at a press conference held immediately after the H.Res. 121 was passed. Photo by Yong Sok Chung.

Post H.Res. 121: Memorial Movement and More

Subsequent to the passing of H.Res. 121, activists involved in the H.Res. 121 campaign realized that something more substantial was needed to pressure the Japanese government, which had not budged an inch from its previous position of inaction and denial, despite the unanimous passage of the H.Res. 121 and numerous other similar resolutions in the United States, Japan, and other countries. It was again the KAVC that took the initiative and built the first "comfort women" monument at a public site in October 2010 in Palisades Park, New Jersey. Successful installation of the monument in Palisades Park Public Library motivated other groups to do the same. Former members of the 121 Coalition in California formed a non-profit organization, Korean American Forum of California (hereinafter KAFC), which now includes key individuals such as Joachim Youn, Phyllis Kim, Roy Hong, Keun Hwang, Jung-ran Shin, and Yooha Song. Since the first memorial in Palisades Park was erected, grassroots activism spread across the U.S. like wildfire as groups raced to erect more "comfort women" memorials and monuments in many public locations (Bergen County, NJ, two memorials in Nassau County in Long Island, NY, Glendale, CA, Fairfax County, VA, Union City, NJ,

Brookhaven, GA, and San Francisco, CA) and in some private locations (Southfield, MI, Garden Grove, CA, and New York, NY) with less impact. The effort to raise awareness about the "comfort women" issue did not end with building memorials but expanded to many other creative activities, such as art exhibits, speaking events, film screenings, and book donation campaigns. Certainly, these various efforts to raise the profile of the "comfort women" issue is a reflection of and pro-active reaction to the success of the campaign to pass H. Res. 121 of 2007 and the legitimacy it brought to mainstream America, but it was also a pro-active response to Japan's Prime Minister Abe and the history deniers and their efforts to directly challenge and undermine the movement to remember Japan's various past war crimes. The grassroots effort was, indeed, propelled by the very realization that the efforts in the United States were having a huge impact on Abe's regime and the history deniers.

Along with grassroots activists, many artists of various mediums stepped forward with creative ways to present the "comfort women" issue in the United States. Most notable and consistent among the artists are Steve Cavallo of New Jersey and Chang-jin Lee of New York. Their exhibits of paintings, photos, and video art have received local and national attention, in both ethnic and also mainstream media. Julie (Jungsil) Lee of WCCW has organized and curated multiple exhibits featuring artwork about the "comfort women" issue both in the United States and South Korea. A number of films have also been made about "comfort women," including *Silence Broken* (2004) by Dae Sil Kim-Gibson, which is a docu-drama that was brought back in 2016 for showing around the country. Christopher Lee's documentary film *The Last Tear* (2015), which focused on one particular "comfort woman" survivor from Korea, won numerous awards and was shown in the U.S. and other countries. Canadian filmmaker Tiffany Hsiung and her documentary film *The Apology* (2016), which followed three survivors from Korea, China, and the Philippines, is a masterpiece that was highly acclaimed and was shown in the U.S. and around the world. *Spirits' Homecoming* (2016), the first Korean blockbuster feature film about the plight of the "comfort station" victims, based on the true story of the survivor Kang Il-chul, was widely screened in the United States and other countries in 2016 and 2017, contributing a great deal to raise awareness about the issue outside of Korea. *I Can Speak* (2017), another hit film made in South Korea and shown in the United States and other countries, dramatized the story of Lee Yong-soo, who testified at the U.S. Congressional hearing in 2007 for the passage of House Resolution 121.

One of the most effective efforts to raise awareness of the nature of the "comfort women" atrocity was to bridge the experiences of the "comfort women" survivors and the Holocaust survivors. The first of such efforts was successfully made by KAVC, in collaboration with the Kupferberg Holocaust Center at

Queensborough Community College in Queens, New York in December of 2011. Holocaust survivors Hanne Liebmann and Ethel Katz formed a sisterhood with the Korean survivors Lee Yong-soo and Lee Ok-sun when they met for the first time at speaking events at Queensborough Community College. They went to Columbia University to speak and later to a joint protest event at the office of the Representatives of Japan to the UN in New York. KAVC jointly hosted several more similar events at the Kupferberg Holocaust Center.

Glendale Peace Monument and the Lawsuit

In commemoration of the fifth anniversary of the H.Res. 121 and the proclamation of the "Comfort Women Day" at the City of Glendale in 2012, KAFC hosted two "comfort women" exhibits—one in Glendale and another in Los Angeles. Since then, KAFC campaigned and raised funds to install the first Peace Monument (aka the "Girl Statue") outside of South Korea in the City of Glendale's Central Park, amidst strong opposition from deniers. In fact, our initial plan was to install a gravestone-type memorial with an inscription and a drawing of one of the Grandmas, but when the City Council members saw the photos of the Peace Monument in front of the Japanese Embassy in Seoul, they requested that we bring the Peace Monument instead of the design we had prepared. The level of opposition exceeded anyone's imagination. The Japanese Consul General of Los Angeles sent letters to the City Council to request meetings, and even published an op-ed in the *Los Angeles Times* saying "Japan did enough to remedy the 'comfort women' issue." Through the letter campaign organized by the Nadeshiko Action and Happy Science in Japan, hundreds of opposition emails were sent to the City of Glendale. During a public hearing in July 2013 in Glendale City Hall where the placement of the memorial was discussed, dozens of history deniers—mostly of Japanese descent—showed up to speak against the plan, making absurd claims that the women were paid prostitutes and willing volunteers. These blatant denials, captured and archived on video by the city, did nothing to persuade the City Council members who taught them a lesson instead. "Whether they were considered prostitutes at the time or forced, to me, is a moot argument because there is no such thing as a willing 14-year old prostitute," said Council member Laura Friedman. "One of the speakers said you never heard about it. You never heard about it because the Japanese government chose not to teach its people the reality and the truth of what that Imperial Army did in the second World War," said Council member Frank Quintero. A group of Japanese politicians came to visit Glendale to meet and demand removal of the statue after its installation, but they were turned away without a meeting with the Glendale Council members.

In conjunction with the unveiling of the Glendale memorial, KAFC co-hosted a joint forum with the globally recognized Museum of Tolerance, where the Holocaust survivors, Grandma Kim Bok-dong, and human trafficking survivors, as well as the Honorable Rabbi Cooper, met and addressed the issue. The unveiling of the Peace Monument on 30 July 2013 put the small City of Glendale on the world map. About 50 local and international media outlets and hundreds of supporters turned up to witness the historic moment with the survivor Kim Bok-dong.

Fig. 2: Unveiling ceremony for Peace Monument in Glendale, CA on 30 July 2013. Photo by Roy Hong.

Japanese history deniers' working against their own agenda became most apparent when it was widely reported that a lawsuit was filed against the City of Glendale in February 2014, in a rather farfetched effort to remove the Peace Monument and send a threatening message to all the cities and governmental entities contemplating the same move to remember "comfort women" around the country. Mera Koichi, a former Clinical Professor of International Management at the University of Southern California, put himself out there as the leader of the history deniers and an avid Abe supporter when he filed a lawsuit against the City of Glendale in federal court asking the judge to hand down an order to remove the Peace Monument in the park in Glendale. (Gingery, et al. v. City of Glendale. Case No. 2:14-cv-1291)

Upon being served the complaint, the concern of the Glendale city officials was not the lawsuit itself—most lawyers viewed it as an absurd and frivolous action, filed only to intimidate other cities and government entities from erecting a "comfort women" statue, out of fear of a potential lawsuit. The bigger concern for the lawyers was the reputation of the law firm for the plaintiffs, Mayer Brown. Mayer Brown is the fifteenth largest law firm in the United States, and when it comes to legal action, it's no secret in the legal world that the size and reputation of the law firm handling the case matters as much as the merits of the case. KAFC immediately started searching for an equally reputable and sizable law firm, with a First Amendment specialist in its Los Angeles office. Soon, we were able to secure pro bono representation for the City of Glendale from Sidley Austin, LLP, the seventh largest firm (in 2014) in the United States. Bradley Ellis, a renowned First Amendment expert, and Christopher Munsey, led the case. KAFC then contacted different victim communities to garner support for the City of Glendale, which stood firm to defend the Peace Monument, and conducted a joint press conference with community groups from various victim communities, including the Japanese American community, as well as the local Armenian and women's groups in Glendale on International Women's Day in 2014.

Interest around the lawsuit exploded after an article by Eamonn Fingleton appeared in *Forbes* magazine on 13 April 2014, heavily criticizing Mayer Brown for taking such a shameful case. Soon, a whirlwind of debate about the case in the legal community ensued. By the end of April, Mayer Brown withdrew from the lawsuit, going so far as to offer to refund the retainer fee and to provide free services until the plaintiffs found a suitable replacement, in order to soothe the unhappy client and get out of the case.

Major media outlets around the globe including BBC, Associated Press, CNN, New York Times, Kyodo News, Arirang News, and Al Jazeera came and interviewed KAFC about the pending lawsuit. In the summer of 2014, KAFC invited two survivors from Korea—Grandma Lee Ok-sun and Kang Il-chul from the House of Sharing—to counter the lawsuit. KAFC worked with Paul Hoffman, a human rights attorney who had represented the survivors at the 2000 Tokyo Tribunal on Japan's military sexual slavery, and Catherine Sweetser, another human rights attorney from the same firm as Hoffman, to prepare *amicus curiae* briefs with the declarations of the two survivors in support of the defendant Glendale. KAFC also travelled with the two Grandmas to Washington, DC to meet with representatives of the Obama administration at the White House and the State Department to explain why it is so important for the Japanese government to officially accept its responsibility and properly resolve the issue with the victims. It was again Dong-suk Kim of KACE who arranged these meetings in DC. Global Alliance in the Chinese community also submitted its *amicus curiae* brief for the defendant Glendale.

As expected, the District Court Judge dismissed the case in the summer of 2014, but the plaintiffs appealed. When the case was dismissed again by the 9th Circuit Court in August of 2016, KAFC threw a victory party, inviting the community supporters, City Council members of Glendale, as well as the attorneys on the case to thank them, believing that in the unlikely event of appeal to the U.S. Supreme Court, it was most certain that the court would refuse to review the case. That is exactly what ended up happening, despite the Japanese government's interference in the lawsuit with big strides of its own *amicus curiae* brief submitted in the U.S. Supreme Court, stating that the removal of the Glendale Peace Monument was Japan's "national core interest." In March of 2017, the District Court's decision became final. Mera Koichi and others also filed a separate case in the State Court in 2014 when the District Court dismissed the case. The case was dismissed at the State Court and the 9th Circuit Court, and Glendale won an anti-SLAPP (i.e., strategic lawsuit against public participation) decision against the plaintiffs, resulting in a U.S. $300,000 award for the defendant's legal fees.

After installing a Peace Monument in Glendale, KAFC started campaigning to install another "Girl Statue" in Fullerton, California, about 25 miles southeast of Los Angeles. The city council members were on board and cooperative, but things started slowing down when the word got out and the Japanese Consul General started having multiple meetings with the mayor and the city manager. Everyone in Glendale City Council and the legal team was confident that the lawsuit against the city was frivolous and that the city was going to prevail, but it did inflict certain damages in our efforts in Fullerton, or at least it was used as an excuse for the infinite delay. Also, Fullerton is a small city where the city manager is referred to as the "real boss" who controls all city affairs, while the city council members were changed every two to four years. We didn't realize until much later that the city manager was laying hurdles in front of us, significantly delaying the process, blocking us from promoting the project to the board members of the Fullerton Museum, which was designated as an installation site for the monument. In 2015, the city manager started making various excessive demands under his sole discretion, such as a requirement of a $2 million liability insurance package to cover the entire City of Fullerton for accepting the gift of the Peace Monument, while failing to put the matter on the agenda for more than a year. In June of 2015, KAFC concluded that the city leadership was not ready to accept the gift of the Peace Monument and fully appreciate the struggle of the Grandmas through the Peace Monument, and we withdrew our proposal to donate the Peace Monument to the City of Fullerton.

Japan's "History War" in the United States

News broke in December of 2013 that Prime Minister Abe Shinzō had visited the Yasukuni Shrine to pay respect to the war dead, including dozens of convicted war criminals of World War II. China and South Korea immediately condemned Abe in the strongest language. Many viewed his actions as a sign of unrepentance of the war crimes committed during World War II. In addition, his actions seemed to glorify Japan's failed attempt to dominate half of the world through military aggression, and whip up nationalistic jingoism that preceded his real goal: to revise Japan's Peace Constitution and re-militarize with authority to invade other countries again.

Attempt to Revise American Textbooks

In November of 2014, Japanese diplomats demanded a revision or deletion of the section of a McGraw-Hill textbook[4] that mentions "comfort women." Their argument was that the description in the section does not conform with the Japanese government's position on the issue. Instead of granting the request, the publisher refused and spoke with the press about this ridiculous demand from the Japanese government, which was widely reported in major news outlets such as the *New York Times* and the *Washington Post*. Later, one of the authors of the book, Professor Herbert Ziegler of the University of Hawaii, spoke with the *Japan Times* to recount the unannounced and discourteous visit by a Japanese diplomat who barged into his office without an appointment to make forceful demands to delete or revise the section. In February 2015, concerned scholars of Japanese studies and historians, led by Professor Alexis Dudden of the University of Connecticut, got together and issued a statement to condemn the Japanese government's attempt to skew history inside and outside of Japan, and to support the publisher and the author Herbert Ziegler's perseverance. The initial statement by 19 scholars grew to collect nearly 500 signatures around the globe by 19 May 2015. In the aftermath of the dismissal of the Glendale lawsuit in the District Court and the

---

4 Jerry H. Bentley and Herbert Ziegler, *Traditions and Encounters: A Global Perspective on the Past* (New York: McGraw-Hill Education, 2010).

diplomacy failure around the McGraw-Hill textbook, Prime Minister Abe Shinzō "pledged to increase efforts to alter views abroad on Japan's actions in World War II by disseminating the 'correct' view, as he put it." (*Japan Times*, 29 January 2015). Sure enough, Abe tripled the budget to $500 million per year to improve Japan's image in the international community.

Abe's Visit to the United States

2015 marked the 70th anniversary of the end of World War II. In the spring of 2015, we learned that Japanese Prime Minister Abe was pushing to give a speech at the Joint Meeting of Congress in the United States. KACE (Korean American Civic Empowerment, formerly Korean American Voters Council), KAFC (Korean American Forum of California), and WCCW (Washington Coaltion for Comfort Women Issues), which had been commemorating the passage of H.Res. 121 together annually, again worked together to send a strong message to Abe and the Japanese government that he would not have the chance to speak at the Joint Meeting of Congress if he continued to deny Japan's war crimes and refuse to offer an official and unequivocal apology to the victims of the "comfort women" atrocity. The three organizations formed a national network and started a petition drive to the members of Congress, collected 10,000 signatures, conveyed our concerns to the State Department, and raised funds to place a full-page advertisement in *The Hill* and *The Washington Post*. We also invited Grandma Lee Yong-soo to follow Abe wherever he was going to give a speech—Harvard University in Boston, Washington, DC, and Los Angeles. In addition, multi-ethnic demonstrations were organized in San Francisco and Stanford University, in addition to those held at Harvard, Washington, DC, and Los Angeles, mobilizing thousands of people from multiple communities. Abe did give a speech at the Joint Meeting of Congress where he never mentioned "comfort women," but the campaign received wide media attention, sending a strong message to American politicians and the public that Japan's ongoing denial and evasion of the responsibility of the war crimes it committed during World War II is not acceptable.

San Francisco Memorial

In August of 2015, KAFC made contacts with people who were organizing to pass a resolution to build a "comfort women" memorial at a public site in San Francisco. The leaders of this effort were Lillian Sing and Julie Tang, two Chinese

American judges who have served in the San Francisco Superior Court for over 30 years and 20 years, respectively. At the time, Eric Mar was a Supervisor (equivalent to a city council member) who spearheaded the resolution in the San Francisco Board of Supervisors. Judge Sing and Judge Tang have been active in the redress movement for the Rape of Nanjing for the past 20 years through RNRC (Rape of Nanking Redress Coalition) in San Francisco. Later they said that they had been following the series of successes led by Korean Americans since 2007, starting with the passage of H.Res. 121, the Glendale Peace Monument, and the lawsuit, and they were inspired to erect a monument dedicated to the Asian women victims during World War II in San Francisco. When we learned that some of the Supervisors who had previously supported the San Francisco "comfort women" memorial resolution were having second thoughts due to the lobby efforts by some local Japanese Americans and others backed by the Japanese government, we decided to invite one of the survivors from South Korea to speak at the Board of Supervisors hearings. KAFC funded Grandma Lee Yong-soo's travel to San Francisco, and she spoke multiple times at the city hearing (17–22 September 2015) in front of the Board of Supervisors and hundreds of audience members, some of whom had to be redirected to separate media rooms because the main hall had become too crowded.

The forces behind the history deniers bused in their followers, including Mera—the lead plaintiff of the Glendale lawsuit—and others to speak against the resolution. Grandma Lee stated, "I hate the crime people committed, but I do not hate people because I want the next generation from Japan and Korea to be friendly to each other." Her testimony was powerful. When Mera stood at the podium and insulted Grandma Lee that she was lying in her testimony and in fact, she had volunteered to become a "comfort woman" for money, waving around a copy of C. Sarah Soh's book,[5] it not only enraged Grandma Lee, who shouted, "[w]ere you there to see it yourself? How dare you lie in front of the person who actually went through it?" but also moved the Supervisors such that in the end, the resolution passed unanimously on 22 September 2015. After two years of tireless work, CWJC (Comfort Women Justice Coaltion), a coalition of a dozen community organizations in the San Francisco and Bay Area, unveiled the unique design of its own "Comfort Women's Column of Strength" in St. Mary's Square extension on 22 September 2017. Judith Mirkinson, the President

---

5 C. Sarah Soh is an anthropology professor of Korean descent at San Francisco State University. Her book, *The Comfort Women: Sexual Violence and Postcolonial Memory in Korea and Japan* (Chicago: Chicago University Press, 2008), is controversial because it challenges the view that the Japanese government were the main perpetrators behind the victimization of "comfort women." Many people believe that Soh's book has helped the cause of Japanese history deniers.

of the CWJC, will discuss the campaign to erect this monument in greater detail in her chapter.

California Textbook Campaign

Anyone interested in Asian or Asian American history (including teachers) would have been following the development around the "comfort women" issue in California with great interest. From the 2013 controversy over the placement of the Glendale Peace Monument and the lawsuit against Glendale in 2014, to the Japanese government's demand to revise a section in the McGraw-Hill textbook, the publisher's refusal, and the subsequent 500 scholars' statement against historical revisionism by the Japanese government, all of these incidents were widely reported in the media. So it is not surprising at all that the "comfort women" issue made its way into the proposed revision in the California High School's History-Social Science curriculum guideline that was to be revised in the spring of 2016. In fact, the San Francisco Unified School District had already adopted the "comfort women" issue in the revised curriculum for the district in 2015, and it seemed only natural for the California Education Board to do the same in 2016— that is, unless you are up against the Japanese government.

KAFC formed an alliance with other groups in Southern California and CWJC in Northern California to lead a state-wide campaign to have the "comfort women" history adopted in the curriculum guideline as proposed in the revision. We created a website and posted a letter in English, Spanish, Chinese, Korean, Japanese, and Tagalog, where people could send a form email to the California Department of Education (DOE) Quality Instructional Commission where public comments were supposed to be sent, and collected signatures on the paper petition for the people who preferred to sign on paper. During the two months designated for the online public comments in January and February, we collected 20,000 signatures online and offline. The Japanese history deniers started an online campaign at change.org claiming that the "comfort women" were paid prostitutes and that the California DOE should not adopt this history in the textbook. In August, hundreds of people gathered in the Sacramento Department of Education building where the public hearing was held. Among them was a group of history deniers, including Mera, and others we've seen in Glendale, Fullerton, and San Francisco. They argued that the "comfort women" history should not be included in the California textbook. Members of KAFC and CWJC also attended the hearing to support the inclusion of the "comfort women" history in the textbook. After the public comment session was over, the deputy superintendent Tom Adams took the microphone and explained the pressure they were under from both sides of the "comfort women" issue, and said that it was decided to include the link to the controversial 2015 Agreement in the curriculum revision, in consideration of the strong opposite positions, without presenting it to the public, thus giving us no opportunity to comment on it. The revision was adopted with the link. During a private meeting a month later, Adams said that not only the Japanese government, but also the Korean government, lobbied him to include the link in the revision.

Atlanta Comfort Women Memorial Task Force

In 2016, Baik-kyu Kim of Atlanta, Georgia contacted KAFC in search of advice in order to erect a "comfort women" memorial in Atlanta. We advised him to build a multi-ethnic community coalition to work with the local government to understand that this issue is as American as the Holocaust, since it pertains to all women when it comes to the nature and the magnitude of the crime. He recruited Helen Kim Ho, an attorney and activist, to organize the Atlanta Comfort Women Memorial Task Force, a multi-ethnic, community organization that conducted educational events, raised funds, and approached public officials to explain the memorial project. When the news broke in early 2017 that the Center for Civil and Human Rights in Atlanta had entered into an MOU (memorandum of understanding) with the Task Force to place the "comfort women" statue on its grounds, the Japanese government and the deniers immediately started working behind the scenes to influence the Center to cancel the plan. The Japanese Consul General pressured the board members of the Center for Civil and Human Rights and made a threat to the Metro Atlanta Chamber of Commerce that if the Center went ahead and installed the monument, all Japanese businesses would leave the State of Georgia. After a few weeks, the Center backed out of the plan, providing an unconvincing excuse that the Center's landscape plan never included any outdoor sculpture.

The Center's decision to give in to the history deniers' intimidation tactic outraged the proud local residents in Atlanta, the home of the Civil Rights Movement and Dr. Martin Luther King. Jr. Op-eds (editorials) criticizing the Center's decision popped up in local newspapers and some citizens who are not affiliated with the Task Force went ahead and started a change.org petition, demanding that the Center keep the original promise to host the statue. John Park, a City Council member in the nearby City of Brookhaven, took this issue to heart and worked with Helen Ho to persuade the City Council of Brookhaven to host the monument. Undeterred by the Japanese Consul General's lobby and opposition emails from Japan, the City Council reached a unanimous decision and its citizens welcomed the statue in a Brookhaven park in June of 2017, celebrating the seventh "Comfort Women" memorial in a public space in the United States.

Concurrent Campaigns, Events and Lectures

In addition to resolutions passed at various levels of government and memorials that have been established in public sites, art exhibits and movie screenings provide strong emotional awakening and raise awareness effectively. Books can also be as powerful, if not more, than artwork and public memorials. *Daughters of the Dragon* (2014), a novel based on the testimonies of "comfort station" survivors, written by William Andrews and published in the United States, is one such book that can leave an indelible impression on readers' minds. KAFC invited the author in January 2015 to have two book signing events in Southern California and started a book donation drive, sending copies of the book to public libraries in the United States. We sent more than 400 copies to public libraries in different states, hoping that this novel will spread awareness and promote understanding of "comfort women" and the "comfort station" system much as *The Diary of Anne Frank* did for the Holocaust. The rights to make a film based on this story has been sold and the movie will come out very soon.

Another book that bears a great significance is *Chinese Comfort Women: Testimonies from Imperial Japan's Sex Slaves*, co-authored by professors Su Zhiliang and Chen Lifei of Shanghai Normal University and Peipei Qiu of Vassar College. Until this book came out, the common estimate for the number of victims in the Japanese military sexual slavery system was as little as 50,000 and as much as 200,000, with about 160,000 from the Korean Peninsula. However, the more than ten years-long research that is based on more than 100 interviews with the survivors, conducted by professors Su and Chen, established that the number of victims of the military sexual slavery system during the Japanese occupation in China alone was at least 200,000, excluding those women who were randomly raped or killed. That means the total number of victims throughout the Asia-Pacific region was as many as 400,000. This research has changed our understanding of the scale and characteristics of the Japanese military sexual slavery system in a manner we have not seen before. It is very fortunate that professors Su and Chen are both active in giving talks in various conferences and symposiums, in addition to their dedicated work as the founders and directors of the Nanjing "Comfort Women" museum and the museum/archive at Shanghai Normal University in China.

In Glendale, California, the site of the Peace Monument, KAFC has offered memorial rituals whenever surviving victims passed away. Anglican, Protestant, and Buddhist clergy help lead the rituals in three religions and the supporters come and pay respects and offer incense for the Grandmas. Ed Royce, the Chairman of the Foreign Affairs Committee in the House of Representatives, Adam Schiff, the Representative for the district that covers Glendale, and other local politicians have visited the Glendale Peace Monument memorial rituals to pay respect to the deceased. Each year since 2015, a team of cyclists consisting of a few college students (Triple A Project: Acknowledge, Apologize, Accompany) visit Los Angeles from South Korea to take a cross-country bicycle ride from Glendale to New York, to promote the "comfort women" issue along the way in the United States. For three years, KAFC has supported their endeavor by helping them to get ready for the rough days ahead and to receive effective media attention. In 2017, Congressman Adam Schiff recognized the work led by KAFC to promote awareness and justice for the "comfort station" victims in the United States, and presented the Congressional "Woman of the Year" award to KAFC's executive director Phyllis Kim.

As the campaigns led by KAFC succeeded year after year, more media is paying attention to the unresolved issue of the "comfort women." Student groups, college professors, and local high school teachers invite us to come and speak to the students. We are also invited to present at international conferences to give perspectives from our movement in the United States. These speaking opportunities allow us to reach out to young people who may become interested and passionate about the "comfort women" issue or gendered crimes against humanity, so the next generation can continue this struggle for justice in the years to come.

2015 Japan-South Korea Agreement

On 28 December 2015, the Foreign Ministers of Japan and South Korea held a joint press conference and announced that the two governments had decided that the "comfort women" issue was "finally and irreversibly resolved" with Abe's vague apology and 1 billion yen to provide "assistance" to the survivors through a foundation set up by the South Korean government.

The agreement was welcomed by the major Western media and the U.S. government and politicians, but it was immediately rejected and denounced by the surviving Grandmas and their advocates. The problems with this agreement were that it addressed *none* of the seven demands that the Grandmas have been asserting in the past two and half decades as a way to properly resolve the "comfort women" issue, according to international standards. They are: 1. Full acknowledgement of the Japanese government's responsibility for the sexual enslavement of women for its military, 2. Official apology, 3. Direct, legal reparations, 4. Thorough investigation of the crime, 5. Prosecution of any surviving perpetrators, 6. Ongoing education in Japan's public schools, and 7. Building of museums and memorials. Rather, the agreement was an attempt to muzzle the victims and erase history by prohibiting the Korean government from advocating for the victims in international fora such as the UN, obligating the Korean government to not use the term "sex slave," and not supporting the overseas efforts to build "comfort women" memorials, and requiring it to try and remove the Peace Monument in front of the Japanese Embassy in Seoul. Another even greater problem was that no non-South Korean victims were included in the 2015 Agreement, which was brazenly declared a "final and irreversible" resolution of the issue with a 1 billion yen payment by the Japanese government. The surviving Grandmas in other countries such as China, the Philippines, and Taiwan were rightly outraged and demanded that the Japanese government properly resolve this issue for them.

The Japanese government turned a deaf ear to these demands. Instead, it took a two-faced approach and utilized this agreement to deny and downplay its responsibilities to the full extent. While the South Korean government dismantled all "comfort women" related research and programs following the 2015 Agreement, including the publication of White Pages and the subsidy to the efforts to register the "comfort women" dossier at UNESCO Memory of the World, the Japanese government launched a full-scale offensive in the UN and other international fora, including UNESCO. In 2017, Japan delayed the payment of the UNESCO dues to pressure the organization from accepting the "comfort women" dossier at its Memory of the World. Later in the same year, UNESCO announced that it will postpone the decision whether or not to accept the dossier, and recommended that the victim parties and the perpetrator party engage in a discussion to resolve differences in opinions. Japanese diplomats have argued that the "comfort women" were not sex slaves and that there is no evidence of coercion in the recruitment of the "comfort women." Whenever U.S. cities try to remember the victims through a small monument or resolution, the Consul General of Japan in the area, without failure, would lobby heavily against any and all such projects—in Glendale, CA, Fullerton, CA, Chicago, IL, Atlanta, GA, Brookhaven, GA, San Francisco, CA, Washington, D.C., in the United States and Freiburg, Germany. In 2017, while South Korea was going through a revolutionary democratic movement that impeached its scandal-ridden President Park Geun-hye, Prime Minister Abe recalled Japan's Ambassador to South Korea and the Consul General of the City of Busan, in protest of the new Peace Monument that was placed in front of the Japanese Consulate General in Busan. Also, the Japanese government submitted an *amicus curiae* brief at the U.S. Supreme

Court and argued that the removal of the Glendale Peace Monument was Japan's national core interest.

As of January 2018, the Japanese government under Prime Minister Abe's leadership seems to be as far as it can be from properly resolving the "comfort women" issue. Instead, it is escalating its efforts to deny, downplay, and erase this dark past from the memory of the world. Further, it has been proactively misusing the 2015 Agreement to silence the victims and erase this chapter of history, instead of acknowledging its past wrongdoing and pledging to eradicate such crime from the world.

Conclusion

In the past ten years of activism in search of justice for the Grandmas in the United States, we have learned that the role of grassroots efforts in the United States was one of the most essential elements that has had a huge impact in terms of pressuring Abe and Japan and its attempt to whitewash, deny, and cover up history. Having the battlefront open up in the United States—a "history war," as the *Sankei Shimbun* dubbed it—through all of the activities aforementioned in this paper may have been the single most important development for the "comfort women" movement. It has further elevated the issue on the global stage in support of the Grandmas and their efforts, and it has infused vigor to a movement led by South Koreans that appeared to have run out of ideas and energy to go on prior to 2007. In fact, according to the head of The Korean Council for the Women Drafted for the Military Sexual Slavery, the passage of H.Res. 121 "reinvigorated Korea's movement."

The United States is the strongest ally of Japan, and Japan is a key strategic ally of the U.S. in the Northeast Asian and Pacific Region. In the context of this geopolitical dynamic, the "comfort women" movement in the U.S. represents a serious threat to Japan and its positive public image as a friend of the U.S. and/or as a victim of the nuclear bombing by the U.S. that occurred at the end of World War II. This explains the Japanese government's strong—often absurd—reactions towards the public memorials, resolutions, and textbooks that teach the "comfort women" history in the United States. However, the U.S. has a long tradition and culture of standing on the side of the victims of human right issues, and the rising awareness in mainstream U.S. society has become the gravest concern for Japan and its efforts to deny history and to silence this issue once and for all.

Even in the United States, the true heroes and the driving engine of this movement were the courageous Grandmas who broke the silence, overcoming deeply embedded trauma, shame, and anguish. At the sunset of their lives, these Grandmas took long and exhausting flights to travel to the other side of the world to tell people about the horrors that they have endured. They did this not only for themselves, but for all victims of Japanese military sexual slavery who have passed away, who could not travel to foreign countries themselves, and who could not come to the Wednesday demonstrations. It is also important to note that I am not just talking about Korean women, but all victims, including those from China, Taiwan, Indonesia, East Timor, and the Philippines. Inspired by the overwhelming power of these activist Grandmas, the Korean American community throughout the United States raised its own understanding of the universal human rights and women's issue, turning that understanding into a positive and explosive energy in the grassroots movement to bring justice for the victims of Japanese military sexual slavery. Without the persistent and focused community-based grassroots activism led by the Korean American leaders and organizations, we wouldn't have seen many of our victories in the United States.

Then, what is to be done? The petitions, statements, monuments, press events, theater, art, and many other grassroots actions along with the Wednesday demonstrations in South Korea did a great deal to raise awareness about the issue around the world, but they weren't enough to pressure the Japanese government to sit down with any of the victims to own up to its past crimes. It was the pressure from the U.S. government, the closest ally of Japan, that pushed Japan to the negotiation table with the South Korean government. The effective grassroots activism in the U.S., combined with growing awareness in the international community and media, were major factors that led to the U.S. government's recognition and understanding of the importance of the issue.

Again, this is where the movement in the U.S. can exert great impact in the efforts to resolve this issue. In order to continuously put pressure on the Japanese government, we should support the various efforts in the public sector of the U.S. to remember and spread awareness and education about the "comfort women" issue by building memorials and museums, including it in textbooks, making films, and holding exhibits and international conferences. Also, it is crucial to work with the diverse victim communities in the United States, where all victim communities exist and thrive. We should also continue to work with our government and politicians from both sides of the aisle to urge Japan to overcome its shameful past by squarely facing it and accepting its historical responsibility, as urged in the H.Res. 121. The U.S. government brought long-awaited closure and healing to Japanese American citizens who were interned in camps during World War II by officially apologizing and passing a law in U.S. Congress. In the U.S., we commemorate this event through the annual Day of Remembrance, to remember and educate younger generations so we don't make the same mistake again. Also, the U.S. government has played a vital role as a mediator in negotiations of many complicated cases, such as the negotiation between victims of the Holocaust and the German government. Perhaps the U.S. may play a role in bringing the "comfort women" survivors and the Japanese government to a meaningful negotiation.

The South Korean government has a special obligation to provide leadership in resolving this issue, particularly with the election of President Moon Jae-in. President Moon replaced the impeached Park Geun-hye, who struck the secret 2015 deal with Japan. Thus far, since Moon was elected, the South Korean government has commendably announced that the 2015 deal did not resolve the "comfort women" issue according to the international standard. Furthermore, it has reasserted the nature of the issue as a universal human rights issue, and has urged the Japanese government to show its sincere intention to repent and apologize in a victim-centered manner. Like it or not, because of the 2015 Agreement, and the fact that it was the Korean Grandmas' fierce activism that attracted the attention from the international community, the South Korean government has been put in a position to represent the voices of the victims, and it was only proper and correct to announce that the government will make every effort to recover the victims' honor and dignity.

Ten years ago, no one could have imagined in their wildest dreams that there would be a beautiful and dignified statue of Asian women depicting a Korean, a Chinese, and a Filipina girl and the Grandma Kim Hak-sun in the heart of San Francisco. In addition, no one imagined that Japan would come to a negotiation table with any one of the victim countries to "resolve" the "comfort women" issue. With strong international solidarity that puts continuous pressure on Japan, the time when the Japanese government will sit down again at a negotiation table to resolve the "comfort women" issue may arrive more abruptly than we expect. When it does happen, we should be able to demand in unison that the Japanese government must come to the table with all victim countries, not with any one country. Also, we need to be ready to negotiate with the Japanese government to draw a comprehensive resolution of the "comfort women" issue according to the Grandmas' seven demands. Only then will the burden on the shoulders of the Grandmas be lifted, and they will be able to fly like butterflies.

Part III: **Legacies of "Comfort Women" in Arts**

Bonnie B.C. Oh
Legacies of "Comfort Women"

The Question of Legacies

"I don't have anything to give," Grandma Gil Won-ok, originally from Pyongyang, North Korea, said in *Apology*,[1] a docudrama on the "comfort women" of China, Korea and the Philippines. The film was recently screened at Northwestern University in Evanston, Illinois, and drew nearly 150 people on a fine late summer evening, when people of this cold-climate area would rather be outdoors in the last remaining days of the summer.

Such a sentiment that the "comfort women" were without value was widely shared at the beginning of the "comfort women" movement in 1992, when Mrs. Dongwoo Lee Hahm founded the Washington Coalition for the Comfort Women Issues, Inc. (WCCW). It was the same four years later, on the last day of September 1996, when Professor Margaret Stetz, I, the WCCW, and the Korea Society Washington Office (which is no longer in existence) co-convened the first academic conference on "comfort women" at Georgetown University. In fact, I must confess that I was a late convert in endowing value to "comfort women." As a conventional historian, I didn't see what Professor Stetz, a feminist scholar, saw—that the "comfort women" would have value, and therefore, legacies. She argued as follows, which she articulated in our co-edited volume, "To consider ... the 'comfort women' as having any legacy to give is to begin by assigning value to women who have been designated ... as without value ... To affirm their value now is in itself an act with broad, political implications. It *deliberately challenges* so-called racial hierarchies that allowed the Japanese ..."[2] Deliberately challenged we did! It was one of my most enlightening moments in my academic life. As a Korean native, raised in a genteel upper-middle class family, in which men were revered and husbands were supposed to be "so-ch'on, small heaven," challenging the established norm was not in my consciousness. I had to come out of the "box," which I did, and began to rethink. It was a delib-

---

[1] Anita Lee (producer), *The Apology*. Documentary film. Directed by Tiffany Hsiung. (Montreal, Quebec and New York, New York: National Film Board of Canada, 2016).
[2] Margaret Stetz and Bonnie B.C. Oh, "Introduction," *Legacies of the Comfort Women of World War II*, eds. Margaret Stetz and Bonnie B.C. Oh (Armonk, NY/London: M.E. Sharpe, 2001), xii, author's emphasis.

erate and conscious act. I adopted the feminist thinking of my esteemed colleague and together we forged ahead to plan our meeting.

We were forewarned of consequences of dealing with such an inconsequential but toxic subject, although I don't know how it can be toxic if it's inconsequential. We were not yet consciously building a field of study as a legacy, but soon it became clear that the movement would leave something behind.

The symposium was, quite unexpectedly, a phenomenal success, having significance far beyond the scope of an academic forum.[3] It appeared as though a logjam had been broken. Within a short time, scholars of various disciplines, students, and activists sponsored "comfort women"-related conferences, symposia, and discussion groups. There was not a major U.S. university that did not hold "comfort women" meetings. The U.S. Holocaust Museum and the Philadelphia Free Museum were just two among many that sponsored "comfort women" meetings.

A totally unanticipated result was that it even influenced the decision of the U.S. Department of Justice to issue a list of sixteen Japanese individuals on the "Watch List," who were prohibited from entering the United States.[4] Three of the sixteen had been involved in some aspects of the "comfort women" system during the Pacific War. On 4 December 1996, *The Washington Post* editorialized the DOJ decision.[5]

Another impact of the conference was that its proceedings became the basis for the first academic book on "comfort women." Following the forum, we responded to our colleague's plea that we edit a book from the conference proceedings. We solicited and added several extra scholarly pieces. In 2001, the book was published with the title, *Legacies of Comfort Women of World War II.*[6] Even then, five years after our conference, the soundness of our thinking was questioned about the title of the book. Legacies? What legacies—from "comfort women"? They were considered worthless and poor. What could they possibly leave behind? Now, over twenty-five years later, the question is not whether there are legacies, since it is very clear that there are. Rather, the more relevant

---

[3] It is given credit for having influenced the U.S. Department of Justice in issuing a list of Japanese war criminals from entering the United States. The decision was announced in an editorial in the *Washington Post,* December 4, 1996.

[4] John Y. Lee, "Placing Japanese War Criminals on the U.S. Justice Department's Watch List of 3 December 1996," in *Legacies of the Comfort Women of World War II,* eds. Margaret Stetz and Bonnie B.C. Oh, (Armonk, NY/London: M.E. Sharpe, 2001), 151–163.

[5] Washington Post Editorial, December 3, 1996.

[6] Stetz and Oh, *Legacies of the Comfort Women.*

questions are connected to the utility of discussing all of them, since they are so numerous.

In fact, their legacies are significantly abundant that it will not be possible to enumerate them all and engage in meaningful deliberations. Therefore, this chapter will focus on what will be, at least to me, the most enduring: developing and establishing educational materials and fields of study. It will focus on how delving into "comfort women" issues has facilitated the advancement of emerging and recently rising non-traditional academic fields in American higher education, such as women's studies, oral history, and interdisciplinary studies.

Women's Studies

The "comfort women" issues have taken up spaces in numerous, non-"comfort women"-focused conferences, especially those related to women's studies. In 2017, the prestigious Berkshire Conference on the History of Women, Genders, and Sexualities had several panels on the subject. It is fitting that discussions of this topic have been included in women's studies conferences, because without feminist thinking, scholarship, and activism, the silence of "comfort women" might have continued to this day. From total muteness of the victims and complete ignorance of the existence of the "comfort women" system, it has now become a subject of consideration, not just in academic institutions and fora, but also a heated issue among involved nations and international organizations.

In the political and international sphere, issues related to "comfort women," in particular, the erecting of statues and memorials, have caused a stalemate between South Korea and Japan. Since it has not been resolved even after 25 years, it might be considered a failure. On the other hand, as an area of academic discourse, it has been a phenomenal success. Few topics encompass such an amalgam of fields, ranging from humanities to the arts, and now even to social sciences and sciences.

No other field has contributed more in exposing the "comfort women" system than women's studies. When former "comfort woman" Kim Hak-sun (1924–1997)[7] broke her silence on 14 August 1991, forty-six years after the end of World War II and perhaps over a half-century after she had suffered, she was not alone. Next to her were representatives from the Korean Church Women United, the Ko-

---

7 Kim Hak-sun's face has become an iconic image of "comfort women." Her portrait is part of the permanent collection of the Illinois Holocaust Museum, Skokie, IL; Kim Hak-sun's name is sometimes Romanized as Kim Hak-soon, Kim Hak Soon, or Kim Hak-Sun.

rean Council for the Women Drafted for Military Sexual Slavery by Japan (hereafter, The Korean Council), and Professor Yun Jung-ok[8] of Ewha Womans[9] University. Professor Yun had been quietly uncovering, documenting, and recording the narratives of "comfort women's" experiences in the 1980s. In 1987, she came forward with definitive proof of the existence of the "comfort women" system and the victims. Most importantly, she, along with other early supporters, created a climate that enabled Kim Hak-sun to overcome her scruples, to break her long silence, and to make a public announcement that she had indeed been a former "comfort woman."

> Kim was born in 1924 in Jilin (Kirin) Province, Manchuria, but grew up in Pyongyang until she was seventeen, when her stepfather took her to China for business. Upon arriving in Beijing, the Japanese police arrested her father, and a Japanese military officer dragged her into an empty building and raped her. Thus began her life as a military sex slave. She managed to escape the "comfort women" facility in the company of an itinerant Korean merchant, who was twice her age and also abusive, citing her past as justification for his actions. She had two children, one of whom died soon after returning to Korea. Before she was 40, she was bereft of her family. Despondent and lonely, she attempted suicide more than once, but did not succeed in her attempts. For the next twenty years, she led an invisible life, roaming the countryside, drinking, and taking on odd jobs. In the early 1980s, she returned to Seoul, and worked as a domestic servant for several years. When she left the job due to a heart problem, she rented a room with a roommate, who was a volunteer for atom bomb victims. They shared stories of their hard life. Kim Hak-sun talked about her life as a "comfort woman." It was her roommate who informed the Korean Council, which had been established just a few months earlier.[10]

> The Korean Council, the Christian women, and Professor Yun encouraged Kim Hak-sun to speak out. Still she resisted. She could no longer endure hearing repeated Japanese denials of the existence of the "comfort women" system and refusal to take responsibility for it. She went to the Korean Council's office, which was then located in the Christian women's establishment. She first testified in July. Then, she met Yi Mi-kyung, former National Assembly woman, who urged her to announce on the media on 14 August 1991, the day before the

---

8 As early as the 1980s, before the "comfort women" system became known, Yun Jung-ok of Ewha Womans University explored and disclosed the "comfort women" system's existence; Yun Jung-ok's name is also sometimes Romanized as Yun Chong-ok, Yun Jeong-ok, Yun Chung-ok, or Yoon Chung-ok.

9 This is the official name of the university, not a typographical error.

10 This account is largely based on Kim Hak-sun's testimony, "Doe puri hagi jocha sirun kiuk dul [Memories that I hate to repeat]," *Gangjero Kkullyeogan Joseonin Gunwianbudeul* [The Forcibly Drafted Korean Comfort Women, Vol. 1], ed. The Korean Council for the Women Drafted for Military Sexual Slavery by Japan and The Research Institute for Chongshindae(Seoul: Hanul, 1993), 32–44.

Korean National Independence Day.[11] The rest is history. Kim could not have come forward on her own, had she not been encouraged and supported by scholars like Professor Yun and a group of supporters, such as the Korean Council.

As a professor of literature and a feminist scholar, Yun's approach characterized mutual relations rather than exclusivity, unlike the practices of other traditional fields, which were marked by competitiveness. She employed feminist methods of caring, nurturing, sharing, and mutual concerns. She also abided by the feminist principles of not accepting traditional conceptions and challenging pre-existing norms about women.[12]

By thus appropriating the "comfort women" issues as a field worthy of her exploration, research, and study, Yun endowed value to "comfort women," who had hitherto been considered without value. Kim Hak-sun was empowered by feminist principles, backed up by the long-time research of a credible scholar like Professor Yun. Thus, Kim Hak-sun gained sufficient confidence to present her story because she was deemed worthy and her story credible enough to be heard.

Testimony as Oral History[13]

Thus began the "comfort women" narrative, which was woven into the history of the Pacific War (1931–1945). Kim Hak-sun's account of her experiences as a "comfort woman" was quickly followed by numerous others, not just in South Korea, but also in all other victim countries that had been occupied by the Japanese military during the Pacific War. Their stories became part of previously non-existing collections of oral testimony. Their first-person accounts were the very first, essential, and only sources for constructing the narratives of the "comfort women" as a legitimate field of history.

In the case of "comfort women," not only were there no written histories of their ordeal, but even the existing documentation of the system they served under had been destroyed by the Japanese government to conceal evidence.[14] In-

---

11 Mee-hyang Yoon, the current president of the Korean Council, texted me the story on 9 January 2019.
12 Hunter College Women's Studies Collective, *Women's Realities, Women's Choices* (New York & Oxford: Oxford University Press, 1983), 5.
13 Joan Tumblety, *Memory and History: Understanding Memory as Source and Subject* (London/New York: Routledge, 2013).
14 Yoshiaki Yoshimi, *Comfort Women: Sexual Slavery in the Japanese Military During World War II*, trans. Suzanne O'Brien, (New York: Columbia University Press, 2000); Norimitsu Onishi, "In

itially, the only information on "comfort women" came from the accounts of "comfort women" survivors themselves. This is precisely the rationale that the current Japanese government is using; how can one believe the accounts of those lowly, worthless women, who were probably prostitutes?

But other people heard them differently. It was indeed the "comfort women" story that triggered the memory of Dr. Yoshimi Yoshiaki,[15] a Japanese historian at Chūō University. He had seen, in the Japanese Self-Defense Agency archives, something that might have been related to "comfort women." Because Professor Yoshimi Yoshiaki took "comfort women" oral accounts seriously, he was able to return to the documents he encountered earlier and began serious research. Thus, he became the first and foremost of numerous Japanese scholars on the "comfort women" subject. Once historians like him transcribe oral testimonies into writing, they become legitimate parts of written history.

The first edited volume of survivor testimonies, *Comfort Women Speak: Testimony by Sex Slaves of the Japanese Military*,[16] was published in 2000. Though the book was edited by Sangmi Choi Schellstede, it was actually the result of the labor-intensive efforts of Mrs. Dongwoo Lee Hahm, the founder and first president of WCCW (Washington Coalition for Comfort Women Issues). It is an emotional, empathetic, and affectionate rendering of aging former "comfort women." Interspersed with photos, it is a treasure trove of raw material and is indeed an invaluable primary source of history of "comfort women." This volume is an example of how oral testimonies, when transcribed, organized, edited, and placed in historical context, can become invaluable sources for proper and legitimately recognized history.

A recent compilation of oral narratives, *Can You Hear Us? The Untold Narratives of Comfort Women*,[17] is a more up-to-date example of oral presentations transformed into history proper. Victims were chosen according to their ability to give "credible memory among those who were able to give oral testimonies on their own."[18] Eleven of the oral testimonies were taken between 2005 and 2006, but one 90-year old victim reported as late as 2012, past the deadline

---

Japan, a Historian Stands by Proof of Wartime Sex Slavery," *New York Times*, March 31, 2007. Accessed February 27, 2019. https://www.nytimes.com/2007/03/31/world/asia/31yoshimi.html.
15 Yoshimi, *Comfort Women*; Onishi, "In Japan."
16 Sangmi Choi Schellstede, *Comfort Women Speak: Testimony by Sex Slaves of the Japanese Military* (New York/London: Holmes & Meier, 2000).
17 Jeff Jungho Lee, *Can You Hear Us?* (Seoul: Commission on Verification and Support for the Victims of Forced Mobilization under Japanese Colonization in Korea, 2014).
18 Ibid., 19.

for the project, and it had to be reported to the Ministry of Gender Equality and Family of the Republic of Korea.[19]

This 443-page book is more than just a collection of oral narratives; it also includes a summary of the 380 pages of testimonies of twelve victims, descriptions of their current status, the interviewer's postscript, a human rights movement activist's account, and the chronology of the worldwide "comfort women" redress movement, including the dates and locations of when and where "comfort women" memorials and statues have been installed.

The mode of presentation of *Can You Hear Us?* is also unique. It preserved the interview format of questions and answers. The questions are printed in red while the responses are in black, helping the reader to visualize the interview process. Except for one, neither the names nor photos of the survivors are revealed, but other specifics are provided in minute detail, such as family background, mode of recruitment, living conditions, vivid description of their victimization, and the route of their travel, which are marked in maps. Having the diagrams of travel was especially useful in visualizing and imagining the length of time, distances traversed, and ordeals that these women—who were young girls at the time of their coercion into Japanese military brothels—must have endured. Two maps from Lee's *Can You Hear Us?* show one victim's route of movement, and the other, the location of "comfort stations" spread out throughout the Pacific region.

Can You Hear Us? is an essential collection for up-to-date information on various aspects of "comfort women," their status, and their movement. It is also a classic example of oral history transitioning into history proper.

In the past half-century, the discipline of history has undergone a transformation. History is one of the oldest fields of scholarship. As such, it had been skewed to be narrow and rigid, considering the accounts of organized states' political history of establishment classes as the only legitimate material of study. Slowly, however, it had to accommodate rapidly changing social situations and expanded into economic and social histories of not only the ruling and well-to-do strata, but also of social groups and classes that had been neglected. This included social histories of the underclass. During this process, it quickly became evident that there were few written documents about under-represented and under-privileged groups, thus leading to the rise and importance of oral history.

In the United States, the field of oral history came into its own in the 1960s of the Civil Rights Movement and the 1970s of anti-Vietnam War activism. When

---

19 Ibid.

investigating "history from below,"[20] reporters, researchers, historians, and marginalized groups such as African Americans and recent immigrants, found little paper trail. Interviewing, recording, and transcribing of individuals' narratives were, often, the only way to construct stories. Doing so had a surprising advantage. It's often said that "Oral history has one great virtue over document-based research—its immediacy."[21] Studs Terkel, a Chicago-based radio journalist, was one of the first and best-known of oral historians.[22]

Despite the importance of personal narratives of "comfort women," however, the Japanese government continues to dismiss their veracity and their significance in constructing the narrative. The reason for this is not just because Japanese officials do not want to admit the involvement of their government in this system. It is also due to the Japanese government officials' refusal, first of all, to render *credibility* to "comfort women," whom they consider to be "insignificant," and secondly, to accept feminist principles, such as: 1) challenging existing norms and 2) endowing value to women, in general. Finally, Japanese government officials had not caught up with the importance of oral history as a legitimate historical inquiry, nor have they recognized or acknowledged that oral history significantly enhances the traditional historical discipline.

Interdisciplinary Studies

Interdisciplinary Studies also appeared in academia only since the 1970s. Still, most scholars from more traditional and well-established fields took a dim view of it until recently. In the late 1980s and early 1990s, I, as Assistant Dean, was in charge of the "Independent Studies" major at the University of Maryland, College Park. It was a program that entailed student-created majors, "independent" of existing traditional majors, such as history, political science, or sociology. Students would pull together courses from various disciplines and devise their own majors, such as "fish farming" and "environmental studies," when the latter terminology was hardly heard of. Despite the short history of the Independent Studies program, we graduated fifty students every semester and had our own graduation ceremonies. In addition, after graduation, students

---

20 A.L. Morton, *A People's History of England*, (New York: International Publishers, 1938); E.P. Thompson, "History from Below," *The Times Literary Supplement*, April 7, 1966; Howard Zinn, *A People's History of the United States* (New York: Harper and Row, 1990).
21 Tumblety, *Memory and History*, 20.
22 Ibid.

from our interdisciplinary program were hired in cutting-edge new fields in far greater numbers than students from traditional discipline majors.

Ethnomusicologist Joshua Pilzner's *Hearts of Pine*[23] is a quintessential example of interdisciplinary scholarship. Ethnomusicology, itself, is an interdisciplinary field, a fusion of ethnic studies, a subfield of anthropology and musicology, a relatively young field of scientific and historical study of music, theory, and the physical nature of the sound of music. And in his soulful book, Pilzner, a young white American man living in Canada, attempts to enter the minds of three old Asian, Korean women, through songs and by living with them off and on for several years. Even if Pilzner was not consciously crossing over disciplinary boundaries when he put his extraordinary experiences into writing, he had to draw widely from history, politics, social studies, and psychology, as well as from music and musicology.

Dai Sil Kim-Gibson also embodies the characteristics of a multi-disciplinary scholar. After many years as an associate in the National Endowment for the Humanities in Washington, D.C., she produced documentary films, such as *Sakhalin Koreans* (1995) and a "comfort women" docudrama, titled *Silence Broken: Korean Comfort Women* (2000). She also published *Silence Broken: Korean Comfort Women*, a book on Korean "comfort women" that preceded the film of the same name.[24]

In June 2017, Frank Joseph Shulman, a former colleague of mine at the University of Maryland, College Park and a long-time bibliographer, now retired, generously responded to my request and excerpted for me the "Entries for doctoral dissertation about comfort women" from the advanced draft of *The First Century of Doctoral Dissertations on Korea, 1903–2004*.[25] It is a comprehensive, multidisciplinary, descriptively annotated, subject classified, chronologically arranged, cross-referenced, and very extensively indexed bibliography of 14,855 Western-language (Czech, Dutch, English, French, German, Hebrew, Hungarian, Italian, Latin, Polish, Portuguese, Russian, Spanish, Swedish, Turkish, and Ukrainian) dissertations that deal in their entirety or just in part with Korea.

---

23 Joshua D. Pilzner, *Hearts of Pine: Songs in the Lives of Three Korean Survivors of the Japanese "Comfort Women"* (Oxford: Oxford University Press, 2011).
24 Dai Sil Kim-Gibson, *Silence Broken: Korean Comfort Women* (Parkersburg, IA: Mid-Prarie Books, 1999).
25 Frank Joseph Shulman, *An Annotated Bibliography of Studies in Western Languages Concerned in Their Entirety or in Part with Korea*; Accompanied by notes about the academic backgrounds and Master's theses of many of the authors. Forewords by Young-Key Kim-Renaud, William B. McCloy, and Robert C. Provine (2017).

There were thirty-two doctoral dissertations that dealt exclusively, mostly, or partly with "comfort women." The ethnic origins of the authors were as diverse as their fields: Korean (10), American (6), Japanese (4), Chinese (4), German (4), Canadian (1), Thai (1), English (1), and Vietnamese (1). It was even more difficult to put their dissertation topics into disciplinary categories because they represented even more varied fields: literature (9), Asian American studies (6), women and gender studies (3), international studies (3), theology (3), history (2), political science (2), East Asian studies (1), art (1), Japanese studies (1), and ethno-biography (1). Thus said though, it was clear to me that this cataloguing was done according to the field of the respective supervising faculty members and did not do justice to the true content of the actual dissertations.

One dissertation, only partially dealing with "comfort women," attracted my attention.[26] The author was a woman of Korean origin, Soyang Park, studying at the University of London, and was receiving her degree in historical and cultural studies. Dealing with works by various artists and filmmakers, including Byeon Yeong-ju/Byun Youngjoo (*Murmuring*, a "comfort women" movie), Park "examined how the emergent culture—a 'visual culture of haunting'—was instigated and formed by numerous haunted subjects and the return of repressed memories." Her study also explored "how repressed and silenced 'subaltern' groups, especially the former Korean comfort women, gradually came into historical light as they provided their testimonies in this emergent cultural and political milieu."[27]

So, here is a young female scholar working in literature, receiving a degree in historical and cultural studies, examining the works of artists and filmmakers dealing with haunted subjects and repressed memories. Her work alone covers several traditionally boxed-in disciplines, such as history, literature, art, psychology, and perhaps more.

Similarly, one could not understand the complex experiences of "comfort women" by simply steeping in a single discipline. It is a multi-faceted endeavor. We must transcribe their testimonies from their memory, put them into historical context, endeavor to comprehend what they remember, what they don't, and why. We need to understand how memories function in the brains of old women, especially those with severe trauma, and the "comfort women's" experiences were certainly traumas. Scholars, journalists, or novelists must go far beyond the disciplinary boundaries of history and other humanities and encom-

---

26 Soyang Park, "The Visual Culture of Haunting in Post Colonial Korea," Originally submitted under the title "The Visual Culture of Haunting: The Ethics and Aesthetics of the Real in Modern South Korea," (Ph.D. diss., University of London, 2004).
27 Ibid.

pass social sciences, arts, music, and even cognitive psychology and neurosciences.

More recently, Jungsil Julie Lee, the current president of the Washington Coalition for Comfort Women Issues (WCCW), conducted a Webinar course. As many disciplines were represented as the number of weeks (10) it covered. It was truly an interdisciplinary course. Because of the involvement of an art historian like Lee (who has a Ph.D. in art history), art and art history have become integral parts of understanding "comfort women" issues. She has curated a number of exhibits on "comfort women;" in 2014, at the Catholic University of America in Washington, D.C., among others, and most recently in June and July of 2017, a series of four-city itinerant shows in South Korea. These were truly interdisciplinary exhibits, featuring artwork and artifacts of many varieties, including maps, historical documents of recruitment orders, daily logs, notebooks, currencies of the time, the iconic artwork[28] of Hung Liu (which features images of "comfort women"), and of course, the exhibit also featured photos of "comfort women" memorials and statues.

Throughout many parts of North America, interdisciplinary educational materials on "comfort women" are also in preparation for a number of public school systems. In Chicago, for example, a retired teacher and an administrator in the Chicago public school system, have started collecting materials with a view to hold seminars for teachers.

Conclusion

After a quarter century of activist movement and slow but steady theorization, the basic facts of the "comfort women" issues are well-known. These facts are a composite of uncovering of hidden documents, journalists' accounts, and testimonies of "comfort women." All three of these components are essential in constructing "comfort women" narratives. The most disputed are the testimonies, as the Japanese government continues its attempts to challenge their historical veracity.

Nonetheless, "comfort women" testimonies have now become archival documentation, the most valued of traditional historians' sources. It began early in

---

28 Hung Liu, *Strange Fruit* (comfort women), 2001, oil on canvas, 80 x 160 inches. Based on a photograph taken by the Chinese American Allied forces in September 1944 in China. It didn't include the Japanese soldiers in the photo but emphasized unique characterization and expression of individual "comfort women." Description in Korean by Jungsil Julie Lee for the exhibit in Seoul, July 2017.

the history of "comfort women"—in 1973, with the publication of *Military Comfort Women* (*Jūgun-ianfu*) by Senda Kakō, a wartime Japanese journalist. Senda's story might have been too fantastic to believe. Almost a decade and a half would pass before two scholars, Yun Jung-ok of South Korea in the late 1980s and Yoshimi Yoshiaki of Japan in the early 1990s, appeared with their research results.

At present, only 37 of 238 "comfort women" survivors, originally registered with the South Korean government, are living in South Korea. It will not be long before all of them will no longer be with us. Even when none of them are on this earth, we will have many of their legacies: their stories will have been carved in our brains, of their painful pasts, their resilience, and their untiring participation in their movement, including over a thousand weekly Wednesday noontime demonstrations in front of the Japanese Embassy in Seoul, and traveling overseas, like Grandma Lee Yong-soo, to present their testimonies to international audiences.

We have begun to hear the words, "comfort women studies." In time, if not already, it will become a recognized field of study. When a student goes into it, he/she will not be limited to only studying specific disciplines such as history, arts, literature, politics, science, and international relations.

Japan, under Prime Minister Abe, can agitate all it wants and deny the "comfort women" system ever existed. But the legacies of "comfort women" are now part of human and world history, as issues of women's rights, of human rights, and as crimes against humanity. Most of all, we will remember them because future generations of students, scholars, and the general public will learn about them through women's studies, history, and interdisciplinary studies of "comfort women studies." Learning about "comfort women" will measurably enhance and enrich their lives. This is my fondest hope.

Margaret D. Stetz
Making Girl Victims Visible: A Survey of Representations That Have Circulated in the West

In a 2017 volume of essays titled *The Big Push*, the feminist political scientist Cynthia Enloe reminds readers of the importance of language in shaping thought and, therefore, in shaping governmental and non-governmental policy-making in the field of human rights. She draws her example from recent controversies over the plight of refugees from the conflict in Syria—controversies, as she points out, that have also involved the subject of so-called "child marriage" in refugee communities. That very way of naming the problem affects both attitudes toward it and the kinds of initiatives being proposed, for by "adopting the phrase 'child marriages,' one is suggesting that boys are just as likely as girls to be married while still in their childhood, and this is not true"[1]; instead, as she makes clear, "in reality, these are not 'child marriages.' They are *girl* marriages."[2] Why does this matter? As Enloe asserts, "[e]ach of us helps to sustain patriarchal ideas and practices when we hide the workings of gendered inequities behind a curtain of ungendered language," and this has significant consequences in terms of action or inaction, as well as in terms of who will ultimately benefit or lose out.[3]

Almost from the first moment when, in the early 1990s, reports began appearing in the West about the organized system of war crimes that were committed against Asian women during the Second World War by the Japanese Imperial Army, this subject has been inextricably bound up with the issue of language, and of what language makes visible or invisible. On 28 November 2014, the online *Bloomberg News* reported that the *Yomiuri Shimbun*—one of the major national daily newspapers published in Japan—had just issued an apology to its readers for using "the term 'sex slaves' in stories about Asian women trafficked to Japanese military brothels before and during World War II."[4] That same U.S.

---

[1] Cynthia Enloe, *The Big Push: Exposing and Challenging the Persistence of Patriarchy* (Berkeley: University of California Press, 2017), 15.
[2] Ibid. 16; italics in original.
[3] Ibid.
[4] Isabel Reynolds, "Japan's Biggest Newspaper Apologizes for 'Sex Slave' Stories." *Bloomberg News*, November 28, 2014. Accessed February 27, 2019. https://www.bloomberg.com/news/articles/2014-11-28/japan-s-biggest-newspaper-apologizes-for-sex-slave-stories.

news source went on to include the reaction of an unnamed "official at the South Korean foreign ministry" who raised objections to the alternative euphemism: "Japan's refusal to use the term 'sexual slavery' and forcing the international community to use the ambiguous term 'comfort women' distorts the core of the problem and can only be seen as an effort to whitewash its past mistakes."[5] Of course, some of the other ways of referring to these victims that have circulated in the West—especially the terms preferred by Japanese nationalists—have been even more offensive, as well as misleading. As recently as 17 March 2015, the *Washington Post* detailed the efforts of a "group of Japanese historians and academics" to persuade the American firm of McGraw-Hill, publishers of a college-level history textbook, to remove all mentions of the so-called "comfort women" as having been "forcibly recruited" and to accept and reflect instead their notion that "the women were simply prostitutes" and thus volunteers, allegedly responsible for their own sexual exploitation.[6]

Even if one rejects the false idea that these victims were "simply prostitutes" and chooses between either "military sex slaves" or "comfort women"—the two English phrases most common in Western political discourse—there is, however, still an inherent problem. As Cynthia Enloe helps us to recognize, a category such as "military sex slaves" is, like "child marriage," ungendered; thus, it obscures the workings of gender inequities in having underpinned and supported the atrocities in question, which were designed to target and to subjugate female victims on a large scale. But the alternative phrase, "comfort women," also masks and encourages us to overlook a different reality. The so-called "comfort system" was built on the organized sexual assault of underage girls, who were often the preferred victims in this governmentally approved plan for the mass trafficking, forcible confinement, and exploitation of their bodies by Japanese soldiers in war zones. That so many of the Korean, Chinese, Filipina, Indonesian, and other Asian survivors who have testified about their experiences were between the ages of twelve and nineteen when they were imprisoned in brothels for use by the Japanese military demonstrates that this was no anomaly. It was instead a deliberate strategy that, among other things, ensured a greater power differential between the girl captives and the men who, on a daily basis, raped them, even when the latter were young soldiers themselves. It made the girl victims more vulnerable and thus easier to intimidate and to man-

---

5 Ibid.
6 Anna Fifield, "Japanese Historians Contest Textbook's Description of 'Comfort Women,'" *Washington Post*, March 17, 2015. Accessed February 27, 2019. https://www.washingtonpost.com/world/japanese-historians-contest-textbooks-description-of-comfort-women/2015/03/17/6e5422e3-09a3-4d96-a520-8a5767ab93e4_story.html?utm_term=.1bcd334d8c57

age. As mere girl children and adolescents, they were less resourceful, less knowledgeable in general, and less likely to plan or survive escapes or to be equipped to plot rebellion.

In terms of political ramifications, moreover, targeting underage girls was an advantageous move and a low-risk decision for the Japanese officials who made it, for in almost every culture around the world, young girls—those not yet wives or mothers—have long been considered the least valuable and most expendable members of families and of society as a whole. That is nearly as true today as it was in the 1930s and 1940s. The removal and the disappearance of large numbers of girls has always been less likely to incite mass uprisings than the taking of any other population. Not surprisingly, in the case of the "comfort system," it was the survivors themselves and their allies in the human rights sphere, rather than their home communities or their governments, who had to come forward in the early 1990s to lodge the first protests, as well as to initiate the calls for official apologies and reparations from the Japanese government. Scholars have pointed to the factor of class, given the lower-class status of many of those subject to the "comfort system," as influencing the lack of widespread public outrage and the seeming indifference to these girls' fates across Asia and the West, during that long period between 1945 and 1991, before Kim Hak-sun's testimony.[7] But we cannot discount the fact that girl children have never embodied the same degree of what is known as "social capital" as the so-called "sons of a nation." Girls were and are considered of lesser worth to their own societies and to the world as a whole.

At certain moments in history, representations of young girls as victims of sexual assault and exploitation by military forces have been created and disseminated in the West, and these have, in fact, provoked strong reactions. This is not necessarily a sign, however, that the welfare of girls themselves has ever been of great concern; rather, images of helpless girl children attacked by monstrous enemy soldiers sometimes have proven useful for achieving specific political ends, unrelated to any interest in the welfare of the victims themselves. From April through October 2017, for instance, visitors to the Museum of the City of New York were shown, in an exhibition titled *Posters and Patriotism: Selling WWI in New York*, an excellent example of this phenomenon. A well-known 1918 poster by the American artist Ellsworth Young (1866–1952), promoting the sale of bonds to support the war in Europe (which the U.S. had entered one year earlier), featured the warning, "Remember Belgium." Beneath these

---

[7] Margaret D. Stetz and Bonnie B. C. Oh, "Introduction," in *Legacies of the Comfort Women of World War II*, eds. Margaret Stetz and Bonnie B. C. Oh (Armonk, NY: M.E. Sharpe, 1999), xii.

words the artist had depicted the silhouettes of two figures: a large, adult male German soldier wielding his phallic gun with one hand and, with the other hand, dragging behind him a young girl with long, loosened hair—clearly carrying her away for the purpose of rape.[8] As Susan Kingsley Kent explains in *Gender and Power in Britain, 1640–1990*, similar images had originated in Britain in 1915, as fuel for the "efforts to legitimate and justify the war itself."[9] Thus the "official propaganda presented the war as a fight for, and on behalf of, Belgium, casting Belgium in the role of a violated maiden left to die by cruel, inhuman invaders."[10] The focus was less on the experiences of any actual young Belgian girls who may have been subject to sexual assault, and more on the political need to personify the Belgian nation as feminized and helpless, as well as the German military as, in contrast, brutal and dangerously animalistic. When considering, therefore, some of the visual representations of recruitment and forcible confinement of underage Asian girls by the Japanese Imperial Army that have circulated over the course of nearly three decades, we must be cognizant of this history—a history, at least in the West, of making girl victims in general visible *not* for their own sake, in acknowledgment of their individual human value, but purely for their political utility as symbols.

Since the early 1990s, when reports reached the West of the testimony by Kim Hak-sun and other survivors—many of whom spoke of being forced into the "comfort system" before their bodies had even reached the point of first menstruation and sexual maturity—a wide variety of non-visual, literary representations have been made available to English-speaking audiences. Many of them have featured young protagonists. These have included memoirs, such as Maria Rosa Henson's *Comfort Woman* (1999), along with mass-market fictional texts, such as William Andrews's novel, *Daughters of the Dragon: A Comfort Woman's Story* (2014)—both of which concentrate on the perspectives of girls who were fourteen-years-old when first raped by Japanese soldiers and imprisoned in military brothels. While American literary fiction has continued to be a frequent vehicle for the stories of adolescent "comfort system" victims, works such as Therese Park's *A Gift of the Emperor* (1997) and Roger Rudick's *Story of a Comfort Girl* (2012) have not circulated as extensively as the visual images created by filmmakers, nor have they exercised as potent an influence. Visual representations enjoy an unmatched immediacy, whether audiences in the

---

[8] *Posters and Patriotism: Selling WWI in New York*, Exhibition, Museum of the City of New York (2017). Accessed February 27, 2019. http://collections-static-7.mcny.org/Gallery/24UAKVKMVASC.
[9] Susan Kingsley Kent, *Gender and Power in Britain, 1640–1990* (London and New York: Routledge, 1999), 273.
[10] Ibid.

U.S. encounter them through the medium of network television or as feature films that are streamed on their home computers or shown in cinemas.

Indeed, the one representation related to the "comfort system" likely to have been viewed by the greatest number of people across the U.S. was "Open Wounds," a roughly seven-minute-long segment of the popular weekly TV news magazine, *CBS Sunday Morning*. Produced by Marsha Cooke and Marisa Pearl, "Open Wounds," which was broadcast around the nation via one of the main television networks on the morning of 18 March 2007 and then archived on the program's website (as "Japan's Comfort Women Fight for Justice" by Caitlin Johnson), was occasioned by Congressional hearings that led to the passage, on 30 July 2007, of House Resolution 121 by the U.S. House of Representatives. This groundbreaking Resolution, authored by Rep. Michael ("Mike") Honda of California, called on the Japanese government to "formally acknowledge, apologize, and accept historical responsibility" for what it described as the "coercion of young women into sexual slavery."[11] The *CBS Sunday Morning* feature began with a few stills drawn from the now-familiar images of small groups of "comfort system" survivors—a sparse handful of documentary photographs that were taken immediately after the end of the Second World War and preserved. (It did not, however, reproduce any of the illuminating autobiographical paintings or drawings created by survivors, in which they have depicted themselves as girl children or adolescents—images that have been displayed at the War and Women's Rights Museum in Seoul).

In the photographs shown onscreen, it was impossible to tell precisely how old those whose presence in the liberated "comfort stations" was recorded by the camera in 1945 actually were. But the producers of this television segment did not let the issue of age go unremarked. One of the now-elderly survivors who briefly spoke on camera, near the start of the report, was Virginia Villarama, a Filipina victim of the "comfort system," who declared (in an English voiceover translation), "[t]hey," meaning the Japanese military, "destroyed our lives. We have no bright tomorrows because of what they did to us."[12] Before she uttered those words, Barry Peterson, the CBS news correspondent who served as narrator, had announced, "Virginia Villarama was fourteen."[13] It certainly would have

---

[11] Mike Honda, "Time for Abe to Apologize, Properly," CNN.com, April 29, 2015. Accessed February 27, 2019. https://edition.cnn.com/2015/04/28/opinions/honda-abe-comfort-women-issue/index.html.

[12] Caitlin Johnson, "Japan's Comfort Women Fight for Justice," CBS Sunday Morning, March 18, 2007. Accessed February 27, 2019. https://www.cbsnews.com/news/japans-comfort-woman-fight-for-justice/.

[13] Ibid,

been clear, therefore, to viewers of this segment that a fourteen-year-old was by no means a "comfort *woman*," and that the issue at hand was one that had involved child rape—or, with Cynthia Enloe's proviso about gendered language in mind, the rape of *girl children*. In this part of "Open Wounds," moreover, the focus was, both literally and figuratively, on Virginia Villarama—not only as she appeared in 2007, while denouncing the war crimes committed against her and others, but as she appeared while still a girl, for the screen filled with the poignant black-and-white image of her young self. Unlike the generic silhouette of the First World War Belgian rape victim, which existed as a mere prop and stand-in for a larger argument, Virginia Villarama was allowed, if only briefly in this news report, to impress upon the audience the sense of her existence as a unique individual, while also speaking of the collective suffering shared by many in her situation.

Yet, admirable as the sensitivity of the producers of this 2007 TV news segment may have been, their approach still fell into the trap that Dai Sil Kim-Gibson had outlined nearly twenty years earlier in her important 1999 volume, *Silence Broken: Korean Comfort Women*. As she warned there, the form that attention to the survivors takes often risks being reductive: "It is as if their existence is justified solely by the horrendous years they suffered; nothing before or after that seems to matter. ... They have largely become issues, numbers, things, and objects of studies, not full blooded human beings."[14] From "Open Wounds," viewers did learn that many of the victims of the "comfort system" were underage girls. They did not, however, learn anything about the lives of the girls at the time when they were targeted for this war crime, or about how the experience of it at such a young age affected all that followed.

Dai Sil Kim-Gibson herself had tried to counter this limited form of representation, not only in her book, but in a 1999 documentary film with the same title, *Silence Broken*, that aired in the U.S. on PBS television, the network of the Corporation for Public Broadcasting, in the year 2000. The televised version of Kim-Gibson's film, however, had to be edited drastically to approximately one hour in length, which meant the removal of a great deal of footage. Much of what was cut involved docudrama—that is, staged re-enactments of episodes from the lives and experiences of "comfort system" survivors. Thus, some of the dramatic impact of making visible the visceral experience of what it meant to be a very young girl living through horrendous war crimes was lost. Nonetheless, the edited version retained the footage of interviews with survivors, including Kim Hak-

---

[14] Dai Sil Kim-Gibson, *Silence Broken: Korean Comfort Women* (Parkersburg, IA: Mid-Prairie Books, 1999), 9.

sun, who came alive onscreen as fully realized individuals, with powerful personalities. So, too, the shortened documentary repeatedly underscored the age at which girls had been victimized, with one of the elderly speakers testifying to having been only twelve-years-old when she was taken, and saying of others, "[s]ome of them looked twelve, thirteen, fourteen, fifteen. Such young children."[15]

In recent years, human rights activists have been paying greater attention to the sex trafficking of children, while feminist activists have highlighted the trafficking of girl children, bringing these to light as ongoing global problems. At the same time, this enhanced awareness has encouraged representations of the issue not only as a violation of law that must be recognized and eradicated in the present, but as one with historical roots—as a crime that occurred in the past, then was left unaddressed and unresolved. In terms of the circulation of visual images related to the "comfort system" of World War II, this new concern has certainly helped to spur and to shape contemporary representations of the victims as underage girls.

Through South Korean feature films, in particular, screenwriters and directors are dramatizing what it meant to be a girl child subjected to sexual enslavement by the Japanese military; what the fates were of those taken away and exploited; and also what the impact has been on the later lives of those who survived. These films are now receiving wider distribution in the West, as well, through screenings on campuses, in theaters, and through the circulation of DVDs with English subtitles. Hand-in-hand with the increased dissemination of these images, and certainly as no mere coincidence, has come a shift in language, with the phrase "comfort women" often being supplemented and even supplanted by the words "women and girls" or just "young girls" alone, especially in journalistic discourse.

Among the influential visual representations that have reached Western audiences through mass and popular culture are two feature-length commercial films: *Spirits' Homecoming*[16] from 2016, written and directed by Cho Jung-Rae; and *Snowy Road*,[17] written by Yoo Bo-Ra and directed by Lee Na-Jeong. (The latter was released theatrically in 2017, after having first aired in 2015 as a drama on South Korean television.) These two films have much in common, as well as

---

15 *Silence Broken: Korean Comfort Women*. Documentary film, directed by Dai Sil Kim-Gibson (Ho-Ho-Kus, NJ: Dai Sil Productions, 2000).
16 *Spirits' Homecoming*. Film, directed by Cho Jung-Rae (Seoul, South Korea: Jo Entertainment, 2016).
17 *Snowy Road*. Film, directed by Lee Na-Jeong (Seoul, South Korea: KBS at9 Films, 2015).

some interesting differences, in terms of what they make visible about Japanese military sexual slavery and about those who did or did not survive it.

Both *Spirits' Homecoming* and *Snowy Road* interweave the past and the present. Each film features a female protagonist who is now an elderly woman and who, after having lived for decades with the secret of her history as a survivor of the "comfort system," is at last compelled to confront it. Each protagonist lives alone but, in the course of the action, forms a bond with an adolescent girl who is in some way an outsider or outcast. In the case of *Spirits' Homecoming*, the young girl is herself the survivor of a criminal assault, who has subsequently developed psychic powers as a spirit medium, and who is brought by the "comfort system" survivor into her own home. In *Snowy Road*, the aged woman rescues a seventeen-year-old school dropout, living on her own, who has fallen into the hands of a pimp, and who has been subject to sexual exploitation and beatings by an adult male customer. We see, therefore, both of these survivors of Japanese military sex slavery as highly positive figures who function as moral agents; they are women concerned not only with exposing the crimes of the past, but with concrete, personal activism in the present, especially on behalf of at-risk girls.

In both films, too, the present is juxtaposed and intercut with recreations of life in the Second World War, when the two protagonists were young girls themselves. *Spirits' Homecoming* focuses on a girl who was fourteen years old, when she was violently torn from her parents in rural Korea and shipped to a "comfort station" in China. *Snowy Road* does not refer to its protagonist's precise age in 1943, at the time of her recruitment under false pretenses, but has the main character played by a very young teenaged performer. *Spirits' Homecoming* differs from *Snowy Road* in re-enacting explicitly the rapes of the protagonist and of the other underage girls in the "comfort station," while the latter film merely alludes to them. Both films, however, dramatize the brutal beatings of girls throughout their imprisonment in military brothels, making it plain how much violence was involved in keeping them there against their will. So, too, both films depict the disposal, at the end of the War, of the now-inconvenient evidence of this war crime through mass executions by Japanese soldiers of the girls in the battlefront "comfort stations," as well as, in each case, the fortunate escape of the protagonist, in the company of a female friend who ultimately does not survive.

Each film could, of course, be accused of heightened melodrama or of sentimentality in its representations of suffering girl children; yet each also offers an effective and powerful historical recreation of testimony that has been given by actual "comfort system" survivors. In so doing, these films put a face—individual, detailed, and impossible to forget—on the present-day issue of the movement for official apologies and redress. The face is not that of a so-called "comfort woman," or of an undifferentiated "military sex slave," but of a particular underage girl. This image does not replace the one already burned into the popular Western imagination, of groups of elderly survivors demanding their human rights and legal rights; instead, it stands alongside it and enriches it.

Western audiences can perhaps see this dual focus illustrated most clearly in *Spirits' Homecoming* (*Gwi-Hyang*, in Korean)—which, of the two films, has received the wider distribution and was even the subject of an article in the *New York Times*, several months in advance of its U.S. premiere.[18] Unlike *Snowy Road*, Cho Jung-Rae's film opens not in the world of historical fiction, but of historical documentary, with these words: "Taken when I was seventeen years old. I cannot talk about all of it. I cannot express in words."[19] So reads the onscreen English translation that accompanies an image of the late Kim Hak-sun recorded in 1991, as she testified in Seoul about her years as a military sex slave for the Imperial Japanese Army during World War II. In *Spirits' Homecoming*, which begins with Kim's voice and then face, it is not only the cinema audience today that observes her in the process of making these statements. Also watching in the year 1991, via a small television set, is the film's fictional protagonist, an elderly Korean woman who is engaged in sewing at home. As the camera cuts between the televised face of Kim, bearing witness, and that of the unidentified woman, it is clear that the latter is deeply affected by what she hears and, as the film's viewers will soon see, by the memories that she, too, has repressed for nearly fifty years.

The rest of the 127 minutes of *Spirits' Homecoming* shows why this testimony is so distressing to this particular fictionalized woman, even as it illustrates what Kim suggests here—that no single survivor could or should be expected to describe fully what it was like to live through imprisonment in a Japanese wartime military brothel. Cho's film is dedicated to the idea that there was more to this history, as Kim herself stated, than mere words can convey, but also, that the inhumane treatment Kim endured at the age of seventeen was far from unique. The visual and aural medium of film becomes a way both to transmit the general outline of historical fact and, in effect, to embroider upon it the details of personal experience—to re-envision the past and to make tangible its emotional weight, through the creation of a set of imaginary, yet representative, characters who undergo what Kim Hak-sun and others like her did, at a similarly early age. These individual stories reflect the sufferings of the many girls who did not survive the

---

18 Amy Qin, "From Cho Junglae [sic], a Film on Japanese Wartime Brothels." *New York Times*, March 24, 2015. Accessed February 27, 2019. https://www.nytimes.com/2015/03/25/movies/from-cho-junglae-a-film-on-japanese-wartime-brothels.html.
19 *Spirits' Homecoming*, 2016.

daily rapes, beatings, and other atrocities in military "comfort stations," as well as of the few who did, and who maintained decades of silence, because their accounts were unwelcome not only by subsequent Japanese governments, but by their own Korean communities. The conclusion of Cho's screenplay will emphasize to cinematic audiences their need to bring home, in both a literal and a figurative sense, the souls of these young victims who were forgotten or otherwise made spiritually homeless through cultural and political exclusion, especially during the postwar years.

As a period drama, *Spirits' Homecoming* does not come with the precise truth-bearing claims of a documentary—any more than, for instance, Steven Spielberg's 1993 *Schindler's List* did, in its depiction of Holocaust experience. Yet this film grounds itself throughout in the testimony of Korean survivors of Japan's "comfort system"—perhaps most importantly in its emphasis on the extremely young age of those who were the targets of organized military sexual slavery—and thus it enters the fray of current international conflicts over the legal status of these gendered war crimes, as well as over the question of what it will take to heal the still open political and personal wounds left by them. It is a work of cinema engagé—of art taking on the imperative of a moral mission. The "homecoming" to which it points as a solution depends, in the end, less upon governmental or diplomatic action between Japan and South Korea than upon contemporary audiences—and especially on young people—acknowledging and weaving into the fabric of present-day life those, whether living or dead, who were victimized and whose fates were treated for many years as a shameful matter, never to be spoken about. In what seems, moreover, an admirable example of feminist polemical filmmaking on the part of its male creator, the screenplay endows an otherwise culturally marginal figure—a teen-aged girl, acting as a shaman in 1991 to channel the spirits of the long-dead victims, who were also underage girls—with the greatest power to effect a communal reconciliation for the good of the Korean nation and ultimately for the world as a whole.

In an interview with the *Korea Times* in March 2016, shortly after the release of *Spirits' Homecoming*, the writer-director Cho Jung-Rae explained that he was inspired to make this film by his acquaintance, over a decade earlier, with one of the few remaining Korean survivors of the "comfort system," Kang Il-Chul. When he met her at the "House of Sharing," the group residence outside Seoul, he saw the drawing she had made of an event from 1945—a time when the Japanese military was facing defeat, in retreat from its outposts across Asia, and aware of the need to destroy the evidence of its wartime misdeeds: "The picture . . . depicted a group of hanbok-clad Korean comfort women set on fire alive, with armed Japanese soldiers guarding them against fleeing."[20] That image, which continued to haunt him, later resulted in his staging of a related scene near the conclusion of his film. The fictional protagonist becomes a witness-participant, as she and the dear friend she has made—another young Korean who was also trafficked in 1943 to a "comfort station" in Jilin province, China—are, at the end of the war, brought by Japanese soldiers to a pit where they are to be shot and buried, along with other military sex slaves. They are saved from mass execution, however, by the timely and quite miraculous intervention of Korean soldiers, who attack and kill the Japanese troops, although one Japanese officer does succeed in fatally wounding the protagonist's friend just as she is about to escape. It is obvious here that, as a filmmaker, Cho Jung-Rae has taken liberties (some might say melodramatic liberties) with the particulars that Kang Il-Chul depicted in her drawing, while giving them powerful emotional resonance by involving viewers in the fate of two individual fictional characters.

Spirits' Homecoming, nonetheless, has been faithful in a different way to its origins in survivor testimony. Kang Il-Chul's own story, as recorded in 2008 by a correspondent for the UK-based newspaper, the *Independent*, also included an account of having been taken from Korea and shipped to a "comfort station" in Manchuria, when she was only fifteen years old. As she told the British reporter, "On her second night, before her first menstruation, she was raped. Soldiers lined up night after night," and she was left with "scars below her neck from cigarette burns," as well as a lifetime of pain in her head "from a beating ... at the hands of a Japanese officer."[21] The article in the *Independent* made plain that, according to a spokesperson from Amnesty International, this was no anomaly: "Thousands of Asian women—some as young as 12—were 'enslaved ... and repeatedly raped, tortured and brutalised [sic] for months and years."[22]

What gives these war crimes a special degree of horror, both in actuality and in Cho Jung-Rae's 2016 dramatized recreation of them—where the two fictional characters whom we follow are aged fourteen and fifteen, during their first experience of sexual assault—is that they frequently involved victims who could not have been defined legally as women, whether at the time of the Second World War or today, even under Japanese law. Despite the continued insistence on

---

[20] Si-Soo Park and Da-Hee Kim. "A Movie Made to Heal Tortured Souls of 'Comfort Women,'" *The Korea Times*, March 2, 2016. Accessed February 27, 2019. https://www.koreatimes.co.kr/www/news/culture/2016/03/141_199491.html.

[21] David McNeill, "Korea's 'Comfort Women': The Slaves' Revolt," *Independent*, April 23, 2008. Accessed February 27, 2019. http://www.independent.co.uk/news/world/asia/koreas-comfort-women-the-slaves-revolt-814763.html.

[22] Ibid.

the part of Japanese nationalist right-wing factions that the occupants of the military "comfort stations" were actually well-paid prostitutes, who had volunteered to perform sex work for the Japanese Imperial Army, the fact that so many were too young to exercise any legal agency or power to make this alleged choice renders such claims null and void. At the same time, it emphasizes why the establishment, organization, and implementation of a system that often used girl children this way was both a war crime and also an egregious violation of the 1910 International Convention for the Suppression of White Slave Traffic, to which Japan had agreed decades before the Asia-Pacific War began.[23] *Spirits' Homecoming* brings these arguments before Western audiences in strikingly visual terms.

Cho Jung-Rae's 2016 historical film is certainly a political intervention. It wades deliberately into the thick of current controversies over the subject of the so-called "comfort system" and by cinematic means, through its unambiguous assignment of guilt to the Imperial Japanese Army for the atrocities visualized and dramatized onscreen, implicitly indicts past and present Japanese governments for their long refusal to accept full legal responsibility. The film's release in February 2016 could not have been better timed to underscore this latter point. It coincided with the immediate aftermath of the late-December 2015 announcement of an "agreement" between the governments of South Korean President Park Geun-Hye and Japanese Prime Minister Abe Shinzō. This "agreement" supposedly was intended to resolve the historical conflict over the "comfort system," yet failed to do so and instead generated tremendous negative political and public fallout in South Korea, as well as among human rights groups in the West and elsewhere, for its absence of attention to the demands of the remaining elderly survivors.[24]

Spirits' Homecoming ends, however, not with accusations or indictments, based on its reenactments of war crimes, but with two sentimental tableaux of loving reconciliation that are also lessons for the audience. One of these scenes occurs in the "real" world of 1991, and one in a timeless realm of fantasy. With the assistance of a teenaged girl—who, acting as shaman, has absorbed the spirit of a victim killed by a Japanese officer in 1945—the elderly "comfort system" survivor, now terminally ill, is able briefly to embrace and reunite with her murdered friend, and thus to find peace. More important, however, viewers watch

---

[23] Yoshiaki Yoshimi, *Comfort Women: Sexual Slavery in the Japanese Military During World War II*, trans. by Suzanne O'Brien (New York: Columbia University Press, 2000), 157.

[24] Laura King, "Dispute Flares Anew Between Japan and South Korea Over World War II Sex Slaves," *Los Angeles Times*, December 30, 2017. Accessed February 27, 2019. http://www.latimes.com/world/la-fg-south-korea-japan-comfort-women-20171228-story.html.

as the shaman wakes up from the trance in which she has channeled the voice of the dead girl and goes on to perform the dancelike ritual of the spirits' homecoming.

The camera cuts away from this whirling figure. Onscreen, the pit containing the corpses of young girls murdered in 1945 appears, while animated butterflies rise in a cloud from their still intact bodies, fly over the water, and cover the beautiful, green, pastoral landscape of the Korean countryside. Finally, the elderly survivor's murdered friend returns, smiling, once more in the form of a happy girl child, walking down the road to the rural home of her parents. The audience watches as they greet her ecstatically and share with her a feast. With this cinematic image of domestic harmony, Cho Jung-Rae chooses to blot out, at least for the moment, the question of whether the Japanese government will ever settle the claims of its legal responsibility—which, in the end, remains a doubtful proposition. What Cho's film offers instead is a path forward toward a more achievable goal that is within the power of audiences in the West, as well as in Korea, to effect. Not merely to acknowledge, and not to treat as reminders of a shameful episode, but to value the victims, and to embrace the memory of their brief lives as treasured individuals, will be the answer. The spirits of these girls must at last be welcomed home, and the film's final segments show them precisely as that—i.e., re-embodied in the form of *girls*, who are being remembered and honored.

Why does this shift in the terms of representation matter—both the linguistic change toward greater inclusion of the words "girls" and "girl children," in discussions of the Japanese "comfort system," and the change in visual representation, to highlight explicitly the issue of age, rather than the gender, class, or ethnicity alone of those who were victimized? For Western allies of the survivors and their supporters, such a shift ought to mean an equivalent change in how we represent and educate about this history. We need to recognize, teach, and write about this war crime not only as an example of wartime sexual slavery, but as having been—frequently and in numerous cases—a violation of the rights of those who were defined as minors under Japan's own laws, which at the time of the Second World War set the age of adulthood as twenty-one.[25] The "comfort system" *often involved the conscious and deliberate sex trafficking of minor girls and thus was a crime of institutionalized and gendered child rape.*[26] Even in the 2015 "agreement" with South Korea, the Japanese government offered neither

---

25 Yoshimi, *Comfort Women*, 157.
26 Italics emphasis added by the editors.

an apology for nor official acknowledgment of that universally abhorrent criminal act.

This would surely be the Japanese government's worst nightmare, come to life: to be exposed widely as having instituted and overseen, throughout the Asia-Pacific War, a military brothel system that knowingly targeted minor girls —girls who, under no legal definition of consent, even under Japan's own laws, could have been capable of consenting to such recruitment. It perhaps explains the vociferous protests by that same government against the proliferation of copies of what is known as the "Peace Statue" or the "Peace Monument"—an unambiguous and unmistakable representation in bronze, which has been positioned outside Japanese embassies in South Korea and elsewhere around the world, of a "comfort system" victim who is not a woman, but a girl child. In 2016, photographs of this statue began to circulate repeatedly and extensively throughout the West, especially via newspaper and magazine accounts, and to reach many viewers in the U.S., even in places where the statue itself has not yet been erected.[27] Knowledge of this visual representation of violated girlhood has been disseminated further in the West through the 2016 Canadian documentary *The Apology*, written and directed by Tiffany Hsiung, about the movement for legal and financial redress to the elderly "comfort system" survivors. In its DVD release, this film includes a special feature that shows the unveiling of the first "Peace Statue" in Seoul in 2011, at one of the weekly demonstrations staged in front of the Embassy of Japan by the Korean Council for the Women Drafted for Military Sexual Slavery by Japan.

Although controversies over the "comfort system" have been raging for nearly three decades, and there is no sign of their abating, different facets of this historical war crime continue to move from the background to the foreground over time. New aspects of it begin to stand out with greater clarity and prominence to audiences in the West, as these topics enter popular awareness through a variety of media. Today, thanks largely to an increase in visual representations, these newly important elements include the issue of age. More than ever before, it is being made clear to Western audiences that the story of the "comfort system" cannot be told without a focus on its victimization of underage girls and its organized trafficking of girl children. Knowing this fact should challenge professional educators everywhere to make it part of their teaching of history to future generations and encourage those concerned with human rights to incorporate it

---

[27] Erin Blakemore, "'Comfort Woman' Statue Stokes Old Tensions Between Japan and South Korea," *Smithsonian Magazine*, January 3, 2017. Accessed February 27, 2019. https://www.smithsonianmag.com/smart-news/comfort-woman-statue-stokes-old-tensions-between-japan-and-south-korea-180961628/.

in their activism and legal strategies, as they pursue justice and oppose sexual exploitation. This work must and will go on.

Part IV: **The Neo-Nationalist Movement in Japan and the United States**

Tomomi Yamaguchi
The "History Wars" and the "Comfort Woman" Issue: The Significance of *Nippon Kaigi* in the Revisionist Movement in Contemporary Japan

Introduction

In December 2012, Abe Shinzō became Japan's Prime Minister for the second time. From the beginning of his political career in 1993 as a new member of the House of Representatives from the conservative Liberal Democratic Party (hereafter, LDP), Abe has been a politician committed to historical revisionist causes. Both times that he served as the prime minister in 2006–2007 and then since 2012, Abe showed extensive interest in denying Japan's responsibility over the "comfort woman" issue, and the issue gained lots of political attention, both in Japan and abroad.[1] At the national political level, the revision of the Kōno statement issued on 4 August 1993, by then-Chief Cabinet Secretary, Kōno Yōhei, became the topic of intense discussion. The statement includes the phrase, "[a] government study has revealed that in many cases they were recruited against their own will, through coaxing, coercion, etc., and that, at times, administrative/military personnel directly took part in the recruitments."[2] Rightwing forces argue to this day that the Kōno statement's indication that the "comfort women" were forcibly recruited by the Japanese military is false.

After the building of the "comfort woman" statue (Statue of Peace) in front of the Japanese Embassy in Seoul in December 2011, the Japanese right-wing and the government have been obsessed with "comfort women" statues and memorials in different overseas locations, given their heavy interest in the international reputation of Japan. The building of the first "comfort woman" memorial in the U.S. in front of a library in Palisades Park, New Jersey, in 2010, gained attention of Japanese conservatives in spring 2012. Subsequently, statues were built in

---

[1] The term "comfort women" was a euphemism used during WWII, which does not reflect the harsh realities of women forcibly engaged in sexual slavery. When used in English-language activism and academia this term is often put in quotation marks.
[2] Yōhei Kōno, "Statement by the Chief Cabinet Secretary Yōhei Kōno on the Result of the Study on the Issue of 'Comfort Women' Kōno statement," Ministry of Foreign Affairs of Japan, 1993. Accessed January 24, 2019. http://www.mofa.go.jp/policy/women/fund/state9308.html.

multiple locations in the U.S., resulting in mass protest emails being sent from Japan to mayors, city council members, and others. In July 2013, a "comfort woman" statue was built in Glendale, California. While right-wing groups encouraged sending protest emails and faxes, some local Japanese residents in the Los Angeles area attended the public hearing. Using Glendale as an opportunity to initiate a new movement, the conservative intellectuals, activists and the ruling LDP of Japan started to focus on the United States as their *shusenjō* (main battlefield) of the "comfort women" issue. They have criticized the "comfort woman" memorials, resolutions, museum exhibits, and coverage of "comfort women" in history textbooks and curricula in the U.S.

In this context, the concept of *rekishisen* (history wars) was introduced in 2014. The term was initially coined by Japan's most conservative national paper, *Sankei Shimbun*, in April 2014, with its new series entitled "The History Wars," which still continues today. The series focuses on Japan's disagreements with South Korea and China concerning historical events pertaining to Japan's colonial history, and the "comfort women" issue is the most prominent issue in the series. The "history wars" imagined by the conservatives are occurring in the U.S., the "main battlefield" of the "comfort women" issue. Moreover, it puts forth the narrative that Japan is a victim of "false indictments" by South Korea and China, and thus has no choice but to fight against the accusations. Arimoto Takashi, the head of the "history wars" reporting group of *Sankei*, writes that "the comfort women issue is no longer simple difference of opinion on historical understandings; it is a 'war.'"[3] The use of the "war" metaphor in the "history wars" is closely connected to revisionist history. According to Japanese historical revisionists, the "comfort women" issue was fabricated to inflame diplomatic tensions and to put forth a one-sided, unfair evaluation of Japan in the international community, by China, South Korea and also the Japanese left, including *Asahi Shimbun*, the nation's second-largest paper, which is known for its liberal stance. For example, a conservative journalist, Sakurai Yoshiko, characterizes "history wars" as "a full-fledged information war now waged against Japan, with China as the chief adversary and the U.S. as the main battlefield."[4] Critic Nishioka Tsutomu also writes, "unscrupulous forces"—likely meaning South Korea and China in this context—"suppress the facts and malign Japan."[5]

---

[3] Sankei Shimbun, *Rekishisen: Asahi Shimbun ga sekai ni maita"ianfu" no uso wo utsu* [*History Wars: Shooting the Lies about "Comfort Women" that Asahi Shimbun Disseminated to the World*] (Tokyo: Sankei Shimbun, 2015), 4.
[4] Ibid.
[5] Ibid., 1.

Intellectuals who have promoted the idea of "history wars," such as Sakurai and Nishioka, are the key conservative ideologues,[6] and they closely work with Japan's largest conservative organization, *Nippon Kaigi* (Japan Conference), and its allied organizations. Formed with the merger of two conservative organizations in 1997, *Nippon Kaigi* became an umbrella organization encompassing traditionally conservative groups and individuals, as well as the religious right—including *Jinja Honchō* (the Association of Shinto Shrines) and many other right-wing new religions and moral education groups.[7] Activist Tawara Yoshifumi points out that the organization appointed business leaders and intellectuals as board members, in addition to religious leaders, and hid its right-wing priorities, yet the right-wing nature of the organization remained unchanged.[8] *Nippon Kaigi* has local headquarters in all 47 prefectures, along with many local branches in cities across Japan. There are also various affiliated organizations of *Nippon Kaigi*, such as its Parliamentary League and Municipal Council Members' League, and its women's section called *Nihon Josei no Kai* (Japan Women's Association). In addition, there are organizations that work closely with *Nippon Kaigi*, including *Nihon Seisaku Kenkyū Sentā* (Japan Policy Institute), a conservative think-tank headed by Itō Tetsuo who is said to be one of the advisors to Prime Minister Abe.[9] Hence, despite having the different names of the organizations,

---

6 Ryuichi Kitano, "Neraware tsuzukeru 'ianfu hōdō'" [The 'Reporing of Comfort Women' Targeted Continuously], in *Tettei kenshō, Nihon no ukeika* [Thorough Examination, Japan's Leaning To the Right], ed. Hotaka Tsukada (Tokyo: Chikuma Shobō, 2017), 278.

7 There were two organizations that merged in 1997 to form *Nippon Kaigi*; *Nihon o Mamoru Kai* (Association to Protect Japan) was a right-wing organization formed in 1974 as a Shintō and Buddhist-affiliated religious group. *Nihon o Mamoru Kokumin Kaigi* (The National Conference to Protect Japan) was formed in 1981 as a standing right-wing organization, after the passage of the reign era name law in 1979. Yoshifumi Tawara, "What is the Aim of Nippon Kaigi, the Ultra-right Organization that Supports Japan's Abe Administration?" transl. by Asia Policy Point, William Brooks, and Lu Pengqiao, Introduction by Tomomi Yamaguchi, *The Asia-Pacific Journal: Japan Focus* 15–21, no. 1 (2017). Accessed February 28, 2019. https://apjjf.org/2017/21/Tawara.html.

8 Ibid.

9 Journalistic literature on *Nippon Kaigi* came out in 2016, though still very few scholarly works exist (Nogawa et al. 2017). See Narusawa 2016; Tawara 2016; Yoshifumi Tawara, "What is the Aim of Nippon Kaigi, the Ultra-right Organization that Supports Japan's Abe Administration?" Translated by Asia Policy Point. *The Asia-Pacific Journal: Japan Focus* 15 (21), No. 1, November 1, 2017. Accessed April 2, 2017. https://apjjf.org/2017/21/Tawara.html ; Aoki 2016; Fujiu 2017 for journalist works that were published recently. All of these works point out that the religious group House of Growth (*Seichō-no-ie*) played a significant role in the establishment of the precursor organizations of *Nippon Kaigi*, and impacted many of the core leaders of the current *Nippon Kaigi*. It is, however, important to note that *Seichō-no-ie* became split in the early 2000s under the

many of the organizations have common leaderships, and close relationships with *Nippon Kaigi*.

The estimated membership of *Nippon Kaigi* itself is close to 40,000, which may not sound massive, but considering the number of followers of the religious and moral education organizations affiliated with *Nippon Kaigi*, the number of people whom they can organize to attend rallies, join signature drives and vote is significant. Mobilizing local branches and various affiliated organizations across Japan in national and local levels, *Nippon Kaigi* operates a "grassroots right-wing movement," while maintaining strong ties with the Abe administration. Moreover, current Prime Minister Abe is heavily backed by *Nippon Kaigi*. Abe has participated in *Nippon Kaigi*'s Diet representatives' league since its beginning, and as of September 2019, 16 out of 20 cabinet members, including Abe himself, belonged to the organization.[10] Maintaining close ties with politicians such as Abe, *Nippon Kaigi* is the driving force involved extensively in the "history wars" in Japan, in North America, and at the United Nations, and has been working closely with the Japanese government.

This paper examines the significance of *Nippon Kaigi* and its involvement in the "history wars" as it pertains to the "comfort women" issue, both within and outside of Japan. The main data sources are based on my anthropological field research with right-wing Japanese groups in Japan and in the U.S., my observations of court sessions and rallies, as well as archival research. By discussing their claims and the major activities related to "history wars," I will demonstrate the impact of *Nippon Kaigi* and its related organizations, due to their close ties with the current government and the ruling party, combined with their grassroots movement strategy. After reviewing the background of *Nippon Kaigi*'s involvement in historical revisionism, especially on the "comfort women" issue, I will discuss *Nippon Kaigi*'s two major activities related to the "history wars": 1) the court battle in Japan against *Asahi Shimbun* regarding its "comfort women" coverage, and 2) its work to disseminate information internationally, particularly in English, and their activism to intervene in the adoption of "comfort women" records for UNESCO's Memory of the World program. By doing so, I will demonstrate how the influence of *Nippon Kaigi*, as the largest conservative organization with close ties to the current Japanese government and the ruling party, is signif-

---

third-generation leader of the organization, and he even openly criticizes the Abe administration and *Nippon Kaigi*. The core leaders of *Nippon Kaigi* follow the more orthodox, extremely nationalistic teaching of the religion's founder, Masaharu Taniguchi, than the current *Seichō-no-ie*.
10 Yoshifumi Tawara, "Shiryō Daiyoji Abe Shinzō Saikaizō Naikakuno Chō Takaha (Kyokuu) no Daijin Tachi" [Documents, The Hawkish (Extreme Right-Wing) Ministers of the Re-reshuffled Fourth Abe Cabinet.], September 22, 2019.

icant. They are, in fact, mainstream in the current political context in Japan, regardless of how their claims are not accepted as valid in the scholarly community, both in Japan and elsewhere. Despite their losses in multiple lawsuits, Japanese conservatives are still energized about the "history wars," and they continue to engage in them, especially in the U.S. and at the United Nations. At the time of this writing, they are attempting to disseminate more information representing their position, especially in English. The Japanese government and *Nippon Kaigi*, working with more "fringe" right-wing groups, engage with "history wars" collaboratively to deny the memories of "comfort women" and the systematic nature of sexual slavery.

Nippon Kaigi and Historical Revisionism

While the issue of "comfort women" first gained widespread attention in Japan in 1991, when Korean surviving "comfort woman" Kim Hak-Sun came forward for the first time, attacks and controversy around the issue have become much more intense since the mid 1990s, with the emergence of a new revisionist history textbook movement. By 1997, information about "comfort women" had been added to all junior high school history textbooks; when the plan was exposed in 1996, it triggered a sense of urgency and anxiety among right-leaning citizens. Since then, intense controversy has re-emerged among Japanese conservatives surrounding the issue. Many conservatives deny that there was any government involvement in, or corresponding responsibility for, a system of sexual slavery, and argued that Japanese history education was "masochistic."[11]

With the revisionist history movement, two organizations, *Jiyū Shugi Shikan Kenkyūkai* (The Liberal View of History Study Group) led by scholar Fujioka Nobukatsu in 1995, and *Atarashii Rekishi Kyokasho o Tsukurukai* (The Society for History Textbook Reform) in 1996, were established. They effectively widened the range of people, including self-proclaimed "ordinary citizens"[12] or "newcomers"—the word used by my informant who was a *Nippon Kaigi* member—who came to be involved in the movement. Politicians came to be involved in the revisionist history movement as well, with the founding of a group of 87 young

---

11 Franziska Seraphim, "Relocating War Memory at the Century's End: Japan's Postwar Responsibility and Global Public Culture." In *Ruptured Histories: War, Memory, and the Post-Cold War in Asia*, eds. Shiela Miyoshi Jager and Rana Mitter (Cambridge, MA: Harvard University Press, 2007), 43.
12 Eiji Oguma and Yōko Ueno, *Iyashi no Nashonarizumu* [*Comforting Nationalism*] (Tokyo: Keio Daigaku Shuppankai, 2003), 69–186.

LDP politicians, *Nihon no Zento to Rekishi Kyōiku o Kangaeru Wakate Giin no Kai* (The Young Diet Members' Group for Japan's Future and History Education).[13] A lower-house representative, Nakagawa Shōichi, became the group's leader, and Abe Shinzō, also a lower-house representative then, was the group's secretary.[14]

Nippon Kaigi was founded in 1997, in the midst of the intense controversy surrounding the inclusion of the "comfort women" issue in history textbooks. While *Nippon Kaigi* deals with a wide range of issues, such as the promotion of the emperor system, family values, patriotic education, and the revision of the post-war Constitution, the people of *Nippon Kaigi* have always demonstrated deep interest in the issue of historical consciousness. When the first large-scale rally of *Nippon Kaigi* was held on 6 November 1997, for example, the leader Nakagawa gave a speech entitled "The 'comfort women' and 'forced mobilization' (*kyōsei renkō*) are fake," criticizing history textbooks that included "comfort women" and also the Kōno statement of 1993.[15]

The basic line of revisionist arguments regarding "comfort women" was prepared primarily in the early and mid 1990s, around the time of the establishment of *Tsukuru Kai*[16] and *Nippon Kaigi*, and shared via conservative media and conservative organizations' publications. They deny the forcible recruitment of "comfort women" and the characterization of the "comfort station" system as military sexual slavery. They dispute the number of "comfort women" recruited for the Japanese military. Revisionists often point to 200,000 as the number of "comfort women" suggested by leftists, claiming it as being too large and imprecise. While the definite number remains unclear partly due to the lack of histor-

---

[13] The Young Diet Members' Group for Japan's Future and History Education published a book entitled *Rekishi kyōkasho e no gimon* [Doubts about History Textbooks] in December 1997, summarizing their activities for ten months since February 1997 (*Nihon no Zento to Rekishi Kyōiku o Kangaeru Wakate Giin no Kai* 1997).

[14] Nihon no Zento to Rekishi Kyōiku o Kangaeru Wakate Giin no Kai, *Rekishi kyōkasho e no gimon* [Doubts about History Textbooks] (Tokyo: Tentensha, 1997).

[15] Shōichi Nakagawa, "'Jūgun ianfu,' 'kyōsei renkō' wa kyokō da" [The 'Military Comfort Women' and 'Forcible Removal' are Fake], *Nippon no Ibuki* 121 (1997), 9–10. In 2000, when right-wingers protested against the International Women's War Crimes Tribunal, it was reported that Nakagawa and Abe pressured the public TV station NHK to censor the content of a documentary on the tribunal. *Asahi Shimbun* was the paper that broke that story in 2005; Lisa Yoneyama, "NHK's Censorship of Japanese Crimes Against Humanity," *Harvard Asia Quarterly* 6, no. 1 (Winter 2002): 15–19; Kōzō Nagata, *NHK to Seiji Kenryoku: Bangumi Kaihen Jiken Tōjisha no Shōgen* [NHK and Political Power: The Testimony by a Person Directly Affected by the Incident of Censorship and Forced Edits of the Documentary] (Tokyo: Iwanami Shoten, 2014).

[16] *Tsukuru Kai* is short for *Atarashii Rekishi Kyokasho o Tsukuru Kai*, which translates to "Association to Write New History Textbooks" or "Japanese Society for History Textbook Reform." This group was founded in December 1996 to promote a nationalistic view of the history of Japan.

ical documents, many of which were destroyed by the Japanese military, the number would not change the nature and existence of sexual slavery. Furthermore, the "comfort women" issue itself came to be targeted as consisting only of false accusations and fabrications, and testimonies of "comfort women" were characterized as untrustworthy.

It is also significant to note the revisionist denial of Japan's war crimes judged under the International Military Tribunal for the Far East (the Tokyo Tribunal), and also their rejection of the historical course that Japan has taken under the post-war Constitution of 1947. For example, *Nippon Kaigi*'s prospectus, released on 30 May 1997, states that "the spread of the historical interpretation based on the Tokyo Tribunal led to a subservient 'apology first' diplomacy toward foreign countries, and has made the new generation of young people lose pride and confidence in our country."[17] Moreover, in an interview in a free conservative magazine for the APA hotel chain, a scholar heavily involved with *Nippon Kaigi*, Takahashi Shirō, commented on "history wars," alleging that it is other countries who are warping history, such as in the cases of the Nanking Massacre and "comfort women." He continues that "this is all a part of the information propaganda war. This information propaganda war started against Japan after the war as part of the occupation policy of the United States military—the WGIP."[18] Takahashi explains that the WGIP is an abbreviation of SCAP's (Supreme Commander for the Allied Powers) "War Guilt Information Program" that existed during the occupation period. According to Takahashi's theory, the Japanese public in the post-war period was brainwashed by the WGIP.[19] This, he explained, is the reason for the widespread belief in pre-war and wartime atrocities by Japan, such as the "comfort women," the Nanking Massacre, and other history-related issues; the acceptance of the post-war constitution, the lack of a "real" military, and declining family values. Takahashi claims that all are connected under the "information propaganda" disseminated by the United States since the Tokyo Tribunal, and that it is still very much alive.[20]

---

17 "Setsuritsu Sengen" [Declaration of Establishment], Nippon Kaigi website, May 30, 1997. Accessed January 23, 2019. http://www.nipponkaigi.org/about.
18 Shiro Takahashi and Toshio Motoya, "Disseminating the Truth of Japan to the World in English," *Apple Town*, December 22, 2015, 295.
19 Ibid.; Shirō Takahashi, *Nihon o Kaitaisuru Sensō Puropaganda no Genzai: WGIP no Genryū o Saguru* [The current state of the wartime propaganda that is destroying Japan: looking for the source of the War Guilt Information Program] (Tokyo: Takarajimasha, 2016); idem., "Kaichō Takahashi Shiro no Kinkyō Hōkoku" [President Takahashi Shiro's Updates], *Ippan Zaidan Hōjin Oyagaku Suishin Kyōkai Mēru Magajin* [Parental Studies General Incorporated Foundations, Email Magazine] 94, November 15, 2017.
20 Takahashi, "Kaichō Takahashi Shiro."

According to scholar Nogawa Motokazu, the theory of WGIP, originally proposed by conservative critic Etō Jun[21] with his work on SCAP's censorship in the occupation period, is promoted not only by Takahashi but also by other conservative writers, such as Sekino Michio and Kent Gilbert.[22] The theory questions the entire post-war system under the current constitution. Nogawa states that the theory now spreads widely as "the true post-war history" for certain conservative people on the Internet.[23]

Hence, the interpretation of Japan's colonial history, including the "comfort women" issue, cannot be separated from discussion on constitutional revision, which is *Nippon Kaigi*'s ultimate goal.[24] As Tawara Yoshifumi writes, the revision of the post-war constitution, the promotion of nationalistic education, and a strong defense are all interlocking issues for *Nippon Kaigi*.[25] While national politicians affiliated with *Nippon Kaigi*, such as Abe, played prominent roles in the promotion of revisionist history, the network of *Nippon Kaigi*'s municipal council members who formed the *Nippon Kaigi* Municipal Members' League in 2006 was an indispensable component in the movement to promote revisionist history textbooks and education, and also to pass assembly resolutions nullifying the past resolutions to resolve the "comfort women" issue.

Nippon Kaigi and related organizations, along with the conservative media and intellectuals, have been spreading revisionist claims and engaging in activism, not only domestically but also toward the international community. For example, in 1999, *Nippon Kaigi* launched *Kokusai Kōhō Iinkai* (The Committee for International Affairs), and in 2000, the committee published a bilingual book in English and Japanese, entitled *The Alleged "Nanking Massacre": Japan's Rebuttal to China's Forged Claims*,[26] as a reaction to the best-selling *The Rape of Nanking* by Iris Chang, published in 1997. Abe became Prime Minister for the first time in 2006, and in March 2007, he made a statement denying the forcible

---

[21] Jun Etō, *Tozasareta gengo kūkan: Senryō-gun no ken'etsu to sengo Nihon* [*The Closed Linguistic Space: The Censorship by the Occupation and Post-War Japan*] (Tokyo: Bungei Shunjū, 1989).
[22] Motokazu Nogawa, "'Rekishisen no kessen heiki,' 'WGIP' ron no genzai," in *Tettei kenshō, Nihon no ukeika*, ed. Hotaka Tsukada (Tokyo: Chikuma Shobō, 2017), 256–275.
[23] Nogawa, "Rekishisen," 256.
[24] Takao Sakamoto, "Kenpō kaisei rongi to rekishi kaishaku" [The Discussion on the Revision of the Constitution and the Interpretation of History], *Nihon no Ibuki* (1998): 4–5; Motokazu Nogawa and Tadanori Hayakawa, *Zōo no kōkoku: Uha-kei opinion-shi 'aikoku' 'kenchū', 'kenkan' no keifu* [*Advertisements of Hatred: Right-Wing Opinion Magazines and their Genealogy of 'Patriotism,' 'Hate-China, Hate-Korea'*] (Tokyo: Gōdō Shuppan, 2015), 46.
[25] Tawara, "What is the Aim."
[26] Tadao Takemoto and Yasuo Ōhara, *The Alleged 'Nanking Massacre: Japan's Rebuttal to China's Forged Claims* (Tokyo: Meisei-sha, 2000).

nature of the "comfort women" system, which angered the international community—especially the United States, which later passed House Resolution 121, asking the Japanese government for a formal apology for its engagement in the "comfort women" system. It was at this time on 14 June 2007, when an advertisement entitled "The Facts," denying the involvement of Japan in the "comfort women" system, was put out by the Committee for Historical Facts, and conservative intellectuals, journalists and politicians were the signatories.[27]

In April 2012, journalist Okamoto Akiko, affiliated with *Nippon Kaigi* at the time, published an article about the Palisades Park memorial in *Seiron*, a conservative magazine published by *Sankei Shimbun*, claiming that Japanese children in the U.S. are bullied because of the memorial.[28] It was the first time that anyone had problematized the "comfort women" memorials in the United States. Okamoto was the core secretariat of the *Nippon Kaigi* Municipal Council Members' League, and the secretary general of *Kazoku no Kizuna o Mamorukai* (The Family Values Society, FAVS), which was established in 2007 based on the network of municipal council league. Okamoto was also a core member of *Nippon Kaigi*'s women's section—the Japan Women's Association. The Japanese consulate based in New York attempted to persuade the city to remove the monument in May 2012, followed by a visit by four Diet representatives of the LDP, Furuya Keiji, Yamatani Eriko, Tsukada Ichirō, and Takemoto Naokazu, to the city of Palisades Park.[29] There was a petition movement to submit to the White House, led by the Japanese right wing, entitled "Remove the monument and not to support international harassment related to this issue against the people of Japan," that began in May. Moreover, on 6 November 2012, immediately before he became the Prime Minister for the second time in December, Abe signed his name to a revisionist paid advertisement again by the Committee for Historical Facts, entitled

---

[27] The Asia Policy Point, "Signatories to the June 14th *Washington Post* 'The Facts' Advertisement Politicians, Professors, and Journalists." June 25, 2007. Accessed January 23, 2019. http://www.jiaponline.org/documents/Jun14AdALLSignatoriesLIST.pdf. On the content of the advertisement, see the article by one of the leading figures who was involved in the ad, Kōichi Sugiyama, "Paid Advertisement Concerning 'Comfort Women' Run in the *Washington Post*." Accessed January 23, 2019. http://www.sdh-fact.com/CL02_1/33_S4.pdf.
[28] Akiko Okamoto, "Beikoku no hōjin shitei ga ijime higai: Kankoku no ianfu hannichi senden ga man'en suru kōzu" [Japanese Children in the U.S. are Victims of Bullying: the System of the Permeation of the Anti-Japan PR by South Korea], *Seiron*, (May 2012): 126–133.
[29] Kirk Semple, "In New Jersey, Memorial for 'Comfort Women' Deepens Old Animosity," *The New York Times*, May 18, 2012; Keiji Furuya, "Washinton shucchō" [Business Trip to Washington], *Furuya Keiji Tsūshin*, May 8, 2012.

"Yes, We Remember the Facts" in a local New Jersey paper, *The Star-Ledger*, along with a group of Japanese conservative intellectuals, journalists, and politicians.[30]

Subsequently, statues were built in multiple locations in the U.S. and Canada, resulting in mass protest emails being sent from Japan to mayors, city council members, and others.[31] Nadeshiko Action, a women's right-wing group founded in 2011 by Yamamoto Yumiko, a former secretary of *Zainichi Tokken o Yurusanai Shimin no Kai* (the Citizens' Group Refusing to Tolerate Special Rights of Koreans in Japan, also known as *Zaitokukai*), infamous for its intense hate speeches against Koreans, encouraged the Japanese right wing in Japan and North America to fight against resolutions, museum exhibitions, and the building of memorials. The Japanese consulates in the U.S. also intervened in attempts to build monuments and statues in public locations, as in the case of Southfield, Michigan in 2013, where the initial plan to build the Statue of Peace in front of the city library was cancelled, followed by multiple failed attempts to build it in a public location in the metro Detroit area.[32]

The "comfort women" statue in Glendale, California that was built in 2013 became a symbol of the "history wars." In January 2014, a group of municipal council members visited the City of Glendale to protest against the statue in January 2014.[33] Also in 2014, right-wing activists in both Japan and California filed a lawsuit against the City of Glendale at the Federal District Court, and later at the California State Court. The plaintiffs, along with the Japanese right, established a new organization, the Global Alliance for Historical Truth (GAHT), which Emi Koyama discusses in more detail in this collection. A day before the unveiling of the Glendale statue on 29 July 2013, non-mainstream right-wing groups in Japan founded *Ianfu no Shinjitsu Kokumin Undō* (People's Campaign for the Truth of Comfort Women) as a "counter-propaganda" movement to "protect Japan's honor," especially in the U.S. and abroad, and the organization started to work closely with GAHT and its lawsuits. The highly visible protests against statues and monuments in the U.S., such as in San Francisco and Atlanta,

---

[30] For the actual advertisement, see "Yes, We Remember the Facts (2012)" in Japan-U.S. Feminist Network for Decolonization (FeND). Accessed April 2, 2018. http://fendnow.org/encyclopedia/yes-we-remember-the-facts-2012/.

[31] As of April 2018, there are the total of thirteen "comfort women" memorials in North America.

[32] Interviews with Sue Konarska, Sonyoung Moore, Bruce Park in Southfield Michigan, and Moon Jae Pak in Rochester Michigan, on 14 March 2018.

[33] The leader of the group, the assemblywoman of Suginami Ward, Yoshiko Matsuura, is a member of the Nippon Kaigi Municipal Council Members League, and a long-time member of *Seichō-no-ie*.

have been mobilized by the People's Campaign for the Truth of Comfort Women and GAHT, and not *Nippon Kaigi*. In fact, in my interviews with individuals closely affiliated with Nippon Kaigi, many of them were critical or ambivalent toward the lawsuit by GAHT, as they simply did not see the possibility of GAHT winning the case.

However, *Nippon Kaigi* was deeply concerned with the Glendale memorial and other "comfort women" statues in the U.S., as illustrated by the fact that one of its core members, Takahashi Shirō, visited all of the statues and monuments in the United States.[34] Yet *Nippon Kaigi* chose a different path from GAHT; it chose to fight a court battle in Japan, not in the U.S., although the content of their claim is still very relevant to the "history wars" in the U.S., especially on the Glendale statue. Its target, however, was not the City of Glendale. Instead, *Nippon Kaigi* filed a lawsuit against Japan's liberal paper, the *Asahi Shimbun*, at Tokyo District Court. I will now examine *Nippon Kaigi*'s court battle in Japan against the *Asahi Shimbun*.

The Glendale Statue and *Nippon Kaigi*'s Court Battle with the *Asahi Shimbun*

Since the early 1990s, the liberal media, especially *Asahi Shimbun*, Japan's second-largest daily newspaper, has become the revisionists' target and has been called out as a "fabricator" of the "comfort women" issue. Not only has the paper been criticized for its coverage of the testimony provided by the late Yoshida Seiji, in which he stated that he captured and forcibly transported "comfort women" in Korea during World War II, but then-*Asahi* reporter Uemura Takashi, who was the first to cover Kim Hak-Sun's story, was accused of having "fabricated" the "comfort women" issue.[35] In addition, the late Matsui Yayori, a former *Asahi* reporter, extensively covered the "comfort women" issue as a journalist; later, as an activist, she organized the Women's International War Crimes Tribunal on Japan's Military Sexual Slavery, which took place in December 2000. In

---

34 Shirō Takahashi, *Nihon o kaitaisuru sensō puropaganda no genzai: WGIP no genryū o saguru* (Tokyo: Takarajima-sha, 2016), 156–206.
35 Takashi Uemura, "Labeled the Reporter who 'Fabricated' the Comfort Woman Issue: A Rebuttal," trans. Tomomi Yamaguchi, *The Asia-Pacific Journal: Japan Focus* 13, no. 2–1 (January 12, 2015); Tomomi Yamaguchi, "Press Freedom Under Fire: 'Comfort Women,' the *Asahi* Affair and Uemura Takashi," in *Press Freedom in Contemporary Japan*, ed. Jeffrey Kingston (New York: Routledge, 2017), 135–151.

2005, another reporter, Honda Masakazu, broke the story of Abe's and Nakagawa's efforts to censor the NHK documentary on the Women's Tribunal. In addition, the *Asahi* and their journalists have been under intensive attacks from the right on the "comfort women" issue.

On 22 August 2014, *Asahi Shimbun* released the results of its reexamination of decades-old coverage on "comfort women" in an article titled "Thinking about the Comfort Women Issue."[36] In the article, the paper announced that its careful reexamination revealed that some articles published in *Asahi Shimbun* about Yoshida Seiji contained errors, which they then retracted, while many other articles had withstood the test of reexamination and contained no errors. Since this reexamination, however, right-wing attacks against *Asahi Shimbun*, former "comfort women," and activists, scholars and journalists working on this issue have become extensive. Numerous criticisms against the *Asahi* and the "comfort women" issue have appeared in the mass media, and have been seen in various right-wing organizations' rallies, statements, and actions. In particular, attacks against former reporter Uemura became so intense that he lost his prospective job at a women's college, and he and his family members received death threats.[37] Moreover, Japan's ruling LDP and its politicians have openly criticized the *Asahi* for its errors and have said that its failure to truly acknowledge them was ruining Japan's international reputation.[38]

With the spread of the *Asahi* bashing, conservatives thought that they had won the comfort "comfort women" in Japan.[39] However, the problem of Japan's international reputation still remains. In 2015, three right-wing organizations filed collective lawsuits against the *Asahi Shimbun*. An *Asahi* reporter, Kitano Ryūichi, writes that the right wing situated the lawsuits to "settle and finish the 'history wars' that concluded domestically."[40] While each lawsuit differed in its claims, all of them addressed and emphasized the damage to Japan's rep-

---

36 "Thinking about the Comfort Women Issue," *Asahi Shimbun*, August 22, 2014. Accessed January 23, 2019. http://www.asahi.com/topics/ianfumondaiwokangaeru/en/.
37 Uemura, "Labeled the Reporter."; Yamaguchi, "Press Freedom."
38 For example, the LDP's Committee on International Communications (Chair: Yoshiaki Harada) released a report condemning the *Asahi* on its "comfort women" reporting in 2015. See his interview in the LDP website. Accessed April 2, 2018. https://www.jimin.jp/english/news/126507.html. The party's Policy Research Council also reacted and criticized the *Asahi*. Accessed April 2, 2018. https://www.jimin.jp/english/news/126508.html.
39 Tomomi Yamaguchi, Motokazu Nogawa, Tessa Morris-Suzuki, and Emi Koyama, *Umi o wataru "ianfu" mondai: Uha no rekishisen o tou* [*The "Comfort Women" Issue Goes Overseas: Questioning the Right-Wing "History Wars"*] (Tokyo: Iwanami Shoten, 2016).
40 Kitano, "Neraware," 284.

utation in the international community, due to the *Asahi Shimbun*'s coverage—or rather, "fabrication"—of the "comfort women" issue.

The first case was called *Asahi Shimbun o Tadasu Kokumin Kaigi* (The National Conference to Correct the *Asahi Shimbun*), led by Mizushima Satoru, the president of the right-wing television and online production company, Channel Sakura, and its activist organization, *Ganbare Nippon*. The National Conference, with 25,000 plaintiffs, filed its collective lawsuit at Tokyo District Court on 26 January 2015. Each plaintiff asked for 10,000 yen for the defamation of their characters as Japanese, resulting from the *Asahi's* report, and also demanded that the *Asahi* issue an advertisement of apology. The group tried to mobilize the right wing to hear the court sessions via the Internet and Channel Sakura, and held large-scale events on the case multiple times. The plaintiffs lost the case at Tokyo District Court in July 2016, and Tokyo High Court in September 2017. The courts' rulings were based on the fact that the articles in the *Asahi* focused on the pre-war government and military, and the defamation of character does not apply to the specific plaintiffs as individuals.[41] The plaintiffs did not appeal to the supreme court, and the ruling was finalized.

Another lawsuit was filed on 9 February 2015 by a new group called *Asahi o Tadasu Kai* (Group to Correct the Asahi), with about 480 plaintiffs. The group also filed a suit at Kōfu District Court in Yamanashi Prefecture with about 150 plaintiffs in August 2016. Both lawsuits argued that the plaintiffs' right to knowledge was denied as the *Asahi* did not issue a correction of the Yoshida testimony sooner. The Tokyo case was dismissed by the Supreme Court in October 2017, and the Kōfu case was also dismissed by the high court in November 2017, which was finalized as the plaintiffs did not bring the case to the Supreme Court.[42]

The third case, called *Asahi Glendale Soshō* (Lawsuit), backed by *Nippon Kaigi*, filed a collective lawsuit against *Asahi Shimbun* on 18 February 2015. A total of 2,557 Japanese individuals were named as plaintiffs then; while most of them lived in Japan, three of the plaintiffs were Japanese people living in Southern California. Later, on 3 August 2015, 46 additional Japanese residents in Southern California (Los Angeles and Orange Counties) joined the suit.[43] The National Conference to Correct *Asahi Shimbun* and *Asahi*-Glendale Lawsuit initially planned to file a lawsuit together, but in the middle of their planning, they became split into two factions and ended up filing separate suits. The attorney for the *Asahi*-Glendale Lawsuit, Tokunaga Shin'ichi, explained to me that

---

41 Ibid., 285.
42 Ibid.
43 Ibid.

their approaches were different in that the National Conference wanted to prioritize creating a mass movement via this lawsuit, by having a massive number of plaintiffs, while *Nippon Kaigi* wanted to focus more on the legal aspect of the fight.[44] While he and others in *Nippon Kaigi* did not explain it clearly, another personal relationship-level problem may have been a factor as well.

The complaint by the *Asahi*-Glendale Lawsuit declares that the *Asahi's* fabricated coverage of the "comfort women" issue had a major impact on the international community's understanding of the issue, and damaged Japan's reputation, as well as the lives of Japanese people in the United States. The *Asahi* coverage, the plaintiffs claim, impacted the following: 1) public opinion in South Korea; 2) reports in the Euro-American media; 3) UN reports such as the "Coomaraswamy Report" of 1996,[45] the "McDougall report" of 1998,[46] and other UN recommendations to Japan; 4) the U.S. House Resolution 121 of 2007; 5) the building of memorials and statues in the U.S.; and 6) the introduction of "comfort women" in the McGraw Hill history textbook used in U.S. high schools. The complainant then asks for one million yen in damages for the three plaintiffs living in Southern California, and demands that *Asahi* publishes a paid advertisement containing a "written apology by the *Asahi Shimbun* company" in *The New York Times*, *The Los Angeles Times*, and *The Guardian*, as well as in major Japanese papers. The "written apology" was to include the following points: 1) The testimony of Yoshida Seiji was fabricated; 2) The Japanese Army never forcibly recruited any "comfort women;" 3) *The Asahi Shimbun* is responsible for spreading misinformation worldwide; 4) We ask for the "comfort women" problem to be reevaluated (which includes the declaration that the *Asahi Shimbun* retracts "all of its distorted coverage on the 'comfort women' problem").[47] This list clearly indicates that they are not only interested in criticizing the *Asahi*, but also that they reject widely accepted claims on the "comfort

---

[44] Conversation with Shin'ichi Tokunaga in Tokyo, February 18, 2015.
[45] Radhika Coomaraswamy, "Report on the Mission to the Democratic People's Republic of Korea, the Republic of Korea and Japan on the Issue of Military Sexual Slavery in Wartime," E/CN.4/1996/53/Add.1, the Economic and Social Council, the United Nations.
[46] Gay J. McDougall, "Contemporary Forms of Slavery: Systematic Rape, Sexual Slavery and Slavery-Like Practices during Armed Conflict," Final Report Submitted to United Nations Commission on Human Rights, Sub-Commission on Prevention of Discrimination and Protection of Minorities, 50th session, (June 22, 1998), UN Doc. E/CN.4/Sub.2/1998/13. Appendix: "An Analysis of the Legal Liability of the Government of Japan for 'Comfort Women Stations' Established during the Second World War," 52, paragraph 55.
[47] Asahi Glendale Soshō o Shiensuru Kai, "Written Apology of the Asahi Shimbun Company," (2015), Accessed January 23, 2019. http://www.ianfu.net/pdf/270526besshi1_0610.pdf.

women" issue.⁴⁸ In their claims, the plaintiffs demonstrated major concern over the reputation of Japan in the international community, especially in English-speaking countries, and connected the *Asahi*'s coverage to the building of "comfort women" statues and monuments in the U.S., especially using the Glendale statue as the major example of damages done to Japanese residents in the U.S.

It was obvious that the *Asahi* Glendale lawsuit was fully supported by *Nippon Kaigi*. Besides the admission of the fact by the lead attorney Tokunaga, I went to Tokyo District Court to see the *Asahi* Glendale trial's court sessions several times, and saw that most of the attendees were elderly people likely mobilized by *Nippon Kaigi*; I saw that people were holding flyers made by the organization. The intellectual leaders of *Nippon Kaigi*, such as scholars Momochi Akira and Takahashi Shirō, were present at nearly all of the sessions, as well as the executive secretary of *Nippon Kaigi*, Kabashima Yūzō, who was also the secretary general of a right-wing organization, Japan Council (Nihon Kyōgikai). Momochi also led the support group of the lawsuit as its representative.⁴⁹ In addition to the *Asahi*, other media who were at the courtroom and the gathering after the court session hosted by the plaintiffs' support group were reporters from the paper put out by Shintō shrines, *Jinja Shinpō*, the organ of the Japan Council, *Sokoku to Seinen*, and the organ of *Nippon Kaigi*, *Nippon no Ibuki*. The size of the courtroom assigned was not big, which is an indication that *Nippon Kaigi* was not interested in mobilizing a mass range of citizens beyond those who were already committed to *Nippon Kaigi*'s activism. Rather, the court was primarily for core *Nippon Kaigi* supporters.

Moreover, the *Asahi* Glendale lawsuit used the report by the Independent Examination Committee of the Japan Policy Institute, released a day after the lawsuit, as the basis for their argument. The Japan Policy Institute is a conservative think tank closely connected to mainstream conservatives such as *Nippon Kaigi* and Prime Minister Abe. It established its own Independent Examination Committee after the *Asahi* had created an independent third-party committee to ex-

---

48 A conservative think tank close to *Nippon Kaigi*, the Japan Policy Institute, which had been criticizing the *Asahi* since 1992, started to extensively cover the *Asahi*'s problem with its "comfort women" coverage in its monthly magazine. It has also established its own Independent Examination Committee after the Asahi had created an independent, Third-Party Committee to examine its "comfort women" coverage and the company's re-examination process in its response to heavy criticism from the public. The Independent Examination Committee of the Japan Policy Institute, chaired by conservative scholar Terumasa Nakanishi, had six members, many of whom were key theorists of *Nippon Kaigi*. Its final report was released on 19 February 2015, a day after *Nippon Kaigi* filed a lawsuit against the Tokyo District Court.
49 See the website of the support group, *Asahi Glendale Saiban wo Shiensuru Kai*, http://www.ianfu.net. Accessed April 4, 2018.

amine its "comfort women" coverage and the company's re-examination process in its response to heavy criticism from the public. The Independent Examination Committee was chaired by conservative scholar Nakanishi Terumasa and had six members, many of whom were key theorists of *Nippon Kaigi*. The Committee released its final report on 19 February 2015,[50] and criticized the result of the *Asahi's* third-party committee's report released on 22 December.[51] The Independent Committee claims that even though the third-party committee pointed out the *Asahi's* problems with its re-examination to a certain extent, there was no analysis on why the *Asahi's* reports on the "comfort women" issue went wrong, and the third-party committee did not reach a consensus on the issue of the impact of *Asahi's* coverage on international society. Instead, the Independent Committee argued that the core problem of the *Asahi's* reporting on the "comfort women" issue was the paper's spreading propaganda from the 1970s till January 1992, on the issues of Yoshida's testimony, as well as confusion regarding the women's volunteer corps with the "comfort women", testimonies by former "comfort women", and documents indicating the involvement of the Japanese military. The Independent Committee called it the "Forcible Recruitment Propaganda of January 1992," insisting that the *Asahi* did not correct this propaganda and instead, the paper supported the ideas of a "broad sense of coercion" and "women's human rights" for the "comfort women" issue.[52] The Independent Committee then argued that the "fabrication" had a major impact on the wrong impression of Japan in media reports in newspapers in the U.S. and South Korea, and caused psychological damage to Japanese residents in the United States. The Independent Committee also stated that bullying incidents against Japanese children from six years of age to high school were widespread, and that there were ten reported cases just in the states of California and New Jersey.[53]

---

[50] The members of the committee are: Chair Terumasa Nakanishi; Vice-chair Tsutomu Nishioka; members: Nobuko Araki, Yōichi Shimada and Shirō Takahashi; and secretary general Kanji Katsuoka.

[51] The abridged version of the report is available in English. "Report (Abridged): The Asahi Shimbun Co. Third Party Committee." Accessed on April 3, 2018. http://www.asahi.com/shimbun/3rd/report20150728e.pdf; Other information, including the entire report in Japanese, is posted on the *Asahi Shimbun* website, http://www.asahi.com/shimbun/3rd/3rd.html. Accessed on April 3, 2018.

[52] Dokuritsu Kenshō Iinkai, "*Asahi Shimbun* 'ianfu hōdō ni kansuru dokuritsu kenshō iinkai hōkokusho" [Independent Examination Committee Report on the *Asahi Shimbun's* News Reports on the "Comfort Women"], (2015), 3–4. Accessed March 1, 2019. http://www.seisaku-center.net/sites/default/files/uploaded/dokuritsukensyouiinkai20150219-C20150227.pdf

[53] Ibid., 13.

The core plaintiffs of the *Asahi* Glendale Lawsuit were Japanese residents of the U.S., and "shin issei" residents, who were new migrants to the United States in the post-war period, especially during the post-1980s "bubble" economy era.[54] The attorneys looked for plaintiffs in the U.S., and three people in Los Angeles initially responded and became main plaintiffs, and another person from New Jersey joined the suit later as a plaintiff. Writer Nobuhiro Baba and his son, both living in Southern California, were contacted by Takahashi Shirō on this case, as Baba's son organized Takahashi's lectures at the Los Angeles Mokkei Club group (the readers' organization of the conservative business and ethics magazine, *Chichi*) that he was involved in. In the Los Angeles area, they formed the group, True Japan Network, to "offer an alternative view of the 'comfort women' statues," with some other Japanese residents in the area, according to Baba's son. Baba, his son, and a Buddhist priest, Ryūzen Hayashi, met each other via their movement over the "comfort women" issue. Baba recalls the public hearing at the Glendale City Council as a frustrating occasion and they were furious as they thought that they were looked down upon by the council members. The Japanese residents' feelings of not being heard, combined with their right-wing political orientation, and perhaps the fear of losing their reputation in the local community where Japanese residents are increasingly outnumbered by other Asians, led to the fear that many more statues would be built in Southern California, and they would lose further ground in the area. Baba and his son, as well as Hayashi, said that they did not know much about *Nippon Kaigi*, nor the organization's heavy involvement in this case when they joined the lawsuit. Although both were against the Glendale statue, they did not join the GAHT lawsuit as they were skeptical of the view of its leader Kōichi Mera and others in GAHT, so they decided to join the *Nippon Kaigi*'s case instead.[55]

For the *Asahi*-Glendale lawsuit, scholar Takahashi Shirō and lawyer Tokunaga Shin'ichi have visited the U.S. many times to prepare for the case, and also to organize local residents as supporters. Takahashi writes that he visited all the memorials in the U.S. and saw the memorials' inscriptions with his own eyes, and took photos of himself with each memorial.[56] Local Japanese residents or-

---

54 Katsuya Hirano, "A Reflection on Uemura Takashi's Talk at UCLA," *The Asia-Pacific Journal: Japan Focus* 13–33, no. 4 (August 17, 2015); Tomomi Yamaguchi and Emi Koyama, "What Are the Responses of Japanese Americans and Japanese Nationals Residing in the U.S. Toward the 'Comfort Women' Issue?" *Fight for Justice*. Accessed April 3, 2018. http://fightforjustice.info/?page_id=4300&lang=en.
55 Interview with Nobuhiro Baba, June 9, 2017, and interview with Ryūzen Hayashi and Nobuhiro's son, June 10, 2017.
56 Takahashi, "*Nihon o Kaitaisuru*," 180.

ganized events at which Takahashi, Tokunaga, and others spoke about the trial and the "history wars" in various North American locations, especially in the Los Angeles and New York areas. The most recent rally was held on 24 August 2017, sponsored by New York *Rekishi Mondai Kenkyūkai* (History Issues Research Group), with Nishioka Tsutomu, Takahashi Shirō, and Yamaoka Tetsuhide, all of whom are core theorists behind the *Asahi*-Glendale Lawsuit, as speakers.[57] In order to host the events and engage in activism, new organizations of Japanese residents, such as Himawari Japan in New York-New Jersey and *Toronto Seiron no Kai* in Toronto, Canada, were formed. The religious group, Happy Science, played a significant role in helping to organize these events.[58] Moreover, the roles of Japanese business as well as moral education organizations in the U.S. seem crucial in the "history wars." A network of Japanese residents with common business interests formed a revisionist study group in the case of the New York History Issues Research Group, which sponsored the above event. Free papers for the Japanese communities, such as *New York BIZ* and Los Angeles' *Nikkan Sun*, distributed at Japanese grocery stores and restaurants in the areas, often cover right-wing, revisionist news stories in Japanese, and possibly function as an important connection point for Japanese residents in the U.S.

The plaintiffs lost the case in Tokyo District Court on 22 December 2016, as the court did not recognize any causal relationship between the *Asahi*'s reports and the damages that the plaintiffs claim to have suffered, which included bullying of Japanese residents and children. Tokyo High Court supported the lower court's decision on February 2018, and the plaintiffs did not appeal the deci-

---

[57] "NY Rekishi Mondai Kenkyūkai, Dai 60-kai Reikai (8gatsu Kaisai), Nishioka Tsutomu Sensei, Takahashi Shiro Sensei, Yamaoka Tetsuhide Sensei ga Kōen, Sekai ni Hiromatta Uso to Tatakaitai." (NY Historical Issues Research Group, No. 60 regular meeting (held in August), Mr. Tsutomu Nishioka, Shirō Takahashi and Tetsuhide Yamaoka gave lectures, "We want to fight against the lies that spread in the world",) *New York BIZ*, September 9, 2017. "NY Rekishi Mondai Kenkyūkai, Dai 60-kai Reikai (8gatsu Kaisai), Nishioka Tsutomu Sensei, Takahashi Shirō Sensei, Yamaoka Tetsuhide Sensei ga Kōen 2, 'NY Hatsu no Kyōiku wo Hasshin Shiteikitai,' 'Mina ga Kyōryoku shiatte Taishowo.'" (NY Historical Issues Research Group, No. 60 regular meeting (held in August), Mr. Tsutomu Nishioka, Shirō Takahashi and Tetsuhide Yamaoka gave lectures 2, "I would like to disseminate education out of New York," "Let's deal with the issue with everyone's cooperation."). *New York BIZ*, September 23, 2017.

[58] Emi Koyama, "Amerika 'Ianfu' Hi Secchi eno Kōgeki" [The Attacks Against the Building of 'Comfort Women' Monuments in the U.S.], in *Umi wo Wataru Ianfu Mondai*, eds. Tomomi Yamaguchi et al. (Tokyo: Iwanami Shoten, 2016), 41–68. My interviews with multiple conservative individuals also indicate the deep involvement of Happy Science in organizing events in the U.S.

sion.⁵⁹ The ruling was thus finalized, and as a court battle, it was a failure for the plaintiffs and *Nippon Kaigi*. Yet as a movement, they successfully spread their theory that the widely accepted history of "comfort women" among scholars and in the international community, and testimonies of "comfort women" as "fake" via multiple gatherings, media and online reports, and the stories in the free papers among the Japanese residents in the U.S., and mobilized them to participate in their movement.

After the verdict was delivered at the Tokyo High Court on 8 February 2018, the supporters of the *Asahi* Glendale held a gathering, entitled "The Front Line of the History Wars: Anti-Japan Sentiments are Spreading with the 'Fake' reporting of the *Asahi*."⁶⁰ Despite the loss, the lead attorney, Tokunaga Shin'ichi, emphasized the positive outcomes of the lawsuit. First, he said that both the lower court and high court judgements admitted the existence of damages against Japanese residents in the U.S., such as bullying, threats and insults. The *Asahi* simply did not fight over this issue, and yet, it was interpreted by Tokunaga that it was the formal admission by the court on the existence of bullying. Tokunaga also claimed that "comfort women propaganda" is "hate speech" against the Japanese, utilizing and flipped the meaning of the term, "hate speech," that was used against anti-Korean group *Zaitokukai* that he defended multiple times for different trials. Secondly, according to Tokunaga, the court stated that it was difficult to say that the *Asahi's* false reports had no impact on the reputation of the Japanese abroad, and it was a major achievement for the movement. The *Asahi Shimbun*, however, explained that the court pointed out that "there was not enough evidence to say that the *Asahi*'s reporting created the rumors. The newspaper company interprets that its claim that the *Asahi*'s coverage did not have any causal relationship between the paper's coverage and the damages on the plaintiffs was fully supported by the court.⁶¹ Tokunaga criticized the *Asahi*'s attitude not to deal with and fight the issue of damages in court, as a newspaper company's attempt to minimize the impact of the false reporting.

Despite the fact that the story of bullying was raised as one of the major achievements of this lawsuit by Tokunaga, it did not necessarily function as a unifying theme for the plaintiffs and their supporters. In fact, it also worked to split the Japanese residents. At the appeals court of the *Asahi* Glendale lawsuit, the

---

59 *Asahi Shimbun*, "Ianfu hōdō wo weguru saiban no kiji wo keisai shimashita" [We Posted an Article on the Court Cases Related to the Reporting of "Comfort Women"], February 9, 2018. Accessed March 1, 2019. http://www.asahi.com/corporate/info/11350921
60 The video of the gathering is posted on YouTube. Accessed April 2, 2018. https://www.youtube.com/watch?v=4IdFRXtO3qM
61 *Asahi*, "Ianfu."

number of plaintiffs, originally about 2,500, decreased to 62, and more significantly, two main plaintiffs, Baba and Hayashi, withdrew. The main reason they mentioned was that they did not agree with the theory of "bullying" against Japanese children and residents that the lawyers and theorists supporting the case had been pushing. Baba repeatedly told me that they needed concrete evidence if they were going to argue about the existence of the bullying, but they had not been able to present any, despite their claim that the bullying existed. If bullying incidents were truly happening, why hadn't anyone brought up the issue to the schools, the Board of Education, or the police, Baba wondered. Hayashi also complained that the legal team fabricated his own claim about bullying in the complaint; he generally agreed with Baba on the case of bullying, but the complaint was written in the way that he was concerned about the bullying.[62]

As discussed before, the story of bullying was originally brought up by Okamoto Akiko, a former member of *Nippon Kaigi*, in 2012. Since then, without any concrete evidence provided even in court, the story spread in Japan via writings of conservative intellectuals such as Takahashi,[63] and more popular publications such as manga.[64] As a result, a good number of Japanese residents in Southern California and people in Japan came to believe that the "comfort woman" statue had caused the cases of bullying against Japanese children in the region. The story may have functioned to unify the Japanese in the U.S.— especially mothers whose role was defined to be the protectors of bullied children, to a certain extent. At the same time, the extensive use of the bullying allegations by the attorneys and the supporters of the lawsuit, without concrete evidence, certainly led some of the residents to wonder about the motivation of Nippon Kaigi to push forward with their lawsuit, whether they were truly thinking of the welfare of Japanese residents in the U.S., who had to live in the community, or if they were simply using them to advance their own interests in criticizing the Asahi, and changing the rhetoric on the "comfort women" issue. Regardless of the di-

---

62 Interview with Nobuhiro Baba, June 9, 2017, and interview with Ryūzen Hayashi and Baba's son, June 10, 2017.
63 Michael Yon, Mio Sugita, Shirō Takahashi, Tsutomu Nishioka, Shin'ichi Tokunaga, and Tetsuhide Yamaoka "*Ianfu*" *bōryaku-sen ni tachimukae! Nihon no kodomotachi wo dare ga mamorunoka?* [To Fight Against the Plot of "Comfort Women": Who is Going to Protect Japanese Children?] (Tokyo: Meiseisha, 2017).
64 Manga that fits into the "hate-Korean" genre, such as Sharin Yamano's *Manga dai-kenkanryū* (*Manga Big Hate Korean Wave*), and Akiko Tomita's *The Girls Trying to Bring About National Pride*, both described the scenes where Japanese girls are bullied and attacked violently due to the Glendale statue; Sharin Yamano, *Manga Dai Kenkanryū* [Manga Big Hate Korean Wave] (Tokyo: Shinyūsha, 2015); Akiko Tomita, *The Girls Trying to Bring About National Pride*, English Edition, Vol. 2 (Wilmington, DE: Amazon Services International, 2016).

versity of opinions among the original plaintiffs, the legal team's court documents make the claim about the bullying the core part of its argument, a position that *Nippon Kaigi* have firmly maintained since the article on Palisades Park by Okamoto in 2012.[65]

Historical Records, New Publications, and the Accusation of "Comfort Women" Stories as "Fake News"

The prime concern of the *Asahi* Glendale Lawsuit is the reputation of Japan and the Japanese abroad. The individuals involved in the lawsuit published a book composed of relevant articles and the final brief for the case.[66] In the book, Yamaoka Tetsuhide writes that the current situation is far beyond what the term "history wars" represents; rather, Yamaoka refers to it as a massive "information propaganda war" to the extent that bullying incidents against the Japanese abroad are happening.[67] The language that the right wing now uses includes "propaganda," "fake news," "plot," and "anti-Japan hate," which indicates that Japanese conservatives try to portray South Korea, China, and leftist Japanese as stronger enemies filled with hidden political, anti-Japan agendas, and emphasize the scale of their (imagined) impact. The demands to the *Asahi* to publish advertisements of apology in the English language media, and their extreme concern over the use of the term, "sexual slavery," or even "forced to provide sex"[68] in the media report highlights their extensive interest in publishing and spreading their version of "comfort women" history in English, which does not include any depiction of sexual slavery, and also the Japanese government's responsibility over the system of sexual slavery.[69]

---

65   Yon et al,, "*Ianfu*," 123.
66   Ibid.
67   Tetsuhide Yamaoka, *Nihon yo, mō ayamaruna! Rekishi mondai wa jijitsu ni fumikomazuni kaiketsu shinai* [Make Apologies History! Letting the Facts Be Our Guide] (Tokyo: Asuka Shinsha, 2017).
68   Ibid., 82–96.
69   In fact, Japan's biggest paper, *Yomiuri*, published an apology in its editorial for using the term, "sex slave" in 2014 in its past coverage; Jonathan Soble, "Japanese Newspaper Prints Apology for Using the Term 'Sex Slaves,'" *The New York Times*, November 28, 2014. Accessed April 4, 2018. https://www.nytimes.com/2014/11/29/world/asia/japan-yomiuri-shimbun-apology-sex-slaves.html.

To solve the perceived information discrepancy for Japanese conservatives, a lack of publications with their spin on the "comfort women" issue in English has been considered to be a major weakness of their activism. They have spread information primarily in Japanese on websites and in publications, but very few exist in English. In particular, while quite a few academic books and articles have been published on the topic, there are few peer-reviewed papers and books from the academic press that reflect their views in English. The publication of academic books in English from a prestigious publisher seems to be one major goal.

Conservative organizations, such as the Japan Policy Institute and GAHT, have started to disseminate pamphlets in English. In October 2015, a LDP Upper House representative, Inoguchi Kuniko, sent two non-academic revisionist books, Sankei's *History Wars* and Oh Sonfa's *Getting Over It! Why Korea Needs to Stop Bashing Japan*, to Japan Studies scholars in the U.S. and Australia, as well as to foreign correspondents stationed in Japan.[70] Responding to my interview, Inoguchi said that she sent them as "a part of LDP's team effort."[71]

On 1 October 2016, intellectuals involved with *Nippon Kaigi* established *Rekishi Ninshiki Mondai Kenkyūkai* (Historical Awareness Research Committee). Currently, its chair is Nishioka Tsutomu, its vice chairman is Takahashi Shirō, and its secretary general is Yamaoka Tetsuhide, all of whom are behind the *Asahi*-Glendale Trial. On the issue of historical consciousness, the organization states:

> We, concerned Japanese volunteers, have heretofore responded to domestic anti-Japanese forces with arguments grounded in historical fact. We have seen some success emerge from our efforts, such as when the *Asahi Shimbun* newspaper admitted to errors in some of its comfort woman reporting and duly apologized. However, the influence of anti-Japanese forces in the international community remains strong. The Japanese government has still not mounted a full-scale rebuttal to these forces in a systematic, organized fashion.

---

[70] Tessa Morris-Suzuki, "Historical Revisionism Undermines Abe's Apology," *East Asia Forum*, October 26, 2015. Accessed March 1, 2019. http://www.eastasiaforum.org/2015/10/26/historical-revisionism-undermines-abes-apology/; David McNeill, "Nippon Kaigi and the Radical Conservative Project to Take Back Japan," *The Asia-Pacific Journal, Japan Focus* 13–50, no. 4 (December 14, 2015). Accessed March 1, 2019. https://apjjf.org/-David-McNeill/4409; Tomomi Yamaguchi, "Inoguchi Kuniko giin kara ikinari hon ga okuraretekita – Rekishisen to Jimintō no taigai hasshin" [Senator Inoguchi Kuniko Sent Me Books Out of the Blue – 'History Wars' and the LDP's Communication Outside of Japan], *Synodos*, October 21, 2015. Accessed March 1, 2019. https://synodos.jp/politics/15387.

[71] Ibid.

Wherefore, we have gathered in this association in order to engage in basic research for the purpose of defending the honor of Japan.[72]

The above statement clearly shows their understanding of the *Asahi's* admission of its errors as their success, and yet, their efforts to win the "history wars" are not successful in the international community, due to the lack of the Japanese government's rebuttal. The Committee also sees its own view as neutral, as seen in the short explanation of the aim of the committee on its Japanese-language website, "in order to make the historical awareness issue neutral." The Committee opened its website consisting of both Japanese and English pages, held some symposiums, and initiated a new academic journal, and published five volumes of it and a special issue as of October 2019.

The Committee is housed within the Institute of Moralogy located at Reitaku University,[73] in Kashiwa City, Chiba Prefecture. Moralogy is a quasi-religious, moral education organization, and one of the core member groups of *Nippon Kaigi*. The role of moral education organizations in the "history wars" is significant, with its resources, and their ability to spread the grassroots movement to the general public.

For *Nippon Kaigi* and its new Historical Awareness Research Committee, the United Nations became another battleground of the "history wars," as the right-wingers consider it to be dominated by leftist lobbyists and NGOs.[74] *Nippon Kaigi* leaders have been directly influencing the direction of the Japanese government, and the most notable case is the influence of *Nippon Kaigi* leaders, especially scholar Takahashi Shirō, in the Japanese government's stance against UNESCO's Memory of the World Program. Takahashi is a scholar of education, not of histo-

---

72 Historical Awareness Research Committee, "A Message of Appeal from the Historical Awareness Research Committee," (2016). Accessed April 4, 2018. http://harc.tokyo/en/?page_id=10.
73 Reitaku University employs significant number of conservative scholars, including Hidetsugu Yagi and Jason Morgan.
74 In the mid 2000s, Akiko Okamoto of *Nippon Kaigi* and FAVS wrote articles in conservative *Seiron* magazine criticizing the family-related policy direction of the United Nations as "the Red United Nations" influenced by feminists of the United States and Europe. Okamoto, along with the Parliamentary and Municipal Council representatives of *Nippon Kaigi*, established the Family Value Society (FAVS) in April 2007, and aimed to become an NGO that could participate in United Nations' meetings. Since 2014, the Truth about Comfort Women National Movement has sent their delegations to Geneva and New York for the UN NGO meetings, and one of the regular participants is Kiyoshi Hosoya of FAVS. Nadeshiko Action and others also encourage the Japanese right-wing groups to send their opinions to the UN. My interviews with conservatives uncovered that Okamoto is the figure who initially advised the people to attend meetings and send their opinions to the UN.

ry, yet he submitted his expert opinion to UNESCO on behalf of the Japanese government in 2015, when documents about the Nanking Massacre were registered under the Memory of the World program. He also attended the UNESCO meeting in Abu Dhabi as an observer with the Japanese government. He has been writing on the UNESCO issue extensively in various conservative magazines and newsletters. That is, he has been playing the role of a spokesperson of this issue, while working closely with the Ministry of Foreign Affairs.

On 27 September 2017, the Historical Awareness Research Committee held the "Emergency Symposium: Don't Let UNESCO accept the Registration of 'Comfort Woman' Documents!" The panelists were the usual *Nippon Kaigi* theorists: Sakurai Yoshiko, Nishioka Tsutomu, Takahashi Shirō, and Yamaoka Tetsuhide. The Committee then adopted an emergency statement at the symposium: "We oppose the registration of 'materials related to comfort women' with the UNESCO Memory of the World Program." Their statement lists three "problems" with UNESCO's program, headlined as below:

1) The application has not been open to the public and there has been no consultation whatsoever with concerned parties, such as with Japanese scholars.
2) The application was made by groups holding biased views that the "comfort women" were "sex slaves" and the "comfort women system" was equivalent to the Holocaust conducted by Nazi Germany.
3) Their application is politically charged, as the applicants are opposing the governmental agreement to resolve the "comfort women" issue between Japan and South Korea.[75]

Later, the committee also issued "Statement of Scholars of Japan Opposed to the Joint Registration of the "Voices of 'Comfort Women'" of the Japanese Military with UNESCO's 'Memory of the World' Program," that 103 scholars signed.[76] In addition to these "Japanese scholars," the Historical Awareness Research Committee also mentioned Nadeshiko Action, an organization without an official NPO status and with an unclear membership other than its leader, Yamamoto Yumiko. According to the committee, because some groups including Nadeshiko

---

75 Historical Awareness Research Committee, Emergency Statement: "We oppose the registration of 'materials related to the comfort women' with the UNESCO Memory of the World Program," (2017). Accessed April 4, 2017. http://harc.tokyo/en/?p=114.

76 Historical Awareness Research Committee, "Statement of Scholars of Japan Opposed to the Joint Registration of the "Voices of 'Comfort Women'" of the Japanese Military with UNESCO's 'Memory of the World' Program," October 9, 2017 (2017). Accessed April 4, 2018. http://harc.tokyo/en/?p=135.

Action submitted "the same documents related to 'comfort women' from a different perspective,"[77] it should be the group that should be consulted by the NGOs of the eight countries participating in the submission of "comfort women" documents. The Committee also criticized the eight countries' NGOs for insisting that "comfort women" were sex slaves, claiming that it is a "prejudice" against not only the Japanese government's views but also "the views of many renowned Japanese, Korean, and American scholars who have studied the comfort women issue."[78] Their opposition to the South Korea-Japan diplomatic agreement is also considered to be "politically charged." The Committee demands that "We strongly oppose this and request that the Japanese government cease all contributions to UNESCO should the application be forced through."

As a result, UNESCO, and the International Advisory Committee of the Memory of the World Program, decided on 16 October 2017, that the nominations for "Voices of the 'Comfort Women,'" submitted by the international coalition of "comfort women" support NGOs, and "Documentation on 'Comfort Women' and Japanese Army discipline," submitted by four revisionist groups, including Nadeshiko Action, based in Japan and the U.S.,[79] were recommended to be postponed, pending a "dialogue" among concerned parties, to "leading to a joint nomination to encompass as far as possible all relevant documents."[80] That is, UNESCO went with the claim by the Historical Awareness Research Committee—and likely the Japanese government—in suggesting the "dialogue" among the parties involved, including revisionist groups. It means that the two versions of history—including the revisionist one that denies the Japanese government's responsibility for the "comfort women"—are evaluated on the equal grounds by the international authority, which is the obvious leap from the past stances taken by the United Nations.

The Japanese Committee for Joint Nomination to the UNESCO Memory of the World (MoW) Register, composed of six Japan-based NGOs working in support of

---

77 Historical Awareness Research Committee, "Emergency Statement."
78 Historical Awareness Research Committee, "Emergency Statement."
79 The four Japan-US groups include The Alliance for Truth about Comfort Women, The Study Group for Japan's Rebirth (USA), The Institution of Research of Policy of Media and Broadcasting, Japanese Women for Justice and Peace (Nadeshiko Action). Hideaki Kase, Kōichi Mera, Kazunobu Ōyama, and Yumiko Yamamoto. "Statement Concerning the Decision of UNESCO's Memory of the World Register on 'Documentation on 'Comfort Women' and Japanese Army discipline': United Nations Mark a Great Turning Point on the Comfort Women Issue," *Society for the Dissemination of Historical Fact*. Posted October 31, 2017. Accessed April 3, 2018. http://www.sdh-fact.com/CL/Mow_statement_English.pdf.
80 "UNESCO Memory of the World Nominations List 2016–2017." Accessed January 14, 2019. https://en.unesco.org/sites/default/files/mow_recommended_nominations_list_2016–2017.pdf.

"comfort women," released a statement on 27 October 2017, entitled "*Statement Concerning the IAC Review for the UNESCO's Memory of the World Register: Towards the 'Culture of Memory', not the 'Culture of Oblivion.'*" The Committee points to the reported pressure from the Japanese government onto UNESCO, and "reports indicate that the strong opposition of the government of Japan to the registration of the 'Voices of Comfort Women' has seen it take the extreme measure of suspending the payment of its UNESCO contribution in order to have amendments made to the rules of the Memory of the World Register." The committee states that the set of records that they submitted "is of universal value concerning women's human rights," and points to the significance of them to be included in the program as "registration this year would have guaranteed their preservation as materials valuable for the world. In addition, the few remaining women survivors would have been assured that their ordeal was not in vain even long after they are finally gone." The committee continues,

> What the government of Japan seeks is oblivion. To counter the "culture of oblivion," "dialogue" has little role to play. Rather, in responding to the "culture of oblivion," the role to play expected of the global community, and the UNESCO Memory of the World Register in particular, is nothing other than pushing it back and building a "culture of memory."[81]

The Historical Awareness Research Committee, on the other hand, praised the UNESCO's decision in its statement released on 31 October. It states, "[u]nfortunately, UNESCO and other UN-related organizations have functioned as a place where organizations with biased view used to disseminate their anti-Japan propaganda," and "With the achievement this time, we will demand that they will argue against the anti-Japan propaganda to protect our nation's honor."[82]

What became clear out of the registration for the UNESCO "Memory of the World" program is the influence of the Historical Awareness Research Committee and *Nippon Kaigi* on the direction of the Japanese government, as well as their visible collaboration with the more "fringe" groups, such as Nadeshiko Action. The revisionist version of "comfort women" history that is supported by these

---

[81] "Statement Concerning the IAC Review for the UNESCO's Memory of the World Register: Towards the 'Culture of Memory', not the 'Culture of Oblivion,'" The Japanese Committee for Joint Nomination to the UNESCO MoW Register 2017, October 27, 2017, Women's Active Museum on War and Peace. Accessed April 4, 2018. http://wam-peace.org/en/20171028/.

[82] Historical Awareness Research Committee, "Rekishi Ninshiki Mondai Kenkyūkai. UNESCO no Sekai no Kioku eno Ianfu Shiryō Tōroku o Kangei suru Rekininken Seimei" [The Statement to Welcome the Postponement of the Registration of Comfort Women Materials to UNESCO's Memory of the World Program]." (2017) Accessed April 4, 2018. http://harc.tokyo/en/?page_id=10.

organizations was recognized as valid and worthy of having a "dialogue" by UNESCO, an entity that was likely under the pressure from the Japanese government that threated to withdraw its funding.

Conclusion

The influence of *Nippon Kaigi*, as the largest conservative organization with close ties with the current government and the ruling party, cannot be ignored. This is true for *Nippon Kaigi* and also its related organizations such as the Japan Policy Institute and Historical Awareness Research Committee. While their revisionist claims may sound very far away from the widely accepted claims on the "comfort women" issue in the international community, they are in fact mainstream in the current political context in Japan. Despite their loss in the *Asahi*-Glendale lawsuit, conservatives are still energized about the "history wars." The leaders of *Nippon Kaigi* maintain a close relationship with the current government's leaders and bureaucrats. Their activist approach is not overly radical, and they tend to choose a more realistic approach so that they can make concrete progress to advance their claims. Moreover, as we saw in the case of UNESCO's "Memory of the World" program, the Japanese government and *Nippon Kaigi* are trying their best to block the voices and memories of "comfort women" and the systematic nature of sexual slavery to be considered as valid and meaningful historical record.

In the meantime, statues and memorials continue to be built in the U.S. and beyond. In September 2017, the first statue in a major city in North America was built in San Francisco. As the City of Osaka terminated the sister city relationship with San Francisco in October 2018 due to the building of the statue, the news was reported widely, in and outside of Japan. Responding to the San Francisco statue, Chief Cabinet Secretary Suga Yoshihide said in his press conference on 24 November that "erecting comfort women statues in the United States and other countries is in conflict with our country's stance and extremely regrettable."[83] *Sankei* also reports that Prime Minister Abe reportedly said "San Francisco was a failure. We seriously need to prevent this from happening."[84]

---

83 Jacey Fortin, "'Comfort Women' Statue in San Francisco Leads a Japanese City to Cut Ties," *New York Times*, November 25, 2017. Accessed March 1, 2019. https://www.nytimes.com/2017/11/25/world/asia/comfort-women-statue.html.
84 Kei Ishinabe, "Jimintō medatsu donkanburi: Abe shushō, San Furanshisuko wa shippai datta" [LDP's Insensitivity Is Standing Out: Prime Minister Abe, "San Francisco was a failure"], *Sankei News*, December 14, 2017.

While the government is more openly fighting against the "history wars" and the building of "comfort women" memorials overseas, in January 2018, Sugiyama Shinsuke, former vice minister for foreign affairs, was appointed as an ambassador to the United States. Sugiyama said in an interview in February 2018 that he "will work hard to gain acceptance of Japan's position against statues built in the United States, as well as other countries, that symbolize the 'comfort women.'"[85] The "history wars," and the pressure from the Japanese government against the "comfort women" issue and other history-related issues in the U.S. and beyond are continuing, and may become even more intensified.

---

[85] Jiji, "Japan's Next Ambassador to the U.S. firm on Stance against North Korea," *The Japan Times*, February 16, 2018. Accessed March 1, 2019. https://www.japantimes.co.jp/news/2018/02/16/national/politics-diplomacy/japans-next-ambassador-u-s-firm-stance-north-korea/#.WsUsrSNjZYI.

Emi Koyama
Japanese Far-Right Activities in the United States and at the United Nations: Conflict and Coordination between Japanese Government and Fringe Groups

"Japanese consul general: Brookhaven memorial is 'symbol of hatred'" stated the headline of an article published on 23 June 2017 by *Reporter Newspapers*, the publisher of several local newspapers in Georgia, a mere week before the planned unveiling of a "comfort women" memorial in Brookhaven, a suburb of Atlanta, Georgia.

Citing a recorded interview with Shinozuka Takashi, Japan's Consulate General for Atlanta, journalist Dyana Bagby reported that Shinozuka not only stated that the memorial dedicated to the victims of WWII-era Japanese military sexual slavery was a "symbol of hatred," but also argued that "there is 'no evidence' that the military sexually enslaved women," and that the women were, in fact, "paid prostitutes." This shocking statement was a testament to how far Japan's organized effort to distort history and attack victims and survivors of Japan's wartime atrocities had advanced.

After Shinozuka's comment received widespread condemnation from across the world, he and the Japanese government clarified that the Consulate General had not actually used the phrase "paid prostitutes." But in the recording released online by Bagby, Shinozuka can be heard stating that "in Asian culture, in some countries, we have girls who decide to go to take this job to help their family." In the context, "this job" clearly refers to voluntary forms of prostitution, so Bagby was correct to interpret his statement as arguing that "comfort women" were voluntary "paid prostitutes."

Shinozuka was, of course, not criticized for using the specific phrase "paid prostitute" but for negating the historical fact that many women and girls were forced to serve as "comfort women" under various combinations of force, fraud, coercion, or debt bondage, and for suggesting that these "girls," as Shinozuka calls them, voluntarily became "comfort women" as a career choice.

I was shocked not by the fact that someone like Shinozuka holds such a repugnant view, which I already know that many Japanese officials share, but by the increasing boldness of the Japanese government, where officials no longer even feel the need to conceal their true feelings on this issue. This is an important shift that has taken place over the last several years during which I have

https://doi.org/10.1515/9783110643480-014

been observing and exposing various anti-"comfort women" efforts within the U.S. by Japanese diplomats and far-right activists.

My Initial Engagment with the "Comfort Women" Issue

I first began following the "comfort women" issue in the U.S. around July 2014, when Glendale, California proposed to install a "peace memorial" dedicated to the victims and survivors of the Japanese military "comfort women" system on public land. Mera Koichi has been one of the most consistent leaders of the Japanese nationalist movement that denies the history of "comfort women," and he was especially active in opposing the memorial in Glendale. In 2006, he founded the Study Group for Japan's Renewal, a monthly nationalist history discussion group in Los Angeles, but his activity was not known outside of the small community of Japanese nationals because it was publicized and held in the Japanese language only. But as Mera and his followers descended to the Glendale City Hall en masse to speak out against the proposed memorial, arguing that "comfort women is a myth" and that "the memorial leads to bullying and hate crimes against Japanese residents," the presence of a vocal Japanese nationalist movement in the U.S. became widely reported by U.S. media for the first time.

To be clear, it was not U.S.-born Japanese Americans (most of whom do not speak any Japanese) who opposed the memorial. It was "shin issei," or "new first generation" immigrants and Japanese nationals from Japan, especially those who came to the U.S. during or after the 1980s. And yet, media often inaccurately described them as "Japanese American," leading to confusion and frustration among Japanese Americans who did not recognize any of the protesters as members of their community. In response, local Japanese American leaders expressed their support for the memorial in solidarity with the Korean American group that was spearheading the establishment of memorial, culminating in speeches and participation by leaders of local Japanese American groups Nikkei for Civil Rights and Redress (hereafter, NCRR) and the San Fernando Valley chapter of Japanese American Citizens League at the official unveiling of the memorial. And when Mera and others filed a lawsuit against the City of Glendale seeking the removal of the memorial, the Japanese American Bar Association of California issued a joint statement with the Korean American Bar Association and other Asian American groups to denounce the frivolous lawsuit.

NCRR was founded in 1980 to seek apology and redress for Japanese Americans unjustly incarcerated by the U.S. government during World War II. After

Japanese Americans achieved their goal in 1988, NCRR continued working on defending the rights of ethnic minorities both in the U.S. and in Japan, including resisting the persecution of immigrants and Muslims post-9/11 and after Donald Trump's presidential inauguration, as Japanese Americans had faced similar persecution during the 1940s. In a speech given at the Glendale unveiling, NCRR's Kathy Masaoka described how important the U.S. government's decision to issue a formal apology and provide compensation was to the healing of historical trauma for Japanese Americans, and urged the Japanese government to follow suit.

Japanese American incarceration during World War II was a result of the racist prejudice that alleged Japanese Americans to be unpatriotic and potentially loyal to an enemy, the Japanese Empire. It has been well-established in studies since then that the racial targeting had no basis in reality, but Japanese Americans continue to feel the deep impact of the historical trauma within their families and communities. It was not surprising that many Japanese Americans reacted negatively when Japanese nationalists and recent immigrants who do not share that history falsely represented themselves as Japanese Americans while exonerating the Japanese Empire of its massive war atrocities.

GAHT and Japanese Historical Revisionism

The Global Alliance for Historical Truth (hereafter, GAHT) was founded by Mera Koichi in February 2014, two weeks before the organization filed a lawsuit against the City of Glendale. Its board roster is a who's who of Japan's far-right historical revisionist movement, including Fujioka Nobukatsu (Japanese Society for History Textbook Reform), Yamamoto Yumiko (Nadeshiko Action, and former vice president of anti-Korean extremist group *Zaitokukai*), Kase Hideaki (Society for the Dissemination of Historical Fact), and other well-known right-wing agitators.

To its Japanese supporters and donors, GAHT pledged to "expose historical fallacy of 'comfort women' narrative" through the lawsuit. But in the legal complaint, GAHT's main argument was that the City of Glendale violated the federal government's exclusive foreign affairs powers by involving itself in a contested foreign affairs issue like the "comfort women" issue. GAHT also failed to allege concrete harms caused by the establishment of the memorial, even as it fueled unsubstantiated claims of widespread bullying and harassment of Japanese children in the Glendale area in Japanese media (members of JACL-SFV and other local Japanese American groups are not aware of any such incidents).

The legal battles continued for three years in state and federal courts, but plaintiff Mera et al. lost in all five courts. Furthermore, California state courts imposed a fine on the plaintiffs under the state's anti-SLAPP (strategic lawsuit against public participation) statute, calling GAHT's claim "contrary to the fundamental principles of federalism and democracy."

As the lawsuit was pending, Mera and other Japanese nationalists continued holding revisionist panels and other events in many cities across the U.S., including San Francisco and New York City (in addition to Los Angeles), aimed at mobilizing other Japanese people living in the U.S. to oppose efforts to memorialize "comfort women." Speakers for these events included Mera, Yamamoto, pro-Japanese American YouTuber Tony Marano, his representative in Japan (and the person who recruited Marano in the first place) Fujiki Shun'ichi, "Rompa Project" founder and "Happy Science" religion affiliated Fujii Mitsuhiko, former Member of the Parliament Sugita Mio (who has since returned to the Parliament), Japan Conference-affiliated Takahashi Shirō, Hosoya Kiyoshi of the Researchers of History on Modern Japan, who is also affiliated with Japan Family Values Society as well as GAHT, and others. Logistics for many of these events are taken care of by representatives of Happy Science, which has chapters all over the U.S.

Almost all of these right-wing events are publicized and held in Japanese, so they used to take place without being noticed by Japanese Americans or anyone else outside of small Japanese enclaves. But since one such event in the San Francisco area was protested by a coalition of Asian American, peace, women's, and labor activists in December 2014, progressive Japanese and other activists began monitoring and protesting them wherever they happen.

In March 2015, Japanese nationalists organized a "comfort women" denier panel featuring Marano, Yamamoto, and Takahashi at the New York Japanese American Society, who had been told only that they were holding a "history study group." The New York Japanese American Society cancelled the reservation after activists had alerted them about the nature of the event being held in their space. The history deniers moved the event to a nearby restaurant, but members of the Japanese American-led activist group Sloths Against Nuclear State, along with women visiting New York to attend the United Nations Commission on the Status of Women, showed up to protest the event.

The most amazing example of resistance against "comfort women" denial in the U.S. took place in April 2015 at Central Washington University, two hours southeast of Seattle, where Japanese language instructor Mariko Okada-Collins had invited Taniyama Yujirō, the producer of a historical revisionist fauxmentary (i.e., fake documentary) film on "comfort women," to speak and show his film on campus. Unlike almost all other revisionist events in the U.S., it was held on an American college campus in English for an American audience.

When the campus community heard about the upcoming lecture and screening by a "comfort women" denier, students and faculty organized various events to counter it. The largest among these was a panel organized by anthropologist Mark Auslander, which brought together experts from anthropology, history, political science, literature, and other fields, and was attended by hundreds of students. The Department of History issued a statement signed by every member of its faculty denouncing historical revisionism and calling for a just and equitable solution to the "comfort women" issue.

Students also organized a film screening of a short documentary in which former "comfort women" tell their stories, and students in the Theatre department held a reading of survivor testimonies. Finally, a group of Chinese and other exchange students quietly held a sign protesting the revisionist film screening outside of the right-wing event.

San Francisco as a Battleground for "Comfort Women" Memorials

When San Francisco became the largest city in the U.S. to ever consider enacting a memorial dedicated to "comfort women" in July 2015, it became the battleground between Japanese nationalists and activists from across the U.S. who support survivors. Several days before the proposal was to be introduced at the Board of Supervisors (San Francisco's city council), revisionist group Nadeshiko Action sent out an alert to its supporters to contact the Supervisors to oppose the proposal. Hundreds of angry emails were sent to the Supervisors, and dozens of Japanese nationalists lined up to testify in opposition, including GAHT's Mera, Taguchi Yoshiaki of Happy Science, and Okada-Collins from Central Washington University. In response, the Board of Supervisors decided to hold a formal hearing in a committee before voting on the proposal.

The memorial was originally proposed by the Rape of Nanking Redress Coalition, a group comprised mainly (but not exclusively) of Chinese Americans. After the controversy erupted in the City Hall, they were joined by activists who had protested the right-wing event the year before, including Asian American, Japanese, *Hisabetsu Nikkei* (Okinawans, Ainu, Zainichi Koreans, and others who came from Japan but are considered minority in Japan), as well as women's, peace, and labor activists, scholars, and faith leaders.

At the same time, there was some organized resistance from Japanese American leaders toward the proposal. Unlike the *"shin issei"* Japanese nationalists, these were generally liberal individuals who play important roles in Japantown and Asian American communities in San Francisco, and are not revisionists. Their main concern had to do with the potential negative influences of the proposed memorial, fueled by the unsubstantiated claims of bullying and harassment against Japanese children and adults in Glendale.

In difficult conversations with these individuals, supporters of the memorial realized that there was a concerted effort not just by the Japanese nationalists, but also by the Japanese Consulate General of San Francisco to deceive and even threaten Japanese American leaders and institutions. According to them, the Japanese government told them about massive anti-Japanese bullying and harassment in Glendale, and at least one person was told that the Chinese government was behind the "comfort women" redress effort to split the Japan-U.S. alliance. In addition, Japanese American leaders who work for non-profit organizations that receive financial support from Japanese companies doing business in San Francisco were told that their funding may be withdrawn if San Francisco proved itself to be a less than hospitable place to continue doing business in.

For years, the Japanese government has tried to interfere with municipalities' decisions to address the "comfort women" issue, starting with Palisades Park, New Jersey, the site of the first memorial to "comfort women" in the U.S. in 2010. But it was mostly through formal diplomatic and governmental channels, or through Japanese corporations (like Japanese auto parts maker Denso in Detroit) rather than directly deceiving and threatening Japanese Americans as they apparently did in San Francisco. As in the case of Atlanta Consulate General Shinozuka's statement, this demonstrates increasing boldness on the part of Japanese government.

In the end, the Board of Supervisors voted unanimously to support the establishment of the memorial in September 2015 after Japanese nationalists self-destructed during a public hearing. Many people on both sides testified at the hearing, including survivor Lee Yong-Soo, who flew from South Korea to attend the hearing at the invitation of a Korean American group.

Mera and several other Japanese nationalists took the opportunity to attack Lee, who was sitting in the front row, selectively quoting anthropologist C. Sarah Soh's book *The Comfort Women: Sexual Violence and Postcolonial Memory* (2008) to suggest that Lee's testimony was inconsistent and unreliable, despite the fact Soh herself cautions against such (ab)use of her scholarship: "The fact that some individual survivors and their advocates have given accounts that are exaggerated or only partially true, however, does not warrant the assertion by conservative leaders in Japan that Japan is being 'condemned based on propagandistic accounts of things that simply did not happen'."[1]

Supervisor Eric Mar, who presided over the committee, interrupted Mera, asking if he was calling Lee a liar, and Supervisor David Campos repeated, "shame on you" four times before voting for the proposal, adding that he "hoped" that the Japanese government wasn't behind such offensive comments. To many observers, Mera's and his colleagues' actions were convincing evidence that a memorial was necessary to defend the honor and dignity of victims and survivors and to remember the historical truth.

Governmental Attempts to Bury History of the "Comfort Women" Issue

The Japanese government's hidden diplomacy to bury the historical memory of "comfort women" goes beyond opposition to "comfort women" memorials. For example, a month after the Board of Supervisors of San Francisco voted in support of establishing the memorial, the Japanese Embassy in Washington, D.C. seemingly created a fake "Vietnamese American" astroturf (i.e., a sponsored organization with an ulterior motive; a play on the term "grassroots") organization, Voices of Vietnam, through a lobbyist firm.

"Voices of Vietnam" registered its web domain on 4 October 2015 and had no prior existence whatsoever. And yet on 15 October the group bought a full-page color advertisement in the *Wall Street Journal* to coincide with the visit of then-South Korean President Geun-Hye Park to the White House to criticize the South Korean government's inaction on sexual violence committed by the South Korean military during the Vietnam War. They also held a press conference at the National Press Club, where former U.S. Senator Norm Coleman attacked the South Korean government, even though the Korean military was under U.S. command in Vietnam. While Coleman was simply introduced as a former U.S. Senator, his current employer was international law firm Hogan Lovells, a registered agent of the Japanese government. In addition, lawyers at Hogan Lovells later authored the Japanese government's amicus curiae brief on behalf of GAHT in the Glendale memorial case.

---

[1] C. Sarah Soh, *The Comfort Women: Sexual Violence and Postcolonial Memory* (Chicago: Chicago University Press, 2008), 104.

The 2015 Agreement between Japan and South Korea

When foreign ministers of Japan and South Korea announced a "final and irreversible solution" on the issue of "comfort women" in late 2015, it was the National Security Advisor Susan Rice who welcomed the bilateral agreement on behalf of the White House, which lent credence to the analysis that the agreement was a product of political pressure on both countries from the U.S. government in order to address national security and diplomatic concerns of the United States. The 2015 agreement was received favorably by the U.S. government and U.S. media, making it difficult for the average reader to understand that the remaining survivors of the Japanese military "comfort women" system were not involved or consulted in the negotiation between the two governments, or how it fell far short of meeting demands made by survivors and various United Nations committees, as well as by U.S. Congress. But as activists from Glendale to San Francisco and beyond voiced opposition to the "solution" that excluded and silenced survivors, the media began reporting these criticisms.

After the governments of Japan and South Korea agreed to mutually avoid criticizing each other at international forums, the Japanese government intensified its efforts to fight the "history war," as it was referred to by conservative Japanese newspaper *Sankei Shimbun*. The turning point was the statement made by Foreign Ministry official Sugiyama Shinsuke (who was later promoted to the Deputy Minister of Foreign Affairs and then the Ambassador to the U.S.) at the United Nations Committee on the Elimination of Discrimination against Women (hereafter, CEDAW) in March 2016.

In response to questions by members of the CEDAW, Sugiyama stated that the "myth" of "forcible recruitment" of "comfort women" was a result of erroneous reporting by the liberal media which turned out to be false. Further, he argued that there was no basis for the estimate of the number of "comfort women" as 200,000, and that they were not "sex slaves." This approach clearly deviates from Japanese government's longstanding public stance since the mid-1990s, in which they maintained that the Japanese government has already apologized (however vaguely) and done everything they could to take accountability under the 1993 Kōno Statement. This three-point set—no forcible recruitment, no basis for the 200,000 figure, and no "sex slaves"—is a milder restatement of the right-wing view that "comfort women" were voluntary "paid prostitutes," and was welcomed as the de facto repeal of the Kōno Statement.

In early 2017, when the Japanese government submitted an amicus curiae brief to the U.S. Supreme Court in support of GAHT in its lawsuit against the

City of Glendale, Hogan Lovells attorneys invoked the same three points as reasons that the Japanese government is interested in setting the record straight. By then, GAHT had lost all previous contests and paid a large fine to the City of Glendale. Since they could not afford to keep their high-powered lawyer, Mera, Yamamoto, and Hosoya, none of whom have legal backgrounds, came together to draft briefs, which was edited by a local attorney hired for a fixed amount. And since the Supreme Court takes up less than two percent of cases they were petitioned to hear, there was almost no chance that they could possibly prevail. It is hard to comprehend why the Japanese government chose to intervene at that point, but the Supreme Court refused to hear the case, and rulings against GAHT became final.

Japanese Opposition to the Brookhaven Memorial

The day before the "comfort women" memorial was unveiled in Brookhaven, Georgia, ten Japanese nationalists and their supporters (including Tony Marano) attended a City Council meeting to ask them to cancel the memorial. Consulate General Shinozuka, who had notoriously described "comfort women" as "girls who took the job" as prostitutes to help out their family, did not attend, but his deputy Consulate Ōyama Tomoko testified, once again invoking the same three points.

While Japanese diplomats have worked behind the scenes in past attempts to convince or pressure municipalities, Japanese Americans, and others to oppose the memorial, this was probably the first time that a representative of a Japanese government gave a one-on-one interview to local media or spoke at a public meeting of a municipal government in opposition to the memorial, which is another sign of its increasing boldness.

However, it is not clear whether the increasing boldness of the Japanese government has helped their cause. Similar to how Mera's self-inflicted explosion might have led to the unanimous vote in favor of the memorial at the San Francisco Board of Supervisors, it is possible that the Japanese government's aggressive efforts may be backfiring in some places. Even the conservative Japanese newspaper *Sankei Shimbun*, which runs the "history war" series in its pages, cautioned on 8 July 2016 that Korean groups sometimes "exploit" the Japanese government's involvement in opposition to the memorials as an argument for the need for such a memorial.

Since the beginning of the backlash against the "comfort women" redress movement in the mid-1990s (for example, the Japanese Society for History Textbook Reform was founded in 1996), Japan's political leaders have consistently denied the history of "comfort women" domestically while telling the rest of the world that Japan has already acknowledged its responsibility in the Kōno Statement and has made amends through Prime Ministers' "personal" letters of apology and the Asian Women's Fund. But Shinozuka's statement at the CEDAW and the Japanese government's actions thereafter demonstrate that this two-decade-long doubletalk has finally ended.

And it is not likely that the Japanese government, with its (ironically named, since it is quite conservative) Liberal Democratic Party majority would reverse its course anytime soon, whether or not Prime Minister Abe remains in power. Moreover, opposition party leaders do not appear to be prepared to challenge the course: according to the *Sankei* newspaper on 1 July 2017, supposedly liberal Democratic Party leader Renho argued that it was "unacceptable" that a "comfort women" memorial was erected in Brookhaven, and that the Ministry of Foreign Affairs must do more to address the issue.

Similarly, University of Kyoto professor Takezawa Yasuko, a highly respected expert on race and racism who has extensive connections to Japanese American communities due to her work on the racial identity formation of Japanese Americans, emailed a member of a Japanese American group in Southern California that had supported the Glendale memorial with "reliable" information on the issue, all of which were those representing the views of the Japanese government and nothing from survivors or their advocates. The fact that even supposedly liberal leaders and scholars are promoting views that only conservatives felt free to express just a decade ago shows how far to the right the Japanese public discourse on the issue of "comfort women" has shifted in the past several years.

Conclusion

Japanese Americans are facing an important turning point today. With the Trump administration's hostile policies toward immigrants, Muslims, and other minorities, Japanese Americans are recognizing the need to use their own experience of similarly being targeted by the U.S. government as a bridge to reach out to those facing persecution today and building alliances. At the same time, the Japanese government is increasing funding for cultural exchange programs, academic research centers, and pro-Japan think tanks under the banner of "strategic external communication" in an effort to strengthen its hold over Japanese American and other influential institutions, intensifying conflict between progressive

Japanese American youth who view themselves as Asian Americans and part of a broader anti-racist social justice struggles and the older leadership of Japanese American groups who fund and manage Japanese American institutions. Japan's historical revisionism appears to continue to play a role in shaping and sometimes disrupting Japanese American and other Asian American communities, as well as international relations.

Part V: **New Sources and Theories**

Peipei Qiu
Documenting War Atrocities Against Women:
Newly Discovered Japanese Military Files in Jilin Provincial Archives

Since the "comfort women"[1] redress movement arose in the late 1980s, history revisionists in Japan have continuously denied the forcible drafting of hundreds of thousands of "comfort women" and the torture these women suffered at the hands of the Imperial Japanese forces. Despite ample historical materials and victims' testimonies confirming the crimes, Japanese officials insist that no evidence has been found to prove the existence of the sexual slavery in the Japanese military. At the same time, the Japanese government continues supporting efforts to remove the "comfort women" memorials and information concerning the issue in history textbooks.

Facing the steadfast revisionist campaigns, Chinese researchers have put great effort into archival research in recent years and unearthed new evidence for the Imperial Japanese military's direct involvement in setting up the "comfort women" system. This paper discusses the dedicated work and research findings of the Jilin Provincial Archives.[2] These findings show undeniably that the "comfort women" system was implemented by the Japanese nation-state to further its aggression in Asia; that women from Japan and its colony were drafted into the "comfort stations" under Japan's "National Mobilization Law;" that a large number of Chinese women in occupied areas were enslaved in the Japanese military "comfort stations;" and that the Japanese military authorities had purposely concealed information regarding the "comfort women" even before the war ended.

---

[1] I use quotation marks around the terms "comfort women," "comfort stations," and "comfort facilities" to acknowledge that "comfort" was a misleading euphemism coined by the Japanese military to refer to sexual slavery. However, to maintain the historical integrity of documents, when quoting from historic Japanese military files, I have not added quotation marks around these terms.

[2] I would like to express my deep thanks to Zhao Yujie, Senior Research Archivist at the Jilin Provincial Archives, for her time and generosity in providing information and archival materials for this study. I would also like to thank Yi Baozhong, Professor at the Center for Northeast Asian Studies, Jilin University, for facilitating my contact with Zhao Yujie.

https://doi.org/10.1515/9783110643480-015

The Jilin Provincial Archives

Jilin Province lies in the center of China's Northeast plain. The area was occupied by the infamous Japanese Kwantung Army in 1931, from the very beginning of Imperial Japan's aggressive war. In 1932, the provincial capital, Changchun, was renamed Xinjing (also spelled Hsinking, meaning "New Capital") and became the capital of the puppet state Manchukuo (Manzhouguo in pinyin) set up by Japan. The Kwantung (Guandong in pinyin) Army also set up its headquarters there.[3] "Kwantung" literally means "east of the Shanhai Pass." It was a guarded pass, east of which was Manchuria. Following the Russo-Japanese War, Japan occupied Kwantung Leased Territory and established the Kwantung Garrison to control the region, which became the most prestigious army group in the Imperial Japanese Army in the 1930s and was largely responsible for the creation of Japan's puppet state Manchukuo.

A staggering number of military and administrative documents were kept in the capital area during the fourteen years of Japanese occupation. At the end of the war, Japan carried out a national action to destroy the wartime documents, but the Kwantung Army was unable to destroy them all before the city was taken over by the Soviet forces in a lightning offensive in August 1945,[4] leaving behind a large number of the files that were later preserved in the Jilin Provincial Archives.

Jilin Provincial Archives is one of the many national archives in China. Established in 1959, it preserves both historical and contemporary documents produced by the local administrations. Currently Jilin Provincial Archives preserves about 520,000 volumes/files (*juan jian*) of historical documents dating from 1754 to 1949, of which 100,000 volumes/files in 65 case-sets (*quan zong*) were produced during Japan's invasion of China (*Riben qin-Hua dangan*, hereafter, RQD).[5] These documents came from different places, including both materials

---

[3] This paper uses the pinyin system to write Chinese names and titles except for "Kwantung," "Manchou," and "Manchukuo," which are commonly used in English publications.

[4] In August of 1945 the Soviet Red Army defeated the Kwantung Army in Manchuria area with a well-structured offensive within seven days. See LTC David M. Glantz, "August Storm: The Soviet 1945 Strategic Offensive in Manchuria," *Leavenworth Papers* (Combat Studies Institute, U.S. Army Command and General Staff College, 1983), 173.

[5] Jilin Provincial Archives followed the categorization method of the former Soviet Union. The historical documents were first sorted into volumes (*juan*) and files (*jian*), which were then placed into case sets (*quan zong*) according to the agents or institutions that produced them. A volume contains multiple files, but some files were directly placed into a case set without

left by the Japanese military police and the puppet state administrations in the area, and relevant files collected from other archives outside the province.

Among the RQD documents, there is a unique set of files left by the Kwantung Army Military Police Regiment (Kempeitai). On 11 November 1953, Chinese military construction workers in Changchun accidentally found a large number of Japanese files buried at the site of the former Headquarters of the Kwantung Army Military Police. Hirota Toshimitsu, former head of the Guard Squad of Xinjing Military Police detained at Fushun War Criminals Detainment Camp (*Fushun zhanfan guanlisuo*) at the time of the files' discovery, confirmed that these documents belonged to the Kwantung Military Police Regiment, which failed to destroy them completely at the end of the war.[6] Having been buried deeply in soil for more than eight years, these documents were in very poor physical condition when they were unearthed. Mr. Sun Yi, a retiree of the Archives, recalled that many of the files were stuck together and, when exposed to air, hardened like bricks. They had to separate and repair the damaged files page by page.[7] After the initial cleaning and repair, the local Public Security Bureau collected and preserved these files before handing them over to the Jilin Provincial Archives in 1982.

The Jilin Provincial Archives carried out more systematic categorization and research of the RQD files in the 1990s, as China opened its doors to the world and the country's National Bureau of Archives issued provisional guidelines allowing organizations and individuals from the international community to use archives in China.[8] For more than a decade, four archivists (the number was later increased to eight) at the Jilin Provincial Archives worked on the RQD files with the help of a number of retirees from local administrations, and finally

---

being organized as volumes first, so both "volume" and "file" are used as the basic counting units.

6 Zhuang Yan, "Yong lishi dangan huanyuan lishi zhenxiang" [Reconstruct Historical Truth with Historical Files], in *Tiezhengrushan: Jilin-sheng xin fajue Riben qinhua dangan yanjiu* [Irrefutable Evidence: Studies on the Newly Discovered Files on Japanese Invasion in Jilin Province. Henceforth, *Tiezheng*], ed. Zhuang Yan (Changchun: Jilin Publishing Group, 2014), 2.

7 Written interview with Zhao Yujie, Senior Research Archivist of Jilin Provincial Archives, July 29, 2017.

8 "Waiguo zuzhi he geren liyong woguo dang'an shixing banfa" [Provisional Guidelines Regarding the Use of Archives in China by Foreign Organizations and Individuals] was put into effect on 1 July 1992. The provisional guidelines allowed foreign organizations and individuals to read, copy and cite the declassified archive files in China's national archives directly or by mailing request, but require the users to submit an application to the relevant archives 30 days prior to using the files. Currently only 25 files that contain information on Japanese military "comfort women" have been released for public use.

completed the volume-level catalogue of these files in 2005. The task was both mentally and physically challenging. According to Senior Research Archivist Zhao Yujie, a leading member of the team, these files were mostly written in old-style Japanese—very different from the modern Japanese language that the archivists had learned, and most of the files produced by the puppet Manchukuo administration were written in classical Chinese. The translation and categorization of each file took a long time. At a 2014 interview with *Xinjing-bao* newspaper, Zhao Yujie recalled that for a long period of time, she suffered from nightmares and insomnia while working on these files, as the translation was mentally demanding and the Archivists often had to deal with records of brutal killings and torture.[9]

Despite the difficulties and limited manpower, researchers at the Archives worked hard, and by 2005, have published ten volumes of research reports and collections of selected files from the RQD archives. They have also collaborated with Chinese and international institutions to produce TV documentaries and have held exhibitions of the archival materials. Starting from 2011, facing the steadfast denial of Japan's war atrocities, the new leadership of Jilin Provincial Archives commissioned a larger team of specialists and graduate students to translate and conduct research on the RQD files. Three professors from Jilin University and a senior researcher from the Provincial People's Political Consultative Conference (PPCC) served as expert advisors.[10] The Archives also began digitizing the RQD files. Yet the size of the RQD is immense, and the portion that has been translated is only the tip of the iceberg. Zhao Yujie estimated that it would perhaps take 50 translators more than 70 years to finish translating the 100,000 volumes of RQD documents.[11]

In 2014 the Jilin Provincial Archives published a 730-page volume of 89 files left at the site of the former Headquarters of the Kwantung Military Police Regiment. The volume, a project funded by the National Social Science Foundation, provides photocopies of the original Japanese files, grouped under eight subjects: the Nanjing Massacre; the invading Japanese troops' forcible recruitment

---

[9] "Jilin-sheng dang'anguan yanjiu guanyuan Zhao Yujie: Gongbu qin-Hua Rijun dang'an, rang zhengju fasheng" (Interview with Zhao Yujie, Research Archivist at the Jilin Provincial Archives: Publishing the Archival Documents Produced by the Japanese Military During Its Invasion of China, Letting the Evidence Speak for Itself), *People.cn*, May 5, 2014. Accessed August 24, 2017. http://gs.people.com.cn/n/2014/0505/c188871–21133889.html.

[10] They are Yi Baozhong, Shen Haitao, and Chen Jingyan from Jilin University and Jiang Dongping from the Jilin Province People's Political Consultative Conference.

[11] "Jilin-sheng dang'anguan yanjiu guanyuan Zhao Yujie," *People.cn*, May 5, 2014. Accessed August 24, 2017. http://gs.people.com.cn/n/2014/0505/c188871–21133889.html.

of "comfort women;" the "special transfer" of people to Unit 731; forced labor; various Japanese military atrocities; Japan's invasion of Northeast China by immigration; and the torture of American and British prisoners of war. Of the 89 files, 25 contain information concerning the Japanese military's "comfort women" system. Amid the revisionists' clamor denying the Japanese military's sexual slavery, the remarkable work of the Jilin researchers contributed indisputable new evidence for the studies of the "comfort women" issue and Imperial Japan's other war atrocities.

The "Comfort Women" System as Japan's War Apparatus

The Japanese military began detaining women as sex slaves and setting up "comfort stations" in the early 1930s, as soon as Imperial Japan escalated its aggression in China. After full-scale war broke out in 1937, particularly around the time of the notorious Nanjing Massacre, the Japanese forces expanded the "comfort women" system rapidly, setting up "comfort facilities" throughout the occupied areas. This process, as I have noted in *Chinese Comfort Women: Testimonies from Imperial Japan's Sex Slaves,* shows a close correlation between the proliferation of the "comfort stations" and the progression of Japan's war of aggression.[12] The Japanese military police's wartime documents discovered by the Jilin researchers provide further evidence for the nature of the "comfort women" system as a war apparatus.

Two reports submitted by Ōki Shigeru, Commander in Chief of the Japanese Military Police Regiment of Central China Detachment (*Naka Shina haken kempeitai*), on 19 and 28 February 1938 summarized the situation of the "comfort facilities" in Nanjing and its surrounding areas two months after the Nanjing Massacre. Each of the reports contains a table with information on the "comfort facilities" in Nanjing, Xiaguan, Jurong, Zhenjiang, Jintan, Changzhou, Danyang, Wuhu, and Ningguo, which lists the total number of Japanese soldiers stationed, the number of "comfort women," and the ratio between the soldiers and these "comfort women" (see Tables 1 and 2).

As shown by the tables, from the very beginning of full-scale warfare, the Japanese military had already systematically planned and implemented the "comfort women" system, and a large number of military men used the "comfort

---

[12] Peipei Qiu with Su Zhiliang and Chen Lifei, *Chinese Comfort Women: Testimonies from Imperial Japan's Sex Slaves* (London and New York: Oxford University Press, 2014), 13.

Table 1: Comfort Facilities[a]

The situation of comfort facilities in different [missing text] is as the follows:[b]

Place Name	Nanjing	Xiaguan	Jurong	Zhenjiang	Jintan	Changzhou	Danyang	Wuhu	Ningguo
Round Number of Soldiers Stationed	25,000	1,200			1,200	6,440	1,700		
Number of Comfort Women	141	6		109	9	46		25	
Number of Soldiers Per Comfort Woman	178	200			133	140			
Notes			No comfort station.	In the past 10 days 5,734 personnel, soldiers and officers used the comfort station.					Unclear.

[a] English translations of the Japanese and Chinese texts in this paper are all done by Peipei Qiu unless noted otherwise. In this and the translations of the following pages, brackets are used to indicate where there are missing words due to file damage, and italicized font is used where there are illegible characters, or the meaning of the missing text can be inferred based on the context.

[b] Jilin Provincial Archives, Quan zong, J315. The photocopy of the file is published in Zhuang, *Tiezheng*, 119–120. The pages of the report are partially damaged so the title and the first sentence are incomplete. Judging from the identical format of this report and the report produced ten days later on 28 February, their titles are likely to be the same. The report on 28 February is titled "Chian kaifuku jōkyō chōsa ni kansuru ken hōkoku (Tsūchō)" [An Investigation Report on the Restoration of the Order (Memorandum).] See Zhuang, *Tiezheng*, 48.

Table 2: The Situation of Comfort Facilities for the Army
The situation of comfort facilities in different areas is as the follows:[a]

Place Name	Nanjing	Xiaguan	Jurong	Zhenjiang	Jintan	Changzhou	Danyang	Wuhu	Ningguo
Round Number of Soldiers Stationed	25,000	1,200		[mis. text]	[mis. text]	[mis. text]	[mis. text]		
Number of Comfort Women	141	17		109	9	46	6	109	
Number of Soldiers Per Comfort Woman	178	71		137	133	140	267		
Notes	Besides the above, there are 17 *geishas*.	On February 20th, 11 more comfort women were added to the initial 6.	No comfort facilities yet.	In the past 10 days 8,929 personnel, soldiers, and officers used the "comfort station."	In the past 10 days 338 personnel, soldiers and officers used the comfort station.		Due to the insufficiency [of comfort women] we are now recruiting comfort women in the local area.	48 Japanese, 36 Korean, 25 Chinese.	Situation unknown due to the cessation of communication.

[a] Jilin Provincial Archives, Quan zong, J315. The photocopy of the file is published in Zhuang, *Tiezheng*, 125–126. The table was included in the "Chian kaifuku jōkyō chōsa ni kansuru ken hōkoku (Tsūchō)" [Investigation Report on the Restoration of the Order (Memorandum)] made by Ōki Shigeru, Chief Commander of Military Police Regiment of Central China Detachment, February 28, 1938.

facilities." At Zhenjiang, for example, 5,734 Japanese military men used the "comfort stations" during the ten-day period from 1–10 February 1938.[13] Table 2 shows that ten days later, this number increased to 8,929, about 56% more than in the previous ten days.[14] Within that ten-day period, more women were sent to the "comfort stations" in the following: at Xiaguan, the numbers increased from 6 to 17; at Danyang, from none to 6; and at Wuhu, from 25 to 109. The rapidly growing "comfort stations" drafted women from Japan, the Korean Peninsula, and local occupied areas. The notes in Table 2 indicate that at Wuhu, there were "48 Japanese, 36 Korean, 25 Chinese;" and at Danyang: "due to the insufficiency [of "comfort women"] we are now recruiting comfort women in the local area."[15] The same table shows that six local women were drafted as "comfort women" during the period of 11–20 February, and that the ratio between the women and the soldiers was 1 woman to 267 military men. Although the ratio cannot be taken directly as the number of rapes each of the "comfort women" suffered during the ten-day period, the number does reveal the horrifying reality of the sexual exploitation of the "comfort stations."

On a different page, the report dated 19 February 1938 states that immediately following the Nanjing Massacre, the Japanese military had "finished setting up comfort facilities for each army; and within the ten-day period of the report, the newly established comfort stations in the areas controlled by the Military Police Regiment" are seven, two in Wuxi, one in Changshu, two in Longcui-zhen, and two in Huxi.[16] The same report also mentions that an increasing number of women were drafted into the "comfort stations" even though the number of troops decreased in some areas. "Since the Kuwana Brigade moved to Huzhou," the report states, "the number of troops stationed in this area has decreased, but a special comfort station was added, [*missing text*]." [17] At the same time, the number of "comfort women" in the area "has also increased from the previous period (now there are 11 Chinese and 29 Korean comfort women), and the comfort stations were all established through the good offices of the military commissariat. The first has 6 Korean women (frequency of service: 1 woman [*missing text*] men); the second has 11 Chinese women (6 to 7 men on average); the third has 15 Korean women (14 to 15 men on average); and the fourth has 8 Ko-

---

[13] Jilin Provincial Archives, Quan zong, J315. The photocopy of the file is published in Zhuang, Tiezheng, 119.
[14] Jilin Provincial Archives, Quan zong, J315. The photocopy of the file is published in ibid., 125.
[15] Ibid., 126.
[16] Ibid.,121–122.
[17] Ibid., 117. Part of the sentence is missing due to the damage sustained by the original file page.

rean women (7 to 8 men on average)."[18] "Frequency of service" is a translation of the Japanese term, *"sekkyaku-ritsu,"* used in the report, which seems to refer to how many military men a "comfort woman" served during a designated period of time. Due to the file damage, it is unclear what period of time the reporter used to calculate the "frequency of service." The place name was also missing. However, the overall contents of the report indicate that it must have been one of the towns or counties near Nanjing.

It is well-known that Japanese troops committed mass murder and rape in Nanjing and the surrounding areas when the capital of China was occupied by the Japanese forces in December of 1937. The International Military Tribunal for the Far East (hereafter, IMTFE) described the ruthless sexual violence perpetrated by the Japanese soldiers during the Nanjing Massacre in its judgment, stating that throughout the city, young girls and old women were sadistically raped and that a large number of women were killed after being violated, and their bodies mutilated. The IMTFE estimates that there were approximately twenty thousand cases of rape within the city during the first month of the occupation.[19] The atrocities of the Japanese troops outraged the Chinese people and evoked condemnations from the international community. Considering the mass rape to be harmful to Japan's image and a potential hindrance to its military advance in China, the Japanese military leaders ordered the implementation of "comfort stations" throughout the frontlines and occupied areas. In a memorandum sent out on 27 June 1938, Okabe Naozaburō, then Chief of Staff of Japan's North China Area Army, wrote that "[a]ccording to different sources, the strong anti-Japanese sentiment has been caused by the widespread raping by Japanese troops in many places" and that "the frequent occurrence of rapes in different areas is not merely a matter of criminal law; it is serious treason that damages the order under our occupation, that obstructs the military actions of our entire army, and that harms our country." He concluded: "Therefore, the acts of individual military personnel must be strictly controlled. At the same time, facilities for sexual comfort must be established immediately to prevent inadvertent violation of the rules due to the lack of such facilities."[20] Okabe's statement made plain that the goal behind the establishment of the "comfort stations" was to the

---

18 Ibid., 117–118.
19 HyperWar Foundation, "HyperWar: International Military Tribunal for the Far East," IMTFE Judgement (English Translation), Chapter 8, "Conventional War Crimes (Atrocities)," 1012. Accessed September 15, 2017. http://ibiblio.org/.
20 Yoshimi Yoshiaki, *Jūgun ianfu shiryōshū* [*A Collection of Documents on the Military Comfort Women*] (Tokyo: Otsuki shoten, 1992), 210.

advancement of Japan's aggressive war rather than the prevention of widespread rape.

Ōki Shigeru's reports demonstrate clearly that the "comfort women" system was set up and operated by the Imperial Japanese state from the early stages of its aggressive war. His reports deceitfully summarize the situation as "the Restoration of the Order," but in reality, the rapid expansion of the "comfort stations" was carried out through both extensive human trafficking from Japan and its colonies and the brutal abduction of women from the occupied areas. A 1939 written report from Fang Zhiyuan, the chief of the Liyang City Police Bureau, states that, on 25 February 1938, Japanese soldiers abducted Mrs. Jiang Wu and other local women at Liyang, a county about 70 miles southeast of Nanjing, taking them to their barracks and detaining them, naked, in an empty room, thus making a temporary "comfort station." A woman named Xue Fengying was abducted from Wuxi. The soldiers cut off one of her breasts and thrust a stick into her lower body when she resisted their sexual abuse. She bled to death. Within a month, the women detained there increased to fifty. Many of these women were killed by being forced to endure multiple gang-rapes or drowned.[21]

Clearly, the implementation of "comfort stations" sanctioned sexual violence instead of preventing rapes. It institutionalized the soldiers' sexual violence as part of the military's war act.

Human Trafficking Operated by the Japanese Empire

Among the files found by the researchers at the Jilin Provincial Archives, there are two telephone records produced by the Foreign Funds Office, the Treasury Department of the Central Bank of Manchou.[22] Written on the bank's official forms, the records documented the transaction of large military funds for the procurement of "comfort women." Below is a translation of the first record.

---

21 Fang Zhiyuan, "Yige xiuru de baogao" [A Humiliating Report], in Chen Sibai, *Yeshou zai jiangnan* [*The Monstrous Troops in South China*] (Shangyao: Qianxian ribaoshe, 1939), 89–90.
22 Description of the file in Zhuang, *Tiezheng*, 150.

Telephone Record 1:

Time: 10:40 AM, 30 March, the 12th year of Kangde Reign (1945)
Caller: Anshan Branch Office; Fukami, Acting Manager of Anshan Branch
Subject: Regarding funds for the procurement of comfort women (*imonfu*)
Amount remitted: 252,000 yen
Remitting location: Xuzhou
Remitter: Huaihai Province, Communication Division (Unit 7990)
Receiver: The Anshan Management Headquarters
The above transaction is in the form of a public fund, but the actual receiver is Yonei Tsuru in Anshan, who has received large funds as noted below. This branch office has restrictions on term-deposit, but it is inferred that exemptions might be made to treat the case as official military funds.
Last year   17 November 50,000 yen
               16 December 150,000 yen
               This year 24 January 80,000 yen

This case requires a certificate issued by the 4th Division of the Kwantung Army, therefore a notification is submitted.[23]

The record above bears the seals of three persons: Ishikawa, Maekawa, and [*illegible character*]hayashi,[24] who seem to be the recorders and/or reviewers of the telephone record. The subject sentence used a Japanese word "*imonfu*" instead of "*ianfu*," the euphemism more commonly used by Japanese military men to refer to the "comfort women." In Japanese, "*imon*" means "console," "comfort," or "sympathy call." Because the subject line of the record did not use "*ianfu*," questions have been raised as to whether the phone call recorded the procurement of "comfort women." However, as we will see below, the second telephone record concerning the same matter used *ianfu* to write about the same matter immediately after the first call.

Telephone Record 2:

Telephone Call: Anshan; Fukami, Acting Manager

This office does not have the authority to approve the acceptance of over 200,000 yen for the procurement of comfort women (*ianfu*) in the name of a military unit, so the case has been forwarded to the Ministry of Economic Affairs, and the transaction of the above-mentioned fund has been approved by it.

---

23 Jilin Provincial Archives, Quan zong, J350. The photocopy of the file is published in ibid., 151–152.
24 The image of third seal is unclear and the first character of the name is unreadable.

(We deem that judging from the difficult nature of the case, the decision of the Ministry of Economic Affairs is appropriate.)²⁵

This second record was not dated, but the sequential pagination of the two records shows that the second call must have been made not long after the first. The last sentence in the parentheses seems to be the response made by the Central Bank of Manchou as it is a common format of the RQD files that the response to a report is written at the end of the report with parentheses.²⁶ The phrase "*ianfu shiire shikin*" (funds for the procurement of comfort women) in the second telephone record is almost identical to that in the subject line of the first record, except that the second one uses *ianfu* instead of *imonfu*. Judging from the textual correlations of the two records, it is clear that "*imonfu*," as used in the first telephone record, also concerned the procurement of "comfort women."

In fact, the use of the word "*imon*" as a euphemism for sexual servitude is also found in former Japanese military men's testimonies. Tomishima Kenji, a former Corporal and Squad Leader in the 59ᵗʰ Division, 54ᵗʰ Brigade, 110ᵗʰ Battalion of the Japanese Imperial Army, related that his unit abducted eight Chinese women and made them the troops "*imondan*" (comfort delegation) in a small coastal village near Bohai Bay on 8 December 1943. He states:

> Beyond a bushy area there was cropland. The ground next to it was sunk about one meter deep. In the middle of the sunken area were the remains of a house that had been looted and destroyed by the Japanese troops. There we saw eight women pressing themselves closely together, using a sunny corner of the remains as shelter against the cold winds from the sea. All were in ragged clothes and shivering; they seemed to have been crying for days. Their eyes were filled with hatred of the warfare. Staring at the Japanese soldiers surrounding them, they pressed their bodies closer to each other and held each other's hands.
>
> "Yeah! Finally found something good! It'd be a shame to kill them! Now let me show you some good stuff. Ready for that? Here is a comfort delegation (*imondan*). Today is the 8 December Holiday! Ha, ha, ha..." Second Lieutenant Aoki said, leaning on his military sword. He and Warrant Officer Tanida looked at each other with broad grins and nodded.²⁷

The account goes on to describe how the Japanese troops forced the women to have sex with an old Chinese man, who was taken by the troops as a road

---

25 Jilin Provincial Archives, Quan zong, J350. The photocopy of the file is published in Zhuang, *Tiezheng*, 155.
26 This information is from my written interview with Zhao Yujie on 29 July 2017.
27 Kenji Tomishima, "Inu" [Dog], in *Sankō: Kanzenban* [The Three Alls: A Complete Edition], comp., Chūgoku kikansha renrakukai (Tokyo: Banseisha, 1984), 102–108.

guide, so the soldiers could watch; how they made a young girl crawl naked for their entertainment; and how the troops eventually gang-raped the women and burned the road guide to death. 8 December [28] was Japan's Imperial Edict Day celebrating the Emperor's declaration of war against the United States and Great Britain in 1941. The Japanese troops celebrated their holiday by abducting the village women as their sex slaves and viciously calling them the "comfort delegation." Second Lieutenant ordered the army interpreter to "tell the women today we will make an exception to spare them from execution. They will all die sooner or later anyway, or they can be found by some other troops and be a comfort delegation again. Ha, ha..."[29]

Tomishima's account testifies to the Japanese military's blatant abduction and enslavement of local women under the military's "comfort women" system. As Second Lieutenant Aoki's words indicate, the "comfort women" system sanctioned the Japanese troops' sexual violence in the occupied regions, where the occupying forces not only paid nothing to the local women they enslaved, but also often forced the families of the abductees to pay large ransoms.[30] Not to mention, the huge fund sent by the Unit 7990 stationed in Huaihai, a place not far from the Bohai Bay where Tomishima's troops held the local women as their "comfort delegation," was not for procuring "comfort women" from the local area, but more likely was for trafficking "comfort women" from Japan and its colonies.

As the telephone records show, between November 1944 and March 1945 a total of 532,000 Japanese yen in the form of official military funds was sent to Yonei Tsuru, who appears to be a Japanese procurer or proprietor, via the Central Bank of Manchou, for the procurement of "comfort women." It is unclear whether the four funds noted in the record were all from the Unit 7990 or from different military units, but the frequency of the transactions and the large amounts remitted during such a short period suggest the existence of an extremely large military budget for the implementation of the "comfort women" system during the war. Moreover, the records reveal that the transactions of the funds for procuring "comfort women" involved the authorization of the 4th Division of the Kwantung Army and the Ministry of Economic Affairs of Manchukuo, and that the Central Bank of Manchou functioned as a supporting agent.

---

28 While, in the United States, 7 December 1941 is regarded as Pearl Harbor Day, or the day that Japan declared war on the U.S., 8 December is the recognized day in Japan, simply because of the 13- or 14-hour time difference (depending on the status of Daylight Savings Time in the U.S.).
29 Tomishima, "Inu," 107.
30 For more information on the ransom Japanese military forced local people to pay, see Qiu, *Chinese Comfort Women*, 65–66 and 92.

The Central Bank of Manchou was established in 1932 by the puppet state Manchukuo under Japanese control as Japan advanced its invasion in Northeast China. With its head office in Xinjing, today's Changchun in Jilin Province, the bank acted as a repository for the funds of the Manchukuo State Treasury, controlling the money market of Manchukuo, and also serving as Japan's agent in China. The Acting Manager of the bank's Anshan Branch Office indicated in his phone call that although the bank had restrictions on term-deposit, it could make an exemption to allow for the transaction of large funds in the name of official military funds for "the procurement of comfort women."

It needs to be noted that the huge amount of military funds for procuring "comfort women" should not simply be taken as the money paid to the "comfort women." As mentioned earlier, the vast majority of the women abducted by Japanese troops from the occupied regions received no monetary payment. Confined in improvised "comfort facilities," these women were forced to live in slave-like conditions; many of them were abused to death or killed by the troops after being brutally raped. Their enslavement was rarely mentioned in the Japanese military records.

Even for the "comfort women" who reportedly received monetary payment, their experiences still amounted to forced prostitution. The offering of cash advances was a common method used by procurers when rounding up "comfort women" from Japan and its colonies. In order to support their families, women from impoverished families accepted a cash advance before being taken into the military "comfort stations." Once in the "comfort stations," however, it was not easy for these women to pay off their debt because the costs of clothing, cosmetics, and other daily necessities were added to their debts. The "Regulations for the Operations of Comfort Facilities and Inns" (1943) issued by the Malay army administrative inspector provides some detailed information. According to the regulations, "comfort women" were to receive 40 to 60 percent of the fees based on the cash advances they received.[31] The rules also indicated that three of every one hundred yen the women received were to be put into savings, and over two-thirds of the money the "comfort women" received was to be applied to the repayment of their cash advances. In addition, if the "comfort women" became pregnant or fell ill while working, they were required to pay 50% of the medical treatment expenses. For other illnesses, the women had to

---

31 Marai gunseikan, "Ian shisetsu oyobi ryokan eigyō junshu kisoku" [Regulations for the Operation of Comfort Facilities and Inns], *Gunsei kiteishū* 3, 11 (1943), cited in Yoshimi, *Jūgun ianfu* [Military Comfort Women]. (Tokyo: Iwanami shoten, 1995),145.

pay 100 % of the expenses.³² What the regulations issued by the Malay army administrative inspector described was the best-case scenario, but even in that case it was extremely difficult for the "comfort women" to become debt-free.³³

The fees charged by the relatively formal "comfort stations" have been used by history revisionists to portray "comfort women" as well-paid prostitutes, and the military funds for procuring "comfort women" as evidence of that. However, the fees that soldiers paid to "comfort stations" did not function in the same way as did fees paid to prostitutes, because the vast majority of "comfort women" were coerced and then held captive in the "comfort facilities." In addition, most of the money the soldiers paid went to those who ran the "comfort stations," while the "comfort women" themselves received either nothing or only a very small portion of the payments. Grandma Mao Yinmei,³⁴ for example, was deceived by a procurer and taken from the Korean Peninsula to China in 1945. She thought she was going to get a job in a factory but was put into the Jiqingli military "comfort station" in Wuhan instead. She was forced to service more than 15 Japanese troops every day, even during her menstrual period. If in a day she could not submit 15 or more tickets collected from the military men, she would be beaten and not allowed to eat.³⁵

The telephone records of the Central Bank of Manchou shed light on a hitherto unclear aspect of the operation of the military "comfort women" system: the Japanese military and the Imperial Japanese nation-state jointly financed extremely large-scale human trafficking for the implementation of the "comfort women" system. Evidently, the massive procurement of "comfort women" and human trafficking effort required colossal funds to cover the overseas and cross-continental transportation, the procurers' fees, and other expenses in the operation process. The field-unit of the Japanese military, the authority of the Kwantung Army, and the Manchukuo state of the Japanese Empire collaborated to sponsor and carry out the unprecedented human trafficking and sexual enslavement. This extent of human trafficking, as shown in a seized letter written by a Japanese military man to be discussed in the following pages, was propelled by Japan's "National Mobilization Law."

---

32 Ibid., 145.
33 Ibid.,146–148.
34 "Comfort women" survivors are often affectionately referred to as "grandma," usually combined with their family name or their full name in their respective languages. This indicates the advanced ages of those survivors who are still alive.
35 Li Xiaofang, *Jiushiwei xingcun weianfu shilu* [Records of 90 Comfort Women Survivors] (Hangzhou: Zhejiang renmin chubanshe, 2016), 266. Grandma Mao's Korean family name was Park. She stayed in China after the war ended and adopted a Chinese name.

The Hidden Atrocities and Japanese Military Censorship

In order to conceal the atrocities committed by the Japanese troops and also tighten its ideological control over the military men, Japanese military leaders imposed strict information censorship during the Asia-Pacific War (1931–1945). Even the soldiers' personal letters were regularly inspected. The newly discovered evidence from Jilin Provincial Archives' RQD files shows that letters containing information about the military "comfort stations" and "comfort women" were seized by the military inspectors, who would either delete the relevant part from the letter or not allow its delivery. The following "Monthly Mail Inspection Report" kept by the Beian Inspection Bureau recorded the contents of a seized letter. It was written by Takeda Takejirō, a Japanese military man stationed in Heihe, in 1941.[36]

> There can be seen a comfort station set up using the corner part of the army officers' residence building that stands from east to west. Speaking of the comfort station, it looks somewhat like a playhouse or show tent. It's a place for the soldiers living in these barracks to discharge their precious energy. The number of troops (*heiryoku*) in the comfort station is only 20 Korean women, and they are all bound by the National Mobilization Law (Kokka sōdōin hō). Pink-color rationing tickets are divided with different names such as "Yoshiko" or "Tatsuko" written on them, which is a spectacle one cannot see anywhere else except in the army. Worse yet, it sets officially fixed prices that are not fit for men who get meager pay. The rationing tickets have also been used exclusively by the commissioned officers as part of their abuse of power.
>
> The rest of the letter is omitted.[37]

The censored contents of the letter reveal plainly the nature of Japanese military "comfort stations": it was no ordinary brothel but an integral part of the military unit. The station was physically set within the barracks. Particularly noteworthy is that Takeda used the term "*heiryoku*"—literally meaning "number of troops"— to talk about the number of "comfort women." In addition, the prices of the rationing tickets of the "comfort station" were officially determined and used exclusively by the high-ranking officers.

---

36 Zhuang, *Tiezheng*, 174.
37 "Tsūshin kenetsu geppō teishutsu ni kansuru ken hōkoku" [Monthly report on the mail inspections], November 5, 1941. Jilin Provincial Archives, Quan zong, J 315. The photocopy of the file is published in Zhuang, *Tiezhang*, 175.

More significantly, the letter tells us that the "comfort women" were taken to the "comfort station" under Japan's "National Mobilization Law." "The National Mobilization Law" was issued by the Japanese government in March 1938 to put the Empire of Japan on war-time footing after its full-scale aggressive war broke in China. In the following year, a supplemental law, "The National Service Draft Ordinance" (*Kokumin chōyō rei*) was promulgated by Prime Minister Kōno as part of the "National Mobilization Law." It allowed the government to draft civilians in order to ensure an adequate supply of labor for the aggressive war. Under "The National Mobilization Law," hundreds of thousands of men and women were mobilized from Japan and its colonies as draftees to serve the needs of the war, including a large number of women who were forced into the military "comfort stations." The number of "comfort women" trafficked to the Chinese continent was so massive that even those who worked for Japan's puppet state Manchukuo expressed concerns. In a letter sent to Shin Ok-Tae at Suibin County Supervision Department of the Youth Division of the Concordia Association of Manchukuo, [*illegible character*] Eung-seon expressed that "[t]he large number of the special comfort women is disturbing."[38] This letter was censored by the Kwantung Army Military Police and marked as "deliver after deletion."[39] Another letter, sent by Kitabori Kōji from the headquarters of the Harada Unit, Jiancheng Unit, and Ogiwara Unit in Kaifeng, mentioned his visits to a "P house," a derogative term used by the Japanese troops to refer to the "comfort stations." The military police ordered to delete the relevant section from the letter.[40]

Among the mail inspection reports published by the Jilin Provincial Archives, the following letter has drawn controversial views. In order to give a full picture of the controversy, I provide a complete translation of the contents of the letter recorded in the military police's inspection report below.

> There are about 50 P houses (prostitution house) controlled by the army, where [military men] became crazy even for the women in that kind of place. The [women's] partners are mostly high-ranking officers and non-commissioned officers. Some of the high-ranking officers formed a perfunctory relationship with the women, taking them as their temporary frontline wives. When the troops have to move, for example, to [...] (the place name is omitted in the report), their women just pack up their belongings and go to where their lovers go. At the new place the women will enter that kind of place again, and the men will come

---

38 Jilin Provincial Archives, Quan zong, J315. The photocopy of the file is published in Zhuang, *Tiezheng*, 172.
39 Ibid.
40 "Tsūshin kenetsu geppō (Nigatsu)" [Monthly Report on the Mail Inspections (February)], Jilin Provincial Archives, Quan zong, J315. The photocopy of the file is published in Zhuang, *Tiezheng*, 133–4.

to visit frequently, thus starting a peculiar cohabitation. An exceedingly large number of women followed their lovers to move from one frontline to another like this.[41]

The letter above was written by Tomura Hideo of the Watanabe Regiment of the 84th Field Force in February 1941 when his unit was stationed in Kaifeng, a city in Henan Province, China. The peculiar relationship between Japanese military officers and the "comfort women" described in the letter has been taken by some readers as evidence to prove that "comfort women" were camp-following prostitutes. However, a close reading of the letter in the historical context suggests otherwise: rather than proving the "comfort women" to be prostitutes, the letter reveals the corruption of the high-ranking military officers in the hierarchical "comfort women" system.

As Tomura's letter shows, by 1941 the "comfort stations" had been so proliferated that in a prefecture-level city such as Kaifeng, as many as 50 military-controlled "comfort stations" had been established. Investigations of the Japanese military "comfort stations" in China have shown that the military-controlled "comfort stations" in the occupied regions were typically guarded by armed soldiers and free exit of the "comfort women" was prohibited. In addition, after the outbreak of full-scale warfare, Japanese authorities tightened control over travel from Japan and its colonies to Mainland China as well as travel within the occupied areas. Identification papers issued by Japanese authorities were required in order to obtain permission to travel. Moreover, the movement of the troops was a military secret and was kept highly confidential from civilians. As seen in the mail inspection report above, even a mention of the destination of the military unit's movement was carefully deleted from the censored letter. Given this kind of wartime environment, even though there might have been isolated cases in which some "comfort women" traveled with the Japanese troops, it would have been impossible for a large number of prostitutes to follow the Japanese troops around freely.

When reading the letter in question more carefully, we can see that, similar to Takeda's letter cited earlier, Tomura's letter is not talking about the lives of ordinary soldiers but complains about the abuse of power of the "high-ranking officers." He criticizes the "high-ranking officers" who had the privilege to keep "temporary frontline wives" and form a "peculiar cohabitation" even as the troops moved from one frontline to another. Judging from what Tomura wrote,

---

[41] "Tsūshin kenetsu geppō (Nigatsu)" [Monthly Report on the Mail Inspections (February)], Jilin Provincial Archives, Quan zong, J315. The photocopy of the file is published in Zhuang, *Tiezheng*, 129–130.

the "peculiar cohabitation" became possible not because all "comfort women" could follow the troops freely, but because the high-ranking officers had the power to bring selected women alongside the mobile troops. Not surprisingly, the military police would not allow Tomura's letter to be delivered until the aforementioned part was cut, since it revealed not only the existence of a large number of military "comfort stations" but also the high-ranking officers' corrupt lifestyle in relation to them.

The stern censorship that the Japanese military authorities imposed during the war confirms the fact that the Japanese military "comfort women" system was an intentional and carefully-planned war crime. In order to conceal the unspeakable war atrocities, the Japanese military not only carried out mass destruction of the incriminating evidence at the end of the war, but also painstakingly concealed the relevant information when the "comfort women" system was in operation during the war. Today when history revisionists continue to insist that there is no evidence for the direct involvement of the Japanese military and government in forcing women into the "comfort stations," and that the issues of war compensation have been resolved by the relevant postwar treaties between Japan and other countries, the new evidence from the Jilin Provincial Archives is a powerful rebuttal to them.

As the major theater of the Asia-Pacific War, China witnessed unfathomable atrocities committed by the Imperial Japanese forces. The RQD files concerning the military "comfort women" discussed above are only a small part of the wartime documents left by the Japanese military.[42] As the Chinese researchers' investigations progress, their findings will continue to contribute to the transnational movement for justice and historical truth.

---

42 As noted earlier in the paper, a large number of the RQD files have not been released yet. Among the 25 released files that contain information on the "comfort women," there are also 17 of the Japanese military's investigation records on the military personnel's misconducts and offenses at "comfort stations." Due to space limitations, this chapter is unable to discuss all of the files.

Angella Son
The Japanese Secret: The Shame Behind Japan's Longstanding Denial of Its War Crime against Korean *Comfort Girls-Women*

Introduction

In this chapter, I argue that shame is behind Japan's longstanding denial of their war crimes against Korean *comfort girls-women*. I propose that Japan's refusal to acknowledge guilt in enslaving Korean girls and forcing them to work as sex slaves is not simply a claim of innocence on their part, but that it also reveals the deep sense of shame associated with such an atrocity. They inadvertently employ guilt language to cover up their own sense of shame, thus creating the Japanese secret. Japan's inability to embrace its own sense of shame will be analyzed by consulting Heinz Kohut's self psychology and Gershen Kaufman's discussion on defenses against shame. In addition, I will argue that *Sonyeosang* (the Statue of Peace), a major display of activism by the Korean Council for Women Drafted for Military Sexual Slavery by Japan, stands to adjudicate Japan's effort to conceal its own shame and guilt for enacting utter violence against Korean *comfort girls-women* and violating their human dignity.

Before I get into the substantive part of my chapter, I want to note that I created the term *comfort girls-women* to replace the widely used term "comfort women," often placed inside quotation marks. This term has three significant aspects: (1) the italics signify that the word, *comfort*, has a different meaning—sexual slavery—than its usual meaning in the term "comfort women" of entertaining and providing pleasure to men; (2) the addition of the word *girl* underscores the young age of the victims who were put into sexual slavery; and (3) the word *woman* reflects the long period—about three quarters of a century—that they endured without a satisfactory resolution to their situation. In addition, it is critical to note that I make the distinction between Japanese people and the Japanese government and that the scope of this work does not apply to Japanese people and is limited to the actions of the Japanese government. Moreover, when I refer to the Japanese government, I am aware that not everyone associated with the Japanese government agrees with and/or holds the same position of denying the guilt of the Japanese government for its horrific violation and violence to Korean *comfort girls-women* and I limit the scope of this discussion as applicable only to those responsible for the Japanese government's atrocity and for the denial of its guilt. Lastly, while the discussion is only about Korean *comfort girls-women* for specificity, this discussion extends to *comfort girls-women* from other countries, such as China, Taiwan, the Philippines, etc.

Korean *Comfort Girls-Women:* Historical Backdrop[1]

Japan's patriarchal culture commodified women, so the practice of being a "comfort woman" was a culturally accepted and legally approved profession in Japan. Japanese prostitution took place in what was called the "pleasure quarters." Yoshiwara was the first pleasure quarters in Tokyo,[2] approved and licensed for this purpose in 1617.[3] Japan's licensed prostitution system extended to other pleasure quarters in Japan and to military quarters as the government expanded the war that had the grandiose purpose of saving Asia from adulteration by Western influence by conquering Asia and ultimately the world. The notion of "comfort women" progressed through various transformations, especially during the intense period of heightened war conflict toward the latter part of World War II. Ideally, it was understood as a profession by which women offered comfort to stressed soldiers during wartime by performing (singing and dancing) and providing companionship. By legalizing prostitution, Japan normalized the exploitation of women by creating the practice of "comforting," which often was a euphemism for prostitution, and by establishing it as a licensed profession that could be chosen voluntarily by women. On top of this deceitful sexual violence towards women, Japan started recruiting not just women but also—or mostly—girls. Moreover, the practice of recruiting became increasingly involuntary, and the recruiters used deception and force often mingled with violence. Furthermore, the working conditions and nature of the work did not stop at objectifying women as "comfort women" or licensed prostitutes, but more and more frequently, turned them into sexual slaves. "Comfort women" serving as sexual slaves be-

---

[1] Much of the material in this section is from my article, Angella Son, "Inadequate Innocence of Korean *Comfort Girls-Women:* Obliterated Dignity and Shamed Self," *Pastoral Psychology* 67, no. 2 (2018): 175–194. Accessed March 2, 2019. http://www.springer.com/-/0/AVyEqFvklsZN9k3LjEbF.

[2] For clarity, I use the contemporary names for cities and countries, such as Korea instead of Chosun and Tokyo instead of Edo.

[3] C. Sarah Soh, *The Comfort Women: Sexual Violence and Postcolonial Memory in Korea and Japan* (Chicago: Chicago University Press, 2008), 110.

came most evident as the war became more intense. As Japan was struggling in its effort to advance into and occupy other nations and even to defend itself, the number of Japanese soldiers had to be increased and, as a result, so did the number of "comfort women." Japan eventually became brutal in its effort to recruit young girls and force them into sexual slavery.

The very first "comfort station" was established in Shanghai in March 1932[4] after the Manchurian Incident on 18 September 1931, when Japan commenced a war against China after blaming the Chinese for what they themselves had done (exploding track belonging to the South Manchuria Railway in Liutiaohu in northeastern China). Within four months of seizing territory in northeastern China, in January of 1932, Japan instigated another hostile attack, which has become known historically as the First Shanghai Incident. During the First Shanghai Incident, Lieutenant-General Okamura Yasuji, Vice Chief of Staff of the Shanghai Expeditionary Force, after 223 reported cases of rape of Shanghai residents by his troops, requested the governor of Nagasaki Prefecture to send "comfort women" in order to prevent further rapes of Shanghai residents by Japanese soldiers as well as the spread of venereal diseases among the soldiers. Japan's previous war experiences in Siberia had alerted the military to the devastating effects of the spread of sexually transmitted diseases, and the preventative measure the Japanese government took was to provide "comfort women," who had to undergo regular medical examinations. The governor approved the request and sent "comfort women," mostly Korean women living in the Kyushu mining region who were initially drafted as laborers and had been transported to places in Japan such as this area in 1909.[5] In March of 1932, this became the first "comfort station" outside of Japan established by the Japanese military; by the end of World War II, one-third of Japan's labor force was composed of drafted Korean workers.[6] This first "comfort station" was the beginning of the military sexual exploitation and slavery of Korean *comfort girls-women*, i.e., this was the onset of the obliteration of dignity and the creation of the shamed self of Korean *comfort girls-women*, and the brutality and cruelty only escalated.

The expansion of "comfort stations," however, was ignited by the 1937 Nanking Massacre, in which mass rapes of women and girls in Nanking occurred

---

[4] Yoshimi Yoshiaki, *Comfort Women: Sexual Slavery in the Japanese Military during World War II*, translated by Suzanne O'Brien (New York: Columbia University Press, 2000), 43–48.
[5] Bruce Cumings, *Korea's Place in the Sun: A Modern History* (New York: W. W. Norton, 1997), 177.
[6] Yoshimi points out that technically the first "comfort station" was established by the navy in China long before the first "comfort station" had been set up by the Japanese army (*Comfort Women*, 43–44).

along with murder, looting, setting fires, etc.[7] Japan initiated a full-scale war against China in July 1937. The Japanese military was very sensitive about distressing the Chinese people, especially since the Chinese considered rape the most horrible violation, because they were struggling to bring the Chinese people under control of the Japanese regime. The Japanese military immediately decided to expand and establish "comfort women" on or near military bases throughout China and other parts of Asia such as Japan, Taiwan, Korea, the Philippines, and the Dutch East Indies. Their urgency stemmed from preventing both further rapes of residents by the Japanese military and the spread of venereal diseases among Japanese soldiers. On 11 December the Central China Area Army officially ordered "comfort stations" to be established. The occupation of Nanking began on 13 December and Chinese women were forced into the role of "comfort women" immediately after the seizure of Nanking. It is ironic that one Japanese medical officer reported that alcohol and "comfort women" were not effective solutions to ease the stress of soldiers from the drastic changes from an intense conflict from battle into a period of sudden rest. His recommendation was to reduce the time of their engagement in battle, provide more recreation such as entertainment, sports, movies, etc., and screen out detrimental soldiers.[8] Just as "comfort stations" were widespread geographically in numerous nations, the recruiting also took place in many countries. What is alarming, however, is that most of the recruits were Korean girls, whose age could be as young as 11; usually they were not older than 18. Some estimate that Korean "comfort women," or rather girls, comprised at least 80 % of all the "comfort women."[9]

---

[7] Ibid., 49–56.
[8] George L. Hicks, *The Comfort Women: Japan's Brutal Regime of Enforced Prostitution in the Second World War* (New York, NY: W. W. Norton, 1994), 44.
[9] Ibid., 11; Keith Howard, ed. *True Stories of the Korean Comfort Women*, trans. Young Joo Lee (London: Cassell, 1995), v. Chan and Su provide a conflicting estimate, arguing that Chinese women made up more than half of the recruited comfort women (*Chūgoku no ianjo ni kansuru chosahokoku* [Research report on the comfort stations in China], in *"Ianfu": Senji seibōryoku no jittai II* [*"Comfort women": Actual Conditions of Wartime Sexual Violence*], eds. VAWW-NET Japan, Puja-Kim, and Yon-ok Song (Tokyo: Ryokufū Shuppan, 2000), 81.)

Silence of Half a Century: Korean *Comfort Girls-Women* Shamed into Nonexistence[10]

What was tragic was the silence about this horrific situation for about a half a century because Korean *comfort girls-women* were shamed into nonexistence.[11] The experiences of Korean *comfort girls-women* are a paradigmatic example of how military sexual violence can obliterate the dignity of women and shame them into nonexistence. I propose that these girls and women's horrific experiences of sexual slavery by the Japanese military caused intense and lasting shame that resulted in their sense of self being entrenched in shame. Moreover, I argue that the innocence of Korean *comfort girls-women* was and continues to be inadequately recognized. The Japanese government refuses to admit its legal accountability for this and to provide just reparations to Korean *comfort girls-women* for its treacherous and systematic sexual enslavement of Korean and other *comfort girls-women*. The Korean government and people have been too slow to accept the innocence of these women and to embrace their pain, sorrow, and suffering and advocate for justice for them. This turning of their innocence into inadequacy or shame, actively by the Japanese government and passively by the Korean government and its people, compounded their long, miserable suffering for half a century until Kim Hak-sun broke the silence in 1991 with the support of Korean activists.

Obliteration of the dignity of Korean *comfort girls-women* to the point of shaming them into nonexistence or even into negative existence is woefully easy to describe. First, the onset and continuous shaming of Korean *comfort girls-women* was inflicted by the Japanese military.[12] Korean *comfort girls-women* suffered the obliteration of their dignity in multiple and repeated ways, primarily at the hands of the Japanese military, which, at the time, had legitimate authority over them. Japan annexed Korea as a colony in 1910, and it had authority over Korea, including the responsibility to protect Korea and the Korean people. Instead, Japan misused its authority and used Korean people, es-

---

10 Much of the material in this section is from my article, Angella Son, "Inadequate Innocence of Korean *Comfort Girls-Women:* Obliterated Dignity and Shamed Self." *Pastoral Psychology* 67, no. 2, 175–194. Accessed March 2, 2019. http://www.springer.com/-/0/AVyEqFvklsZN9k3LjEbF
11 The fact that Korean people possess a great amount of shame caused by Japan's occupation of Korea as its colony is not a part of this discussion in order to focus on the particular shame experiences of Korean *comfort girls-women*.
12 See Appendix 1 regarding Soh's discussion of "approximate truths" or "strategic exaggerations."

pecially young girls, as mere instruments to function as sexual machines who granted soldiers sexual relief. Various terms and symbols for the "comfort women" used by Japanese soldiers demonstrate the diminishment of their dignity down to the last drop, as illustrated in the following passage from C. Sarah Soh's book, *The Comfort Women: Sexual Violence and Postcolonial Memory in Korea and Japan.*

> The specific terms and images deployed to refer to them vary significantly, from statist euphemisms such as "comfort women," through the paternalistic metaphor of imperial "gifts" and the documentary classification of the women as military "supplies," to the coarse and objectifying *pi* (vagina; pronounced "pea") and the crude metaphor of public "toilet," as well as the ethnic nationalists' reactive representations of the women as either licensed "prostitutes" (primarily by the Japanese) or deceived labor recruits called *chongsindae* (by the Koreans), to the prevailing feminist label of "sex slaves."[13]

These terms and symbols vividly illustrate how Korean *comfort girls-women* were shamed by being reduced to an organ, the function of an organ, a military supply, or even a receptacle of Japanese soldiers' semen. In addition, the recruiting by Japanese military and the working conditions of "comfort stations" demonstrate that these young girls were thoroughly exploited and violated in all aspects of their being by the very government that was responsible for protecting them.

Second, the recruiting of *comfort girls-women* became non-voluntary, and the force that was employed eradicated their sense of agency. As the demand for *comfort girls-women* increased, the Japanese military started using both deception and force to meet the demand. Young girls were promised good-paying jobs, and they were very hopeful and happy about the prospect of making money to contribute to their poor families. Alas, their pride and joy in being a productive member of society and supporting their own families turned instantly into fear and despair as soon as they were taken to "comfort stations" instead of factories or hospitals where they had been promised jobs. Girls who had already been recruited for the labor force were often deceived with the promise of better work or better pay and were transported to "comfort stations." When deception did not work, the Japanese military added the tactic of intimidation by getting the police and military personnel involved. In the end, the effort of going through the charade of having the girls make their own decisions was totally suspended, and brutal force was used to abduct and kidnap girls. Kim Hak-sun's experience testifies to this brutal reality of girls being forcibly abducted and trans-

---

13 Soh, *The Comfort Women*, 32.

ported to unknown "comfort stations" next to Japanese military bases. This complete erasure of these girls' own agency turned them into, at best, prostitutes and, at worst, sex slaves. Fear of this fate spread among Korean girls and their parents, so some girls were married prematurely, some to disabled, abusive, very old, or extremely poor husbands, and they had no choice if they wanted to avoid being abducted and/or sold as *comfort girls-women*.

Third, once the *comfort girls-women* had been violently recruited and transported to "comfort stations," they faced wretchedly inhumane working conditions and experienced an ongoing sense of shame. Their lives as wartime sexual slaves were initiated by multiple rapes by a single person or two or more people. The working conditions at "comfort stations" varied. Some offered services for Japanese military men, so that they were essentially prostitution stations where "comfort women" could save money and have some semblance of personal freedom. At the extreme opposite end were "comfort stations" where "comfort women" were forcibly placed into sexual slavery, often accompanied by intolerable violence and without adequate pay (or any pay). The former usually were facilities for Japanese professional prostitutes, and the latter were what many Korean *comfort girls-women* had to face. Yoshimi[14] points out that whether or not the methods of recruiting involved deception and/or force, the *comfort girls-women*'s experiences at "comfort stations" represented conditions of sexual slavery because of coerced sexual intercourse, harsh scrutiny, physical violence, inability to leave, nominal or no compensation, hunger, and constant exposure to sexually transmitted diseases, among other factors. Kim Hak-sun was subjected to all of these and lived her life as a sexual slave, in fear. It must have been severely dehumanizing for her to go through rituals of washing with antiseptic solution, routine weekly check-ups, and injections of anti-syphilis drugs.

Kim Hak-sun was one of the few who stayed in "comfort stations" for the relatively short duration of four months and then successfully escaped, although she did not really escape since she ended up in an abusive marriage that she agreed to because of her fear of being caught. In most cases, Korean *comfort girls-women* had no wherewithal to leave and no place to go to. They lived in constant fear and were subjected to physical, psychological, and sexual abuse. Moreover, some had to serve a mind-boggling number of Japanese soldiers each day. The number of soldiers they served varied. Some, such as Kim Hak-sun, had sexual intercourse with far fewer than the average number and served seven or eight men a day, especially if the military base associated with the "comfort station" was small and/or located in deep countryside. Many others,

---

14 Yoshimi, *Comfort Women*, 11.

such as Kim Tokchin, Ha Sunnyo, Mun Pilgi, Yi Okpun, Mun Okchu, Pak Sunae, and Yun Turi, served 20 to 50 men a day.[15] Can a human body sustain such brutal injury? Their sexual slavery was accompanied by such severe physical and psychological abuse that some ended up with permanent damage to and disfigurement of their bodies. Some tried repeatedly to take their own lives, and some of these succeeded in taking all their pain and suffering with them from this life. Can the human psyche survive such objectification and degradation? It is too overwhelming even to think about it and to try to grasp the nature of such mechanization of the fragile bodies of young girls.[16] Many young Korean *comfort girls-women* missed growing up due to being enslaved as sexual tools by the Japanese military at a young age. Through repeated sexual intercourse, their sense of self was being eroded until it gradually became empty and instead filled up with shame.

Fourth, when the *comfort girls-women* returned to their lives back in Korea after World War II, they were met with indifference and complacency, at best, and judgment and rejection, at worst, from the Korean government and people. Many or most of the Korean *comfort girls-women* were not welcomed back, nor was their suffering acknowledged by the Korean government and people, even though some had returned at the risk of death. Some were rejected even by their own family members. Some were even cut off from their own sons and daughters who were born after their return to Korea. Their children were afraid that it would be exposed that their mothers had been "comfort women." For instance, Kim Hak-sun, who risked her life and escaped with a stranger, was constantly subjected to verbal and psychological abuse because she had been a former "comfort woman" against her will for four months. She states:

> I had suffered so much, living with this man who had supposedly been my husband. When he was drunk and aggressive, because he knew that I had been a "comfort woman", he would insult me with words that had cut me to the heart. After we had returned to Korea I hadn't wanted him to come near me. My life seemed to be wretched. I had refused

---

[15] Howard, *True Stories*, 45, 61, 84, 99, 107, 162, and 188.

[16] The horrific working conditions do not preclude the formation of lover relationships between some soldiers and "comfort women," nor does the presence of affectionate relationships between soldiers and "comfort woman" disavow the inhumane nature of the working conditions of "comfort women." Ito Keiichi, in his book, *Soldiers' History of the Army*, mentions some cases of affectionate relationships between soldiers and "comfort woman" (Hicks, *Comfort Women*, 79). Yuha Park naively uses this as a piece of evidence for her claim that the Korean *comfort girls-women* were not sexual slaves but volunteered to engage in prostitution for economic gain. (Yuha Park, *Je-guk ui wianbu: Shik min jiji beh wah gi eok ui tu jaeng* [*Comfort Women of the Empire: The Battle Over Colonial Rule and Memory*] (Puriwaipari: Seoul, 2013.)

to do as I was told and I had received more and more abuse from him. When he called me a dirty bitch or a prostitute in front of my son, I cursed him. Now, though, once my husband was cremated, my son and I lived alone. He had tortured me mentally so much that I did not miss him a lot.[17]

For Kim Hak-sun, the last straw came when her son died of a heart attack during a vacation, and she tried several times to take her life. Having failed at committing suicide, she then led a reckless lifestyle. She thought that her life was worthless: "I hadn't been blessed with good parents, I had been unfortunate with my husband and children. Now I lost all my will to live."[18]

According to Margaret Urban Walker, this excruciatingly painful sense of abandonment experienced by Korean *comfort girls-women* is caused by the complacency or rejection by the very authority that could validate the wrong that was done to them. Walker states:

> When these responses [validation and vindication] are not forthcoming, the victim's situation is worse than unaddressed. If the community or authority to whom the victim looks for validation and vindication ignores the victim, challenges the victim's credibility, treats the victim's complaint as of little import, shelters or sides with the perpetrator of wrong, or, worse, overtly or by implication blames the victim, the victim will feel abandoned and isolated. That abandonment is a "second injury" that can be humiliating.[19]

The second abandonment Korean *comfort girls-women* experienced on their return to Korea was indeed devastating since, on top of being abandoned and abused by the Japanese government, they were rejected and abandoned as damaged goods and denigrated as prostitutes, i.e., impure girls and women, by the Korean government and Koreans in general. They were perceived as shameful to Korea as a nation. Helen Merrell Lynd states that shame experiences are very difficult to express because they involve the whole self and not specific acts or non-acts or particular aspects of the self, as is the case in dealing with guilt.[20] This has serious consequences—the victim has trouble expressing her own pain and suffering because she is enveloped by shame, and others in her life have no interest in hearing about her pain and suffering and are more interested in trying to stay away from the victim. As a result, the complicity and abandonment of Ko-

---

17 Howard, *True Stories*, 39.
18 Ibid., 40.
19 Margaret Urban Walker, *Moral Repair: Reconstructing Moral Relations after Wrongdoing* (Cambridge, UK: Cambridge University Press, 2006), 19–20.
20 Helen Merrell Lynd, *On Shame and the Search for Identity* (New York, NY: Harcourt Brace, 1958), 49–56.

rean *comfort girls-women* by the Korean government and people, including their families and friends, did not allow them to recover from their horrific tragedy and furthermore symbolically crushed them yet again by ignoring their suffering and isolating them at such a profound level. The Korean government and people's refusal to expand themselves and embrace the Korean *comfort girls-women* intensified the women's pain and suffering as well as coalesced their sense of self as shameful.

Finally, it is important to recognize that all the shaming imposed on Korean *comfort girls-women* created their shame-based sense of self. Even though they were violently recruited and coerced into sexual slavery, the routine of living at "comfort stations" for various durations of time convinced them of their participation in immoral acts, especially since they were indoctrinated by the Confucian teaching that elevates chastity to the highest virtue for girls and women, and ultimately they saw themselves as impure, immoral, and irredeemable. They viewed themselves as defiled and their experiences of sexual slavery as immoral acts. Their sense of shame and unworthiness as moral beings kept them in isolation and silence. This sense of shame imposed by the self kept many Korean *comfort girls-women* from revealing their unjust treatment by the Japanese military for half a century as well as from requesting financial, housing, and medical subsidies from the Korean government when the issue became public. Neither the Korean government and people nor the Korean *comfort girls-women* were able to rise above their sense of shame.

Lynd's understanding of shame is helpful in shedding light on why the Korean *comfort girls-women* see themselves as embodying shame even though they were wrongly shamed by the Japanese government and its military and by the Korean government and its people. As noted above, Lynd proposes that shame involves the whole self, whereas guilt addresses specific acts or non-acts or specific aspects of oneself. Furthermore, Lynd was one of the first who disagreed with the conventional understanding of the difference between guilt and shame, which was based on psychological schools such as the Freudian school, and suggested an alternative understanding of shame. Lynd, adding to some of the pioneering works on shame, argued that the difference between guilt and shame is not whether one is experienced internally and the other is caused externally. In the conventional understanding of shame and guilt, guilt was associated with one's own conscience and shame with exposure to others' ridicule and disapproval, but Lynd contends that both shame and guilt involve self-judgment, although in the case of shame, exposure to others can be simultaneously present with exposure to one's own perception.

Illustrating experiences of shame in characters in several works of literature, Lynd points out that shame is primarily caused by one's own view of oneself. For instance, she points out how exposure to others can in fact alleviate the excruciating pain of the experience of shame by quoting Dimmesdale in Nathaniel Hawthorne's *The Scarlet Letter:*

> Of penance, I have had enough! Of penitence there has been none! Else, I should long ago have thrown off these garments of mock holiness and have shown myself to mankind as they will see me at the judgment seat. Happy are you, Hester, that wear the scarlet letter openly upon your bosom! Mine burns in secret![21]

The anguished sense of shame of the fictional character of Dimmesdale illustrates the contrast with the conventional understanding of shame as caused by exposure to others' judgment. In fact, Dimmesdale thinks that Hester's exposure to others' view lifts to some extent the weight of her shame. Dimmesdale had an internal eye that shamed and tormented him because of his sexual affair with Hester Prynne, and this reveals the power of shame to completely destroy a life. Unlike Dimmesdale, Korean *comfort girls-women*, forced into lives of sexual slavery, were innocent. Nonetheless, they too experienced intense shame and self-judgment. Having been indoctrinated from a young age about the great importance of chastity in girls, they developed an internal sense of self similar to that of Dimmesdale, one that shamed and tormented them, ashamed of themselves because of their lives as *comfort girls-women*. In addition to being unjustly shamed by others and exposed as defiled in others' eyes, their own assessment of themselves as shameful produced further shame within them. This internalized shame then kept them silent about their experiences of humiliation and objectification and the mutilation of their dignity and lives.

Silence Broken: Healing and Transformation of Korean *Comfort Girls-Women*

It took about half a century after 1937 for the Korean *comfort girls-women* issue to even become an issue and for the world to open its eyes to the erased lives of Korean *comfort girls-women*.[22] Even though World War II ended in 1945, it was

---

[21] Nathaniel Hawthorne, *The Scarlet Letter*, ed. Gross et al., 3rd ed. (New York: W. W. Norton, 1988), 130–131.
[22] Although sexism played a major role in minimizing the issue of the "comfort women" in society, I choose not to include it in this discussion in order to focus primarily on the role of shame in suppressing the issues related to Korean *comfort girls-women*.

not until Kim Hak-sun brought suit against the Japanese government in 1991 that the world opened its eyes to the issue of "comfort women."[23] After World War II, nothing about "comfort women" was a part of the war resolution. Korea did not claim redress for "comfort women" nor did Japan offer to pay or provide care for them. Neither United Nations troops nor the United States suggested any reparation for them. It became a moot point and disappeared from people's attention. It wasn't revived until seventeen years later in 1962, when a newspaper reporter, Senda Kakō, found some photos of non-Japanese women while he was working on a photographic book on war, *Nihon no Senreki* (Japan's War Chronicle) for *Mainichi Shimbun*. He personally got interested in the issue and began his own research. He then found out that those women in the photos were called *jūgun ianfu*. In 1973, eleven years after Kakō found the photos and twenty-eight years after WWII ended, the first written publication on "comfort women" was his book, *Jūgun Ianfu (Military Comfort Women)* in which chapter four focused on Korean "comfort women" with the title, "Tsukoku! 'Teishintai'" (Lamentation! "Volunteers"). Kakō's book awakened or re-awakened some people's awareness about the issue. After Kakō's work, there were other works on issues of "comfort women" in Japan. In 1969, Itō Keiichi first wrote about the regulations at "comfort stations" established in and around Shanghai; Kim Il-myon, a Japanese Korean, published a comprehensive book on "comfort women" in 1976; and Yoshida Seiji's testimonial book or rather memoir[24] was published in 1983. Along with these books, *An Old Lady in Okinawa: Testimony of a Military Comfort Woman*, a movie about the life of Pae Pong Gi, who lived in Japan and was the very first Korean "comfort woman" to come forward in public, was made by Yamatani Tetsuo in 1979. This film was critical for Yun Chung Ok making the connection between the "comfort women" of World War II and post-war prostitution around the Allied base.[25] These books and the movie were important but they were not able to bring the issue of "comfort women" to people's awareness, either in Japan or the world.

In South Korea, religious and secular women's organizations such as Korea Church Women United and Korean Women's Association United, respectively, were very active in addressing women's human rights and societal well-being and focused their work on sex tourism from Japan to South Korea. In the midst of their research and activism (which were funded by the South Korean

---

23 Jan Ruff O'Herne, one of the few non-Korean "comfort women" to give public testimony, made her story public in Tokyo on 9 December 1992 (Hicks, *Comfort Women*, 61).
24 Yoshida Seiji's works were discredited by a Japanese history scholar, Hata Ikuhiko. It is thus more appropriate to consider this a memoir instead of a factual biography.
25 Hicks, *The Comfort Women*, 176.

government) against Japanese sex tourism, they realized that the root of Japanese sex tourism went back to the system of "comfort women" during World War II. They then shifted their focus and centered their activism around the issue of "comfort women." Their work included research and the curation of accurate facts, assistance to former "comfort women" with medical, psychological, financial support, and political activism for redress. One of the major actions they took was in 1990; thirty-seven organizations, both church and non-church women's organizations,[26] came together and prepared a letter to the Japanese Prime Minister Kaifu Toshiki making six specific demands:

For these reasons, we make the following demands of the Japanese government:
1. That the Japanese government admit the forced draft of Korean women as "comfort women;"
2. That a public apology be made for this;
3. That all barbarities be fully disclosed;
4. That a memorial be raised for the victims;
5. That the survivors or their bereaved families be compensated;
6. That these facts be continuously related in historical education so that such misdeeds are not repeated.[27]

To organize their activism more effectively, on 10 July 1990, the Korean Institute on Chongsindae was founded, and then in November of 1990, The Korean Council for the Women Drafted for Sexual Slavery by Japan was founded. Dr. Yun Chung Ok was chosen as the first president and five months later in April of 1991, the Korean Council reorganized and established joint representatives, with Dr. Yun Chung-Ok representing academic research, Dr. Lee Hyo-chae representing Korean Women's Association United, and President Soon Kum Park of Korea Church Women United. The Institute and Council encouraged "comfort women" to break their silence and come forward. One of the women who came forward then made an earth-shattering decision. The "comfort women" issue, which was shrouded in silence but was nonetheless slipping out into people's attention slowly and gradually, suddenly broke out into the public view

---

[26] There were seven from Church Women's Association, twenty-four from the Alliance of South Korean Women's Organizations, and other organizations such as YWCA and student organizations. (Ibid., 183.)
[27] Ibid.,185.

when Kim Hak-sun, along with two other anonymous plaintiffs,[28] brought a suit against the Japanese government in August of 1991. This highly-publicized legal action was widely reported around the world when she gave a Tokyo press conference on 6 December 1991. Kim Hak-sun and other plaintiffs were represented pro bono by a team of Japanese lawyers led by Takagi Ken'ichi. This was the first time since the end of World War II in 1945 that the issue of the Korean *comfort girls-women* captured the world's attention. The shame and suffering of Korean *comfort girls-women* due to their dehumanization by the Japanese military and the shame imposed on them by the Korean government and its people was about to be buried underground for good, but then this brave "comfort woman" stepped forward and her resilience overcame her ineffable suffering, injuries, and the loss of her dignity.

Inspired by Kim Hak-sun, Japanese historian, Yoshimi Yoshiaki remembered seeing some relevant documents in the library of the Self-Defense Agency during his previous research on Japan's use of gas in China and went back to the library and indeed found other crucial documents proving the direct involvement of the Japanese military and government in instituting and running "comfort stations." These and other documents were then published by *Asahi Shimbun*, the oldest and largest daily newspaper in Japan, on 11 January 1992. Yoshimi's research finding was crucial in making Japan's first apology possible. The publication of these documents in the *Asahi* newspaper on 11 January 1992 launched a series of official apologies from the Japanese government. On 12 January 1992, the following day, then-Chief Cabinet Secretary Katō Kōichi publicly acknowledged the involvement of the Japanese military in setting up "comfort stations." Six days after the publication of six documents on 17 January 1992, the Japanese Prime Minister Miyazawa Kiichi issued a statement of apology admitting the role of Japanese government in establishing and running "comfort stations" during his state visit of Korea.

The Japanese government then investigated the issue and issued an official statement of findings after a year and a half of investigation. This statement, made by Kōno Yōhei, then-Chief Cabinet Secretary on 4 August 1993, is known as the Kōno Statement. This statement conceded that the Japanese military was officially involved in establishing and administering "comfort stations" as

---

[28] The suit also represented eleven ex-soldiers (Five were represented by their bereaved families) and twenty-one paramilitary (Eleven were represented by their bereaved families). The suit was considered a class action suit for those belonging to the categories represented by the suit.

well as the use of force in recruiting "comfort women."²⁹ The following acknowledgments including an apology summarizes the Kōno Statement:
1. The Japanese military was "directly or indirectly involved" in the establishment and management of the comfort stations and in the transfer of comfort women.
2. As for the "recruitment" of comfort women, "in many cases they were recruited against their own will, through coaxing, coercion, etc." and "at times administrative/military personnel directly took part in the recruitment."
3. "they lived in misery at comfort stations in a coercive atmosphere."
4. The "recruitment," transfer, and control of comfort women born on the Korean Peninsula were conducted "generally against their will, through coaxing, coercion, etc."
5. The issue of military comfort women is "an act, with the involvement of the military authorities of the day, that severely injured the honor and dignity of many women."
6. To the former comfort women, "the government of Japan would like to take this opportunity once again to extend its sincere apologies (owabi) and regrets.³⁰

However, Yoshimi is astute in pointing out the limitation of these acknowledgments and apology in that (1) the statement is ambiguous enough for diverse interpretation, in particular, the fact of whether Japan's involvement was direct or indirect in recruiting "comfort women" and setting up and running "comfort stations;" (2) the statement mentions only Korean women but not other Asian "comfort women" such as Taiwanese, Chinese, Filipina, Vietnamese, Indonesians, etc.; and (3) the statement stops short of Japan's taking full responsibility for war crimes and recompense thereof.³¹

While the Japanese government denied its legal responsibility, many efforts have been made by Korean activists and *comfort girls-women*, or *halmeonis* (this is the Korean word for "grandmothers," which has become widely used in describing former *comfort girls-women*, since the surviving ones are very old now) since 1991 to address the issue of *comfort girls-women*, and they achieved historic success when the United Nations issued statements acknowledging Japan's guilt and asking Japan to admit its guilt and provide reparations to Korean *comfort girls-women*. The understanding of "comfort women" as sex slaves be-

---
29 See Appendix 2 for statement by the Chief Cabinet Secretary Kōno Yōhei on the result of the study on the issue of "comfort women."
30 Yoshimi, *Comfort Women*, 36, end note 6.
31 Ibid., 36–37.

came official in the early 1990s after the "comfort women" issue was raised at the UN Commission on Human Rights and UN Sub-Commission on the Prevention of Discrimination and Protection of Minorities, and particularly after the 1993 Vienna Human Rights Conference whose slogan was "Women's rights are human rights." [32] A year later in August 1994, Japanese Prime Minister Murayama reiterated that Japan does not have any legal accountability to "comfort women" and rejected making any redress payments to "comfort women" but announced a plan for a private fund. Japanese government cabinet approved the establishment of the Asian Women's Fund to fulfill its moral responsibility in August 1995 and started execution of disbursements a year later in August 1996. While some victims benefitted from the fund, some other victims and activists were dissatisfied with and refused to accept this fund for two primary reasons: (1) The Japanese government was still denying its legal responsibility; and (2) The Asian Women's Fund was not paid by the Japanese government and thus does not reflect the legal responsibility of the Japanese government. It was paid with donations from Japanese citizens to assist "comfort women" on a humanitarian level, i.e., to fulfill moral responsibility in sharing common humanity.

The global scene carried on the opposite plot. In November 1994, the International Commission of Jurists concluded in a special report that the claims by "comfort women" and activists were legitimate, and that the Japanese government had violated and engaged in the sexual slavery of "comfort women."[33] Two proceedings at the United Nations brought hope for bringing justice to "comfort women," although legal accountability is not attached to them. In January 1996, UN special Rapporteur on Violence Against Women, Ms. Radhika Coomaraswamy, presented a report on crimes against "comfort women" to the UN Commission on Human Rights. Moreover, in August 1998, UN Special Rapporteur Gay McDougall made a UN study report calling on the Japanese government to take legal responsibility for the sexual slavery of "comfort women" during World War II. In December 2000, The "Women's International War Crimes Tribunal on Japan's Military Sexual Slavery" was held in Tokyo, and while no mode of holding legal accountability of the Emperor exists, Japan's Emperor was found guilty. Moreover, the United States Congress passed House Resolution 121 on 30 July 2007 sponsored by then-Congressman Mike Honda, who continued the

---

32 Soh, *The Comfort Women*, 33. The horrific and large-scale rapes of Bosnian women by Serb forces in early 1992 brought feminists' attention to the violation of women's rights during wars. National Organization for Women (NOW) invited a representative from the Korean Council to participate in the protest against the mass rape in Bosnia on 24 February 1993.

33 See Appendix 3 for the 1994 International Commission of Jurists Statement on "comfort women," sexual slavery, and the culpability of the Japanese government.

vigilant effort of the late Congressman Lane Evans that resolved the following summarized recommendations to the Japanese government:

> The Government of Japan should (1) formally acknowledge, apologize, and accept historical responsibility for its Imperial Armed Forces' coercion of young women into sexual slavery (comfort women) during its colonial and wartime occupation of Asia and the Pacific Islands from the 1930s through the duration of World War II; (2) have this official and public apology presented by the Prime Minister of Japan; (3) refute any claims that the sexual enslavement and trafficking of the comfort women never occurred; and (4) educate current and future generations about this crime while following the international community's recommendations with respect to the comfort women.[34]

With the confirmations of injustice of *comfort girls-women* globally and resilient struggles for justice for Korean *comfort girls-women* in South Korea and Japan, the reversal of the shame-based identity of Korean *comfort girls-women* occurred gradually over a long period of time and they in fact transformed from victims into activists. Their story is a triumphant story because they not only overcame much, if not all, of their shame which deeply infiltrated into their sense of being, but they also enabled themselves to alter their identity as victims with new identities as activists for justice and peace in the world. Many *halmeonis* who came out and worked with Korean activists such as the Korean Council and the House of Sharing found ways to heal their pain and even became activists for other victims and for peace in the world. Their leadership in the weekly Wednesday demonstrations, their testimonies around the world against war and for peace, and their establishment of scholarship funds and/or the Nabi Fund to help other women and war victims in the world all testify to their activism.

Tragic Story of the Japanese Government

Unlike the *halmeonis* who were both healed and thriving as activists themselves, the Japanese government is stuck in its road to healing. Tragically, the Japanese government denied its culpability and did not take responsibility to redress the harm and wounds perpetrated on Korean *comfort girls-women* for nearly 60 years from 1937 till 1993. As noted previously, there was a turn-around and the Japa-

---

[34] See Appendix 3 in the chapter by Dongwoo Lee Hahm and Jungsil Lee for full text of House Resolution 121 (H.Res. 121), a resolution passed by the U.S. House of Representatives that expressed that the Japanese Government should formally acknowledge, apologize, and accept historical responsibility for its Imperial Armed Forces' coercion of young women into sexual slavery. Accessed March 2, 2019. https://www.congress.gov/bill/110th-congress/house-resolution/121

nese government admitted its guilt. What made the admission of guilt by the Japanese government was the result of resilient activism by Koreans, Koreans living in Japan, and Japanese including the critical finding of evidence by Yoshimi Yoshiaki that was instrumental for this reversal and admission of guilt by the Japanese government. The Japanese government admitted its guilt in the Kōno Statement on 4 August 1993. However, Japan's admission of its guilt was short-lived, lasting 14 years from 1993 to 2007. In 2007, the Japanese conservative party, led by the Abe administration, reversed Japan's admission of its guilt in the Kōno Statement. Abe stated, "[t]he fact is, there is no evidence to prove there was coercion."[35] Ethno-nationalists of Japan argue that "comfort women" were licensed prostitutes and, thus, Japan as a nation has no accountability regarding the "comfort women" issue because no redress was necessary to those women engaged in trade by providing sex for economic gain.[36] They also argue that war created suffering for everyone involved, including Japanese "comfort women" and soldiers, an effort to water down the extreme nature of the crimes and to generalize the specificity of the profound violation of human dignity of Korean *comfort girls-women*. Moreover, Japan's response includes the claim that Japan has no more obligation to Korea because The Japanese-South Korean Basic Treaty of 1965 absolved Japan of any further debts, including that of "comfort women."

Regrettably, to this day, the Japanese government denies its part in causing unjust and undeserved suffering and its inhumane treatment of Korean *comfort girls-women*. There has thus been no progress in Japan's admission of guilt and the effort to provide just reparations to Korean *comfort girls-women*. On 28 December 2015, Japan and Korea entered a "final and irreversible" agreement of reconciliation under which Japan issued a statement of apology and created a fund of one million yen with which to pay Korean *comfort girls-women* and Korea is to remove the *Sonyeosang* in front of the Japanese Embassy in Seoul, South Korea. Korean activists and *halmeonis* are furious about this agreement because it completely ignores the victims; justice is not served. They do not think that Japan's apology is a true apology since it does not include Japan's admission of guilt. Japanese Prime Minister Ābe Shinzō confirmed that apology is

---

[35] Hiroko Tabuchi, "Japan's Abe: No Proof of WWII Sex Slaves," *The Washington Post*, March 1, 2007. Accessed March 2, 2019. http://www.washingtonpost.com/wp-dyn/content/article/2007/03/01/AR2007030100578.html.

[36] The Japanese historian Fujime Yuki, argued that the Japan's licensed prostitution is also a form of sexual slavery (Soh, *The Comfort Women*, 42).

not part of the 28 December 2015 agreement.[37] As a result, twelve of the surviving *halmeonis* are bringing suit against the Korean government. This final and irreversible agreement of reconciliation on 28 December 2015 may erase Japan's guilt on the surface, but the situation remains a tragic story of the Japanese government because the shame of the Japanese government is fully alive in the memories and psyche of the Japanese and Korean people. There does not seem to be any inkling of the Japanese government wanting to own up to its own accountability and redress Korean *comfort girls-women*.

What is noteworthy is that denying one's own guilt does not erase what was done by the guilty party, but instead, it keeps the guilty party stuck in its path to healing. Moreover, I argue that shame is behind Japan's longstanding denial of their crimes against Korean *comfort girls-women*. Japan's refusal to acknowledge guilt in enslaving Korean girls and forcing them to work as sex slaves should not be seen as a straightforward claim of innocence on their part, but instead reveals the deep sense of shame associated with such an atrocity. They inadvertently employ guilt language to cover up their own sense of shame, thus creating the Japanese secret. Japan is not the only country guilty of denying war crimes. For instance, the Korean government ignored the suffering and injustice of or even abandoned Korean *comfort girls-women* by stigmatizing them as shame to the country. Moreover, while the distinction should be made that the Korean government did not willfully nor systematically commit violence or dehumanize Vietnamese people during the Vietnam War, the Korean government is also trapped in redeeming itself from its own atrocity during the Vietnam War. The Korean government has not come forward with its admission of horrific war crimes committed by its soldiers to Vietnamese people during the Vietnam War, nor has it tried to redress wrong done by its soldiers to Vietnamese people. Both of their criminal and/or negligent acts are as apparent as they can be but more importantly, both of their denials can result in undesirable byproducts in the country, such as a lack of trust from its own people and other countries because of the stark inauthenticity on the part of the both governments. Both Hayashi Hirofumi and Yoshimi Yoshiaki, two renowned scholars on issues of "comfort women" in Japan, confirmed the necessity for Japan's apology and compensation to Korean

---

37 "Abe Confirms Japan Not Considering Apology Letters for 'Comfort Women,'" *Japan Times*, October 3, 2016. Accessed March 2, 2019. https://www.japantimes.co.jp/news/2016/10/03/national/politics-diplomacy/abe-confirms-japan-not-considering-apology-letters-comfort-women/#.WjsPVlWnGpp.

comfort girls-women and its benefit for Japan to recover trust from neighboring nations in Asia.[38]

The notion of cohesive self of Heinz Kohut's self psychology and Gershen Kaufmann's discussion on defenses against shame illumine Japan's inability to embrace its own sense of shame. According to Heinz Kohut, shame is a manifestation of injury to the self. Kohut also proposes that when the self is cohesive, the self is less vulnerable to shame or is able to deal with experiences of shame. On the other hand, when the self is not cohesive, the self is more vulnerable to shame. More importantly, the self develops its cohesiveness with the help of a selfobject which is socially an object but is experienced internally as a part of the subject or self.[39] In my work, I expanded Kohut's notion of management of self-coherence by creating new concepts: *self-preservation*, *self-loss*, and *selfobject-augmentation*.[40] I propose that cohesion of the self depends on the dynamic among these three. I define *self-prese*rvation as the level of one's development of a cohesive self; *self-loss* as the level of injuries to the self incurred by external force; and *selfobject-augmentation* as the self shored up by others. I posit that, on a basic level, one's cohesiveness is intact when the level of *self-preservation* is greater than the level of *self-loss*. By contrast, it is not cohesive when *self-loss* is greater than the level of *self-preservation*. On a higher level, however, one's self can still be cohesive or even surpass one's natural level of cohesiveness, even if *self-loss* overtakes the self's capability to withstand it, i.e., *self-preservation*, when the self's function is augmented by others called selfobjects. This *selfobject-augmentation* can make the level of one's cohesiveness match the level of *self-loss* or be buoyed to a level above the level of *self-loss*. To state it differently, one's cohesiveness is intact as long as the level of *self-loss* does not exceed the level of one's *self-preservation* or the combination of the level of *self-preservation* and the level of *selfobject-augmentation*.

What happens when the self is unable to contain its *self-loss* or shame experiences, and how does this apply to the shame experience of the Japanese government? Gershen Kaufman in *The Psychology of Shame* discusses defending

---

[38] Angella Son, "Author's personal interviews with Hayashi Hirofumi, Professor at Kanto Gakuin University in Japan, on May 19, 2017 and Yoshimi Yoshiaki, Professor Emeritus at Chuo University in Japan, on 7 and 8 July 2017"; See also Hirofumi Hayashi, "Disputes in Japan over the Japanese Military 'Comfort Women' System and Its Perception in History," *The Annals of the American Academy of Political and Social Science* 617 (2008): 131.

[39] Heinz Kohut, *The Restoration of the Self* (Madison, CT: International Universities Press 1977), 84.

[40] Angella Son, "Making a Great Man, Moses: Sustenance and Augmentation of the Self through God as the Selfobject," *Pastoral Psychology* 64, no. 5 (2015): 751–768.

strategies to handle excessive shame that the self is unable to contain. They include rage, contempt, striving for perfection, striving for power, transfer of blame, and denial.⁴¹ Among these, denial is enacted when all attempts to avoid or escape shame are futile. Kaufman states: "Denial is a final line of defense when action strategies fail."⁴² Kaufman continues, "Denial ... attempt[s] to exclude shame from awareness by denying its perception, or by denying the perception of anything that might arouse shame."⁴³ I suggest that, considering the Japanese government to be a self, it incurred a greater level of *self-loss* from World War II than its capacity to maintain its coherence, and was consequently unable to contain its *self-loss* or shame experiences. This was due not only to the fact that Japan lost the war to the Allies, but also the way that they lost the war. The critical measure against Japan was the atomic bomb dropped on Hiroshima and Nagasaki in August of 1945 by the United States. This unexpected attack of nuclear bombs from the United States devastated the Japanese government and people. Their sense of cohesive self as a nation was bankrupt. Japanese people thus see themselves as victims of the war, and rightly so, since many innocent civilians and as many as over 100,000 people were killed by the atomic bombs, but unfortunately some Japanese people forget that they were also the culprit when initiating aggression against other Asian countries by committing violence and dehumanizing many, including Korean *comfort girls-women*. The Japanese government thus resorts to defending its excessive *self-loss* or shame to preserve its coherence. It does this by denying its war crimes or its guilt to erase the shame arising out of its horrific violation of the human rights of Korean *comfort girls-women*. The Japanese government has attempted to provide compensation to Korean *comfort-girls-women*, but it was never leveled as such, but instead as humanitarian donations to help Korean *comfort girls-women* such as the Asian Women's Fund in August of 1995 or the fund stipulated in the 28 December 2015 agreement. These attempts at a humanitarian gesture by the Japanese government attest to its admission of guilt, but also reveal its inability to overcome the deep shame associated with its non-humanitarian offenses to Korean *comfort girls-women*.

---

41 Gershen Kaufmann, *The Psychology of Shame: Theory and Treatment of Shame-Based Syndromes* (New York: Springer Publishing Company, 1989), 100–104.
42 Ibid., 103.
43 Ibid.

Symbolic Meanings of *Sonyeosang*, the Statue of Peace: Adjudication of Shame and Guilt of the Japanese Government

Sonyeosang was commissioned by the Korean Council and created by sculptors Kim Seo-kyung and Kim Eun-sung[44] to commemorate the thousand weekly Wednesday rallies held in front of the Japanese embassy in Seoul, South Korea since 8 January 1992. It was dedicated on the 1,000th Wednesday rally on 14 December 2011. The sculptors Kim Seo-kyung and Kim Eun-sung created twelve aspects of *Sonyeosang*, the Statue of Peace, to represent specific symbolic meanings: (1) The statue is a girl representing many underaged girls in Korea placed in sexual slavery by the Japanese government; (2) The girl is wearing a *hanbok*, a Korean traditional costume worn by girls to reflect their Korean nationality in spite of rejection by the Korean government and people; (3) The girl's hair is roughly cut instead of a girl's customary long braided hairstyle tied with a ribbon at the end, the chopped locks representing how *comfort girls-women* went through abrupt and total disruption in their lives due to the Japanese military; (4) A bird symbolizing freedom and peace sits on the girl's left shoulder; (5) The *Sonyeosang*'s feet are tiptoeing, representing the unrest and alienation they experienced even after their return to their own country, especially due to neglect and abandonment from the South Korean government; (6) The shadow of the *Sonyeosang*[45] is not of a girl but of a *halmeoni* or grandmother showing the long period of their lives without any satisfactory apology and redress; (7) The shadow of the *halmeoni* has a white butterfly in the chest area, a symbolic wish for a better life in re-birth or for a visitation by already deceased Korean *comfort girls-women* as butterflies, sharing the lives and the effort of justice for Korean *comfort girls-women* today; (8) The empty chair remembers those Korean *comfort girls-women* already passed and invites others today to empathically join them; (9) *Sonyeosang*'s clenched fists speak to her rage against the shameless Japanese government, which never apologized after violently ruining the lives of so many young girls, and reveal her deep determination to continuously pursue justice and resolution for Korean *comfort girls-women*; (10) *Sonyeosang*'s face displays

---

44 The sculptors are Seo-kyung Kim (김서경) and Eun-sung Kim (김운성). They are husband and wife and often work collaboratively on projects and use the name Kim Seo-kyungEun-sung by combining their first names.

45 Seo-kyung and Eun-sung Kim's daughter, who modeled for *Sonyeosang*, suggested *halmeoni* instead of a girl for shadow.

complexities of the young but confident; the violated but determined for justice; the fearful, sad, and enraged but the fear, sadness and rage overcome; (11) A touch of *halmeonis* is the inscription of the title on the Peace Monument next to *Sonyeosang* written by Won Ok Gil *halmeoni*; and (12) *Sonyeosang* sits across the street from and faces the Japanese Embassy and waits for the Japanese government to come through with heart-felt apology and redress.[46]

Among these twelve symbolic meanings of *Sonyeosang*, I would like to focus on the clenched fists which represent her rage against the Japanese government and her determination for justice as noted above. I suggest that we add another symbolic meaning that moves us beyond the rage and determination portrayed by the two fists clenched tightly. I suggest that one of the symbolic meanings of *Sonyeosang* is an embodiment of the shame and guilt of the Japanese government. This is evident in the Japanese government being particularly keen on eliminating *Sonyeosang*, as is demonstrated by its repeated attempts to remove *Sonyeosang* including the stipulation to remove the *Sonyeosang* facing the Japanese Embassy in the 28 December 2015 agreement. For instance, Japanese Prime Minister Ābe Shinzō pressured the Korean government to remove the new *Sonyeosang* facing the Japanese Embassy in Busan as a part of the fulfillment of the agreement.[47] *Sonyeosang* thus speaks directly to the hidden shame of the Japanese government and the two clenched fists can stand for not just determination to pursue justice against the Japanese government but it itself is the determination of justice for a constructive forward move. As the embodiment of the shame and guilt of the Japanese government, *Sonyeosang* can be seen to represent adjudication or judgment of the Japanese government as the determination of justice. *Sonyeosang*'s clenched fists would then symbolize the judge's gavel used in the court of law in the United States, pronouncing a guilty verdict against the Japanese government. It is the ingenuity of Yoon Mee-hyang, Co-Representative of the Korean Council, and the sculptors Kim Seo-kyung and Kim Eun-sung to create *Sonyeosang* and erect it facing the Japanese embassy in South Korea. It is the fruit of the tireless commitment and dedication of the *halmeonis*, the Korean Council, and many other activists and from the profound artistry by Kim Seo-kyung and Kim Eun-sung that made it possible for the stories of *halmeonis* to live on as an embodied *Sonyeosang*. *Sonyeosang*, the Statue of Peace, also makes itself available for a multiplicity of symbolic meanings and has opened up a dialogue about the *halmeonis* and other victims of

---

46 Seo-kyung Kim and Kim Eun-sung, *Promises Engraved in the Empty Chair* (Seoul: Mal, 2016).
47 "Abe Urges South Korea to Remove 'Comfort Women' Statue at Busan, Claims 2015 Agreement at Stake," *Japan Times*, January 8, 2017. Accessed March 2, 2019. https://www.japantimes.co.jp/news/2017/01/08/national/abe-urges-south-korea-remove-comfort-women-statue-says-agreements-credibility-stake/#.WjsPuVWnGpp.

war crimes. The Japanese government can continue to deny its war crimes against Korean *comfort girls-women*, but *Sonyeosang* stands to adjudicate not only its guilt but also its shame. While no legal platform is available to hold the Japanese government accountable for its war crimes, *Sonyeosang* continues to bear witness to the shame and pronounce the guilt of the Japanese government. I would push it further and claim that *Sonyeosang*[48] invites the Japanese government to the road to healing its shame as the *halmeoni*s did so that peace in the world is further accomplished.

Conclusion

By the end of 2013, 237 Korean *comfort girls-women* had registered with the South Korean government,[49] but of those, only thirty-five are still alive as of 30 October 2017. All are 80 or older and about half are in their 80s and the other half are in their 90s. It is quite plausible that there may be no Korean *comfort girls-women* still alive ten to twenty years from now. It is extremely urgent that justice be resolved before all the Korean *comfort girls-women* leave this life with wrenching *han* in their hearts, such as the *han* evident in Kim Hak-sun's summary of her life appealing for justice for former Korean *comfort girls-women* like herself:

> I harbored a considerable grudge against the Japanese, and my whole life had been loathsome and abhorrent, largely because of them. I had been wanting to talk to someone about my past for a long time, and I told this woman that I had once been a comfort woman. Since then I have been called to speak in many different places, because I was the first

---

[48] Many *Sonyeosang*s and other statues inspired by *Sonyeosang* are erected throughout South Korea and some have been erected in the United States and other nations. They include one in Glendale, CA, Detroit, MI, New York, NY, Toronto in Canada, Sydney in Australia, Shanghai in China, Wiesent in Germany, etc. The most recent one is the peace statue in memory of "comfort women" of Asia in San Francisco which was unveiled on 22 September 2017. The statue of Kim Hak-sun faces statues of three girls—meant to represent girls from Korea, China, and the Philippines—on a pedestal. *Sonyeosang* has also transformed in its forms and sizes particularly by movements by high school students. Spearheaded by high school students from a history club at Ewha Girls' High School, students from 53 high schools collaborated and erected a standing *Sonyeosang* in Seoul, South Korea. Some high school students in South Korea started a movement of erecting 30 cm *Sonyeosang* at each high school. There are 10 cm *Sonyeosang*, which people carry around with them. There are also plastic *Sonyeosang* that people carry with them in buses and cars. (Kim and Kim, *Promises*, 223–329; VOA News. Accessed March 2, 2019. https://www.voanews.com/a/san-francisco-statue-wwii-comfort-women/4041188.html).

[49] Chin-sung Chung, et. al., *20 Years of the Korean Council for the Women Drafted for Military Sexual Slavery by Japan* (Paju, South Korea: Hanul Books, 2014), 62.

of the comfort women witnesses to come forward. I find it very painful to recall my memories. Why haven't I been able to lead a normal life, free from shame, like other people? When I look at old women, I compare myself to them, thinking that I cannot be like them. I feel I could tear apart, limb by limb, those who took away my innocence and made me as I am. Yet how can I appease my bitterness? Now I don't want to disturb my memories any further. Once I am dead and gone, I wonder whether the Korean or Japanese governments will pay any attention to the miserable life of a woman like me.[50]

In reverse, this suggests that the Japanese government is running out of time and may lose its opportunities forever to apologize to and attempt to make amends for its inhumane atrocity against victims of its war crimes, including Korean *comfort girls-women*. *Sonyeosang*, however, carries on the legacy of the *halmeonis*' stories and lives that draws attention to transformation of shame and pursuit of world peace. *Sonyeosang* adjudicates the war crime of the Japanese government so that the Japanese government will move forward on its road to healing from its hidden and secret shame and share the work of world peace side by side with *halmeonis* as companions. *Sonyeosang* is indeed the Statue of Peace inviting all to shed their shame and press forward to accomplish peace in the world.

I thus appeal to the Japanese government and the Korean government as well as the Korean and Japanese people to take courage as the *halmeonis* have done and start their journey to healing from the weighty burden of shame and the guilt of its war crimes against Korean *comfort girls-women* and/or Vietnamese people. I also appeal to Korean activists and *halmeonis* to take pride and celebrate their creative and courageous efforts in creating *Sonyeosang*, an embodiment of judgment against these war crimes and also an invitation to take the courageous admission of its shame and guilt to the Japanese government that can lead to their healing and advancing peace in the world. I also appeal to them to move from a posture of accusation to a posture of invitation toward the Japanese government to admit its shame and guilt and join together as reconciled people and nations in pursuit of the world peace represented by *Sonyeosang*, the Statue of Peace.

Acknowledgment: I would like to express my appreciation to *Pastoral Psychology* for granting me the permission to use my article, "Inadequate Innocence of Korean *Comfort Girls-Women:* Obliterated and Shamed Self" published in *Pastoral Psychology* mainly for the sections, "Korean *Comfort Girls-Women:* Historic Backdrop" and "Silence of a Half a Century: Korean *Comfort Girls-Women* Shamed into Nonexistence" in this work. I would like to express my deep appreciation to Yale Center for Faith and Culture for awarding me the 2017 Open Rank

---

50 Howard, *The Comfort Women*, 40.

Research Grant funded by the John Templeton Foundation that made it possible for my research travel to interview scholars and activists in Japan, South Korea, and the United States for the justice of Korean *comfort girls-women*. I would also like to express my deep gratitude to Yoon Mee-hyang, Co-Representative of the Korean Council, and Artists Kim Seo-kyung and Kim Eun-sung for very moving and inspiring interviews.

Appendix 1

C. Sarah Soh acknowledges the contribution of Korean activists in publicizing the "comfort women" issue to the world but criticizes its using "'approximate truths' or strategic exaggerations" in their simplistic approach to targeting Japanese war crimes. She posits that their approach prevented more adequate measurements to address the issue with a deeper understanding of the complex nature of what she calls "gendered structural violence" generated from the everyday power imbalances weaved into economic (classism, industrial modernization, capitalist imperialism), political (colonialism, militarism, and racism), and cultural (Confucianism, sexism) aspects of the society (xii–xiii, xvii). She asserts that the responsibility lies not only with Japan but also with the Korean people and Korea as a nation. For instance, Soh points out how her research contradicts Korean activists' claim that Korean "comfort women" were deceived and recruited as *chongsindae*. Her research among surviving "comfort women" suggests that most Korean "comfort women" were not recruited as *chongsindae* but instead were enticed by Korean men and women who were entrepreneurs taking advantage of the demands of the Japanese military and the widespread poverty in Korea for their own economic gain. Moreover, some of the girls were sold by their poor families, some were lured in by their efforts to pursue an education or escape from a poor or abusive family situation, etc.[51]

Yun Chung Ok, one of the co-founders of the Korean Council, acknowledged that distinctions should be made between those who were strictly recruited as *chongsindae* and those who were forced into being "comfort women" after being drafted as *chongsindae*. Yun, however, disagrees with Soh that those who were recruited as *chongsindae* and those who were recruited as "comfort women" should not be distinguished in terms of their violation by the Japanese government because they all lost the agency to decide for themselves.[52]

---

51 Soh, *Comfort Women*, 3–4, 18–20, 58–63.
52 Hicks, *Comfort Women*, 187.

Appendix 2

Statement by the Chief Cabinet Secretary Kōno Yōhei on the result of the study on the issue of "comfort women."
4 August 1993

> The Government of Japan has been conducting a study on the issue of wartime "comfort women" since December 1991. I wish to announce the findings as a result of that study.
>
> As a result of the study which indicates that comfort stations were operated in extensive areas for long periods, it is apparent that there existed a great number of comfort women. Comfort stations were operated in response to the request of the military authorities of the day. The then Japanese military was, directly or indirectly, involved in the establishment and management of the comfort stations and the transfer of comfort women. The recruitment of the comfort women was conducted mainly by private recruiters who acted in response to the request of the military. The Government study has revealed that in many cases they were recruited against their own will, through coaxing, coercion, etc., and that, at times, administrative/military personnel directly took part in the recruitments. They lived in misery at comfort stations under a coercive atmosphere.
>
> As to the origin of those comfort women who were transferred to the war areas, excluding those from Japan, those from the Korean Peninsula accounted for a large part. The Korean Peninsula was under Japanese rule in those days, and their recruitment, transfer, control, etc., were conducted generally against their will, through coaxing, coercion, etc.
>
> Undeniably, this was an act, with the involvement of the military authorities of the day, that severely injured the honor and dignity of many women. The Government of Japan would like to take this opportunity once again to extend its sincere apologies and remorse to all those, irrespective of place of origin, who suffered immeasurable pain and incurable physical and psychological wounds as comfort women.
>
> It is incumbent upon us, the Government of Japan, to continue to consider seriously, while listening to the views of learned circles, how best we can express this sentiment.
>
> We shall face squarely the historical facts as described above instead of evading them, and take them to heart as lessons of history. We hereby reiterate our firm determination never to repeat the same mistake by forever engraving such issues in our memories through the study and teaching of history.

As actions have been brought to court in Japan and interests have been shown in this issue outside Japan, the Government of Japan shall continue to pay full attention to this matter, including private researched related thereto.[53]

---

[53] Ministry of Foreign Affairs of Japan, mofa.go.jp. Accessed March 2, 2019. http://www.mofa.go.jp/policy/women/fund/state9308.html

Appendix 3

ICJ Statement
Preface

As mentioned in the introduction, this is the story of people everyone tried to forget. The matter has been raised before many fora, including those of the United Nations. Much has appeared on the subject in the media. Yet very little concrete action has been taken to provide relief to the victims: the Comfort Women from Korea, the Philippines, and other countries in Asia, whose numbers range between 100,000 and 200,000. Why human rights violations on such a massive scale were not discussed in any meaningful way for more than 40 years is inexplicable.

It is for this reason that the International Commission of Jurists (ICJ) sent a mission in April 1993 to the Philippines, the Republic of Korea, the Democratic People's Republic of Korea and to Japan. The mission inquired into the circumstances concerning sexual services obtained from Korean and Filipino women by the Japanese military during World War II. It also inquired into what responsibility the present Japanese Government bears towards these women and, what steps must be taken and by whom, to resolve issues concerning these women. The preliminary report of the mission was issued in May 1993.

The mission consisted of Ms. Ustinia Dolgopol, Lecturer, School of Law, The Flinders University of South Australia and Ms. Snehal Paranjape, an Advocate of the Bombay High Court, India. The mission interviewed over 40 victims, three former soldiers, government representatives, representatives of non-governmental organizations, lawyers, academics and journalists.

Based on documents reviewed and interviews held, the mission concludes that it is clear that the Japanese Imperial Army initiated the setting up of a vast network of comfort stations for the exclusive use of the Japanese Imperial Army, before and during the Second World War. Chinese, Dutch, Filipino, Indonesian, Korean, Malaysian and Taiwanese women and girls were targeted, put into these comfort stations and sexual services were extracted from them under duress. The Japanese military was responsible for the setting up, use, operation and control of the comfort stations. Detailed regulations were framed by the Japanese military in this regard.

The mission also found that life in the comfort stations was living hell for the women. They were beaten and tortured in addition to being repeatedly raped day after day by officers and soldiers. Living conditions were cramped and shabby, food was usually of a poor quality and in short supply. Although medical check-ups by army doctors took place, many women were afflicted by sexually transmitted diseases. When they were brought to the comfort stations, they were healthy in body and spirit. They left the comfort stations, diseased in body and crippled in spirit.

The report also shows that the suffering of these women did not end after the war. After being abandoned by fleeing Japanese soldiers, some of them reached home, only to live lives of isolation. The pain they have endured has continued throughout their lifetime.

The ICJ is grateful to the Governments of the Philippines, the Republic of Korea, the Democratic People's Republic of Korea and Japan for having met the mission. The ICJ would also like to thank the Task Force for Filipino Victims of Military Sexual Slavery by Japan, in the Philippines; the Korean Council for the Women Drafted for Military Sexual Slavery by Japan, and Dr. Tai Young Lee from the Republic of Korea; the Democratic Lawyers Association of the Democratic People's Republic of Korea; the Japan Civil Liberties Union, the Japan Federation of Bar Associations, and Mr. Totsuka, Mr. Uesugi, Mr. Aitani, Ms. Naomi Hirakawa, and especially Professor Yoshimi from Japan for their hospitality and the invaluable assistance they gave to the ICJ mission. We are very grateful to Mr. George Hicks for having given us useful information on the subject and we also sincerely thank Dr. Christian Tomuschat, Ms. Monika Luke and Mr. Hans-Peter Gasser, for their very useful comments on the legal issues.

And, of course, our deepest gratitude to the women, who, despite all the pain and anguish they have been through, with dignity and courage allowed the mission to interview them.

In August 1993, the Japanese Government, for the first time admitted that "the then Japanese military was directly or indirectly involved in the establishment and management of the comfort stations and the transfer of comfort women". The government also admitted that recruitment and transportation of the women were carried out against their will by deceipt and pressure and that the military personnel directly took part in the recruitments. It also stated that "it is apparent that there existed a great number of comfort women" and that life at the comfort stations was miserable. The Japanese Government has recognized that "this was an act that severely injured the honour and dignity of many women" and it apologized to all these women.

On 2 September 1994 a draft of the report was sent to the Governments of Japan, the Philippines, the Republic of Korea and the Democratic People's Republic of Korea inviting them to comment on the report. Written comments have only been received from the Government of the Philippines, most of which have been reflected in the report.

Considering the evidence that has come before the mission it is imperative that the Government of Japan take immediate steps to provide full rehabilitation and restitution to the victims. The ICJ sincerely hopes that this report will make a contribution to provide immediate relief to the victims and to ensure that they do not remain forgotten, forever.

Adama Dieng Secretary General

November 1994[54]

---

54 Accessed March 2, 2019. http://icj.wpengine.netdna-cdn.com/wp-content/uploads/1994/01/Japan-comfort-women-fact-finding-report-1994-eng.pdf.

Major Publications Included in Book Chapters (Reading List)

Andrews, William. *Daughters of the Dragon: A Comfort Woman's Story*. Seattle: Lake Union Publishing, 2014.

Asian Women's Fund. "*Jugun Ianfu ni Sareta Gatanata Tsugunai no Tameni*" [Compensation for Military Comfort Women]. Tokyo: Asian Women's Fund, 1995.

Bentley, Jerry H., and Herbert Ziegler. *Traditions and Encounters: A Global Perspective on the Past*. New York: McGraw-Hill Education, 2010.

Chinkin, Christine M. "Editorial Comments: Women's International Tribunal on Japanese Military Sexual Slavery," *The American Journal of International Law* 95 (2001): 335–341.

Choi Schellstede, Sangmie. *Comfort Women Speak: Testimony by Sex Slaves of the Japanese Military*. New York and London: Holmes & Meier, 2000.

Chung, Chin-song. *Inbongun Sungnoyeje* [The Japanese Military Sexual Slavery System], Second Edition. Seoul: Seoul National University Publishing Company, 2016.

Cumings, Bruce. *Korea's Place in the Sun: A Modern History*. New York: W. W. Norton & Company, Inc., 1997.

Dolgopol, Ustinia, and Snehal Paranjape. *Comfort Women: An Unfinished Ordeal: Report of a Mission*. Geneva, Switzerland: International Commission of Jurists, 1995.

Enloe, Cynthia. *The Big Push: Exposing and Challenging the Persistence of Patriarchy*. Berkeley: University of California Press, 2017.

Hawthorne, Nathaniel. *The Scarlet Letter: An Authoritative Text, Essays in Criticism and Scholarship*, 3 ed. New York: W. W. Norton, 1988.

Hayashi, Hirofumi. "Disputes in Japan over the Japanese Military 'Comfort Women' System and Its Perception in History." *The Annals of American Academy of Political and Social Science* 617 (May 2008): 123–132.

Hayashi, Hirofumi. *Nihongun "Ianfu" Mondai-no Kakushi* (The Essence of the Japanese Military Comfort Women Issue). Tokyo: Kadensha, 2015.

Hein, Laura. "Savage Irony: The Imaginative Power of the 'Military Comfort Women' in the 1990s." *Gender and History* 11, no. 2 (July 1999): 336–372.

Henson, Maria Rosa. *Comfort Women: A Filipina's Story of Prostitution and Slavery under the Japanese Military*. Lanham, MD: Rowman and Littlefield, 1995.

Hicks, George. *The Comfort Women: Japan's Brutal Regime of Enforced Prostitution in the Second World War*. New York: W. W. Norton & Company, 1990.

Jager, Sheila Miyoshi, and Rana Mitter, eds. *Ruptured Histories: War, Memory, and the Post-Cold War in Asia*. Cambridge: Harvard University Press, 2007.

Kim-Gibson, Dae Sil. *Silence Broken: Korean Comfort Women*. Parkerburg, Iowa: Mid-Prairie Books, 1999.

Kim, Il-myeon. *Tenno no Guntai to Chosenjin Ianfu* [The Emperor's Army and the Korean "Comfort Women"]. Tokyo: San'ichi Sobo, 1992.

Kaufmann, Gershen. *The Psychology of Shame: Theory and Treatment of Shame-Based Syndromes*. New York: Springer Publishing Company, 1989.

Kent, Susan Kingsley. 1999. *Gender and Power in Britain, 1640–1990*. London and New York: Routledge.

Kim, Il-myeon. *Tenno no Guntai to Chosenjin Ianfu* [The Emperor's Army and the Korean Com fort Women]. Tokyo: San'ichi Sobo, 1992.

Kim, Seo-kyung, and Eun-sung Kim. *The Promise Engraved on the Empty Chair: The Artists' Notes about "Statue of Peace: The Little Girl,"* 16–17. Seoul: Mal, 2016.

Kohut, Heinz. *The Restoration of the Self.* Madison, CT: International Universities Press, 1977.

Lee, Hyun-Sook. *Hankuk Kyohoe Yosong Yonhaphoe 25 Nyonsa* [A 25 Years' History of Korean Church Women United]. Seoul: Korean Church Women United, 1992.

Lee, Jeff Jungho, ed. *Can You Hear Us?* Seoul: Commission on Verification and Support for the Victims of Forced Mobilization under Japanese Colonization in Korea, 2014.

Lynd, Helen Merrell. *On Shame and the Search for Identity.* New York: Harcourt Brace, 1958.

Morikawa, Machiko, ed. *Mun Ok-chu: Burmes Sensen Tacheshiden no Ianfu Data Watashi* [Mun Ok-chu: I Was a Comfort Woman of the Shield Division on the Burma Front]. Tokyo: Nashinokisha, 1996.

McDougall, Gay J. "Contemporary Forms of Slavery: Systematic Rape, Sexual Slavery and Slave-Like Practices during Armed Conflict." Economic and Social Council, United Nations, 1998.

McNeill, David. "Nippon Kaigi and the Radical Conservative Project to Take Back Japan." *The Asia-Pacific Journal, Japan Focus* 13, issue 50, no. 4 (December 14, 2015). https://apjjf.org/-David-McNeill/4409. Accessed May 22, 2019.

Min, Pyong Gap. "Korean 'Comfort Women': The Intersection of Colonial Power, Gender, and Class." *Gender and Society* 17, no. 6 (December 2003): 938–957.

Mizohata, Sachie. "Nippon Kaigi: Empire, Contradiction, and Japan's Future." *The Asia-Pacific Journal, Japan Focus* 14, issue 21, no. 2 (November 1, 2016). http://apjjf.org/2016/21/Mizohata.html. Accessed February 11, 2017.

Nishino, Rumiko. 2006. "Women's Active Museum on War and Peace: Creating a Space for Hub of Activism for Peace and Gender Justice." *Women's Asia: Voices from Japan* 21, no. 36 (Winter 2006): 35–43.

Nishino, Rumiko, Puja Kim, and Akane Onozawa, eds. *Denying the Comfort Women: The Japanese State's Assault on Historical Truth.* Translated by Robert Rickett. New York and London: Routledge, 2018.

Park, Therese. *A Gift of the Emperor.* Duluth, MN: Spinsters Ink, 1997.

Park, Yuha. *Cheguk-ui Wianbu: Sigminjibae-wa Gieag-ui Tujaeng* [Comfort Women of the Empire: The Colonial Rule and Struggles for Memory). Seoul: Bburi-wa Ippari, 2013.

Pilzner. Joshua D. *Hearts of Pine: Songs in the Lives of Three Korean Survivors of the Japanese "Comfort Women,"* New York: Oxford University Press, 2012.

Qiu, Peipei, with Su Zhiliang, and Chen Lifei. *Chinese Comfort Women: Testimonies from Imperial Japan's Sex Slaves.* New York: Oxford University Press, 2014.

Rudick, Roger. *Story of a Comfort Girl.* Seattle: Amazon Digital Services, 2012.

Sakamoto, Rumi. "The Women's International War Crimes Tribunal on Japan's Military Sexual Slavery: A Legal and Feminist Approach to the 'Comfort Women' Issue." *New Zealand Journal of Asian Studies* 3, no. 1 (June 2001): 49–58.

Schirch, Lisa. *Ritual and Symbol in Peacebuilding.* Bloomfield, CT: Kumarian Press, 2005.

Senda, Kako, *Jugun Ianfu (Military Comfort Women).* Tokyo: Futabasha, 1973.

Soh, C. Sarah. *The Comfort Women: Sexual Violence and Postcolonial Memory in Korea and Japan.* Chicago: University of Chicago Press, 2008.

Son, Angella. "Making a Great Man, Moses: Sustenance and Augmentation of the Self Through God as Selfobject." *Pastoral Psychology* 64, no. 5 (2015): 751–768.

Stetz, Margaret, and Bonnie B. C. Oh (eds). *Legacies of the Comfort Women of World War II*. London: M.E. Sharpe, 2001.

The Korean Council for Women Drafted for Military Sexual Slavery by Japan. *True Stories of the Korean Comfort Women*. Edited by Keith Howard. London: Cassell, 1995.

The Korean Council for Women Drafted for Military Sexual Slavery by Japan, ed. *Ilbongun 'Wianbu' Munche-ui Chinsang* [The Real Picture of the Japanese Military 'Comfort Women Issue]. Seoul: Ryeaksa Bipyongsa, 1997.

The Korean Council for Women Drafted for Military Sexual Slavery by Japan, ed. *2000 Nyeon Ilbongun Wianbu Seongnoye Jeonbeom Gugjebeopjeong: Jaryeojip* [Women's International War Crimes Tribunal on Japanese Military Sexual Slavery of 2000: Sourcebook]. Seoul: The Korean Council, 2000.

The Korean Council for Women Drafted for Military Sexual Slavery by Japan, ed. *Gangjero Kkullyeogan Joseonin Gunwianbudeul*, [The Forcibly Drafted Korean Comfort Women], *Testimonies,* Volume 4. Seoul: Pulbit, 2001a.

The Korean Council for Women Drafted for Military Sexual Slavery by Japan, ed. *Gangjero Kkullyeogan Joseonin Gunwianbudeul* [The Forcibly Drafted Korean Comfort Women], *Testimonies*, Volume 5. Seoul: Pulbit, 2001b.

The Korean Council for Women Drafted for Military Sexual Slavery by Japan, ed. *Yeoksareul Mandeuneun Iyagi* [History Making Stories], *Testimonies,* Volume 6. Seoul: Doseo Chulpan, 2004.

The Korean Council for Women Drafted for Military Sexual Slavery by Japan, ed. *Hanguk Cheongshindae Munje Daecheak Hyeopeuihe 20-Nyonsa* [A 20-Year History of the Korean Council]. Seoul: Hanul, 2014.

The Korean Council for Women Drafted for Military Sexual Slavery by Japan, ed. 2015. *Wianbu Heusaengja-ae Gwanhan Juyo Gukjeh Munseodeul* [Major International Documents on the Japanese Military Sexual Slavery 'Comfort Women') Issue]. Seoul: The Korean Council, 2015.

The Korean Council for Women Drafted for Military Sexual Slavery by Japan and the Korean Research Institute, eds. *Gangjero Kkullyeogan Joseonin Gunwianbudeul* [The Forcibly Drafted Korean Comfort Women], *Testimonies*, Volume 1. Seoul: Hanul, 1993.

The Korean Council for Women Drafted for Military Sexual Slavery by Japan and the Korean Research Institute, eds. *Gangjero Kkullyeogan Joseonin Gunwianbudeul*. [The Forcibly Drafted Korean Comfort Women], *Comfort Women Testimonies*, Volume 2. Seoul: Hanul, 1997.

The Korean Research Institute, ed. *Junggug-euro Kkullyeogan Joseonin Gunwianbudeul* [Forcefully Dragged Korean Military Comfort Women to China], *Testimonies*, Volume 1. Seoul Hanul, 1995.

The Korean Research Institute, ed. *Junggug-euro Kkeullyeogan Joseonin Gunwianbudeul* [Forcefully Dragged Korean Military Comfort Women to China], *Testimonies*, Volume 2. Seoul: Hanul, 2003.

The Korean Research Institute and the Korean Council for Women Drafted for Military Sexual Slavery by Japan, eds. *Gangjero Kkullyeogan Joseonin Gunwianbudeul* [Forcibly Drafted Korean Comfort Women], *Testimonies*, Volume 3. Seoul: Hanul, 1999.

Tokudome, Kinue. "Passage of H.Res. 121 on 'Comfort Women,' the US Congress and Historical Memory in Japan," *The Asia-Pacific Journal, Japan Focus* 5, no. 8 (August 1, 2007). https://apjjf.org/-Kinue-TOKUDOME/2510/article.html. Accessed May 22, 2019.

Tumblety, Joan. *Memory and History: Understanding Memory as Source and Subject*. London and New York: Routledge, 2013.

Uemura, Takashi. "Labeled the Reporter who 'Fabricated' the Comfort Woman Issue: A Rebuttal." Translation and Introduction by Tomomi Yamaguchi. *The Asia-Pacific Journal: Japan Focus* 13, issue 2, no. 1 (January 12, 2015). https://apjjf.org/2015/13/1/Tomomi-Yamaguchi/4249.html. Accessed May 22, 2019.

Wada, Haruki. *Ianfumondai no Kaiketsu no Tameni Ajia-jyosei-kikin no Keiken Kara* [The Resolution to the Comfort Women Issue: From the Experience of Asian Women's Fund]. Tokyo: Heibonsha, 2015.

Walker, Margaret Urban. *Moral Repair: Reconstructing Moral Relations after Wrongdoing*. Cambridge, UK: Cambridge University Press, 2006.

Yamaguchi, Tomomi, and Emi Koyama. "What are the responses of Japanese Americans and Japanese nationals residing in the U.S. toward the "comfort women" issue?" *Fight for Justice* (2016). http://fightforjustice.info/?page_id=4300&lang=en. Accessed April 3, 2018.

Yamaguchi, Tomomi, Nogawa Motokazu, and Emi Koyama (eds). *Umi o wataru "ianfu" mondai —Uha no "rekishisen o tou* [*The "Comfort Women" Problem Crosses the Pacific: Examining the Right's "History Wars"*] (Tokyo: Iwanami Shoten, 2016).

Yoshimi, Yoshiaki. *Comfort Women: Sexual Slavery in the Japanese Military during World War II*. Translated by Suzanne O'Brien. New York: Columbia University Press, 2000.

Yoshimi, Yoshiaki, and Hirofumi Hayashi, eds. *Kyodou Kenkyu Nihongun Ianfu* [Collaborative Studies of Japanese Military Comfort Women]. Tokyo: Otsuki Shoten, 1995.

Yoshimi, Yoshiaki, and Kawata Fumiko, eds. *"Jugun Ianfu" o Meguru 30 no Usoto Shinjitsu* (30 Lies and Truths about the "Military Comfort Women"). Tokyo: Otsuki Shoten, 1997.

Hayashi, Yōko. "Issues Surrounding the Wartime 'Comfort Women." *Review of Japanese Culture and Society* 11–12 (December 1999–2000): 54–65.

Authors' Bios

Dongwoo Lee Hahm is the Founding President of Washington Coalition for Comfort Women Issues, Inc. (WCCW), which was established in December 1992 to conduct research, educate people, and spread awareness about crimes against humanity during World War II. As Founding President of WCCW, Dongwoo served as a pioneer of the "comfort women" movement in the U.S. for ten years, and she was instrumental in the production of audio-visual educational programs about "comfort women." In 1994, she rushed to South Korea to videotape interviews with 15 "comfort women" survivors, and in May 1995, she presented the first published works of the WCCW Exhibit and Video "Comfort Women." She has been involved in many major programs and activities related to the "comfort women" issue, including publications, conferences, speeches at public events and educational institutions, and has received awards for her work. Dongwoo earned a BA from Ewha Womans University.

Phyllis Kim was born and raised in South Korea and moved to California with her family in 1990. After obtaining a BA at UCLA, she became a Court Certified interpreter. She joined the campaign to pass House Resolution 121 in 2007 that urged the Japanese government to accept full responsibility for the "comfort women" atrocity and provide ongoing education about it. After co-founding KAFC, she has worked with others to bring awareness about the unresolved "comfort women" issue in the United States through building memorials, including references to "comfort women" in high school history curriculums, and fighting historical revisionism.

Puja Kim is a Professor of Gender Studies and East Asian History at Tokyo University of Foreign Studies. She is part of the second generation of Koreans living in Japan. She received her Ph.D. from Ochamomizu University, Tokyo in 2001. She was awarded The First Women's History Prize (2007) in Japan for her book, *Shokuminchi-ki Chosen no Kyouiku to Gender* [Education and Gender during Colonial Korea], and has published books on the colonial education system, colonial prostitution system, and the "comfort women" issue. She has participated in the "comfort women" redress movement in Japan since the early 1990s and joined the Women's International War Crimes Tribunal as a member of VAWW-NET Japan (Violence Against Women in War Network Japan). Currently, she serves on the steering committee as co-president of VAWWRAC (Violence Against Women in War Research Action Center), and the executive committee of the "comfort women" website, Fight for Justice (http://fightforjustice.info).

Emi Koyama is a Seattle-based activist and writer who has worked in the movements against domestic and sexual violence, violence against LGBTQ communities and sex workers, and sex trafficking over the past 20 years. In response to the recent rise of Japanese right-wing nationalism and history denial (particularly "comfort women" denial) among Japanese (not Japanese American) communities in the U.S., she co-founded Japan-U.S. Feminist Network for Decolonization (FeND) which documents and analyzes their activities to help progressive Japanese and Japanese American communities and others confront them. She also coordinates the Coalition for Rights and Safety for People in the Sex Trade, a network of community groups in Seattle/King County area working to enact policy changes at state and local levels to enhance safety and rights for sex workers and people in the sex trade.

Jungsil Lee is an art historian, independent curator, and Adjunct Professor at George Washington University. Her Ph.D. in Art History from University of Maryland focused on the significance of public monuments in the nineteenth century French public sphere and their role in healing processes. Her minor area is 20th and 21st century Modern and Contemporary art focused on feminist theory and ritual practice. She is the president of the Washington Coalition for Comfort Women Issues, Inc. (WCCW), where she educates and promotes public awareness regarding sexual slavery during World War II. She has organized numerous academic conferences and art exhibitions and played a central role in the building of the "Comfort Women Memorial Peace Garden" in Fairfax County, VA in 2014. She has also developed the webinar project in which students, scholars, and activists do research and archive historical material of "comfort women."

Judith Mirkinson is a long-term women's and human rights advocate specializing in the role of sexual violence and trafficking of women and their relationship to militarism. A founder of GABRIELA Network, one of the first organizations to discuss "comfort women" and sex trafficking, she began documenting the issue of the "comfort women" in 1993 when she arranged for the first nationwide speaking tour of a former "comfort women" from the Philippines. She has lectured and written extensively on the issue of women's rights and is the author of *Red Light, Green Light*, one of the first articles to discuss sex trafficking. She is currently President of the San Francisco/Bay Area Chapter of the National Lawyers Guild and President of the Board of the Comfort Women Justice Coalition. She lives and works in San Francisco.

Bonnie B.C. Oh retired from Georgetown University as Distinguished Professor of Korean Studies. She started college at the Law College of Seoul National University, received a B.A. from Barnard College, Columbia University, M.A. from Georgetown University, and Ph.D. from the University of Chicago. With her late husband, Dr. John K.C. Oh, a scholar of democracy in Korea and East Asian international relations, she published *Korean Embassy in America*. They jointly received the 2007 Distinguished Achievement Award from the Mid-Atlantic Region Association for Asian Studies. She serves on the boards of the Washington Coalition for Comfort Women Issues, Council of Korean Americans, Seoul National University Alumni Association, the Korean Writers' Association and the Korean Cultural Center of Chicago, and Ewha Girls' High School alumni association of Chicago.

Peipei Qiu is Professor of Chinese and Japanese on the Louise Boyd Dale and Alfred Lichtenstein Chair at Vassar College. She received her master's degree in Japanese Studies from Peking University and M. Phil. and Ph.D. in Japanese Literature and Culture from Columbia University. She is the recipient of a number of honors and grants, including Chinese American Librarians Association 2014 Best Book Award in Non-Fiction Category, National Endowment for the Humanities Fellowship, Mellon Foundation Grant, Japan Society for the Promotion of Science Fellowship, Columbia University President's Fellowship, and The Japan Foundation Fellowships. She has published widely in English, Chinese, and Japanese, including *Bashō and the Dao: The Zhuangzi and the Transformation of Haikai* (2005), *Chinese Comfort Women:*

Testimonies from Imperial Japan's Sex Slaves (2013), and many articles in academic journals and newspapers.

Angella Son is an Associate Professor of Psychology and Religion of the Theological School at Drew University and the Director of Korean Care and Counseling Program at Blanton-Peal Institute & Counseling Center. She received her Ph.D. from Princeton Theological Seminary and taught at New Brunswick Theological Seminary and New York Theological Seminary before joining the Drew University faculty in 2001. She is an ordained Presbyterian minister and a fellow of the American Association of Pastoral Counselors. She published a book, *Spirituality of Joy: Moving Beyond Dread and Duty*, and its translated version in Korean, 기쁨의 영성: 두려움과 의무를 넘어 기쁨으로 향하는 길, and has also published numerous book chapters and peer-reviewed journal articles. She received the Open Rank Research Grant from the Yale Center for Faith and Culture at Yale Divinity School in 2017. The grant was for research on joy and *comfort girls-women* and funded by the Templeton Foundation.

Margaret D. Stetz is the Mae and Robert Carter Professor of Women's Studies and Professor of Humanities at the University of Delaware. In 2015, she was named one of the top 25 women in higher education by *Diverse: Issues in Higher Education* magazine. In addition to co-editing volumes such as *Legacies of the Comfort Women of WWII*, she has published more than 100 essays which have appeared in a wide range of journals, including *Journal of Human Rights Practice*, *Literature/Film Quarterly*, and *National Women's Studies Association Journal*.

In 2017, she was chosen by the Korean Ministry of Foreign Affairs as the sole representative from the U.S. for the Korea Foundation's "Invitation Program for Distinguished Guests in Academia." She has delivered papers and lectures on the WWII "comfort system" at the Graduate Center of CUNY; the Universidad Complutense in Madrid; Loyola University of Chicago; Keio University in Japan; and many others.

Mina Watanabe is a director of the Tokyo-based Women's Active Museum on War and Peace (WAM), established in 2015. WAM focuses on violence against women in war and conflict situations, with particular emphasis on Japan's military sexual slavery, or "comfort women" issue. She was actively involved in the December 2000 Women's International War Crimes Tribunal on Japan's Military Sexual Slavery held in Tokyo, which tried high-ranking officials responsible for Japan's military sexual slavery system. In addition to publishing articles and co-authoring a book on the "comfort women" issue, she has given talks to a wide range of audiences. In order to make the Japanese government accountable for crimes committed under the Japanese military sexual slavery system, she has submitted alternative reports on the issue to various UN human rights bodies over the past fifteen years.

Tomomi Yamaguchi is an Associate Professor of Anthropology at Montana State University – Bozeman. She is a cultural anthropologist and studies social movements in Japan, especially regarding feminist and right-wing movements. She received her Ph.D. in Anthropology from the University of Michigan. She has published co-authored books in Japanese, such as *The "Comfort Woman" Issue Goes Overseas: Questioning the Right-Wing "History Wars"* [*Umi o wataru "ianfu" mondai: Uha no 'rekishisen' o tou, Iwanami shoten*] (2016). She has also co-edited *The Complete Collection of Reprinted Materials of the Women's Action Group, Eight Volumes* [*Kōdō-suru onna-tachi no kai shiryō shūsei, Rikka shuppan*] (2015–16). She has published numerous academic journal and other articles in English and Japanese, including "Revisionism, Ultranationalism, Sexism: Relations between the Far Right and the Establishment over the 'Comfort Woman' Issue," *Social Science Japan Journal* 21, no.2 (2018): 193–212.

Mee-Hyang Yoon is Representative from The Korean Council for Justice and Remembrance for the Issues of Military Sexual Slavery by Japan. She has been an integral figure in the Weekly Wednesday Demonstrations in front of the Japanese Embassy for more than 27 years. As well as being a human rights activist and an author, Ms. Yoon has been a hands-on worker in the Korean Council since the organization's founding in 1990. She helped establish the War and Women's Human Rights Museum, and set up the Peace Monument in front of the Japanese Embassy for the 1,000th anniversary of the Wednesday Demonstration on December 14th, 2011. Following the survivors' honorable decision to help the victims of sexual violence during wartime in the world, she has actively worked for the Butterfly Fund, which supports female victims of sexual violence in armed conflicts. As the mother of a daughter, she has tried to restore honor and human rights of the victims and to make the world better place for the next generation.

Editors' Bios

Pyong Gap Min is a Distinguished Professor of Sociology at Queens College and the Graduate Center of the City University of New York (CUNY), and Director of the Research Center for Korean Community (RCKC) at Queens College. The areas of his research specialization are immigration/ethnic identity, gender/women/the family, and immigrants' religious practices with a research and teaching focus on Korean/Asian Americans, and Korean society. He has published five monographs and 13 edited and co-edited books. Two of the monographs—*Caught in the Middle: Korean Communities in New York and Los Angeles* and *Preserving Ethnicity through Religion in America: Korean Protestants and Indian Hindus across Generations*—received multiple book awards from professional associations. His book, *Changes and Conflicts: Korean Immigrant Families in New York City*, became a popular textbook in social sciences. Two of his 13 edited or co-edited books (*Encyclopedia of Racism in the United States* and *Struggle for Ethnic Identity: Personal Narratives by Asian American Professionals*) received special recognition from professional organizations. He received the Career Distinguished Award in 2012 from the International Migration Section and the Contribution to the Field Award in 2019 from the Section on Asia and Asian America of the American Sociological Association. In addition, he has received the Presidential Award in 2017 from the South Korean government and a dozen other awards from the Korean Association of New York, the New York City government, Korean community organizations, and U.S. university institutions.

Thomas R. Chung is a Ph.D. student in the Department of Sociology at The Graduate Center of the City University of New York (CUNY). He is also an editor, proposal writer, and web content manager for The Research Center for Korean Community (RCKC) at Queens College. His research interests include subcultures, race/ethnicity, media studies, and cultural sociology. Thomas currently teaches at Queens College of CUNY and has co-edited a couple of anthologies about Korean Americans. In his spare time, he enjoys writing fiction and playing guitar and tennis.

Sejung Sage Yim is a Ph.D. student in the Department of Sociology at the Graduate Center of the City University of New York (CUNY). Her main research interests include immigration, race and ethnicity, and transnationalism focusing on contemporary immigrants' experiences in the United States. Sejung currently teaches at Queens College, and she also works part-time at the Research Center for Korean Community (RCKC) at Queens College, where she is involved in various quantitative and qualitative projects related to the Korean American population.

Index

121 Coalition in California   181–182, 184
2010 Japan National Action to Resolve the Japanese Military "Comfort Women" Issue   58
2015 Japan-South Korean Agreement   4–6, 13, 22, 30, 32–34, 39–40, 46, 64–66, 97, 101, 108–111, 121–122, 127, 141–143, 165–166, 177, 180, 194, 196–198, 200, 226–227, 256–257, 268–269, 312–313, 315 317
– "Comfort women's" rejection of   22
– Foundation for Reconciliation and Healing   66
– Invigoration of the movement after   39–40
– UN bodies' and international human rights organizations' rejection of   32, 33, 66

A Gift of the Emperor   218
Ahn, Shin-kwon   vi, 74–75
Amnesty International   180, 225
Apology   139, 185, 203, 228
Asahi Glendale Sosho (Asahi Glendale Lawsuit)   245, 247
Asahi Shimbun   61, 234, 234, 243, 244, 246, 247, 248, 250, 255
Asian Solidarity Conference   25, 48, 62, 63, 82–83, 93
Asian Women's Fund   3, 29, 45, 51, 84, 85, 90, 93
– Charity (sympathy) money   4, 51, 83, 84
– Divided advocacy organizations in Japan   84
– Inadequacy to resolve the "comfort women" issue   51
– Payment to Korean "comfort women"   4
– Rejection of   4, 83, 93
Association of Citizens against the Special Privileges of Zainichi Koreans
Atlanta Comfort Women Memorial Task Force   194

Atarashii Rekishi Kyōkasho o Tsukurukai (The Society for History Textbook Reform)   237

Batavia Temporary Court Martial   103
Brecher, Jeremy   156
Bulova, Sharon   134

California Educational Board   193
Cavallo, Steve   185
Chang, Iris   152, 240
Center for Civil and Human Rights in Atlanta   193
Chen, Lifei   195
Cheonyeo gongchul   16
Chinese Comfort Women: Testimonies from Imperial Japan's Sexual Slaves   279
Chinkin, Christine   10, 87, 125
Cho, Jung-Rae   15, 221, 223, 225, 226, 227
Cho, Sihak   4
Cho, Young J.   117
Chongshindae   16, 17, 300, 320
Chung, Chin-sung   318
Chung, Thomas   1–18, 333
"Comfort Women" Column of Strength   171
Choi Schellstede, Sangmi   7, 125, 208, 325
"Comfort women" memorials   316
"Comfort Women" Revisionism   15, 46, 54, 55, 56, 59, 61, 67, 71, 180, 193, 236, 237, 254, 263, 265, 271, 329, 332
(Korean) "Comfort Women"   1, 10, 16, 17, 18, 69
– Act one Livelihood and Stability for   30
– As prostitutes   51
– Asian "comfort women"   14, 25
– Chinese "comfort women"   15
– "Comfort women" bashing   56, 59
– "Comfort women" monuments   3, 5, 6, 14
– Damaged physical conditions and psychological traumas of   27–28
– Emergence of   2, 24–25, 44
– Hate speech against   60
– House of Sharing   28

– Human rights camps for   28
– International activities   30–31
– Lawsuits against the Japanese government   25, 33, 49, 51, 79, 93
– Legacies of   14, 203–229
– Medical conditions of   27–28
– Poor economic conditions of   29
– Total number of   1, 163, 195
– See Wednesday demonstrations
– Wishes of to the Japanese government   37–38
Constitutional Court of Korea   58
Coomaraswamy, Radhika   10, 17, 31, 52, 81, 85–86, 91, 246, 310
Criticisms of the Japanese government's denials of responsibility   50–52, 55–62, 95–113
Chuburaya, Gyoko   92
Chung, Chin-song   8, 84
Cumings, Bruce   297

Daughters of Dragon   195
Doi, Takako   119

Emperor Shōwa (Hirohito)   53, 87, 88, 105, 121
Enloe, Cynthia   215
Evans, Lane   117, 128, 129, 130, 132, 182

Fifield, Anna   216
Fortin, Jacey   259
Fourth World Conference on Women   9
Franziska, Seraphim   237
Fujioka, Nobukatsu   3, 237, 263

GABRIELA Philippines   157, 330
Gil, Won-ok   22, 203
Gilbert, Kent   240
Global Alliance for Historical Truth (GAHT)   61, 254, 264
Gingrich, Newt   117
Global Alliance for Historical Truth   242, 263, 268, 269

Ha, Sunnyo   302
Hallyu (Korean Wave)   59
Hashimoto, Tōru   153

Hata, Ikuhiko   56
Hawtjorne, Nathaniel   305
Hayashi, Hirofumi   16, 48, 104, 314
Hayashi, Yōko   1
Henry, Nichola   85
Henson, Maria Rosa   7, 218
Historical revisionism, the emergence of   3, 67, 71
Historical Revisionist Activities
– In Japan   3, 55–62, 234–259
– In the U.S.   159–160, 171, 186–191, 261–271
Historical Awareness Research Committee   254, 255, 256, 257, 258, 259
Hicks, George   7, 298, 306, 306
"History war"   8, 15, 62, 190, 198, 233, 234, 236, 237, 239, 242, 243, 244, 250, 251, 253, 254, 255, 259, 260, 260, 268, 269, 328, 331
Historical Museum of Japanese Military "Comfort Women"   75
– Japanese citizens' contributions to, the construction of   75
Hoffman, Paul   184, 188
Hogan Lovells   129, 267, 269
Honda, Mike   117, 121, 129, 130, 132, 181, 182, 219, 244, 310
Hong, Roy   182, 184, 187
House of Sharing   vi, 28, 72, 74, 75, 92, 136, 188, 224, 311
– Pyong Gap Min's stay at   74
House Representative William Lipinski   117, 124, 128, 183
Howard, Keith   7, 298, 302, 303, 319, 327
Hsiung, Tiffany   139, 185, 203, 228
Hwang, Keum-ju   117, 118, 121, 125, 128

Indai, Sajor   52, 86
Inoguchi, Kuniko   254
International Commission of Jurists   39, 91, 125, 130, 310, 322, 325
International Court of Justice   53
International Labour Organization   31
International Military Tribunal for the Far East (IMTFE)   102, 103, 130, 239, 283
International Women's War Crimes Tribunal on Japanese Military Sexual Slavery

10–11, 46, 52–56, 84–89, 93, 95–96, 102–103, 105, 162, 180, 188, 238, 243–244, 310, 325, 326–327, 329, 331
Ishikawa, Itsuko   91–92

Japan Federation of Bar Associations   90–91, 323
Japan Policy Institute   235, 247, 254, 259
Japanese American Bar Association of California   262
Japanese American Citizens League   159, 262
Japanese Society for History Textbook Reform   55, 67, 237–238, 263, 270
Japan Times   88, 171, 190–191, 260, 313, 317
Japan's War Responsibility Center (JWRC)   48–49
Japan's ultranationalist backlash   52
Jinja Honchō (the Association of Shinto Shrines)   235
Jilin Provincial Archives   15, 275–278, 280–282, 284–286, 290–293
Johnson, Caitlin   219
Judge Gabrielle Kirk McDonald   86, 105

Kang, Duk-kyung   80, 87, 136
Kang, Il-chul   185, 188, 224–225
Kang, Soon Im   118–119
KASCON (Korean American Students Conference)   124–125, 128
Katō, Kōichi   308
Kaufman, Gershen   16, 296, 314, 315
Kawata, Fumiko   48, 328
Keam   Mark, 117
Kenpeitai, (the Kwantung Army Military Police Regiment)   276–277, 285, 287, 289, 291
Kent, Susan Kingsley   218, 325
Kim, Baik-kyu   194
Kim, Bok-dong   22, 36, 124, 170, 187
Kim, Chang-rok   4, 78
Kim, Chungmi   125
Kim, Da-Hee   225
Kim, Eun-sung   316–317, 320, 326
Kim, Hak-sun   v, 2, 11, 18–19, 25, 35, 43–44, 47–49, 76–77, 80, 149, 163,

167, 169–170, 176, 179, 200, 205–207, 217–218, 220, 223, 237, 243, 299–303, 306, 308, 318
Kim, Hwa Sun   128
Kim, Hye-won   76–77
Kim, Jane   153, 158
Kim, Kun-ja   131–132, 182
Kim, Phyllis   14, 179–200
Kim, Puja   3, 13, 43–69, 72–73, 88, 298, 326, 329
Kim, Seo-kyung   316–317, 320, 326
Kim, Soon-duk   24, 125, 136
Kim, Yoon-Shim   123
Kim-Gibson, Dae Sil   7, 118, 125–126, 185, 211, 220–221, 325
Kishida, Fumio   65, 165
Kobayashi, Yoshinori   67–68
Kohut, Heinz   16, 296, 314, 326
Kōno Statement   2, 44–46, 57, 60, 63, 71, 85, 106, 179–180, 233, 238, 268, 270, 308–309, 312, 321
– Abe's and other Japanese historical revisionists' rejection of   44–45, 60
Korean American Civic Empowerment (KACE)   121, 132–133, 181, 182, 183, 184, 186, 191
– Korean American Voters Council (KAVC)   132, 181–184, 186
Korean American Forum of California (KAFC)   121, 132, 181, 184, 186–196, 329
Korean Council for the Women Drafted for Military Sexual Slavery by Japan (the Korean Council)   v–vi, 2–4, 6, 8–13, 16–18, 21, 23–30, 35–38, 43, 52, 58, 71–73, 75–87, 89–93, 99–100, 106–107, 118, 121, 127, 179, 198, 206–207, 228, 295, 307, 310–311, 316–318, 320, 323, 327, 332
– International activities   30–34
– Six demands to the Japanese government   2
– See the redress movement
Korean immigrants' transnational redress movement   10–12, 14
Korean-Japanese 2015 Agreement   4–6, 13, 22, 30, 32–34, 39–40, 46, 64–66, 97, 101, 108–111, 121–122, 127, 141–143,

165–166, 177, 180, 194, 196–198, 200, 226–227, 256–257, 268–269, 312–313, 315, 317
– Charity money   4–6, 83–84, 179
– Controversy over   5, 13
– Rejection of by the Korean Council   4, 99
– Secret agreements of   5, 6
– UN's condemnations of   32–33, 100
Korean Research Institute for the Chongshindae   vi
Korean United Methodist Church of Greater Washington   117–118
Kotler, Mindy   117, 131–132
Koyama, Emi   15, 62, 165, 242, 244, 249–250, 261–271, 328–329

Lantos, Tom   130, 183
Lee, Anita   139, 203
Lee, Chang-jin   126, 137, 185
Lee, Daniel   182
Lee, Hyo-jae   121, 307
Lee, Hyun-Sook   2, 326
Lee Hahm, Dongwoo   14, 117–148, 181, 203, 208, 311, 329
Lee, Jeff Jungho   208, 326
Lee, Jungsil   14, 117–148, 181, 185, 213, 311, 330
Lee, Na-young   4
Lee, Ok-Sun   186, 188
Lee, Susan   117, 133
Lee Yong-su   17, 24, 121, 125, 131–132, 158, 170, 182–186, 191–192, 214, 266
Liberal Democratic Party (LDP)   45, 55, 58–59, 65–66, 68, 88, 233–234, 238, 241, 244, 254, 270
Lipinski, William   117
Liu, Hung   213
Lynd, Helen Merrell   303–304, 326
Los Angeles' Nikkan Sun   250
Los Angeles Times   135, 186, 226, 246

Manjoo, Rashida   21, 29, 85
Mar, Eric   153, 156–158, 160, 172, 192, 267
Masaoka, Kathy   159, 263
Matsui, Yayori   52, 56, 58, 84–86, 88–89, 93, 243
Mayer Brown   188

McDougal Littell   164
McDougall, Gay J.   10, 31, 86, 162, 246, 310, 326
McGraw-Hill Textbook   190–191, 193, 216, 246, 325
Mainichi Shimbun   104, 109, 171, 306
McNeill, David   225, 254, 326
Mera, Kōichi   134, 160, 188–189, 192–193, 249, 257, 262–267, 269
Min, Pyong Gap   v–vii, 1–18, 71–94, 326, 333
Min, Yong Soon   126127
Mirkinson, Judith   14, 149–177, 181, 193, 330
Mitchell, John   134
Modern World History   164
Morris-Suzuki, Tessa   244, 254
Morton, A. L.   210
Motooka, Shōji   84
Mun, Ok-chu   25, 79–80, 302, 326
Mun, Pilgi   302
Mutsuko, Miki   123

NAACP   159
Nadeshiko Action   61, 186, 242, 255–258, 265
Nakahara, Michiko   53
Nakasone, Yasuhiro   104–105
Nanjing Massacre   45, 112, 152, 155, 160, 164, 239–240, 256, 278–279, 282–283, 297–298
– Rape of Nanjing or Rape of Nanking   192
National Mobilization Law   275, 289–291
Neo-nationalism   3, 8, 15, 71, 85, 88, 93, 231
New York Biz   250
New York Times   4, 45, 134, 153, 188, 190, 208, 223, 241, 246, 253, 259
Nihon Seisaku Kenkyū Sentā (Japan Policy Research Institute)   235
Nikkei for Civil Rights Justice   159, 262
NHK   56–57, 59–60, 76, 88, 111, 244
Nippon Kaigi (Japan Conference)   55, 233, 235–249, 251–256, 258, 259–260, 326
Nishino, Rumiko   45, 48, 50–51, 54, 56–57, 69, 75, 87, 326

Nishioka, Tsutomu   234–235, 248, 250, 252, 254, 256
Nogawa, Motokazu   62, 235, 240, 244, 328
Nozaki, Yoshiko   8

Oh, Bonnie B.C.   7–8, 14, 16, 117, 181, 203–214, 217, 327, 330
Oh, Sonfa   254
Okamoto, Akiko   241, 252–253, 255
Okamura, Yasuji   297
Onozawa, Akane   45, 50–51, 56, 69, 326
Ōnuma, Yasaki   77
Oogami, Iko   80–81
Oral history   14, 149, 205, 207, 209–210
Oyama, Tomoko   269

Pai, Pong Gi   306
Palisades Park   133–134, 173, 184, 233, 241, 253, 266
Park, Annabel   132, 183
Park, Geun-hye   5, 64, 198, 200, 226, 267
Park, Si-Soo   225
Park, Soyang   212
Park, Sunae   302
Park, Therese   218, 326
Park, Young-sim   54, 137
Park, Yu-ha   302, 326
Peace Nabi (Nabi Fund)   26, 29, 35–36, 311
– Butterfly Fund   332
Pelosi, Nancy   117, 183
Permanent Court of Arbitration (PCA) 91–93
Pillay, Navi, a UN High Commissioner for Human Rights   21
Pilzner, Joshua   211, 326
President Barack Obama   126, 189
President Bill Clinton   121, 124
President Lee Myung-bak   58, 125
President Park Geun-hye   5, 64, 198, 200, 226, 267
Prime Minister Abe Shinzō   3, 4, 6, 32, 39, 45–46, 55, 57, 59–66, 68–69, 88, 99, 101, 108, 112, 121–122, 165, 171, 180, 185, 188, 190–191, 196, 198, 214, 219, 226, 233, 235–236, 238, 240–241, 244, 247, 259, 270, 312–313, 317

Prime Minister Hosokawa Morihiro   121
Prime Minister Murayama Tomiichi   3, 44–45, 64, 68, 80, 83–85, 90, 310
Prime Minister Noda Yoshihiko   58

Qiu, Peipei   7, 15, 163, 181, 195, 275–293, 326, 330
Quintero, Frank   187

Rape in Nanjing Redress Coalition (RNRC) 152, 192, 265
Rape of Nanking   152, 192, 249, 265
Redress movement for the victims of Japanese military sexual slavery   1, 3
– Asian Solidarity   9
– Conference on   6
– Beginning of in Korea   23–24
– Invigoration of   6
– Movement in Japan   44–55, 72–94, 44–55, 71–94, 96–113
– Movement in Korea   22–30
   – Social background of the beginning of the movement   23–24, 47
   – Support for the victims of Japanese military sexual slavery   27–30
   – Transnational   8–12, 21–23, 30–37
– Movement in the U.S.   116–200
   – By Korean American Civic Empowerment 184–185
   – By Washington Coalition for Comfort Women Issues, 14, 117–128, 164, 182, 185, 213
   – By Comfort Women Justice Coalition 14, 149–177, 181, 193
   – By Korean American Forum of California 184–191, 193, 195–196
   – By other organizations   132–134, 181–183, 185–186, 194
– Wednesday demonstrations   30, 34–35, 79
   – Japanese citizens' participation in   73, 74, 79, 80
Report on Japan's War Responsibility   49
Research Center for Korean Community   v, vii, 6, 333
Reynolds, Isabel   215
Rhee, Moon Hyung   119–120

Rosenbaum, Eli   117
Ruff-O'Herne, Jan   7, 28, 131–132, 182, 306
Russell Tribunal   53
Russo-Japanese War   276

Sugiyama, Kōichi   241
Sakamoto, Rumi   10, 326
Sakurai, Yoshiko   234–235, 256
Semple, Kirk   134, 241
Sankei Shimbun   112, 198, 234, 241, 254, 259, 268–270
Schirch, Lisa   134, 326
Shulman, Frank Joseph   211
Sekino, Michio   240
Senda, Kakō   47, 214, 306, 326
Seraphim, Franziska   8, 237
Schellstede, Sangmi Choi   7, 125, 208, 325
Shin, Hei-su   9
Shinozuka, Takashi   112, 261, 269
Silence Broken   7, 118, 125, 139, 185, 211, 220–221, 325
Sim, Young-hee   87
Sing, Lillian   152–153, 156, 192
Six (Seven) demands to the Japanese government   2–3, 38–39, 63, 120, 132, 180, 197, 200, 226, 268, 307
Snowy Road   15, 221–223
Soh, Ok Cha   127–129, 131–132
Soh, C. Sarah   7, 8, 79, 192, 266–267, 296–297, 300, 310, 312, 320, 326
Son, Angella   16, 295–323, 327, 331
Song, Sin Do or Song, Shin Do   25, 79
Spirits' Homecoming (2016)   15, 139, 185, 221–227
Stetz, Margaret   7, 14–15, 117, 181, 203–204, 215–229, 327, 331
Sprits Homecoming II   139
Sugiyama, Shinsuke   171, 260, 268
Suzuki, Yūko   16, 48
Szczepanska, Kamila   8

Tabuchi, Hiroko   153, 312
Takagi, Ken'ichi   77, 308
Takahashi, Shiro   239, 243, 247–250, 252, 254–256, 264
Takezawa, Yasuko   270
Tang, Julie   152, 156, 192

Tawara, Yoshifumi   56, 235–236, 240
Tokudome, Kinue   131, 328
Tokyo War Crimes Trial (International Military Tribunal for the Far East) (1946–1948)   54–55, 85–86, 102–103, 239, 283
Star Ledger   242
Turkel, Studs   210
Totsuka, Etsuro   90, 95, 323
Toyama, Misao   103
Tumblety, Joan   207, 328

Uemura, Takashi   62, 243–244, 249, 328
UNESCO's "Memory of the World Program"   112, 197, 236, 255–259
UN Criminal Tribunals for Yugoslavia and Rwanda   52, 67, 86–87, 105, 163
UN High Commissioner for Human Rights   10, 21, 31–33, 81, 85, 90, 96–98, 310
UN's International War Crimes Tribunal   86
UN General Assembly's adoption in 1993 of the Convention of Elimination of All Forms of Discrimination against Women (CEDAW)   31–33, 51, 96, 99–100, 121–122, 152, 268, 270
UN Special Rapporteurs on Violence against Women   17, 21, 31, 33, 81, 97–98, 100, 130, 162, 310,
U.S. House Resolution   3, 14, 121, 124, 128,–133, 180, 181, 182, 183, 184, 185, 186, 191, 219, 246, 311
Utsumi, Aiko   55

VAWW-Net Japan   52–53, 55–57, 84, 85–86, 88–89, 95, 298, 329

Wada, Haruki   4, 84, 328
Walker, Margaret Urban   303, 328
War and Women's Human Rights Museum   5, 26–27, 34, 75, 219, 332
– Japanese citizens' donations for the construction of   75
Washington Coalition for Comfort Women Issues (WCCW)   14, 117–147, 182, 203, 208, 213, 329–330
Washington Post   45, 57, 121, 123–124, 183, 190–191, 204, 216, 241, 312

Watanabe, Mina   13–14, 78, 89, 95–114, 331
Women's Active Museum of War and Peace (WAM)   5, 13–14, 57–58, 63, 78, 89, 96–97, 114, 258, 326, 331
Women's International War Crimes Tribunal on Japan's Military Sexual Slavery   10–11, 46, 52–56, 58, 84–89, 93, 95, 105, 162, 180, 243, 310, 326–327, 329, 331
World Convention for Human Rights Held in Vienna   9, 90

Yamamoto, Yumiko   242, 256–257, 263–264, 269
Yamaoka, Tetsuhide   250, 252–254, 256
Yamatani, Tetsuo   306
Yamaguchi, Tomomi   15, 62, 233–260, 328, 331
Yang, Hyun-a   4
Yang, Jing-ja   79
Yi, Okpun   302
Yim, Sejung Sage   1–18, 333

Yomiuri Shimbun   215, 253
Yoneyama, Lisa   56, 88, 238
Yoo, Bo-ra   15, 221
Yoon, Mee-hyang   vi, 13, 21–41, 87, 207, 317, 320, 332
Yoshida, Seiji   243–246, 248, 306
Yoshimi, Yoshiaki   1–2, 7, 16, 43, 45, 47–48, 60, 181, 207–208, 214, 226–227, 288, 297, 301, 308–309, 312–314, 323, 328
Young, Ellsworth   217
Yun, Byong-sei   165
Yun Chong-ok   47, 52, 86, 206, 306–307, 320
Yun, Turi   302
Yun, Paul   182

Zaitokukai   59, 61, 68, 242, 251, 263
Zhao, Yujie   275, 277–278, 286
Zhiliang, Su   7, 163, 181, 195, 279, 326
Ziegler, Herbert   190–191, 325
Zinn, Howard   210

www.ingramcontent.com/pod-product-compliance
Lightning Source LLC
Chambersburg PA
CBHW020323170426
43200CB00006B/253